MW01641747

IN AND AROUND THE BOOK OF DANIEL

IN AND AROUND THE BOOK OF DANIEL

by
Charles Boutflower

KREGEL PUBLICATIONS
Grand Rapids, Michigan 49501

IN AND AROUND THE BOOK OF DANIEL
Published in 1977 by Kregel Publications, a division of Kregel, Inc.

Printed in the United States of America

Library of Congress Cataloging in Publication Data

Boutflower, Charles, 1846-1936.
In and around the book of Daniel.

Reprint of the 1923 ed. published by Society for Promoting Christian Knowledge, London; Macmillan, New York.
Bibliography: p.
Includes index
1. Bible. O.T. Daniel—Criticism, interpretation, etc. 2. Babylonia—History. I. Title.
BS1555.B6 1977 224'.5'06 77-7648
ISBN 0-8254-2229-9

PREFACE

CHRISTIAN believers may be divided into two classes—those who believe without interesting themselves greatly in the source of their belief and the land which gave it birth, and those for whom the Semitic east, and especially our Saviour's native land, are the abode of romance and delight. It was the dwelling-place of Abraham and the Patriarchs; and the home of the Jews after the Exodus, when the judges ruled and later the kings held sway. In these latter days, too, Assyria and Babylonia came upon the scene, and we are shown the ways of a still more romantic East—in the case of Babylonia, moreover, an earlier home of the Hebrews, as well as a later one, stands revealed.

Owing to these changes, doubtless, the Book of Daniel has always attracted considerable attention among all classes of students, from the most orthodox to those prominent in the opposite camp; and it may also be said that it has attracted not a little attention from those who would banish Christianity and a belief in God entirely from the world. And this is not to be wondered at, especially when we read the well-reasoned and instructive pages which the Rev. Charles Boutflower here presents to us. If one might in this place make a parallel, the Book of Daniel is in a like case to the Book of Jonah in the matter of historical difficulties. But such difficulties as these are not seldom met with in the Old Testament. Earliest of all is the reference to Nimrod in Gen. x. 10. It is a name which is not found in the records of Babylonia and Assyria, but which we have nevertheless to explain. After this comes the question of the battle of the four kings against five in Gen. xiv., for now we have the complete list of the year-dates of Ḫammurabi, the king who is apparently to be identified with Amraphél, and among them there is no record of an expedition to the Dead Sea region or to any of the lands adjacent thereto. Still later on there is the question of Cushan-rishathaim, king of Mesopotamia (Aram-Naharaim), whose name has still to be discovered or identified. And when we come to the time of Hezekiah, we are confronted with the doubt whether Sennacherib of Assyria made two expeditions against Judah and Jerusalem, or only one. And so the seeming discrepancies between the compiled history contained in the Old Testament and the contemporary documents of the Assyrians and the Babylonians goes on.

But of all the Old Testament books which contain problems requiring solution, none would seem to surpass in importance the Book of Daniel. There is not only in it the question of the status of the Israelites who were captives at Babylon, and their treatment at the hands of their captors, but the reader is also faced by numerous historical questions due to events belonging to the period of their captivity. Did Nebuchadrezzar, king of Babylon, really go mad, and did he, after regaining his reason, become a worshipper of the God of the Hebrews? Was Belshazzar, son of Nabonidus, really the last native king of Babylon, and if so, how is it that Nebuchadrezzar, in Daniel, is stated to have been his father? Both these assertions are against the testimony of the Babylonian contemporary records, and need explanation—how are they to be explained? As to Daniel being appointed the third ruler in the kingdom, that is bound up with the latter of these two questions, and has an important bearing upon it. Of equal difficulty, and of equal importance, is the identity of Darius the Median. Here we are again faced by a ruler whose name is absent from the inscriptions and chronological lists—neither the Babylonians nor the Greek historians know anything of him, and the only personage either in the Babylonian Chronicle or in Xenophon "receiving the kingdom" (instead of Cyrus, the conqueror of Babylonia) from the last of the native rulers, was Gobryas, whom the Babylonians called Gubaru or Ugbaru (variant spellings which suggest the pronunciation G'baru). In no case, however, is he called Darius, which, moreover, is doubtfully a Median name. As to his nationality, the Babylonians describe Gubaru as being of Gutium, a mountainous district identified with "old Media," and the Arabic Jebel Judi. All the identifications, however, are learnedly discussed by the author of this book, and will not fail to provide the reader with the needful material for deciding the question for himself. Incidentally he will acquire much information concerning many other potentates of those ancient days—all of them historical personages and men of renown.

In the end the reader will probably come to the conclusion that there is no more interesting examination of the Book of Daniel than the present work. Not only are the great problems contained in the Book examined and dealt with in the light of the records accessible to the author, but likewise all the lesser problems which the Hebrew record contains. In this book the reader will find explanations of all Daniel's prophetic dreams, and much strange information thereon is brought to light. His remarks upon the difference between Babylonians and Chaldeans are by no means to be neglected, though many an ethnic problem still remains to be solved. Whatever may have been said against it, and however much the Book of Daniel may have been, and may still be, criticised, it remains a most valuable record dealing with a great and proud people, who thought that they had a right to be proud. Was not their land the place of the earthly Paradise, and were not their priests every one of them princes, steeped in celestial lore? Moreover, was not all the wisdom of the old Sumerians and Akkadians, reaching back through untold ages, when the god of wisdom came forth from the sea to teach them the arts and the things which a nation favoured by the gods ought to know—was not all this wisdom theirs?

Daniel and his contemporaries were eye-witnesses of the last glories of Babylon, and also of the assumption of its dominion by a foreign power—that of Persia, the most beneficent rule in the world. We have still to learn what moved the Babylonians to accept it, but we may suppose that there was a feeling of great discontent in the country, and that the people thought that they could not do better than accept this foreign rule. If, however, they expected to retain their proud position in the world, and be considered, as of old, as one of the great nations, they were undeceived before many decades had passed. The Persians were not a nation whose rulers could be absorbed, as were absorbed the Amorites, the Kassites, and the Elamites of the dynasty of Larsa, into the Babylonian empire. "The beauty of the Chaldees' excellency," therefore, continued to decline until Babylon became the desolation which it is at the present day. As in the case of the Book of Jonah, the critics attack the Book of Daniel, aiming, through them, their shafts at the Churches, but both books remain among the most important in the Old Testament, for both contain pictures of phases of Eastern life and teaching not to be found elsewhere.

THEOPHILUS G. PINCHES

CONTENTS

PAGE

Chronological Tables xvii

CHAPTER I: Introduction 1

Statement of the two views with respect to the Book of Daniel: the orthodox and the critical—The critics, guided by chap. xi., do great violence to the rest of the Book—Dr. Wright's explanation of that chapter a concession, but not improbable—Interpolation of Holy Scripture as witnessed by the Targums—The visions of Daniel only to be made clear by their fulfilment—Nevertheless this Book to engage the attention of many, and further light promised.

CHAPTER II: The Four Kingdoms 13

The Grecian and the Roman scheme—Chaps. vii. and viii. not parallels—A curious piece of criticism—The "little horn" of vii. 8 not identical with that of viii. 9—The "ten horns" wrongly treated by the critics—Visions of chaps. vii. and viii. contrasted—Difficulty presented by the words "another kingdom inferior to thee"—Justification of a new rendering—Daniel's silence as to the second kingdom—Why the Grecian scheme first found favour—Additional Note on Ararat, Minni, and Ashkenaz.

CHAPTER III: The Gold, the Silver, the Brass, and the Iron 24

Hint from Josephus as to the meaning of the metals—Their order considered—Babylon the golden kingdom, as testified by Herodotus and the inscriptions—Persia the silver or monied kingdom—Wealth the source of its strength—Brass a picture of the Grecian arms—"Brazen men from the sea"—The leopard of chap. vii. symbolises the rapid advance of Alexander—An argument from the Greek lexicon—With the rise of the Roman power brass gives place to iron—The Roman kingdom pictured by the fourth beast of chap. vii.—Strength of the Roman kingdom proved by its duration—Suitability of the metals from the mythological standpoint.

CHAPTER IV: The Chaldeans of the Book of Daniel 35

The "Chaldeans" one proof of the authenticity of this Book—The word not used as in Juvenal—Its double meaning—Home of the Kaldu—"Nebuchadnezzar the Chaldean"—His father drives out the Assyrians and founds a Chaldean dynasty at Babylon—A feature of Chaldean

PAGE

throne-names—"The Chaldeans" not identical with the Babylonians—Herodotus as to the Chaldean priesthood of Bel—Testimony of Diodorus Siculus confirmed by an inscription of Nabopolassar—Strange absence of the name in Babylonian inscriptions—A possible explanation—An enlightening tablet of the reign of Nebuchadnezzar—High social position of "the Chaldeans"—Correct estimate of them formed by Delattre.

CHAPTER V: THE GREAT MOUNTAIN 45

Shadu Rabu, "The Great Mountain," originally a title of En-lil of Nippur, the chief of the gods—His supremacy and title presently transferred to Merodach of Babylon—The Aramaic *Dhur Rabh* of Dan. ii. 35 the exact equivalent of the Babylonian *Shadu Rabu*—How a Babylonian audience would understand Daniel's interpretation of the king's dream—En-lil the storm-god—His name signifies "lord of the wind"—In this respect also he is superseded by Merodach—This throws further light on the meaning of the dream—The six mountains of the Book of Enoch suggested by Dan. ii.—How they are to be understood—Immense impression made on Nebuchadnezzar by the discovery and interpretation of his dream—Consequent fame of Daniel as attested by Ezekiel.

CHAPTER VI: THE MESSIANIC KINGDOM 55

Striking reference in the Similitudes of Enoch to the vision of Dan. vii. 13, 14—Growth of Messianic doctrine before the birth of Christ—Dan. vii. 13, 14 interpreted by our Lord and His contemporaries as in the Similitudes—Strange interpretation offered by the critics—Driver's argument refuted by the fact that "the saints" belong to the vision and not merely to its interpretation—Further refutation obtained by an analysis of the chapter—Clear view of the author of the Similitudes—The critics blinded by their low estimate of Daniel's Book—A resemblance between the Messianic kingdom and the first of the four kingdoms—Note on the date of the Similitudes.

CHAPTER VII: THE ROYAL BUILDER 65

The legend of Megasthenes—Its connection with the narrative of Dan. iv.—The king walking upon his palace, possibly in the Hanging Gardens—Remarkable structure discovered by Koldewey—Good view of Babylon obtainable therefrom—Nebuchadnezzar one of the greatest builders—The building inscriptions—How they can be arranged in chronological order—Some features of the longer inscriptions—A fragment from the annals—Babylon Nebuchadnezzar's only place of residence—Excavation of the Old Palace rebuilt by him—New palace to the north erected in fifteen days—The rampart of "mighty stones"—The two palaces formed into one acropolis represented by the Kasr mound—A third palace at the north angle of the outer wall of Babylon represented by the mound Babil—The temple of Merodach buried in the mound Amran—The Hanging Gardens the centre of the whole—From this point, close to the Ishtar Gate, may have been uttered the proud boast of Dan. iv. 30.

PAGE

CHAPTER VIII: THE ROYAL WOOD-CUTTER 78

Light thrown by the inscriptions on the narrative of Dan. iv.—Nebuchadnezzar makes Babylon the centre of empire—"Under her everlasting shadow have I gathered all men in peace"—The vision of the great tree an exact picture of the king's idea of empire—Nebuchadnezzar's love for the Lebanon—The Wady Brissa Inscription—Its contents described—Conquest of the Lebanon—Royal visits to the cedar forest—The king cuts down trees with his own hand—Vivid light thrown on Hab. ii.—Tyre a competitor for the Lebanon—Strategic position of Riblah—Typical significance of the cedar—The dream of Dan. iv. genuine—"The basest of men" explained by an inscription of Nabopolassar—This one of the strongest proofs of the authenticity of the Book of Daniel.

CHAPTER IX: THE PERSONALITY OF NEBUCHADNEZZAR ... 92

Different character of the royal inscriptions of Assyria and Babylonia—The personality of the monarch sometimes visible in the inscriptions of the Neo-Babylonian kings—This, in Nebuchadnezzar's case, a strong confirmation of the authenticity of the Book of Daniel—Monotheistic tendency in the Babylonian religion due originally to the supremacy of En-lil of Nippur—That supremacy transferred to Merodach—The Enlilship of Merodach strongly emphasised in passages of the India House Inscription—In such passages can be traced the pen of Nebuchadnezzar—Increasing monotheism of this king in his later years—How it was possible for him to acknowledge the supremacy of the God of Israel—Nabopolassar's exaltation of Shamash—Nabonidus' devotion to Sin and Shamash—Poetic style of Nebuchadnezzar in narrative as well as in hymns of praise—An echo of this in the Book of Daniel—Would an author of the Maccabean age write thus?

CHAPTER X: THE LEGEND OF MEGASTHENES 105

Points of contact between the legend and the narrative of Dan. iv.—The legend, though in a Greek dress, belongs to the early Persian period—Its authors the Chaldean priests—Their hatred to Nabonidus, whose training inclined him to Sin rather than to Merodach—History of his reign—Though united in their hatred to Nabonidus the priesthood are divided over Cyrus—The Cylinder of Cyrus—Its language respecting Cyrus shows an acquaintance with the Book of Isaiah, and is in strong contrast to the contempt expressed in the legend—Light thrown by the Book of Daniel on this division of opinion in the priesthood—The true story of Dan. iv. turned into a legend bewailing the departed Nebuchadnezzar and crediting him with the gift of prophecy—Note on an inscription by the father of Nabonidus.

CHAPTER XI: BELSHAZZAR 114

Belshazzar a distinctly historical personage—Conjecture as to his age—Trained in the cult of Sin, Shamash, and Anunit—Early brought into connection with the court of Nebuchadnezzar—His relation to that

PAGE

king merely a legal one, arising out of the anxiety of his father Nabonidus to legitimise his claim—The "queen" of Dan. v. 10 probably the widow of Nebuchadnezzar—Belshazzar in what sense king—Important tablet from Erech, showing him to have been associated with his father during part of the reign of Nabonidus—Hence the explanation of his "first" and "third" years—Why his name is not found in the dating of the contract tablets—His position as head of the nobility.

CHAPTER XII: THE FALL OF BABYLON 121

Prophecy of Jer. chaps. l., li.—Its fulfilment as recorded in Dan. v. as well as in the pages of Herodotus and Xenophon—Points of agreement between the narrative in Daniel and those of the two Greek writers form a voucher for the truth of all three records, no less than for the genuineness of the prophecy—The native records on the Annalistic Tablet and the Cylinder of Cyrus—Points of agreement with Dan. v. and with the statements of Herodotus and Xenophon—A seeming difference explained by the light of the contract tablets—Note on Cyrus' occupation of Babylon.

CHAPTER XIII: THE HANDWRITING ON THE WALL ... 133

Discovery of the throne-room of the Babylonian kings—Belshazzar's feast pictured—His knowledge at first hand of Nebuchadnezzar's madness—The proffered rewards—Daniel's stern address—The four mystic words, probably written in Aramaic and in alphabetic characters—Their seeming sense nonsense, but significant of some hidden meaning—"The tablets of fate" explain the king's alarm—Daniel's interpretation confirms his forebodings—The closing scene.

CHAPTER XIV: DARIUS THE MEDE 142

Darius the great historical crux of this Book—In what sense he "received the kingdom"—The six proposed identifications of Darius reduced to two—The claim of Gobryas considered—Preference given to Cambyses the son of Cyrus—Evidence from the Annalistic Tablet that Cyrus appointed Cambyses to succeed Belshazzar—Evidence from the contract tablets that for some ten months in the year after the capture of Babylon Cambyses bore the title "King of Babylon," his father being styled "King of the Countries"—The two titles point to a distribution of authority—Babylon formed into a sub-kingdom—Cambyses in what sense a Mede and why so called—Josephus' statement that Darius the Mede "had another name among the Greeks"—Argument to show that this name was Cambyses—"Darius" an appellative rather than a proper name—The "Ahasuerus" of Dan. ix. 1 probably to be identified with Cyaxeres.

CHAPTER XV: DARIUS THE MEDE—*continued* 156

Age of Darius not given in the LXX—If the son of Amytis, the daughter of Astyages, he might be twelve years old when appointed king of Babylon—Argument to show that 12, not 62, is the correct

PAGE

reading in Dan. v. 31—Letters of the alphabet early used for numbers —Close resemblance about 500 B.C. between the letters which stand for 10 and 60—A 10 thus mistaken for 60 in Isa. vii. 8—Attempt to explain the remarkable reading of the LXX—The story of Dan. vi. the best proof of the youthful age of Darius—Cambyses not altogether bad —His kindness to the Jews in Egypt, as related in the letter from Elephantiné, possibly to be explained by the narrative of Dan. vi.— The "satraps" of Dan. vi. 1, 2—Reply to Charles' remarks on the title, sovereignty, and power ascribed to Darius—Possible extent of his kingdom—Explanation of the imperial style of his decree—That style justified in the light of the inscription on the Cyrus Cylinder—Dan. vi. helps to explain the removal of Cambyses from the throne of Babylon —Note on the letters Samekh and Yod.

CHAPTER XVI: THE EVANGELIC PROPHECY 168

Immense gulf between the critical and the orthodox interpretations— Statement of the traditional view and of the critical—Free treatment of Dan. ix. 24–27 at the hands of the LXX translator shown by placing a translation of the LXX side by side with the R.V.—Examination of the mutilation of the passage by the LXX and the reason thereof explained—The action of the LXX a strong proof that the prophecy does not refer to the Maccabean crisis—Interpretation of the passage offered by the critics involves a glaring chronological error in a prophecy remarkable for its exact numbers—Supposed Jewish ignorance of the chronology of the Persian period shown to be utterly unfounded—The attempt of the critics as complete a failure as that of the LXX.

CHAPTER XVII: THE EVANGELIC PROPHECY—*continued* ... 179

Short summary of the traditional interpretation of Dan. ix. 24–27— Occasion of the vision—The seer overcome with the enormity of the national sin—His earnest pleadings with God for the Holy City and the Chosen People—The speedy answer—Gabriel's kindly greeting—Expansion of the seventy years into seventy weeks of years—The order of the vision follows the order of Daniel's prayer; the atonement for sin standing first—The six clauses of verse 24—Translation of verses 25–27 —Punctuation of verse 25 in the A.V. explained and defended— *Terminus a quo* of the prophecy—The "troublous times"—Public appearance of the Messiah at the end of the sixty-nine weeks—"Prince Messiah" a compound title—The title Messiah, whence taken—Like Tsemach in Zech. iii. 8, here used as a proper name—Statements concerning Messiah's death.

CHAPTER XVIII: THE EVANGELIC PROPHECY—*continued*... 194

"The coming Prince" identified with "Prince Messiah"—The term usually points to Christ coming to judgment—Stier on Matt. xxii. 7— Dan. ix. 26b describes the judgment entailed by the crime of 26a—The Prince makes a firm covenant with his subjects during the seventieth week, which ends with the death of Stephen—Noticeable change of

PAGE

popular feeling towards Christianity after that event—Jerusalem's day of grace extends to the close of the seventieth week; but with Messiah's death in the middle of that week the Jewish sacrifices cease in God's sight—The "desolator" of verse 27 not to be confounded with "the people of the coming Prince" of verse 26—The expression points to the Zealots—Their atrocities as described by Josephus—The wrath poured out on the desolator.

CHAPTER XIX: Chronology of the Seventieth Week 206

The prophecy not concerned with literal days and weeks, but only with prophetic year-days—Three independent calculations which point to A.D. 26 as the year in which Messiah was proclaimed present among His people—The length of Christ's earthly ministry points to A.D. 29–30, the fourth "day" of the seventieth "week," as the year in which He suffered—Ramsay places the Crucifixion in A.D. 30, and the death of Stephen in A.D. 33—These two dates complete the chronology of the seventieth week—For the glory of "Prince Messiah" as well as to take in Israel's day of grace the prophecy is carried down to that point at which the Messianic kingdom is proclaimed to the Gentile world.

CHAPTER XX: On the Scenes of the Two Visions concerning the Jewish Church 212

Close connection of the visions in chaps. viii. and x.–xii.—Why the earlier vision of chap. vii. was shown to Daniel on the shore of "the great sea"—Why these more contracted visions on the banks of the Ulai and the Hiddekel—Daniel present there only in spirit—Physical features of Elam—Elam in the Assyrian period—Outlives Assyria—Probable story of her downfall—Western Elam, including Shushan, absorbed into the Babylonian Empire—Shushan later the favourite residence of the Persian kings—The fortress-palace at Shushan as pictured on a bas-relief—The canal Ulai symbolic of the wealth of the Persian kingdom—The Medo-Persian ram stands in front of this canal to guard his treasures—The fabulous wealth captured by Alexander at Shushan—God's voice heard between the banks of the Ulai—The Hiddekel, or Tigris, styled in chap. x. "the great river," a name elsewhere only bestowed on the Euphrates—The broad, still Ulai suggestive of commerce; the deep, rapid Tigris of the onrush of war—Why the vision of chaps. x.–xii. was shown by the Tigris rather than by the Euphrates or Orontes—The word for "river" in xii. 5, elsewhere used only of the Nile—The two names thus bestowed on the Tigris are suggestive of an overwhelming tyranny, a Babylon and Egypt combined, before which Judah must needs go under; but a Divine Person standing above the waters of the river is on her side—This Person is the Christ who walked on the waters of the Sea of Galilee—Note on the site of the ancient Shushan and the reputed tomb of Daniel.

CHAPTER XXI: The Language Evidence 226

Driver's famous verdict modified by its author—The Book of Daniel probably written in Aramaic—Historic facts concerning the Arameans—

PAGE

Babylonia ringed round with Aramean tribes—Aramaic the language of diplomacy and commerce—Not surprising that Daniel wrote in that language—Aramaic inscriptions—Discoveries made at Elephantiné—The Elephantiné legal documents commence about sixty-five years after the time of Daniel—The Elephantiné letter of 408 B.C.—Its purport—English translation with notes—Grammar and syntax of the letter the same as that of the Aramaic of Daniel—A noticeable difference in one respect—How explained—"Eastern" and "Western Aramaic" misnomers—The Aramaic of Daniel suggests that the Book was written in Babylonia rather than in Palestine.

CHAPTER XXII: EVIDENCE OF THE FOREIGN WORDS ... 241

The foreign words in the Book of Daniel a valuable evidence as to its authenticity—Driver's verdict on the Old Persian words loses sight of some important facts—Daniel's position well explains his use of such words—The Aramaic in close contact with the Old Persian for at least two centuries before the time of Daniel—Character of the majority of the Old Persian words used—How the others are to be accounted for—Daniel written in the early Persian period—The Old Persian words stitch the two parts of the Book together—The *fewness* of the Greek words fatal to the theory that the Book was written in 165 B.C.—Greek musical instruments naturally bore Greek names—Contact between the Assyrians and the Greeks in the latter half of the eighth and the earlier half of the seventh centuries B.C.—Sennacherib, for the sake of commerce with the West, keeps open the "Cilician Road" in 698 B.C.—Traces of Greek architecture in Assyria and Ararat in the time of Sargon II.—Striking Greek decorations on the façade of Nebuchadnezzar's palace—The artists probably Greek captives brought from Egypt—The Nebuchadnezzar cameo—Greek soldiers in the Babylonian army—The musical instruments probably from Asiatic Greece—Answer to the objection that two of the Greek words do not occur in classical Greek till long after the time of Daniel—Greek instruments suit the tastes of the reigning monarch—Assyro-Babylonian elements in the Book of Daniel—The foreign words a voucher for the period at which the Book was written—Light thrown by them on the region in which it was written, and on the person of the writer—APPENDICES: I. On the Old Persian Words; II. On the Assyro-Babylonian Words.

CHAPTER XXIII: THE BOOK OF DANIEL AND THE JEWISH APOCALYPSES 268

The Book of Enoch the most famous of the Apocalypses—Driver's description of a Jewish apocalypse—The pseudonymous character of these works, how to be accounted for—The Book of Daniel classed by the critics with the Apocalypses—The idea refuted (i) by the absence in this Book of any plain connecting link with the Old Testament mention of the hero whose name it bears; (ii) but still more evidently by the writer's perfect acquaintance with Babylonian history and the peculiar linguistic features of his work—Cause for thankfulness to God suggested by these facts.

PAGE

CHAPTER XXIV: On the Position of the Book of Daniel in the Canon of the Old Testament ... 276

Little known about the formation of the Canon—The present position of Daniel in the Canon not its original position—The number of the Old Testament books indicated in 2 Esdras xiv.—The threefold division referred to Luke xxiv. 44, and first mentioned in the prologue to Ecclesiasticus—The Palestinian and Talmudic Canons—Two statements from Josephus showing that in his day Daniel was placed in the Prophets—Witness of Melito and Origen to the same effect—In Jerome's day Daniel is found in the Hagiographa—Possible reason for this change—Surprise of Jerome at the position of the Book—The Book depreciated by its new position—Bearing of the above facts on Matt. xxiii. 35—The argument clenched—"The books" in Dan. ix. 2 to be referred, not to a collection of sacred books, but to the writings of Jeremiah

CHAPTER XXV: The Testimony of Christ 286

The view held by Christ, if He be regarded merely as a human teacher steeped in Old Testament lore, demands nevertheless the consideration of doubters—The Book of Daniel treated by Him with special honour—Echoes of this Book in the Revelation—The Revelation throws light on the appearances of Christ in the visions shown to Daniel—It also helps to identify Daniel's Fourth Kingdom with Rome, pagan and papal—That criticism which is higher than Christ must be looked upon as coming from beneath.

Additional Note 294

Indexes 297

ILLUSTRATIONS

FACING PAGE

Plan of Babylon ... ... *Frontispiece*
From Koldewey's "Excavations at Babylon."

Principal Citadel of Babylon, built by Nebuchadnezzar 50
Koldewey, Fig. 98.

Plan of Eastern section of the Southern Citadel, showing the position of the Hanging Gardens 68
Koldewey, Fig. 44.

Stone Wall of Northern Citadel, built by Nebuchadnezzar ... 74
Koldewey, Fig. 110.

The Ishtar Gate 76
Koldewey, Fig. 24.

The India House Inscription 96

Cylinder of Nabonidus, inscribed with a Prayer in behalf of his son Belshazzar 114
British Museum.

Cylinder of Cyrus, with an Inscription describing his Capture of Babylon 128
British Museum.

Plan of the Central Part of the Southern Citadel, showing the Throne-room of the Neo-Babylonian Kings 134
Koldewey, Fig. 63.

The Teima Stone 158

Decoration of the Façade of the Throne-room at Babylon, in the so-called Ionic Style 248
Koldewey, Fig. 64.

Gem in the Museum at the Hague, with an Inscription of Nebuchadnezzar 250

Cameo of Nebuchadnezzar now in the Museum at Florence 250

Head of Shabitoku 252
"Passing of the Empires," p. 360.

Funerary Stele of a Lycaonian Soldier built into the S. Wall of Konieh, the Ancient Iconium 252
Lewin's "Life and Epistles of St. Paul," Vol. I. p. 146.

TABLE 1

Chronology of the New Babylonian Empire

626 B.C. Nabopolassar, king of Babylon, on the death of Ashurbanipal, king of Assyria.

614 B.C. Nineveh besieged by Cyaxares of Media.

612 B.C. Fall of Nineveh before the combined attack of Medes, Babylonians, and Scythians.

610 B.C. Overthrow at Haran by an army of Babylonians and Scythians of the last vestiges of the kingdom of Assyria.

608 B.C. Pharaoh Necho slays Josiah at Megiddo, defeats Babylon at Carchemish; and returning, places Jehoiakim on the throne of Judah in place of Jehoahaz.

605 B.C. Nebuchadnezzar's first visit to Jerusalem. After defeating Necho at Carchemish, he presses on through Judah, and invades Egypt; then, hearing of the death of his father Nabopolassar, returns in haste across the desert to Babylon to receive the crown. Daniel and his friends brought to Babylon, along with other captives, Jewish, Syrian, Phœnician, Egyptian, and of "the nations belonging to Egypt": *Josephus c. Apion*, i. 19.

605–600 B.C. Early inscriptions of Nebuchadnezzar, telling of recent conflicts.

603 B.C. Daniel recovers and interprets the king's dream: Dan. ii. 1.

600–593 B.C. Nebuchadnezzar rebuilds numerous temples, beginning with the completion of the temple-tower at Babylon and the rebuilding at Larsa of the temple of the Sun, the foundations of which had been swept bare by the winds.

597 B.C. Nebuchadnezzar's second visit to Jerusalem: Zedekiah appointed to succeed Jehoiachin. On his way thither he cuts down cedars in the Lebanon.

594 B.C. Nebuchadnezzar summons Zedekiah to Babylon: Jer. li. 59.

592 B.C. Ezekiel's first mention of Daniel: chap. xiv. 14, 20.

588 B.C. The Babylonian army pass through the Lebanon: Wady Brissa Inscription A cut. Cedars cut down and brought into Babylon by the Arakhtu canal between 588 and 586 B.C.

587 B.C. January. Siege of Jerusalem begins: 2 Kings xxv. 1. Ezekiel's second mention of Daniel: chap. xxviii. 3. In this year, according to the LXX and Peshitto, the golden image of Dan. iii. was set up.

586 B.C. Nebuchadnezzar's third visit to Jerusalem; establishes his headquarters at Riblah in Hamath. Wady Brissa Inscription B cut. The city falls in July; after which the siege of Tyre begins.

573 B.C. Tyre taken after a thirteen years' siege: Ezek. xxix. 17–20.

568 B.C. Nebuchadnezzar invades Egypt and encounters Amasis (fragment of the Annals).

562 B.C. Nebuchadnezzar dies, and is succeeded by his son Evil-merodach (=Amel-Marduk, "servant of Merodach").

560 B.C. Neriglissar (=Nergal-shar-utsur, "Nergal protect the king"), son-in-law of Nebuchadnezzar, succeeds Evil-merodach.

556 B.C. Labashi-Marduk, son of Neriglissar, reigns three months, and is succeeded by a usurper Nabonidus. Nabonidus, writing of the events of this year, mentions Cyrus as "king of Anshan," and calls him "Merodach's little servant."

553 B.C. The Median army deliver up Astyages to Cyrus, who after spoiling Ecbatana returns to Anshan.

549 B.C. Belshazzar, son of Nabonidus, in command of the Babylonian army.

547 B.C. Cyrus called "king of Persia" for the first time.

539 B.C. Babylon taken by Cyrus. Nabonidus captured by Cyrus. Belshazzar slain in a night attack on the palace.

538 B.C. First year of Cyrus. Proclamation for the return of the Jews. Cambyses "king of Babylon" for nine months from the beginning of the year.

536 B.C. Third year of Cyrus; date of Daniel's latest vision: chap. x. 1.

TABLE 2

To show the wide diffusion of the Arameans, and their contact with Median tribes speaking the Old Persian some 200 years before the probable date of the Book of Daniel.

1650 B.C. Agum-kakrimi, king of Babylon, styles himself "king of Padan and of Alman" (=Arman, cf. Padan-Aram: Gen. xxviii. 2)

1350 B.C. Pudi-ilu, king of Assyria, conquers the Akhlami, an Aramean tribe.

1150 B.C. Ashur-rish-ishi overthrows "the wide-spread host of the Akhlami."

1120 B.C. Tiglathpileser I. speaks of "the Aramean Akhlami the foes of Ashur" as extending from the country of the Shuhites to Carchemish.

1050 B.C. Saul fights against the Aramean "kings of Zobah": 1 Sam. xiv. 47.

1010 B.C. David smites the Arameans of Syria, Damascus, and Aram-naharaim: 2 Sam. viii. 3-5, and Ps. lx. title.

885–860 B.C. Ashurnatsirpal conquers Bit Adini (cf. 2 Kings xix. 12) and other Aramean states on the Middle Euphrates.

850 B.C. Aramaic inscription of Zakir king of Hamath.

770–730 B.C. Aramaic inscriptions of the kings of Samahla on the E. slope of Amanus, and a little N. of the N.E. angle of the Mediterranean.

745 B.C. Tiglathpileser III. speaks of "the land of the Arameans" as extending from the Tigris to where the Uknu (the river of Shushan) falls into the Persian Gulf, and mentions Aramean tribes conquered by him whose territories extended to the Median border.

744 B.C. Tiglathpileser transports 65,000 Medes and Arameans to other parts of the empire.

722 B.C. Sargon places captive Israelites among the Arameans on the Khabur, and in "the cities of the Medes": 2 Kings xvii. 6.

536 B.C. The Aramaic of Daniel, interspersed with twenty Old Persian words.

471–411 B.C. The Jews of Elephantine write in Aramaic closely resembling the Aramaic of the Book of Daniel.

TABLE 3

To show the contact of Assyria, Babylonia, and Egypt with the Asiatic Greeks for over a century before the age of Daniel.

715 B.C. Sargon clears the E. Levant of Greek pirates: *Cylinder Inscr.*, line 21.

711 B.C. A Greek king in Ashdod: *Khorsabad Inscr.*, line 95.

707 B.C. Seven kings of Cyprus send presents to Sargon at Babylon: *Ibid.* line 196.

698 B.C. Sennacherib, to keep open the trade route, encounters the Greeks in Cilicia, and builds an "Athenian temple" at Tarsus: *Cuneiform Texts from Babylonian Tablets in the Br. Museum*, pt. xxvi.

697 B.C. Sennacherib employs Greek captives to build him a fleet on the Tigris: *Bull Inscr.*, No. 4, lines 56–60.

674 B.C. Ten kings of Cyprus—nine of them with Greek names—send materials to build Esarhaddon's palace at Nineveh: *Esarhaddon, Cylinder B*, col. 5, lines 19–27.

664 B.C. Greeks help Psammetichus I. of Egypt to conquer the Dodekarchy. In return he uses Greek mercenaries, and plants two camps of them at Daphnæ on either side of the Pelusiac branch of the Nile: *Herod.* bk. ii. 152, 154.

605 B.C. Nebuchadnezzar, after his campaign against Egypt, plants colonies in Babylonia, consisting of Jews, Phenicians, Syrians, and "of the nations belonging to Egypt": *Joseph. c. Apion*, bk. i. 19.

595 B.C. Nebuchadnezzar, rebuilding the Old Palace at Babylon, employs Greek architectural decorations on the façade of the throne-room: *Koldewey's Excavations*, pp. 104, 105, and plate opposite p. 130.

587 B.C. In the 18th year of Nebuchadnezzar (according to the LXX.), three instruments with Greek names are found in the king's band amongst "all kinds of music": Dan. iii. 5.

In and Around the Book of Daniel

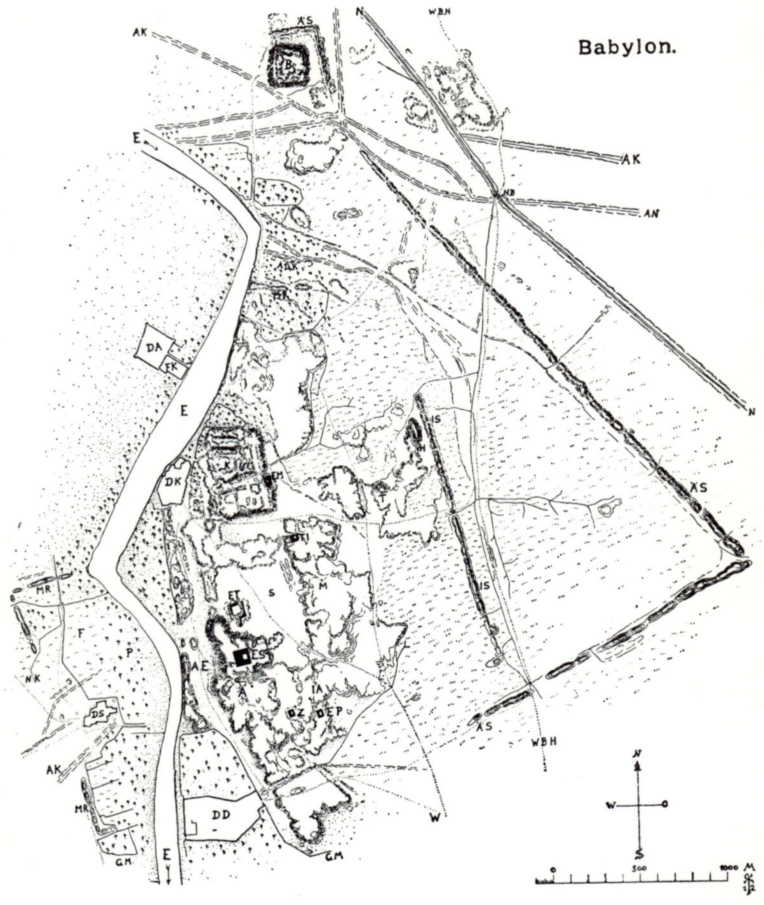

PLAN OF BABYLON

From Koldewey's "Excavations At Babylon"

1

Introduction

WITH the spread of learning and the issue from time to time of fresh commentaries on the Book of Daniel, it is now a matter of common knowledge that two very different views are held respecting that Book, which, for the sake of a name, may be styled respectively the orthodox and the critical—not that all critics are on the same side, but simply that the majority of modern critics incline to the latter view. They may also be styled the Roman and the Grecian, according to the scheme of interpretation adopted with regard to the Four Kingdoms in the vision of Daniel, chaps. ii. and vii. In a book written in defence of the orthodox position it may be well to devote the first chapter to explaining the main difficulty which confronts the upholders of that position, and to showing how that difficulty may be met without having recourse to the solution proposed by the critics—a solution which does great violence to the Book of Daniel as a whole, and creates more difficulties than it removes.

According to the orthodox view, the Book of Daniel is a narrative of some surprising events that happened in the life of a saintly Jewish captive, holding a very high position at the courts of Babylon and of Persia, a fragmentary biography of one who was a special favourite of heaven, including visions such as have been granted to no other man, except possibly the beloved apostle—visions reaching to the end of time. Thus viewed, this Book occupies a unique position in the Old Testament, and as such it was treated by the Founder of Christianity, for there is no other Book of the Old Testament to which Christ pays greater honour than to this Book of Daniel. The estimate, however, of this Book formed by the critics is something far different. To them it appears as one of the Pseudepigrapha, or Jewish religious books, written under a false, or rather an assumed name, which appeared in the second and first centuries B.C., such as the Book of Enoch and the Testaments of the Twelve Patriarchs. They would probably confess it to be the most remarkable of those books, the noblest and the loftiest in its teaching, the grandest in its scope no less than in its descriptions, a literary work of superlative merit; but at the same time a merely human composition. To put the matter in another light, the critics look upon the Book of Daniel as a religious novel, resting upon a shadowy background of history, written about 164 B.C. in the troublous days of the Maccabees, and written with this noble intention, viz. to encourage the faithful in a time of persecution and to support them under very severe trials. Accordingly they see much in this Book that meets with their approval, and are fully awake to its literary beauties. But, all the same, it is in their eyes a mere work of the imagination, cleverly put together, but containing not a few historical inaccuracies, owing to its having been written some three or four hundred years after the times which it describes. To them, therefore, its great facts are pure fancies; its mighty miracles, mere feats of the imagination; its so-called prophecies, past history clothed with the garb of prophecy—a favourite practice in the apocalypses of the Pseudepigrapha. If this view of the matter be the correct one, the puzzle is, How did this Book of Daniel come to be included in the sacred Canon of the Old Testament? and how came it to be treated by our Lord Jesus Christ with such special honour?

The question is altogether such an important one that we may well ask on what ground the critical view is based. And here it is not sufficient to answer that the critics as a body believe neither in miracle nor in prophecy. This doubtless is the case with some, but it is not the whole truth of the matter. To understand their position aright we must turn to the long and striking prophecy of Daniel, chap. xi., which foretells the sufferings of the Jewish people under the Greek empire of Syria, more particularly in the days of Antiochus the Great and his son Antiochus Epiphanes. This chapter is the great crux of the Book of Daniel, and on the remarkable features presented by it the critics base an argument, which at first sight seems unanswerable, to show that the Book was written, as stated above, in or about the year 164 B.C. This argument is admirably set forth by the late Prof. Driver in his Commentary on Daniel. Speaking of chap. xi. Dr. Driver says, "The minuteness of the predictions, embracing even special events in the distant future, is out of harmony with the analogy of prophecy." This is certainly true, for we do not find such detailed prophecies in Isaiah, Jeremiah, or Zechariah; and yet such an argument, taken alone, is not of itself fatal to the authenticity of a Book which in some respects is unique. For surely it may well be granted that the Almighty Ruler of the world knows the end from the beginning, and can, if He sees fit, unfold with minuteness the events even of a far-distant future. The real difficulty is explained by Dr. Driver in the following words: "While down to the period of Antiochus' persecution the *actual* facts are described with surprising distinctness, after this point *the distinctness ceases:* the closing events of Antiochus' own life are, to all appearance, not described as they actually occurred." [1] We venture to think that any honest critic who has studied the matter will be ready to endorse this statement. Thus, in chap. xi. 21–39 we find described many events in Antiochus' remarkable career, *e.g.* his coming into the kingdom by stealth and gaining power by flattery, *v.* 21; his lavish prodigality, *v.* 24; his two expeditions against Egypt (the second, owing to the interposition of the Romans, terminating so differently from the first), *vv.* 25–30; his persecution of the Jews when returning from his first Egyptian expedition, *v.* 28; his attempt to put down and stamp out the temple worship when returning crestfallen from his second expedition, *v.* 31; the early triumphs of the Maccabees, *v.* 34; the assumption by Antiochus of divine honours during the later years of his reign, when he appears on coins as "Antiochus, the God Manifest," *v.* 36; and, finally, the special honours paid by him to Jupiter Capitolinus, "the god of fortresses," *vv.* 38, 39. But when we pass over the evident pause at the close of this 39th verse, this distinctness ceases, and we make what Prof. Charles styles "a transition from history to prophecy" [2]: prophecy which fits in very badly if we restrict and apply it to the closing events of Antiochus' career. Thus, nothing is known from secular history of any further invasion of Egypt such as is described in *vv.* 40–42; whilst Antiochus himself, so far from "having power over the treasures of gold and of silver and over all the precious things of Egypt," *v.* 43, was in sore financial straits towards the close of his life, and died, not in the Holy Land, as *v.* 45 seems to imply, but in Elymais, after a fruitless attempt to rob a temple of its treasures. If, then, we take these closing verses, 40–45, to apply to Antiochus Epiphanes, they appear before us as a prophecy that was never fulfilled; in fact as nothing more than a vain surmise. From the above phenomena the critics have drawn the very evident conclusion

[1] *Cambridge Bible*, Daniel, Introduction, p. lxvi.
[2] *Century Bible*, Daniel, p. 136.

that this seeming prophecy was written just at the point of time where it begins to fail of accomplishment, so that verses 1–39 are nothing more than past history put into the garb of prophecy, and verses 40–45 a speculation on the part of the author as to what he thought likely to happen in the immediate future.

At first sight the above argument seems unanswerable, since it certainly meets the great difficulty presented by this chapter. But it is certain nevertheless that it cannot be the true solution of that difficulty, since, however well it may solve the riddle of chap. xi., we are forced, if we accept it, to do the greatest violence to the rest of the Book. The critics, allowing themselves to be guided by conclusions based on this closing prophecy, use, if one may so say, the tail to waggle the dog, and whenever this is done the dog perforce must exhibit the most unnatural contortions. Thus, then, having arrived at the firm conviction, based on the phenomena presented by chap. xi., that the Book was written about 164 B.C., the critics proceed to make everything fit in with this theory, and treat all the other visions of this Book as so much past history put into the form of Jewish apocalyptic. Hence it follows that the four kingdoms of chap. ii. in their eyes cannot be Babylon, Persia, Greece, and Rome, but must be Babylon, Media, Persia, and Greece, seeing that in 164 B.C. Rome, though on her way to greatness, had not yet developed into a world power. By this wrenching asunder of Media and Persia great violence is done to chap. viii., where the unity of the Medo-Persian kingdom is so distinctly affirmed, first in the vision, where it appears as a ram with two horns of which the higher is seen springing up last, and secondly in the words of the interpreting angel, " The ram which thou sawest that had the two horns, they are the kings of Media and Persia."

Another striking instance of the same thing is found in the treatment dealt out by the critics to the Evangelic prophecy of chap. ix., a prophecy remarkable beyond all others for its exact chronological precision. In endeavouring to make this prophecy fit in with their views they are obliged to admit an error of no less than 67 years in the prophet's reckoning, which they unblushingly ascribe to the writer's faulty information on points of past history ! [1] Other examples of forced interpretation will be given in the course of the next chapter, but enough has been adduced to show that by accepting this view of the critics, derived from the singular phenomena of chap. xi., we only plunge ourselves into far greater and graver difficulties than those which

[1] *Century Bible*, Daniel, p. 107.

confront the orthodox expositor. It is best, then, to turn our attention to another explanation of that remarkable chapter, put forward by the late Dr. C. H. H. Wright in his scholarly work on the prophecies of the Book of Daniel. Dr. Wright maintains that Dan. chap. xi. is of the nature of a paraphrase or targum, in which a genuine prophecy of Daniel lies embedded.[1] In other words, a genuine prophecy is here interpolated and overlaid by real or supposed fulfilments. These interpolations and additions continue down to the end of verse 39, after which we have the original prophecy, copied out pure and simple without any paraphrase, down to its close at chap. xii. 4. Now, it is owing to these interpolations in the first thirty-nine verses of chap. xi. that we naturally look upon the closing verses, viz. 40–45, as a continued description of the events which are to happen in the career of Antiochus Epiphanes; whereas it seems more likely, on further investigation, that these last verses, forming a part of the original prophecy of Daniel, contain an ideal picture of the overthrow of the heathen Greek-Syrian power on the mountains of Israel—a picture called up before the mind of the seer by Isaiah's prophecy of the overthrow of the host of Sennacherib in Jehovah's land and upon His mountains. Thus regarded, the prophecy of verses 40–45 certainly received its fulfilment. It was in the little commonwealth of Judah, and in the days of the Maccabees, that God "chose the weak things of the world to put to shame the things that are strong, and the things that are not to bring to nought the things that are."[2] In the words of Dr. Wright, "The last and final overthrow of Greece, as a world-power antagonistic to truth and to God, took place on the mountains of Judea."[3]

The above explanation as to the earlier and larger part of chap. xi. having been interpolated will come as a surprise to many. In the first place, it certainly contains a concession to the argument of the critics. Dr. Wright himself admits that "the closing prophecy of Daniel, *in its present form*, cannot be proved to go back to an earlier period than 164 B.C."; while he very wisely adds that "it by no means follows that such a statement is true with regard to the Book of Daniel as a whole."[4] In the second place, it will strike some minds that Holy Scripture has here been tampered with, and certainly the allegation is true; and yet it is easily accounted for, if we regard the peculiar circumstances

[1] *Daniel and his Prophecies*, pp. 314, 315, 318.

[2] 1 Cor. i. 27.

[3] *Daniel and his Prophecies*, p. 318.

[4] *Ibid.* p. 318.

under which the Book of Daniel has been handed down to us. As noticed above, this Book is of a fragmentary nature, probably a book of extracts from some larger work. It gives us certain passages from the life of the seer and his friends, with his own account of his visions appended. Two of these visions, viz. those of chaps. viii. and xi., are found to be very closely connected both in subject-matter and in the language employed. They are evidently from the pen of the same author. Now, in both of these chapters the religious persecutions of Antiochus Epiphanes figure largely. This would make the original work, from which we may suppose our present Book to have been taken, an object of especial detestation to the persecuting party, whose evil deeds are therein so clearly foretold. When they rent in pieces the Books of the Law, it is hardly likely that they would spare that Book which foretells so plainly their unrighteous doings.[1] So, then, like some noble cathedral which still bears the marks of the rough treatment which it received at the hands of Cromwell's soldiers, this sacred and venerable Book still shows some evident signs of its having come through the wars. In this way, and no other, can we explain the two languages in which it has come down to us. Chaps. i. to ii. 3, and viii. to xii. are written in Hebrew; while the central portion of the Book, viz. ii. 4 to the end of vii., is in Aramaic, as is explained by the words "in Aramaic," inserted in the text of ii. 4, just as in the *last* clause of Ezra iv. 7.[2] The fact that the change of language in chap. ii. occurs in the very middle of a narrative is proof that the documents used were imperfect. Either the Hebrew copy was used to supplement the Aramaic, or the Aramaic to supplement the Hebrew. Further, it is deserving of notice that in the opinion of most scholars the Book was originally written in Aramaic. In the words of Dr. Charles, "the Aramaic section of Daniel does not give the impression of a translation, and nowhere points to a Hebrew original; the Hebrew sections, on the other hand, favour the hypothesis of an Aramaic original, since they contain frequent Aramaisms."[3] The eleventh chapter of Daniel is, then, in the first place, a translation from the original; and, in the second place, it is a translation that has been added to by way of interpolation; and to this is due the form in which it has come down to us. What has happened to the Greek Septuagint

[1] See 1 Macc. i. 56.

[2] Both in Dan. ii. 4, and in Ezra iv. 7, the words "in Aramaic" ought to be written in italics in the middle of a space left blank.

[3] Dr. Charles is quoting the opinion of Marti and Wright, in which he himself concurs. *Century Bible*, Daniel, p. xxv.

translation has happened also to the Hebrew translation of chap. xi.; *it has been added to,* and the nature of the additions resembles to some extent the expository comments which we meet with in the Hebrew Targums.

The writers of the Targums, or ancient Aramaic commentaries on the Scriptures of the Old Testament, loved to introduce into Scripture prophecies fulfilments, actual or supposed, in such a way that they appear as parts of the original prophecy. "In such paraphrases," writes Dr. Wright, "phrases of the original are retained, although often so modified and obscured by expository comments that if we possessed only the Targum it would be often impossible to restore the original text."[1] Thus, in the Targum of Onkelos, the Blessing of Dan, Gen. xlix. 16–18, is made to include a prophecy of the exploits of Samson, which runs thus:

"From the house of Dan will be chosen, and will arise, a man in whose days his people shall be delivered, and in whose years the tribes of Israel shall have rest together. A chosen man will arise from the house of Dan, the terror of whom shall fall upon the peoples, who will smite the Philistines with strength as the serpent, the deadly serpent lurking by the way; he will smite the might of the Philistine host, the horsemen with the foot, he will weaken the horses and chariots and throw their riders backwards. For thy salvation have I waited, O Lord."[2]

Similarly, in the Palestinian Targum the blessing given to Abraham in Gen. xii. 3, "I will bless them that bless thee, and him that curseth thee will I curse, and in thee shall all the families of the earth be blessed," is paraphrased thus: "I will bless the priests who spread forth their hands in prayer, and Balaam who will curse thee, I will curse, and they shall slay him with the mouth of the sword: and in thee shall be blessed all the generations of the earth." For another example of definite fulfilments introduced into the broad outlines of the original prophecy, take the blessing given by Isaac to Jacob, Gen. xxvii. 29, as we find it paraphrased in the Palestinian Targum: "Let peoples be subject to thee, all the sons of Esau, and kingdoms bend before thee, all the sons of Keturah, a chief and a ruler be thou over thy brethren, and let the sons of thy mother salute thee. Let them who curse thee, my son, be accursed as Balaam the son of Beor, and those

[1] *Daniel and his Prophecies*, p. 253.

[2] *The Targums of Onkelos and Jonathan Ben Uzziel on the Pentateuch,* translated into English by J. W. Etheridge, London, 1862.

who bless thee be blessed, as Moses the prophet, the scribe of Israel." One other instance, of some interest to us as forming an early exemplification of the two systems of interpretation of the Four Kingdoms of Daniel, chap. ii., serves at the same time to exhibit the extravagances of some of these Jewish paraphrases. I allude to the words of Gen. xv. 12: "And when the sun was going down, a deep sleep fell upon Abraham, and lo, an horror of great darkness fell upon him." In the Palestinian Targum this passage is paraphrased thus: "And when the sun was nearing to set, a deep sleep was thrown upon Abraham, and behold four kingdoms rose to enslave his children: Horror, which is Babylon; Darkness, which is Media; Greatness, which is Javan (Greece); Falling, which is Persia, which is to fall and to have no uplifting." In the Jerusalem Targum the interpretation runs on similar lines, while the four kingdoms are identified with Babylon, Media (Medo-Persia), Greece, and Edom (Rome). Similar interpolations to those in the Targums are met with in the Peshitto or ancient Syriac version of the Book of Daniel. According to Wright, they are sometimes written in red ink, but appear in the London polyglot without any distinction of ink. In this version Dan. xi. 6 reads thus:

"And at the end of years they shall agree (the daughter of Ptolemy he has given to Alexander the brother of Antiochus and Peter), and the daughter of the king of the south shall go to the king of the north (Alexander went and took Petra the daughter of Ptolemy to be his wife) to make peace between them (and Ptolemy came against Alexander his son-in-law to kill him), and there shall be no strength in her because of fear that she shall fear (and the daughter of Ptolemy she shall be given to Demetrius after Alexander her husband is dead), and she shall be handed over, she and her bringers and her maidens and her strengtheners at that time."

In one respect it will be noticed that there is a very marked difference between the interpolated prophecy of Daniel, chap. xi., and the examples quoted from the Targums and the Peshitto. In the prophecy there is an entire absence of proper names, whereby a slightly obscuring veil is drawn over the different incidents. In the Targums and the Peshitto, on the other hand, all is made plain, definite, and specific. In this respect Dan. xi. resembles the Jewish Pseudepigrapha rather than the Targums. This is just what might be expected, since the interpolations date, as we have seen, from about 164 B.C., and were therefore made in the age of the Pseudepigrapha.

Before we pass on from the difficulties presented by Daniel's latest vision, it will be well to direct attention to the words of the revealing angel, spoken at the close of that vision: "But thou, O Daniel, shut up the words, and seal the book, even to the time of the end: many shall run to and fro, and knowledge shall be increased." "Shut up the words": the angel is speaking, not merely of this one vision, but of all the visions shown to Daniel in this Book. This may be gathered from chap. x. 1, with which the vision opens, which should be rendered thus: "In the third year of Cyrus king of Persia, a word was revealed unto Daniel, whose name was called Belteshazzar, and the word was true, even a great warfare: and he understood the word, and had understanding of the vision." This last clause shows that the expressions "word" and "vision" are synonymous, as appears also from the last clause of chap. ix. 23, "therefore consider the word [1] and understand the vision." "The two expressions 'word' and 'vision,'" writes Dr. Charles, "mean practically the same thing, denoting its twofold relation, in regard to God and in regard to man." [2] But if "word" is thus equivalent to "vision," then the use of the plural "words" in xii. 4, shows that the angel is speaking, not only of the vision in chaps. x.–xii., but of *all* Daniel's visions, including that of chap. ii., which was shown to Daniel as well as to Nebuchadnezzar,[3] and that we are justified in understanding the words "Seal the book," to apply to all the seer's recorded visions, and in some sense to the whole Book of Daniel so far as it contains aught that is puzzling and mysterious. This wider sense of the words is warranted by the fact that the angel's words come at the close of the Book of Daniel as it has been preserved to us.

In chap. xii. 4, Daniel is told to "Shut up the words and seal the book." Then, a little farther on, in verse 9, we read, "Go thy way, Daniel: for the words are shut up and sealed till the time of the end." The two statements seem to conflict, but the meaning is, that Daniel is to roll up and seal his scrolls of vision, first as being completed and requiring safe keeping, since it would be a long, long time before they would be fulfilled; and secondly, as a symbolic act, indicating that in the Divine intention those visions were—if one may use such a paradox—hidden revelations, which would not be made plain till the far-off time of their fulfilment. "I heard, but I understood not," is the seer's own complaint, xii. 8. And again, in viii. 27, when his vision had been

[1] R.V. "matter."

[2] *Century Bible*, note on Dan. ix. 23.

[3] Dan. ii. 19.

explained to him, he says, sadly, evidently including himself in the statement, " I was astonished at the vision, but none understood it," *i.e.* none fully comprehended it, indeed none could until the day of its fulfilment. How much more would this be the case with this last vision! What commentator, even in this enlightened age, has been able to show the meaning of the mystic 1290 days and 1335 days? Clearly these and other mysteries will remain hidden till the time of their fulfilment. It follows, then, that the best commentary on Daniel xii. 4 and 9, is that offered by Isa. xxix. 11:

" And all vision is become unto you as the words of a book that is sealed, which men deliver to one that is learned, saying, Read this, I pray thee: and he saith, I cannot, for it is sealed: and the book is delivered to him that is not learned, saying, Read this, I pray thee: and he saith, I am not learned."

In the deep things of God the greatest doctor and the most illiterate believer stand in exactly the same position: both are alike unable to explain them.

It was a grief to Daniel that he could not understand the visions vouchsafed to him, therefore in *vv.* 9 and 13 the angel says kindly to him, " Go thy way," or, as it is rendered in Theodotion's translation of *v.* 9, " Come hither, Daniel." Also in *v.* 4, by way of comfort, he is assured that during the long interval between the time of his receiving the visions and the time of their accomplishment " many shall run to and fro and knowledge shall be increased." It is his special honour to have received from heaven the most sublime and astonishing visions, which shall engage the attention of many devout students, whose labours as time goes on shall not be unrewarded. Here was comfort for the prophet, and here, likewise, is a stimulus to those who apply themselves to the study of his writings. The Hebrew word for " run to and fro " denotes earnest vigilance and scrutiny, with a fixed object. Thus, " the eyes of the Lord run to and fro through the whole earth," Zech. iv. 10, taking knowledge of, and paying the closest attention to, all that is going on. So, too, in Jer. v. 1, the same word is used, when the prophet directs a diligent search to be made throughout the streets of Jerusalem to see if there is one upright, honest man left. There also lies in the Hebrew root the idea of quick glancing motion, as in the strokes of a whip and the lashing of the water with oars. Here it is used of the quick motion of the eye glancing across the written page.[1]

[1] From the root שׁוּט are derived שׁוֹט "a whip," and שַׁיִט "rowing," as whipping or lashing the water.

"Many shall run to and fro": as in the case of other Books of Holy Scripture, notably the Book of Isaiah, so in the case of this Book of Daniel, the extraordinary number of commentaries constantly issuing from the press bears witness to the intrinsic worth of the original prophecy. One stands amazed before the vast bibliography given by Wright in the Introduction to *Daniel and its Critics*. To this, then, already well-fulfilled prediction is added the promise, "*knowledge shall be increased*," a promise which the writer ventures to think is also being fulfilled in the vast development of knowledge with respect to the times of the prophet Daniel, opened up through the progress of cuneiform discovery. Thus, to quote some instances, the inscriptions of Nebuchadnezzar, as now made known, bear witness to the truthfulness of the picture of that monarch given us in this Book of Daniel, and are even a voucher for its being the work of a contemporary. The "Chaldeans" of this Book are now identified as the priests of the god Bel, men who formed the *élite* of Babylonian society. Belshazzar, whose very existence was long doubted of, stands before us as the energetic son of Nabonidus, the last king of Babylon, and one of Dr. Pinches' latest discoveries shows that he was associated with his father in the sovereignty. Darius the Mede, despite the difficulty caused by his age as given in chap. v. 31, appears to the writer to be none other than Cambyses the son of Cyrus, who, in the first year after the capture of Babylon, reigned for some ten months as king of Babylon, being probably intended by his father to succeed Belshazzar. A fairly good case can also be made out for Gobryas. This view is adopted by Dr. Pinches; the former one by the celebrated Assyriologist Winckler.[1] The circumstances of the capture of the royal palace in Babylon, as described in chap. v., are found to be in complete agreement with the details given us on the Annalistic Tablet of Cyrus. Finally, the foreign words which occur in the Book of Daniel, and which formed such a stumbling-block to the late Prof. Driver, appear rather to form a powerful proof of the genuineness of this Book, a voucher in fact that its author occupied a position such as was actually held by Daniel at the court of Persia at the close of his long life. In all these respects, which will be dealt with at large in the following pages, the writer sees a wonderful fulfilment of the promise, "knowledge shall be increased": and it is this conviction, along with his deep love for so sublime a Book, that has led him to undertake a task,

[1] See Pinches' *Old Testament in the Light of the Historical Records of Assyria and Babylonia*, p. 419, and Winckler in Schrader's *Die Keilinschriften und das Alte Testament*, p. 288.

congenial enough in itself, but not unattended with difficulties. May the Divine Angel, who stands "above the waters of the river,"[1] be pleased to use this work to stem the rising tide of destructive criticism: or, if it should be His will to let that tide rise yet higher, may it speedily, in the prophet's words, "overflow and pass through."[2] And if this should be so, it will not be the first time that such a thing has happened in the annals of Biblical Criticism.

[1] Dan. xii. 6.

[2] Isa. viii. 8, quoted in Dan. xi. 10 and 40.

2

The Four Kingdoms (Daniel 2, 7, and 8)

REFERENCE has already been made at the beginning of Chapter I. to the two main schemes of interpretation of the Book of Daniel and their bearing on the question of the Four Kingdoms of Daniel, chaps. ii. and vii. The matter may be best presented to our readers by placing it before them in tabular form as follows :

GRECIAN SCHEME

CHAP. II	CHAP. VII	CHAP. VIII	
Golden head.	=Lion with eagle's wings.		= Babylonian Empire.
Silver breast and arms.	= Bear with three ribs, etc.	= First and shorter horn of the ram.	= Median Empire.
Brazen belly and thighs.	= Leopard with four wings.	= Second and longer horn of the ram.	= Persian Empire.
Iron legs, with feet and toes partly iron, partly clay.	= Beast with iron teeth and ten horns.	= Goat with one horn followed by four horns.	= Greek Empire of Alexander and his successors.
	Little horn which sprang up among the ten horns.	= Little horn which sprang out of one of the four horns.	= Antiochus Epiphanes.

ROMAN SCHEME

CHAP. II	CHAP. VII	CHAP. VIII	
Golden head.	= Lion with eagle's wings.		= Babylonian Empire.
Silver breast and arms.	= Bear with three ribs, etc.	= Ram with two horns.	= Medo - Persian Empire.
Brazen belly and thighs.	= Leopard with four wings.	= Goat with one horn followed by four horns.	= Greek Empire of Alexander and his successors.
		Little horn which sprang out of one of the four horns.	= Antiochus Epiphanes.
Iron legs, with feet and toes partly iron, partly clay.	= Beast with iron teeth and ten horns.		= Roman Empire.
	Little horn which sprang up among the ten horns and uprooted three of them.		= The temporal power of the Papacy.

Some of the difficulties which beset the Grecian scheme have already been touched on. It will, however, be necessary to go into them more at length in the course of the present chapter. The advocates of this scheme, as will be evident from the tabular statement just given, look upon chaps. vii. and viii. as parallel visions, saving that chap. viii. leaves out the Babylonian Empire, which was on the point of passing away at the time when the vision was shown to Daniel. According to the advocates of the Roman scheme these chapters are not parallels. In their view the vision of chap. vii. takes a much wider range than that of chap. viii., alike geographically and historically, embracing both the Roman Empire and an entirely fresh power which was to spring up after the disintegration of that empire: whilst the vision of chap. viii. is mainly concerned with a development of the Greek-Syrian kingdom and the sufferings and persecutions entailed thereby on the little Jewish community in Palestine. To put it shortly, chap. vii. is in their eyes a world-vision, chap. viii. only a Jewish vision.

In working out an imaginary parallelism between chaps. vii. and viii. the Grecian critics, if we may so call them, are forced to equate the ram of chap. viii. with the bear and the leopard of chap. vii., that so the ram may stand for two empires, the Median and the Persian, which they affirm to be represented as distinct empires in this Book of Daniel. This, surely, is a very curious piece of criticism, for why should the visions of this Book represent these supposed two empires by two beasts in chap. vii. and by only one beast in chap. viii. ? May it not be said to such interpreters—not irreverently—" those whom the seer hath joined together, let not his critics put asunder." Since Media and Persia are so evidently " one flesh " in the vision of chap. viii., no less than in the history of chaps. v. and vi., why should they be parted in the vision of chap. vii. ?

Another point in this forced parallelism is the identifying the " little horn " of chap. vii. 8, with the " little horn " of chap. viii. 9. It is true that both are persecuting powers, that both for awhile " practise and prosper," and that both magnify themselves against God; but there the likeness ceases. Fundamentally these two powers are quite different. The little horn of chap. vii. is a fresh power springing up among already existing powers, and in some way different from them, able also ere long to uproot three of them and to take their place. The little horn of chap. viii., on the other hand, is described as a horn springing out of a horn, *i.e.* it represents, not a fresh power, nor a different kind of power, but a fresh development of an already existing power. Observe also that nothing is said of its uprooting and superseding any other powers. As regards interpretation, the advocates of the Greek system see in the little horn of chap. vii. and that of chap. viii. one and the same persecuting power, identifying both with Antiochus Epiphanes. To the advocates of the Roman system the little horn of chap. vii. appears as a new and different kind of power, springing up among the ten kingdoms into which the Roman Empire, in its Roman part as distinct from its Greek and Asiatic provinces, was presently to be divided, and is generally interpreted of the temporal power, so cleverly and craftily acquired, and so sternly and ruthlessly exercised by the Bishops of Rome. On the other hand, they regard the little horn springing out of a horn, described in chap. viii., as a fresh development of the Greek-Syrian kingdom, when under Antiochus Epiphanes and his two immediate successors it became a persecuting power.

Also, before we leave the subject, there is one other point deserving of notice. The English reader must needs be warned that the Aramaic for "little horn" in chap. vii. and the Hebrew for "little horn" in chap. viii. are not equivalents. In chap. vii. 8, the Aramaic is correctly rendered "another horn, a little one," in the R.V. But in viii. 9, the Hebrew is remarkable, and admits of two renderings: either "a horn less than littleness," *i.e.* "a very little horn"; or, "a horn from littleness," *i.e.* arising from a small beginning, an expression which lays emphasis on its growth. A third and equally faulty piece of criticism lies in the treatment meted out by the advocates of the Grecian scheme to the ten horns seen on the head of the fourth beast in chap. vii. These are regarded by them as denoting ten *successive* kings of Syria; whereas, according to the analogy of the vision in chap. viii.—where the four "notable horns," which take the place of the "great horn" on the head of the he-goat, represent four co-existing powers—they should rather be regarded as *contemporaneous.* If succession were intended, it would be indicated, as in the case of the Medo-Persian ram, where one horn is seen to spring up after the other. Indeed, it may safely be said that when succession is intended it is always clearly indicated, either in the vision itself by one object appearing after another, or in the interpretation by plain statements admitting of inferences based thereon. Thus, in the vision of chap. ii., though the Four Kingdoms are symbolically presented in the great image at one and the same time, yet the interpretation plainly states that they are successive, and that as we descend from the head to the feet we are really descending through the course of the ages, so that in this case the inference is a sound one that the iron legs, and feet and toes of "iron mixed with miry clay," represent respectively an earlier and later stage of the fourth kingdom, the toes representing the latest stage of all.

But apart from these faults of detail, the greatest error of the critics lies in their blind endeavour to cramp the grand worldwide vision of chap. vii. within the narrow Jewish limits of the vision of chap. viii. In some strange way the writers who advocate the Grecian scheme appear to have completely overlooked the utterly different character of these two visions. In proof of this, notice how the scene of vision in chap. viii., which is at first fairly wide, taking in the great contest for world-power between Persia and Greece, or, as one might say, between East and West, very rapidly contracts to much smaller limits, till it is focussed on the persecution raging in little Palestine, the "glorious land." Henceforth the vision is concerned, not with world-powers, but with the Jewish theocracy and ritual; the atmosphere and colouring become strongly local and Levitical; mention is made of the "host of heaven," "the stars,"[1] the "Prince of the host," the "continual *burnt-offering*,"[2] the "sanctuary and the host"—mark the conjunction—and time is reckoned in the Jewish fashion by so many "evenings and mornings."[3] In the vision of chap. vii., on the other hand, the theatre of vision is not only wide at the commencement, but remains so throughout, and is, if anything, widest at the close. No reference whatever is made in that chapter to the land of the Jews or to their sanctuary or ritual. It is true we read of "the saints," "the saints of the *Most High*"[4]—a wider term by far than "the Prince of the host"—and of a persecutor, who thinks "to change the times and the law"; but we are under no necessity to understand these words in a narrow Jewish sense, for all local colouring is absent. Then, too, the mode of reckoning a period by "a time and times and a half time," chap. vii. 25, is not distinctively Jewish, since a similar expression is used of Nebuchadnezzar's madness, which was to last for "seven times," chap. iv. 16. Further, the expressions used to describe the kingdom of "one like unto a son of man," in chap. vii. 14, cannot be restricted to any merely Jewish kingdom, however widely extended, but must be placed side by side with the statements made respecting the same Divine kingdom, first by Daniel when interpreting the dream of Nebuchadnezzar, chap. ii. 44, and secondly by the king himself when recovering from his madness, chap. iv. 34; while the mention of "the peoples, nations, and languages," chap. vii. 14, carries our thoughts, not to the kingdom of a David or even of a Solomon, but to the then empire of Babylon, with which the kingdom of the God of heaven is both compared and contrasted. Lastly, notice the strong contrast presented by the close of these two visions. The vision of chap. viii. ends with the cleansing of the sanctuary, verse 14; whilst that of chap. vii. widens out into a kingdom embracing all nations, and which is to last for ever;

[1] Israel were to be as many as the starry host, Gen. xv. 5, Jer. xxxiii. 22.

[2] The word "burnt-offering" is absent in the original. "The continual," Hebrew הַתָּמִיד, included besides the daily burnt-offering, the offering of incense in the Holy Place, Exod. xxx. 8, the lighting the lamps, Lev. xxiv. 2, the placing of the shewbread on the table, Lev. xxiv. 8, and the meal-offering, Lev. vi. 20. As all these, with the exception of the shewbread, were attended to daily, it would be better, as Wright suggests, to substitute for "the continual burnt-offering," "the daily service."

[3] Gen. i. 5; the Jewish day commenced at sunset.

[4] Even Nebuchadnezzar, a heathen, speaks of the "Most High God," Dan. iii. 26, and iv. 2, and Daniel speaks to him in similar terms, iv. 24, and also to Belshazzar, v. 18.

in the words of the interpreting angel, *v.* 27, "the kingdom, and the dominion, and the greatness of the *kingdoms* "—note the plural—" under the whole heaven, shall be given to the people of the saints of the Most High; his kingdom is an everlasting kingdom, and all dominions shall serve and obey him."

In view of the above considerations, it will, I think, be admitted that the critics who attempt to make chap. viii. run parallel to chap. vii. are attempting an impossibility. There is, however, one genuine difficulty presented by the Roman scheme which demands our attention. I refer to the description given by Daniel of the second kingdom, when explaining to Nebuchadnezzar the meaning of the composite image seen by that monarch in his dream. The seer's words are: "After thee shall arise another kingdom inferior to thee." [1] This statement that the second kingdom would be inferior to the first is agreeable—so the Grecian critics tell us—to the belief that the writer of this Book was under the idea that a weak Median kingdom followed the Babylonian, and in proof of this they point to the parallel vision of chap. vii., where the bear in their judgment represents a power inferior to that represented by the lion. As regards this pronouncement of the inferiority of the bear compared to the lion, the prophet Amos, a simple countryman, will join issue with them. Amos had rather meet a lion than a bear. "The Syrian bear," says Dr. Horton,[2] "is fiercer than the lion." But apart from this question of natural history, the description of the second kingdom, given in Dan. vii. 5, carries with it no suggestion whatever of inferiority to the first as regards strength, but rather the reverse: "Behold another beast, a second, like to a bear, and it was raised up on one side, and three ribs were in his mouth between his teeth: and they said thus unto it, Arise, devour much flesh." It is the voracity of the bear, not its inferiority to the lion, that is here emphasised. Aristotle calls the bear ζῷον παμφάγον, and this bear in the prophetic vision, though already gorged and unable to swallow down all its food, is seen raising itself up on one side as though preparing to strike, and is at the same moment summoned to seize upon a yet greater prey. Now, if with the advocates of the Roman scheme we understand by the bear the Medo-Persian kingdom, then we may venture the hypothesis that the carcase upon which it has been feasting is the empire of Assyria, and that the three ribs in its mouth, which it has been unable to gulp down, represent three buffer states on the Assyrian frontier, such as Ararat, Minni, and Ashkenaz,

[1] Dan. ii. 39.
[2] *Century Bible*, on Amos v. 19.

mentioned by the prophet Jeremiah, more than half a century after Assyria had succumbed to the attack of the Medes, as semi-independent kingdoms though acknowledging a Median over-lordship.[1] The vision, then, of chap. vii. in no wise represents the second kingdom as inferior to the first, and indeed, had it done so, it would have been belied by the event. For the New Babylonian Empire, under which Daniel lived, stood in no small fear of the Medes. When Cyaxares the Mede put down Assyria, Nabopolassar, king of Babylon, was most careful not to interfere with the military operations of his all-powerful northern ally.[2] The same policy was pursued by his son Nebuchadnezzar. No warlike campaigns, so far as we know, were undertaken by Nebuchadnezzar on the side of Media. This was the side on which he feared attack. Hence the strong fortresses erected by him at Babylon, so successfully excavated by Koldewey; hence, too, the "Median wall," built by him from Sippara on the Euphrates to the site of the modern village of Jibbara on the Tigris, as recorded in the Wady Brissa Inscription and described by Xenophon.[3] Moreover, Nabonidus, the last king of the New Babylonian Empire, rejoices most unfeignedly over the overthrow of the Medes by Cyrus, king of Anshan, whom he styles Merodach's "little servant,"[4] never imagining that this same Cyrus at the head of the Medo-Persian army would, within the next twenty years, overthrow the empire of Babylon.

It is clear, then, that neither in the vision of Dan. vii. nor in historical fact is the Median kingdom inferior to the Babylonian. If, then, we stick to the translation "inferior to thee," in Dan. ii. 39, we are forced to qualify it in some way, *e.g.* inferior in magnificence and outward show, which may very possibly have been the case, just as the bear in outward semblance is much inferior to the lion. But this again is an unlikely explanation, since if there be any comparison between the four kingdoms it must be rather on the score of strength, inasmuch as the iron kingdom, as Josephus well points out,[5] is to be the strongest of them all. There thus appears to be a very real difficulty with regard to this statement as to the inferiority of the Medo-Persian kingdom as compared with the Babylonian. But, as Driver observes, the

[1] See the note at the end of this chapter.

[2] See the very curious extract from an inscription of Nabonidus given by me in the *Journal of Theological Studies* for July, 1913, pp. 512, 513.

[3] See *L'inscription en caracteres cursifs de l'Ouady Brissa*, col. vi. 15–31, pp. 16, 17, by H. Pognon; also Xenophon's *Anabasis*, ii. 4, 12.

[4] *Records of the Past*, New Series, vol. v. p. 169.

[5] *Ant.* x. 10, 4.

two Aramaic words rendered "inferior to thee" mean literally "lower than thou."[1] This literal meaning is here to be preferred, and it must be understood in a strictly topical sense, "below thee," *i.e. lower down in the image ;* for Daniel imagines Nebuchadnezzar to be mentally contemplating the composite image which he saw in his dream, and which had just been recalled to his mind, and what he says to the king may be briefly paraphrased thus : "Thou, O king, art the head of gold, and after thee shall arise another kingdom *lower down in the image*, and then a third kingdom of brass, to be followed by a fourth of iron." In favour of this rendering let it be noted that the parts of the image which belong respectively to the first, third, and fourth kingdoms are expressly mentioned in each case. Thus, the first kingdom is the head of gold, the third is represented by the brazen portion of the image, the fourth by the iron portion. If, therefore, we stick to the rendering "inferior to thee," it follows that the second kingdom alone remains unidentified with any portion of the image. The translation proposed removes this anomaly, for the second kingdom is thus pointed out to the monarch as the one "*below thee*" *on the image*, i.e. *below the golden head*, so that it answers to the breast and arms of silver.[2]

But it will be said that in thus escaping from one difficulty we have fallen into another, and that with the new rendering—"below thee"—we have introduced a second anomaly, seeing that the second kingdom, alone of all the four, is now left undescribed, nothing being said about it except the bare mention of its position in the image. Quite so ; and for this there is a good reason. On the first kingdom, the head of gold, the seer very naturally enlarges, since it is the then existing kingdom and he is addressing its all-powerful monarch. On the third he says a good deal in a few words : it is to "bear rule over all the earth." On the fourth kingdom, its strength and subsequent weakness, he speaks at great length, for this is evidently one of the main features of the vision. But of the second kingdom he says never a word. What is the reason for his silence ? It is that the subject

[1] *Cambridge Bible*, Dan. ii. 39. The Aramaic words אַרְעָא מִנָּךְ mean literally "earthwards from thee." אַרְעָא is an adverb, compounded of אֲרַע "earth" and the adverbial ending אָ "towards." Jastrow in his *Dictionary of the Targummin* has אַרְעָאָה "earthwards, that which is below." *Targ.* Jos. xvi. 3.

[2] That those who understood the Aramaic words אַרְעָא מִנָּךְ in the sense "inferior to thee" felt the miss of some definite statement as to the position in the image occupied by the second kingdom may be gathered from the fact that the Codex Alexandrinus reads, *καὶ ὀπίσω σου ἀναστήσεται βασιλεία ἑτέρα σου, ἥτις ἐστὶν ὁ ἄργυρος.*

is a very delicate one; he is treading on dangerous ground. The great king of Babylon would scarcely like to hear of another power that would presently take his place, and all the more so since it was that very Medo-Persian power of which he was already so apprehensive. Daniel's silence, then, may be compared with the silence of Josephus when he is interpreting this very vision of the four kingdoms. Josephus, living under the iron empire of Rome and professing himself a friend of the Romans, at the same time holding the Roman view with regard to the four kingdoms, very naturally declines to declare the Messianic meaning of the Stone which shattered the image. Evidently he shrank from explaining that the kingdom of the God of heaven, with Messiah at its head, would by and by supersede the empire of Imperial Rome. As this writer is one of the early advocates of the orthodox view and the passage is one of considerable interest, it may be well for me to quote it *in extenso*. Josephus represents Daniel addressing Nebuchadnezzar thus: [1]

"The head of gold denotes thee and the kings of Babylon that have been before thee: but the two hands and arms signify this, that your government shall be dissolved by two kings: [2] but another king, that shall come from the west, armed with brass, shall destroy that government: and another kingdom, that shall be like unto iron, shall put an end to the power of the former, and shall have dominion over all the earth, on account of the nature of iron, which is stronger than that of gold, of silver, and of brass." "Daniel," adds the historian, "did also declare the meaning of the stone to the king: but I do not think proper to relate it, since I have only undertaken to describe things past or present, but not things that are future: yet if any one be so very desirous of knowing truth as not to waive such points of curiosity, and cannot curb his inclination for understanding the uncertainties of futurity, and whether they will happen or not, let him be diligent in reading the Book of Daniel, which he will find among the sacred writings."

While most scholars will admit that the Aramaic of chap. ii. 39 admits of the meaning "below thee" as well as "inferior to thee," I shall probably be reminded that the Septuagint favours the latter rendering, and that in a doubtful case this ought to turn the scale. My answer is that a translator might more easily imagine Daniel saying to Nebuchadnezzar "inferior to thee" than his saying "below thee," and that he would also be guided

[1] *Ant.* x. 10, 4.

[2] Viz. Cyrus and Darius the Mede.

to some extent by the idea of silver being inferior to gold. Further, it must be remembered that the Septuagint translator, writing before the full development of the Roman power, probably adopted the Grecian scheme, and regarded the second kingdom, not as the Medo-Persian, but as the Median. Now, as he could hardly have known much about this Median kingdom, he would see nothing strange in its being described as "inferior" to the Babylonian.

It may be well at this point, and before bringing this chapter to a close, to advert to the statement argumentatively advanced by the critics that the Grecian scheme was first in the field, and that traces of it are seen in a portion of the Sibylline Oracles written not later than 140 B.C. The bare fact we willingly admit, but when they go on to speak of it as the "older and *true* interpretation,"[1] we must needs dissent from the latter statement. "Older" it must of necessity be, inasmuch as the Greek Empire appeared before the Roman, and, offering in the days of Antiochus Epiphanes a fulfilment of a part of Daniel's prophetic visions, was very naturally supposed to offer the fulfilment of a larger portion of those visions than the actual terms of the prophecy warranted. The interpreters of those days would naturally adopt the Grecian scheme, just as Josephus, with more to go upon, naturally adopts the Roman. For as history bit by bit turns the future into the past, true, genuine prophecy is bit by bit unfolded. In the days of the Maccabees we should all have been on the Grecian side, and ready in our study of the Book of Daniel to see Antiochus Epiphanes everywhere. But the marvel is that in these later days scholars should revert to the older, and necessarily cruder attempt to interpret the visions of Daniel, made too at a time when criticism was in its infancy.[2]

Additional Note on Ararat, Minni, and Ashkenaz

Winckler in *Die Keilinschriften und das Alte Testament*, p. 103, speaks of Elam and Ararat as "Puffer-staaten" of Assyria. Ararat is the now well-known kingdom of Urartu, whose in-

[1] *Century Bible*, p. 68. Foot-note on the Four World Empires.

[2] As regards the older commentators on the Book of Daniel, the Grecian scheme is favoured or adopted by the Septuagint, 145 B.C. (Charles), which as a paraphrase may well be called the oldest commentary on Daniel; by Porphyry, A.D. 233–304; and by Ephrem Syrus, A.D. 300–350. It is also alluded to by the author of the Apocryphal Book, 4 Esdras, A.D. 81–96. The Roman scheme is adopted by St. John in the Revelation, A.D. 67 or 96; by the author of 4 Esdras; by Josephus, A.D. 94; by the author of the Epistle of Barnabas, *circa* A.D. 100–120; and by Hippolytus, *circa* A.D. 220.

scriptions have been deciphered and translated by Sayce. This kingdom centred round Lake Van. Minni is the kingdom of the Mannā, which lay to the south of Urartu and north of Lake Urumiah. These two kingdoms rose to importance about 900 B.C.; and Ararat was a powerful rival of Assyria, both in the ninth and eighth centuries B.C. Towards the close of the Assyrian Empire, in the days of Ashurbanipal, Ararat was on friendly terms with Assyria, whilst Minni was under Assyrian governors. Ashkenaz has been identified by Winckler with the Ashkuzā of the Assyrian records, believed by him to be the Scythians. In the time of Esarhaddon, 678 B.C., Ishpakai of the Ashkuzā, with his allies the Mannā, was defeated by Assyria. Esarhaddon gave one of his daughters in marriage to Bartatua, king of the Ashkuzā, whom Winckler identifies with Protothyes the Scythian, the father of Madyes. It was an inroad of the Scythians under Madyes which raised the siege of Nineveh and deferred the downfall of Assyria for a generation (Herod. i. 103). "The kingdoms of Ararat, Minni, and Ashkenaz" (Jer. li. 27) have thus some claim to be regarded as three ribs of the carcase of the old Assyrian lion, which the voracious Medo-Persian bear finds himself not quite able to gulp down (Dan. vii. 5).

3

The Gold, Silver, Brass and Iron (Daniel 2)

ONE of the strongest arguments for the Roman scheme of interpretation of the vision of Dan. ii. may be derived from the metals severally assigned to the four kingdoms. Josephus seems to have had an inkling of this when he thus paraphrases Daniel's description of the advent of the third kingdom: "Another king that shall come from the west, armed with brass, shall destroy that government."[1] It is clear that in the armour of the Greeks he saw some reason for the Greek kingdom being represented by the brazen part of the image. What the Jewish historian thus hints at will form the subject of the present chapter. It will be my object to show that the gold is peculiarly appropriate to represent the Babylonian Empire of Nebuchadnezzar, even more so than a writer of the Maccabean age would be likely to know; that the silver, so far from representing a merely Median empire, represents far more suitably the Medo-Persian power, more particularly in its later or Persian stage; that the brass is far better fitted to represent the Grecian kingdom than the Persian; and the iron a better representation of the firm, strong, and, if need be, severe rule of Rome, than of the irresistible might of Alexander the Great.

Gold, silver, brass, and iron occur in the same order in the Great Triumphal Inscription of Sargon II., save that between silver and brass he interjects vessels of gold and silver and precious stone. The order is seemingly a descending one. In the estimation of Nebuchadnezzar iron would certainly hold the lowest place. It is not even mentioned in his inscriptions.[2] The thoughts of this great king were so much set on the more showy and costly metals that it must have been something of a shock for him to be told that a time was coming when, in the figures of his pro-

[1] *Ant.* x. 10, 4.

[2] Iron circlets were found by Koldewey on the site of Babylon, and on the contract tablets of the reign of Nebuchadnezzar iron is mentioned as used for fetters and brick-moulds.

phetic vision, as given in Dan. iv., he would be indebted to the iron and the brass for the preservation of his kingdom.[1] As regards intrinsic worth, the metals are arranged in descending order, but since they are severally characteristic of the different powers which they represent, and since the seer dwells so emphatically on the strength of the iron kingdom, it may easily be guessed that the real order is an ascending one, and that the silver kingdom is to prove stronger than the gold, the brass stronger than the silver, and the iron strongest of all.

To hear himself described as the head of gold must have been very pleasing to the Babylonian monarch, and if he looked upon the description as a suitable one, we cannot blame him. In any case it described the very temper of his soul, and he appears to have done his best to realise the meaning of the figure. Herodotus, who was at Babylon some ninety years after the era of Nebuchadnezzar, was struck with astonishment at the amount of gold which he found within the precincts of the sanctuary of Bel. In the smaller temple, which stood on the top of the tower of Babylon, was a table of gold. In the second temple below [2] was an image of the god "all of gold," seated on a golden throne with a golden base and in front of "a large golden table." All the gold used to form these sacred objects amounted—so the Chaldeans told him—to eight hundred talents. Outside the temple there was also an altar of "solid gold." [3]

When we turn to the India House Inscription of Nebuchadnezzar the same feature meets us. In the eyes of this monarch nothing is too precious to be bestowed on his beloved Babylon. All his thoughts are centred on beautifying the seat of Merodach, "the great lord, the god, my creator." "Silver, gold, glitter of precious stones, copper, palm-wood, cedar, whatsoever thing is precious, in large abundance; the produce of mountains, the fulness of seas, a rich present, a splendid gift, to my city of Babylon into his presence I brought." [4] Accordingly, the walls of the cell of Merodach must be made "to glisten like suns," the hall of his temple must be overlaid with shining gold, lapis-lazuli, and alabaster; [5] and "the chapel of his lordship, which a former king had fabricated in silver," Nebuchadnezzar declares that he

[1] The expression "a band of iron and brass," Dan. iv. 15, finds its explanation in the fact that iron was sometimes used with a bronze casting round it. Layard's *Nineveh and Babylon*, p. 670.

[2] This was the famous temple of Merodach, E-sag-ila, "the house of towering summit."

[3] Herod. i. 181, 183.

[4] India House Inscription, col. ii. 30–39.

[5] *Ibid.* ii. 43–49.

overlaid "with bright gold." [1] The roofing of E-kua, the cell of Merodach, is also overlaid with "bright gold" [2]; and the cell of Nebo at Borsippa is treated in the same manner.[3] In all this the royal builder was actuated by a double motive. A strain of real devotion to Merodach and Nebo runs through his long inscription, but at the same time he freely admits that all this magnificence and grandeur was designed to impress his subjects. Thus, when speaking of the Northern Citadel at Babylon he writes: "That house I caused to be made for gazings, and for the beholding of the multitude of the people with sculptures I had it filled. The awe of power, the dread of the splendour of sovereignty, its sides begird." [4] So, then, magnificence and display form the characteristics of the golden kingdom; and they are intended, as we see, to set forth the greatness of the king and the greatness of his god. When we are reading the inscriptions of this monarch, we find ourselves, as it were, in the third chapter of Daniel, while a loud-voiced herald calls upon us to "fall down and worship the golden image which Nebuchadnezzar the king hath set up." But is it likely that a writer of the Maccabean age would have known all this? Hardly so. Look at the image of the god Bel, as it is described to us in the apocryphal book, *Bel and the Dragon*. What is it made of? Of gold? No! but of "clay within and brass without"! [5]

With the coming of the Medo-Persian kingdom all this is changed. The gold now gives place to the silver. In the Semitic languages *keseph, kaspu,* "silver," bears also the further meaning of "money," silver being the criterion of value and the medium of exchange. When, then, we speak of the gold giving place to the silver, we mean that with the coming of the second kingdom magnificence and outward show were exchanged for treasure, diligently collected by taxation and carefully hoarded up to form the sinews of war when occasion should require. If, then, we are inclined to act in the spirit of the far-famed vicar of Bray, instead of falling down to worship the golden image, we must now be up and doing, making it our main object to see that the king shall receive no damage, but that toll, tribute, and custom be regularly paid by the subject provinces.

The Medo-Persian kingdom, so Herodotus tells us, had its commencement in the administration of justice by Deioces.[6] His grandson, Cyaxares, reorganised the army,[7] and made it such a

[1] Herod. iii. 1–7.
[2] *Ibid.* iii. 27–29.
[3] *Ibid.* iii. 43–45.
[4] *Ibid.* ix. 29–35. Compare Dan. iv. 30.
[5] Bel and the Dragon 7.
[6] Herod. i. 96, 97.
[7] *Ibid.* i. 103.

formidable instrument that it proved more than a match for the veteran troops of Assyria.[1] A power that paid such attention to justice and military matters would hardly be likely to overlook finance. Accordingly, in the first year after the taking of Babylon, in the reign of Darius the Mede—which synchronises with the first year of Cyrus—we learn from Daniel, chap. vi., that an attempt was made to organise the finances of the empire. It may have been only an attempt, nevertheless Herodotus tells us that during all the reign of Cyrus, and afterwards when Cambyses ruled, though there was no fixed tribute, yet the nations severally brought gifts to the king.[2] He also tells us that the Pseudo-Smerdis, as soon as he came to the throne, in order to make himself popular, granted freedom from war-service and from taxes to every nation under his rule for the space of three years.[3] This shows that under Cambyses—who, in his brief earlier reign as sub-king under his father Cyrus in the year after the capture of Babylon, figures in this Book of Daniel as " Darius the Mede " [4]—there was a system of taxation throughout the empire. However, it was under the second Darius, Darius Hystaspes, that this system was brought to perfection. Herodotus furnishes us with a long and exact account of the twenty satrapies established by Darius and the yearly amount at which each was assessed. The tribute, he tells us, was paid in silver talents, except that of the Indians. The Indian satrapy was the richest of all, and yielded 360 talents of gold-dust, which the historian reckons as equivalent to 4,680 talents of silver, thus showing that silver, as stated above, was the standard of value.[5]

That the Persians kept their eye steadily fixed on this main object, appears as clearly in the pages of the Old Testament as in the pages of Herodotus. The Persian monarchs, it was well known, were bent on raising all they could from the subject provinces. Accordingly, Artaxerxes is implored not to allow Jerusalem to be fortified ; for, " be it known now unto the king, that, if this city be builded, and the walls finished, they will not pay tribute, custom, or toll, and in the end it will endamage the kings." [6] Again, when the same king wishes to show special kindness to the Jews, he exempts all those who minister at the temple from paying taxes.[7] Nevertheless, Nehemiah in his long and touching confession is forced to admit that the Jews are servants in their own land, and that " it yieldeth much increase unto the

[1] Herod. i. 106.
[2] *Ibid.* iii. 89.
[3] *Ibid.* iii. 67.
[4] See Chapter XIV. below.
[5] Herod. iii. 89–95.
[6] Ezra iv. 13.
[7] *Ibid.* vii. 24.

kings whom thou hast set over us because of our sins." [1] So, then, in the prophetic summons to the Medo-Persian bear—" Arise, devour much flesh " [2]—it will be noted that the very tone of the words is suggestive of greed and spoliation rather than of conquest and subjugation. In consequence of this policy of the silver kingdom the Persian kings became rich, and it is foretold in Dan. xi. 2 that the fourth king, Xerxes, " shall be far richer than they all ; and that when he is waxed strong through his riches he shall stir up all against the realm of Greece." The vast host which Xerxes collected for the invasion of Greece, and with which he crossed over into Europe, would have been an impossibility but for the system of finance perfected by his father Darius. So keen was Darius in amassing wealth that, according to Herodotus, he appeared to his subjects as a huckster, " one who looked to making a gain in everything." [3] Xerxes trod in his father's footsteps. As Darius had not hesitated to violate the tomb of Nitocris at Babylon in his vain search for treasure,[4] so Xerxes sent a detachment from his army to plunder the temple at Delphi. " Xerxes, as I am informed," says Herodotus, " was better acquainted with what there was worthy of note at Delphi, than even with what he had left in his own house ; so many of those about him were continually describing the treasures, more especially the offerings made by Crœsus the son of Alyattes." [5]

It thus appears that no metal could so suitably picture the Medo-Persian kingdom as silver, and that this is especially true of the later phases of that kingdom. There may have been times when it could be said of the Medes, they "shall not regard silver" [6]; but that could never be said of Darius Hystaspes and his successors. They, at any rate, were all for riches, and by their riches they were strong. The silver kingdom was stronger than the golden kingdom, and consequently it lasted very much longer. Babylon was master of the ancient world for only 70 years ; Persia for over 200 years.

Silver was stronger than gold ; but, as the Persian kings were soon to learn to their cost, brass was stronger than silver.[7] First

[1] Neh. ix. 37. [2] Dan. vii. 5. [3] Herod. iii. 89.
[4] *Ibid.* i. 187. [5] *Ibid.* viii. 35.

[6] Isa. xiii. 17 : referring to a time prior to the formation of the Median tribes into a nation.

[7] By brass we must understand bronze, an alloy of copper and tin. In three specimens found by Layard at Nineveh the proportions were as follows :

Copper	89·51	89·85	88·37
Tin	10·63	9·78	11·33
	100·14	99·63	99·70

at Marathon, and then at Thermopylæ and Salamis, there were alarming foreshadowings of the coming of the brazen kingdom. The power which wealth commands was soon to be proved inferior to the force of arms wielded by a brave and free people. "Another king shall come from the west armed with brass," is the brief interpretation of the third kingdom which Josephus puts into the lips of Daniel. The Jewish historian saw in the mention of a brazen kingdom an unmistakable prediction of the victorious arms of Alexander and his brazen-clad Greeks. If we glance through the ever fresh and delightful pages of Herodotus, we shall come to the conclusion that the inference is a true one. It is noticeable that when Herodotus is describing to us the equipment of the different nationalities that went to make up the vast host of Xerxes, he makes the not infrequent remark, more especially with regard to the crews of the fleet, that such and such nations were "armed" or "equipped in the Grecian fashion," or that they "wore the Grecian armour."[1] The Grecian islanders and inhabitants of the coastlands of Asia Minor, who, as we know, formed a part of Xerxes' host, would no doubt be armed in much the same way as their brethren on the mainland of Greece, against whom they were compelled to fight; and this Grecian armour, famous from the days of Homer, must have presented a very marked contrast to the soft hat, tunic with sleeves, and trousers, worn by both the Medes and Persians.[2] When at Thermopylæ the Greeks encountered first the Medes and then the famous Persian "Immortals," their brazen armour must have stood them in good stead and given them a decided advantage. In the time of Psammetichus I. of Egypt—664–610 B.C., a little earlier than the era of Nebuchadnezzar—the fame of this brazen armour was already making itself felt. Psammetichus, being driven into banishment by the other kings of the Dodekarchy, went, we are told, to consult the oracle of Latona as to how he might take vengeance on his rivals. The oracle answered that "vengeance would come from the sea when brazen men should appear." Over this answer the king was incredulous at first, but presently a crew of Carians and Ionians, driven by stress of weather, landed on the coast of Egypt, all equipped in their brazen armour. This unwonted sight startled the natives, and one of them hastened to Psammetichus with the news that "brazen men had come from the sea, and were plundering the plain." Seeing in this the accomplishment of the oracle, the Egyptian king made friendly advances to the new-comers, engaged them as mercenaries, and

[1] Herod. vii. 74, 89–95. [2] *Ibid.* vii. 61, 62.

with their help worsted his opponents.[1] In the wonderful list given us by Ezekiel of the wares which the different nations brought to the great mart of Tyre, we are told that Javan, Tubal, and Meshech traded in vessels of brass.[2] By Javan we understand the Asiatic Greeks, in fact the word is only another form of Ἰάϝονες, "Ionians." Also, the Hebrew word translated "vessels" would apply to anything made of brass, and is sometimes used to describe the "entire equipment of warriors, armour or armament, offensive and defensive.[3] It thus appears that the brazen kingdom must represent a Greek kingdom rather than a Persian; for, granting that there were "brazen men" to be found in the vast heterogeneous host of Xerxes, more especially in the contingents furnished by the Greek islanders, yet brazen armour was not the distinctive equipment of Median and Persian warriors, but a dress which, whether depicted in the sculptures of Persepolis or described in the pages of Herodotus, presents the most marked contrast.

The above observations lead to the very evident inference that the third or brazen kingdom represents, not a Persian, but a Greek kingdom; and this inference is confirmed when we turn to the description of the third kingdom given in the vision of chap. vii., where it appears as a leopard with four wings. The symbol points to the amazing rapidity of the career of Alexander the Great, the founder of the Greek kingdom. The leopard is remarkable for speed,[4] and in order to emphasise this point the leopard in the vision is seen to be furnished with four wings. Similarly, in the vision of chap. viii., which is infallibly interpreted for us by the angel Gabriel, attention is drawn to this same striking feature of Alexander's career. The mighty conqueror from Macedon is beheld as a he-goat coming from the west, which appeared not to touch the ground. Compare Lucan's description:

> "fulmenque, quod omnes
> Percuteret pariter populos."

The leopard is further remarkable for craft, vigilance, and circumspection.[5] And this thought is accentuated by the leopard in the vision having four heads, and so being able to look in every direction. Alexander's swift career was guided by the most watchful circumspection. Hence the notable horn on the head of the he-goat, in chap. viii. 5, is seen to be placed between its eyes; an indication that the force and fury of Alexander's attack

[1] Herod. ii. 152.
[2] Ezek. xxvii. 13.
[3] See Francis Brown's *Heb. Lex.* under כְּלִי.
[4] Hab. i. 8.
[5] Jer. v. 6; Hos. xiii. 7.

would be guided and directed by rare intelligence and penetration. Unlike Rehoboam, this great king made use of the advice of his father's councillors.

Passing now to the fourth or iron kingdom, which the advocates of the Grecian scheme seek to identify with the Greek kingdom of Alexander the Great and his successors, it may be allowed me to remark that, if the metals are to guide us in our interpretation of the vision of Dan. ii., a glance at the Greek lexicon is sufficient to refute this idea of the critics. In the eighth edition of Liddell and Scott's Greek Lexicon, 1901, the words compounded with χαλκός, "brass," occupy 5 columns, those compounded with σίδηρος, "iron," only $1\frac{3}{4}$ columns. Brass, as we have already seen, points unmistakably to the Greeks. Iron is a poor description of the Greek kingdom, but a very telling description of the Roman. Further, in passing from the third to the fourth kingdom, we are actually passing from a bronze to an iron age. To the Roman poets bronze weapons spoke of the olden time. Thus, Virgil describing times long gone by, writes:

> "Æratæque micant peltæ, micat æreus ensis."—*Æneid.* vii. 743;

and again, describing the sack of Troy, he pictures Anchises calling out to his son:

> "Nate, exclamat, fuge, nate, propinquant
> Ardentes clypeos atque æra micantia cerno."—*Æneid.* ii. 734.

In this connection the lines of Lucretius (99–55 B.C.), contrasting the past with the present, are especially deserving of notice:

> "Et prior æris erat quam ferri cognitus usus.
> Ære solum terræ tractabant, æreque belli
> Miscebant fluctūs, et vulnera vasta serebant.
> Inde minutatim processit ferreus ensis,
> Versaque in opprobrium species est falcis ahena."—Lucret. v. 1285.

Iron, to be sure, was in use long before the coming of the Romans, but at the time of the development of the Republic into a world-power its use became much more general. Iron swords and breastplates took the place of bronze. The change, as Lucretius points out, was a gradual one, and it was contemporary with the rise of the Roman power. During that period both of these metals were employed in the making of arms and armour. Hence, in Dan. vii. 19 the fourth beast in its most aggressive stage is described as having teeth of iron and nails of brass. In Polybius' description of the arms and equipment of the Roman infantry, written about 140 B.C., we seem as it were to see the brass giving place to the iron.[1] The Roman infantry soldier of the time of Polybius still wore a helmet and breastplate of bronze, but his shield had an iron boss, and the rim of it was plated with iron at the top and bottom. Above all, he carried with him that distinctively Roman weapon the *pilum*, capable of being used both as a pike and a javelin. The *pilum* was a weapon with a stout iron head, and a long iron neck fitted to a wooden shaft, the metal extending for about a third of its entire length. Livy, when contrasting the arms of the Romans with those of the Macedonians, makes special mention of the *pilum*, as follows: "Macedonibus arma clypeus sarissæque; Romano scutum, majus corpore tegumentum, et pilum, haud paulo quam hastâ vehementius ictu missuque telum."[2] From this point of view, then, the Greek kingdom being denoted by the brass, the Roman might with equal suitability be denoted by the iron. But the feature which Daniel so strikingly brings out in his interpretation is the strength of the iron kingdom. "The fourth kingdom shall be strong as iron: forasmuch as iron breaketh in pieces and subdueth all things: and as iron that crusheth all these, shall it break in pieces and crush."[3] These words, it is true, might be used of the onward march of the Greek arms under Alexander, but they are ten times more descriptive of the progress of the Roman power during the second and first centuries B.C. The special feature of Alexander's career was its amazing swiftness, so well pictured by the four-winged leopard, the third beast in the vision of chap. vii. But just as swiftness was symbolised by the aspect of the third beast, so what most impressed the seer in his vision of the fourth beast was its intense ferocity. "After this," he writes, "I saw in the night visions, and behold a fourth beast, terrible and powerful, and strong exceedingly; and it had great iron teeth: it devoured and brake in pieces, and stamped the residue with his feet: and it was diverse from all the beasts that were before it."[4] The critics who favour the Grecian scheme assure us that in the words, "it devoured and brake in pieces, and stamped the residue with his feet," we are to see the overthrow of the older civilisation and its radical transformation by the spread of the Greek Empire, and more especially the thoroughness with which the work was done.[5] But the words mean more than thoroughness; they are descriptive of savage ferocity and ruthless severity. Their fulfilment is seen, not in the great changes wrought in the East by Alexander's conquests, but in the

[1] Polyb. *Hist.* vi. 23, § 8.
[2] Livy, bk. xxxviii. 7.
[3] Dan. ii. 40.
[4] *Ibid.* vii. 7.
[5] *Century Bible* on Dan. vii. 7.

severities practised by the Romans on all who resisted them; witness the destruction of Carthage, the siege of Numantia, the War of the gladiators when the Appian Way was lined with six thousand crosses bearing aloft as many bodies, and, last but not least, the siege of Jerusalem and extinction of the Jewish nationality.

One other characteristic of the fourth beast, which suits best the Roman power, is found in the statement that it "was diverse from all the beasts that were before it."[1] This is best illustrated by the following passage from the First Book of Maccabees, which is eloquent as to the impression made on the Jews by their first acquaintance with the Roman system of government: "Whomsoever they will to succour and to make kings, these do they make kings; and whomsoever they will, do they depose; and they are exalted exceedingly: and for all this none of them did ever put on a diadem, neither did they clothe themselves with purple, to be magnified thereby"[2]; after which follows a description of the senate and of the consular power; the whole passage showing how very much the Oriental mind was impressed by this strange and to them novel form of government. But in the case of Alexander's rule there was nothing of this kind to impress and astonish his subjects. Alexander "liked Oriental splendour and the Oriental ceremony which placed an infinite distance between the king and his highest subjects; great statesmen generally love to be absolute, and Alexander enjoyed Oriental despotism."[3]

But the strongest claim of the empire of Rome to be the actual fulfilment of the iron kingdom must ever be found, *first,* in the length of its duration, the best proof surely of its strength. The empire of Babylon lasted only 70 years; the Persian empire 200 years; the Greek 130 years; whilst Rome, in its undivided state, stood for some 500 years, and in its divided state as the ten kingdoms continues down to the present time.[4] *Secondly,* and this must never be overlooked, there is that wonderful prophecy of the papal power given in Dan. vii. 8 and 19–26, into which I have not entered here, because the subject has been so well and exhaustively treated by our Protestant commentators.[5]

[1] Dan. vii. 7.

[2] 1 Macc. viii. 13, 14.

[3] *Encyc. Brit.* 9th ed., under "Persia," p. 585, col. 1.

[4] It will be said that this criterion of strength fails in the case of the Greek Empire. But that empire, amazingly strong at first, soon became a *divided* empire: no sooner was the "great horn" broken than "four notable horns" sprang up to take its place, Dan. viii. 8.

[5] See *The First Two Visions of Daniel,* by the late Prof. T. R. Birks, and Chapter XXV. below.

The choice of gold, silver, brass, and iron, to represent severally the empires of Babylon, Persia, Greece, and Rome, in a vision granted to a Babylonian monarch, possesses also a marked suitability, arising from the fact that those different metals were assigned by the Babylonians to different gods. Thus, according to a Baylonian tablet,[1] Enlil, with whom, in the time of Nebuchadnezzar, Merodach was identified, was the god of gold; Anu, the god of silver; and Ea, the god of brass, *i.e.* bronze; whilst it may be surmised with a fair amount of probability that Ninib, the "strong one" of the gods, was the god of iron, since the same two cuneiform characters which stand for the god Ninib stand also for *parzillu*, "iron." The fact that Enlil, *i.e.* Merodach, was the god of gold, not only accounts for the great quantity of gold employed in his temple at Babylon, but makes gold the most suitable representation of the Babylonian power, Merodach being the patron god of Babylon. In Anu, the god of silver, and at the same time, as his name signifies, the "sky-god," we see the nearest representative that the Babylonian pantheon could offer of Ahura-mazda, the great god of the Persians, whose eye is the resplendent sun and who clothes himself with a starry robe.[2] Silver would thus most suitably picture the Persian power. Ea, the god of bronze, was also the sea-god, and bore the title "the lord of ships." Thus, the bronze portion of the image would point, not only to brazen-clad warriors, but to a power coming from beyond the sea, to those ships of Kittim which were to afflict Asshur and to afflict Eber,[3] *i.e.* the world-powers beyond the Euphrates. Ninib, the god of iron, has been identified by Jensen with Saturn.[4] Though Ninib was a god of war and Saturn a god of peace, yet both alike were patrons of agriculture.[5] Hence, Saturn is usually pictured with a scythe, iron being as useful in agriculture as in war. Saturn, according to Cicero, was especially worshipped in the West.[6] His connection with Latium, where he reigned during the golden age, and with the Capitoline Hill, where his altar stood even before the founding of Rome, enables us to see in the god of iron, Ninib-Saturn, a not unsuitable representative of the great power that was presently to rise out of the West.

[1] See *Cuneiform Texts from Babylonian Tablets*, pt. xxiv., pl. 49, published by British Museum.

[2] *Story of the Nations: Media*, pp. 61, 62.

[3] Num. xxiv. 24.

[4] See Jensen's *Kosmologie*, pp. 136–139.

[5] Cf. the Monotheistic Tablet given in Pinches' *Old Testament*, 1st ed., p. 58, "Ninib is Merodach of the Garden."

[6] Cicero, *De Natura Deorum*, iii. c. 17.

4

The Chaldeans of the Book of Daniel

IT is one feature of the controversy which has so long raged round the Book of Daniel that points once looked upon as fatal to the early date of that Book are seen on further investigation to be proofs of its authenticity. This is the case with the "Chaldeans" who figure so prominently in the narrative portion. The defenders of the orthodox view would now be as sorry to lose the presence of those jealous, contentious individuals as to have the once much-debated, much-doubted-of Belshazzar removed from the scene.

The term "Chaldeans," being found along with such terms as "magicians," "enchanters," "sorcerers," and "soothsayers," has been supposed by the critics to be used in the same sense in which we find it in the pages of Juvenal,[1] viz. as a synonym for cheats and imposters. "In the eyes of the Assyriologist," writes Prof. Sayce, "the use of the word Kasdim ('Chaldeans') in the Book of Daniel would alone be sufficient to indicate the date of the work with unerring certainty." This conclusion was, perhaps, not unnatural, and yet further investigation has shown that the "Chaldeans," so far from being looked upon as quacks and rogues, the parasites of heathen emperors and courts, were in their day regarded as the very *élite* of Babylonian society, men in whose ranks the monarch himself appears to have been enrolled.[2]

In the Old Testament the name Kasdim, "Chaldeans," is

[1] Cf. *Satire*, vi. 55–58:

"Chaldæis sed major erit fiducia: quicquid
Dixerit astrologus, credent a fonte relatum
Hammonis, quoniam Delphi oracula cessant
Et genus humanum damnat caligo futuri."

Also *Satire*, x. 93, referring to the Emperor Tiberius:

"Principis augustâ Caprearum in rupe sedentis
Cum grege Chaldæo."

[2] See below.

invariably used in an ethnic sense until we come to the Book of Daniel. Thus, we read of "Ur of the Chaldees," of "Babylon the glory of kingdoms, the beauty of the Chaldeans' pride," of "the land of the Chaldeans" being utterly devastated by the Assyrian, of "the Chaldeans in the ships of their rejoicing,"—for they were a maritime people—of "the Babylonians, the land of whose nativity is Chaldea," of "Nebuchadnezzar king of Babylon, the Chaldean," of "the Chaldeans, that bitter and hasty nation, which march through the breadth of the earth to possess dwelling-places that are not theirs," and of "the army of the Chaldeans" come to fight against Jerusalem.[1] When we arrive at the Book of Daniel the ethnic sense of the term is found to be still in use, as, for instance, when Darius the Mede is called "king over the realm of the Chaldeans."[2] But along with the old ethnic sense we meet now with an entirely new usage. Thus, in the narrative of chaps. ii., iii., iv., and v. the term is used of a privileged class, apparently the chief of the five classes into which the wise men of Babylon are divided.

When we turn to the Assyrian inscriptions we find the word *Kaldu,* "Chaldeans," used invariably in an ethnic sense. The Kaldu are first mentioned by Ashurnatsirpal in the account of his campaign undertaken in the year 879 B.C. They are described as settled on the Lower Euphrates to the south of Babylonia proper.[3] From the inscriptions of Shalmaneser II., 860–825 B.C., and of Tiglathpileser III., 745–727 B.C.,[3] we learn that they were a race of Semitic origin, divided into several small states, the chief of which and the most southerly, bordering on the Persian Gulf, was the "Country of the Sea," alluded to in the title of the prophetic burden: "The Burden of the Wilderness of the Sea," Isa. xxi. 1. This was the hereditary kingdom of Merodachbaladan,[4] who, in the days of Sargon king of Assyria, for twelve years wrested the throne of Babylon from the Assyrians. The fact that "Nebuchadnezzar the Chaldean" belonged to the same conquering race as Merodachbaladan, is that which lends point to Isaiah's threatening announcement to Hezekiah when the heart of the Jewish king was unduly elated at receiving an embassy from the Chaldean king of Babylon. "Behold the days come," cries the prophet, "that all that is in thine house, and that which thy fathers have laid up in store until this day, shall be carried to

[1] Gen. xi. 28; Isa. xiii. 19, xxiii. 13, xliii. 14; Ezek. xxiii. 15, R.V.M.; Ezra v. 12; Hab. i. 6; Jer. xxxvii. 10.

[2] Dan. ix. 1.

[3] *Records of the Past,* New Series, ii. 164; iv. 43, 79; v. 122, 123.

[4] See *ibid.* vol. v. p. 123, line 26.

Babylon: nothing shall be left, saith the LORD. And of thy sons that shall issue from thee, which thou shalt beget, shall they take away, and they shall be eunuchs in the palace of the king of Babylon."[1] We quote this prophecy at length, since the first chapter of Daniel shows us its fulfilment. Children of the Jewish royal family are there seen being trained to be courtiers and servants to Nebuchadnezzar the Chaldean king of Babylon.

The Chaldeans were always the bitter enemies of the Assyrians, yet, in spite of this hostility, in the closing years of the Assyrian Empire we find a Chaldean king, Nabopolassar the father of Nebuchadnezzar, seated on the throne of Babylon. How he got there we cannot tell, but he tells us himself that he was a man of very humble origin, and that he drove back the Assyrians out of northern Babylonia. In the final conflict with Assyria, Nabopolassar joined hands with Cyaxares of Media,[2] the result being that the northern portion of the Assyrian Empire passed under the sway of Media, while the southern portion fell to Nabopolassar, and helped to form the New Babylonian Empire. The Chaldean origin of the dynasty of Nabopolassar is gathered chiefly from the Old Testament writers. Jeremiah speaks of the army of Nebuchadnezzar as the "army of the Chaldeans." Ezekiel describes the ruling race at Babylon in the days of Nebuchadnezzar as hailing from Chaldea, whilst in the Book of Ezra, in a letter of the Persian governor Tattenai, Nebuchadnezzar is expressly called "the Chaldean." These statements of Scripture are confirmed by Berosus, a learned Chaldean priest, who in his history of Babylonia, written about 300 B.C., tells us that the Chaldean notables at Babylon kept the throne for Nebuchadnezzar on his father's death.[3] Alexander Polyhistor, in the second century B.C., also speaks of the father of Nebuchadnezzar as being a Chaldean.

During the Assyrian period Babylon was long a bone of contention between that people and their warlike neighbours in the south, and not a few Chaldean princes succeeded as the years rolled on in seating themselves on the throne of Bel. It is this which leads the prophet Isaiah to speak of Babylon as "the beauty of the Chaldeans' pride."[4] From the fact that these princes invariably have the names of the gods Bel and Nebo, the patron divinities severally of Babylon and Borsippa, incorporated in their throne-names, we gather that they were specially devoted to the worship of those gods. This was certainly the case with

[1] Isa. xxxix. 6, 7.
[2] See *Cory's Fragments*, pp. 83–90.
[3] *Josephus against Apion*, i. 19.
[4] Isa. xiii. 19.

Nebuchadnezzar, as his inscriptions [1] testify; with others it may have been a mere matter of policy.

In later times the term "Chaldean" is used in an ethnic sense by classical writers from Herodotus downwards. Herodotus mentions them as one of the many nations who served in the army of Xerxes.[2] Whilst the geographer Strabo, who lived till A.D. 25, tells us that even in his day there were still some relics of this people in their old homeland, which he describes as a district of Babylonia bordering on the country of the Arabs and on the Persian Gulf. It will be evident from the above that we are not at liberty to look upon the "Chaldeans" as Babylonians, or to regard the two terms as equivalents. The Chaldeans, strictly speaking, were not Babylonians at all, though they were often masters of Babylon and probably looked upon themselves as its rightful lords. In the Book of Ezra, as we have seen, Nebuchadnezzar is exactly described as "Nebuchadnezzar king of Babylon, the Chaldean." Josephus styles him "king of Babylon and of Chaldea." [3] And it is worthy of notice that the same writer calls Nabonidus, the father of Belshazzar, "a man of Babylon," but says of the historian Berosus that he was by birth a Chaldean.[4] Similarly, Sennacherib, king of Assyria, in his inscription on the Taylor Cylinder, speaks of Nergal-ushezib as "Shuzub of Babylon," while he styles Mushezib-Marduk "Shuzub the Chaldean." [5] In Dan. v. 29, Belshazzar is called "the Chaldean king," inasmuch as his father Nabonidus, a usurper, the last king of Babylon, though not himself a Chaldean, appears to have united himself by marriage with the Chaldean dynasty of Nabopolassar.

The use of the term "Chaldean" in a class sense, to denote a certain caste among the wise men of Babylon, which forms the second subject of our investigations in this chapter, appears first in the Book of Daniel, and is found next in the pages of Herodotus. Herodotus was born about 484 B.C. His visit to Babylon was probably prior to 447 B.C., when he left Halicarnassus to go and live at Athens. His description of Babylon, which in its correctness of topographical detail bears frequent evidence to the testimony of an eyewitness, gives us a picture of the state of things in that city within ninety years after its capture by Cyrus, and therefore less than a century from the time of the prophet Daniel. Herodotus, then, when describing to us the

[1] See *The Churchman* for December, 1903, pp. 119–121.

[2] Herod. vii. 63.

[3] *Ant.* x. 9, 7.

[4] *Josephus c. Apion*, i. 20 compared with i. 19.

[5] *Records of the Past*, New Series, vi. 94, line 35 compared with 97, line 41.

temple-tower and precincts of the sanctuary of Bel makes mention of the "Chaldeans" as his guides and informers. The "Chaldeans" tell him of the astonishing amount of gold used in the temple at the foot of the tower. Outside this temple he sees a great altar, on which, as he tells us, "the *Chaldeans* burn the frankincense, which is offered to the amount of a thousand talents' weight every year at the festival of the god." Again, speaking of a figure which stood in this temple in the time of Cyrus, he carefully adds: "I myself did not see this figure, but I relate what the *Chaldeans* report concerning it." Finally, that we may be in no doubt as to the identity of these friendly ciceroni, we find in a previous paragraph the plain statement, "*as the Chaldeans, the priests of the god, say.*" On the other hand, it is noticeable that when this chatty old historian leaves his description of the temple and its precincts and goes on to speak of the city of Babylon and the strange customs of its inhabitants, we hear no more of the "Chaldeans," but only of the "Babylonians."[1] It is, then, an error to state that the use of this word "Chaldean," as we find it in the pages of Herodotus, "dates really from a time when 'Chaldean' had become synonymous with 'Babylonian,'"[2] for Herodotus clearly does not use the two words as synonyms. The question, then, as to the identity of the "Chaldeans" of the Book of Daniel is settled by the plain statement of Herodotus. They were the priests of the great temple of Bel-Merodach, E-sag-ila, "the house of towering summit," the chief of the many temples in Babylon, and that in which, as recorded in Dan. i. 2, Nebuchadnezzar placed the vessels taken from the house of God at Jerusalem.

Having thus satisfied ourselves as to the identity of these men, we may reasonably endeavour, from the statements of classical writers compared with those which meet us on contemporary documents, to obtain further information as to this Chaldean priesthood and also as to why they were called "Chaldeans."

Diodorus Siculus, who flourished in the first century B.C., speaking of Belesys,[3] *i.e.* Nabopolassar, the founder of the New Babylonian Empire, calls him "the most distinguished of the priests, *whom the Babylonians call Chaldeans.*"[4] This is the testimony of a late writer, but that some credence may be given

[1] Herod. i. 183, 181 compared with i. 195–200.

[2] *Cambridge Bible:* Daniel, p. 12, foot-note.

[3] Belesys, or Balasu, is a Chaldean name. Possibly it was the name of Nabopolassar before he ascended the throne. See *Records of the Past*, New Series, vol. v. p. 123, line 26.

[4] Diod. Sic. *Bibliotheca*, lib. ii. cap. 24.

to it we gather from an inscription of Nabopolassar, in which he describes the part taken by himself and his two sons, Nebuchadnezzar and Nabu-shum-lishir, in the rebuilding of the temple-tower of Bel-Merodach. The passage runs thus:

"Unto Merodach, my lord, I bowed my neck; I arrayed myself in my gown, the robe of my royalty. Bricks and mortar I carried on my head, a workman's cap I wore, and Nebuchadnezzar, the firstborn, the chief son, beloved of my heart, I caused to carry mortar and gifts of wine and oil along with my workmen. Nabu-shum-lishir, his own brother, the offspring of my body, the junior, my darling, I caused to drag a truck with ropes, and a workman's hat I placed upon him, to Merodach my lord I presented him as a gift." [1]

The spirit of the above description, and the zest with which the king relates the part taken by himself and his two sons in the ceremonial of rebuilding the tower, is suggestive that the founder of the empire was either a priest himself, or at any rate thought it politic to ally himself very closely with the priesthood and to make his younger son a member of that body. In any case we seem now to understand the prominent part taken by the "Chaldeans" in the Book of Daniel and the freedom of speech with which they address the king.

To explain a possible way in which the priests of Bel may have acquired the name "Chaldeans," it will be necessary to advert to a very remarkable fact, which has hitherto received no explanation, viz. that in the documents of the New Babylonian Empire, *i.e.* in the royal inscriptions and the numerous business tablets, the word "Chaldean" is never found, either in an ethnic or in a class sense. The Assyrians, the Hebrews, the Greek and Latin writers, all use the term: the Assyrians only in an ethnic sense; the Hebrews similarly, with the exception of the author of the Book of Daniel; the Greek and Latin writers in both senses from Herodotus downwards. But we never find it used in either sense in the inscriptions of Nabopolassar, Nebuchadnezzar, Neriglissar, and Nabonidus. Further, on the contract tablets, while men are described as "Assyrians," "Egyptians," "Persians," and so forth, they are never called "Chaldeans." Possibly Babylonian vanity has something to do with this. It may be that the name "Chaldeans" was offensive to the Babylonians, as savouring too much of conquest by the foreigner, so that whilst a man

[1] See Eberhard Schrader's *Keilinschriftliche Bibliothek,* vol. iii. pt. ii. pp. 4–7.

might be a Chaldean, yet if he aspired to become a ruler of Babylon, he must both "take the hands of Bel," and call himself a Babylonian. A ray of light on this subject comes to us from the writings of the prophet Ezekiel. Ezekiel, who lived in Northern Babylonia in the days of the New Empire, and was a contemporary of the prophet Daniel, speaking of the overtures made by the kingdom of Judah to idolatrous Babylon, writes thus: "She saw men pourtrayed upon the walls, the images of the Chaldeans, pourtrayed with vermilion, girded with girdles upon their loins, exceeding in dyed attire upon their heads, all of them princes to look upon, after the likeness of the Babylonians, the land of whose nativity is Chaldea."[1] This language is remarkable. Ezekiel is evidently speaking of the ruling race: they are Babylonians by virtue of conquest, but Chaldea is where they spring from. The outside world calls them "Chaldeans," but they call themselves "Babylonians," either as being proud of their conquest, or else to humour the vanity of the conquered people. This may possibly explain how the name "Chaldean" came to be dropped by the Chaldeans themselves, though still applied to them by outsiders, such as the Hebrews, Greeks, and Latins. What still remains a mystery is how, being dropped in a national sense, it became attached to the priesthood of Bel in a class sense. Perhaps the simplest explanation is that in the days of the New Empire that priesthood became exclusive and only admitted to its ranks men of pure Chaldean lineage. Aulus Gellius, *circa* A.D. 130, speaking of the term "Chaldæi" as in his day the right term for astrologers and fortune-tellers, calls it *vocabulum gentilicium*,[2] "a name taken from a race." As, then, the conquerors generally were content to sink their origin, so the Chaldean priesthood may have been no less proud to retain it. In any case, be this as it may, we are now able to adduce evidence from contemporary tablets to show the truth of the statement of Gellius that these men were called "Chaldeans" because of their Chaldean origin.

A very interesting tablet of the seventeenth year of the reign of Nebuchadnezzar, which well indicates the office and high social position of the "Chaldeans," indicates no less certainly their nationality. As we have seen, the chief state of the Chaldeans was called "the Country of the Sea." This state, the Chaldean homeland, as being a specially privileged part of the empire, had a government of its own with a secretary, prefect, and sub-

[1] Ezek. xxiii. 14, 15.

[2] Aul. Gellius, *Noctes Atticæ*, lib. i. cap. 9.

prefect. On the tablet in question a decision is given with respect to the ownership of a house, which had been in the possession of Baladhu, a dependant of the Secretary of the Country of the Sea, and among the judges whose names are affixed to the document we find the Prefect and Deputy-Prefect of that district, the Burgomaster of Uruk (Erech), the Priest, presumably the high-priest, of the temple of the Moon-god at Ur, and the Prefect of "the Other Side," probably that part of Babylon which lay on the right bank of the Euphrates. Here is a veritable concourse of notables; but the two officials who interest us most stand last on the list. They are priests of the god Bel-Merodach, here styled *Shadû Rabû*, "the Great Mountain"; one of them possibly is the high-priest. In these men we detect two undoubted members of the famous Chaldean priesthood, men who may have been present at some of the scenes described in the Book of Daniel. In a matter affecting the interests of a dependant of a great Chaldean official, such as the Secretary of the Country of the Sea, nothing would be more natural than to have two Chaldean priests among the judges. These two priests of Bel come originally from that district. They are Chaldeans as being of Chaldean nationality, and also in virtue of their membership in the priestly caste to which they belong. However, that our readers may be able to form their own judgment on the subject, we will let this tablet speak for itself. It runs thus:

"These are the judges, before whom Shapik-zir the son of Zirutu and Baladhu the son of Nasikatum, the female slave of the Secretary of the Country of the Sea, went to law over an house, viz. with regard to the house and the tablet, which Zirutu the father of Shapik-zir had sealed and given unto Baladhu. They (the judges) made Baladhu and Shapik-zir change places. They assigned the house to Shapik-zir, and they took the tablet and gave it to Shapik-zir:

"Nabu-itir-napshati, the Prefect of the Country of the Sea.

"Nabu-shuzziz-anni, the Deputy-Prefect of the Country of the Sea.

"Marduk-irba, the Burgomaster of Uruk.

"Imbi-ili, the Priest of Ur.

"Bel-uballidh, the son of Marduk-shum-ibni, the Prefect of the 'Other Side.'

"Aplâ, the son of Shuzubu, the son of Babutu.

"Mushezib-Bel, the son of Nadin-akhi, the son of Babutu.

"Mushezib-Marduk, the son of Nadin-akhi, the son of Shanashishu.

"Bania, the son of Aplâ, the priest of the temple of the 'Great Mountain.'

"Shamash-ibni, priest of the 'Great Mountain.'

"Babylon, the 6th day of Nisan, the seventeenth year of Nebuchadnezzar king of Babylon."[1]

On the above tablet the high social position of these priests of the "Great Mountain" is very evident. Neither Bania nor Shamash-ibni, we may feel sure, would be at all flattered to find themselves classed with the wandering fortune-tellers mentioned by Juvenal. These men belong to a privileged class, of which the king's younger brother is a member; they are fit to rank with the notables of the land. No wonder, then, that in the Book of Daniel they come forward so confidently and take such a leading part. No wonder that they exhibit such a jealous spirit towards foreigners when they see them raised to posts of honour. In view of their social position as we now understand it, their conduct as described in that Book is just what we might have expected from them.

Further evidence of a quite different kind, but pointing the same way as that which we have derived from the tablet, comes to us from the excavations made at Babylon by Koldewey. On the south side of the great court, in which stood the temple-tower of Babylon, that explorer discovered the foundations of what appeared to be priests' houses. Concerning these he remarks:

"The priests of E-temen-an-ki (the temple-tower) must have occupied very distinguished positions as representatives of the god who bestowed the kingship of Babylon, and the immense private houses to the south of our *peribolos* agree very well with the supposition in regard to this Vatican of Babylon, that the principal administrative apparatus would be lodged there."[2]

On the whole, then, we may say that the true position of the "Chaldeans" was rightly gauged so long ago as 1877 by A. J. Delattre, an able French writer, with whose estimate we may suitably bring this chapter to a close:

"Parmi les diverses catégories de sages auxquels Nabuchodonosor demande l'explication de ses songes, il en est une que le livre de Daniel distingue par la denomination spéciale de *Casdim*, 'Chaldéens.' Un tel emploi du mot *Casdim* serait étrange si tous les Babyloniens de ce temps avaient été Chaldéens. Il se

[1] *Keilinschriftliche Bibliothek*, vol. iv. p. 188.

[2] *Excavations at Babylon*, p. 190.

justifie sans peine si l'on admet avec nous que les Chaldéens étaient une classe particulière et d'origine étrangère dans le peuple babylonien. Des lors en effet, il était assez natural d'appliquer la dénomination de Chaldéen à un collège de prêtres recrutés exclusivement parmi les hommes de cette classe. Ces docteurs Chaldéens—nous les voyons encore par le livre de Daniel—avaient le pas sur leurs confrères. Lorsque Nabuchodonosor, furieux de ce que les sages consultés par lui sont impuissantes à deviner le songe qu'il a eu, menace de les massacrer tous, ce sont le Chaldéens qui s'efforcent de calmer le monarque, et qui portent la parole au nom de tous. On a fait à propos d'un emploi si remarquable du mot *Casdim* des insinuations peu favorables au caractère du livre de Daniel, tandis qu'il fallait trouver en cela même une marque de son originalité." [1]

[1] See the *Revue des Questions Historiques*, tom. xxi. pp. 536–551.

5

The Great Mountain (Daniel 2)

IN the last chapter the "Chaldeans" of the Book of Daniel were identified with the priests of the god Bel-Merodach, styled on the tablet at which we were looking, *Shadû Rabû*, "The Great Mountain." This title of Merodach belonged originally to Enlil, the patron god of Nippur, to whom the most ancient of Babylonian temples, viz. that at Nippur, was dedicated. Hence, Sargon II. king of Assyria, who was of an antiquarian turn, speaks of "The Great Mountain, Enlil, the lord of the lands, dwelling in E-kharsag-gal-kurkurra," [1] *i.e.* "The House of the Great Mountain of the Lands," the name given to the temple at Nippur. In Babylonian mythology the gods were supposed to dwell in the sacred mountain called "the Mountain of the Lands," and, according to Jastrow, Enlil, as being the chief of the gods, was more particularly associated with this mountain, and from being regarded as the inhabitant of the mountain *became identified with the mountain itself*.[2] However, when Babylon rose into supremacy under Khammurabi, Merodach, its patron god, naturally came into prominence, and took the place of Enlil. In fact, an inscription of his son, Samsu-iluna, represents Enlil as transferring his titles and offices to Merodach.[3] In consequence of this we find Nebuchadnezzar speaking of "the Enlil of the gods, Merodach," and using the term to emphasise the supremacy of the god of Babylon. That this is its true signification may be gathered from the Monotheistic Tablet, which identifies the various gods with Merodach, and on which we read, "Enlil is Merodach of lordship and dominion." [4] Further, in the days of the New Babylonian Empire, if we may

[1] *Great Triumphal Inscription*, line 175.

[2] *Religion of Babylonia and Assyria*, p. 56. Jastrow speaks of the god as Bel, but the two cuneiform characters which used to be read "Bel" are now proved by the transcription given in Aramaic dockets to have the value "En-lil."

[3] See Schrader's *Keilinschriftliche Bibliothek*, vol. iii. pt. i. p. 130.

[4] Pinches' *The Old Testament in the Light of the Historical Records of Assyria and Babylonia*, p. 58, 1st ed.

judge from the contract tablets of Nabopolassar and Nebuchadnezzar this epithet, "the Great Mountain," which belonged to the old god Enlil, came into fashion again and was now bestowed on Merodach. In the Strassmaier collection it occurs on no fewer than twenty-three tablets of the reign of Nebuchadnezzar as an element in proper names, such as Shadû-rabû-uballidh, Shadû-rabû-ushezib; whilst in the important tablet given in the last chapter it is bestowed on Merodach himself. Now, the Aramaic rendering of the Babylonian *shadû rabû* is *dhur rabh, dhur* being the ordinary Aramaic word for "mountain" just as *shadû* is the ordinary Babylonian word, and *rabh* answering to the Babylonian *rabû,* and this very expression, *dhur rabh,* is the one which confronts us in Dan. ii. 35. When, then, the priests of *Shadû Rabû* heard from the lips of a strict monotheist, reciting and interpreting their monarch's dream, a statement to the effect that the kingdom of the God of Heaven, the God whom he worshipped, would become "a great mountain," or "the Great Mountain,"—for the words would convey either meaning to their ears—the announcement must have had for them, as well as for the king himself, an altogether peculiar significance. Identifying kingdoms with their patron gods, they would understand it to mean that just as the supremacy had been taken away from the god of Nippur and bestowed on the god of Babylon, so it would presently be taken from Babylon, and after being bestowed for awhile on a second, third, and fourth kingdom in succession, would eventually, in all its fulness, be given to the kingdom of the God of Heaven, the "great God" [1] who had made known to the king what should come to pass hereafter, the God whose kingdom, starting from a small but mysterious beginning, would develop into, and be identified with, the Great Mountain, *i.e.* with the Godhead itself, until eventually it filled all the earth.[2]

In this closing feature of the vision there was also a further idea, which could not fail to strike the prophet's hearers, an idea that chimed in to some extent with their own mythology, as may be gathered from the pages of Jastrow. For speaking of the temples and temple-towers of Babylonia, this great authority writes thus:

"The sacred edifices of Babylonia were intended to be imitations of mountains. It is Jensen's merit to have suggested the explanation for this rather surprising ideal of the Babylonian temple. According to Babylonian notions the earth is pictured as a huge

[1] Dan. ii. 45.

[2] Dan. ii. 34, 35.

mountain. Among other names, the earth is called E-kur, "Mountain-house." The popular and early theology conceived the gods as sprung from the earth. They are born in Kharsag-kurkura, 'the mountain of all lands,' which is again naught but a designation for the earth."[1]

When, then, the stone which smote the image was described in Daniel's recital of the vision as waxing into a great mountain, or into *the* Great Mountain, and filling the whole earth, it would seem to his Chaldean auditors to realise an idea of their own mythology, since it had developed into the earth-mountain. It only remains to add that in order to convey some idea of all this in our English Bible it would be well to place in the margin of Dan. ii. 35, as an alternative reading, "the Great Mountain," and in verse 45, "Mountain," spelt with a capital letter.

If "The Great Mountain," thus recalling the Enlil-ship of Merodach, was suggestive of a Supreme Power, a Most High God, there was also another feature in the vision which must have pointed in the same direction, viz. the wind which swept away the fragments of the image. For Enlil is the storm-god. His very name signifies "Lord of the Wind."[2] According to Radau, he is "the storm" *par excellence*, and his epithets are "lord of the storm," "storm of terrible strength," "rushing storm."[3] That Merodach in this respect succeeded to the heritage of Enlil is capable of the clearest proof. Thus, in the struggle with Tiamat, the dragon of chaos, Merodach is represented as master of the winds. He sends against her "a hurricane, an evil wind, a storm, a tempest, a fourfold wind, a sevenfold wind, a whirlwind." At first the hurricane follows behind him, but as he draws near to the dragon he sends it in front, and causes it to enter into her so that she cannot even close her lips.[4] An illustration of an entirely different kind may be drawn from the annals of Esarhaddon. Esarhaddon, invading the country of Shupria, lays siege to the royal city Ubbumi, situated on a lofty crag. With some difficulty he erects siegeworks against the city. These the besieged set fire to by night. But "at the command of Merodach the king of the gods, the North Wind blew, and the good lord of the gods turned the tongue of the devouring fire against Ubbumi," so that

[1] Jastrow's *Religion*, p. 614.

[2] See Langdon's *Sumerian Grammar*, pp. 226, 282.

[3] *Babylonian Expedition of the University of Pennsylvania*, vol. xxix. pt. i., series A.

[4] *Keilinschriftliche Bibliothek*, vol. vi. pp. 22–25.

the siegeworks were spared and the town set on fire.[1] But we may take a later instance of Merodach's control of the winds which may very possibly have had some connection with Nebuchadnezzar's dream. Early in the reign of this monarch there took place an event which seems to have made a deep impression on him at the time, and which, if it happened as early as his second year, helps to account for one of the closing features of his dream-vision. The inscription recording the rebuilding of the temple of the sun-god at Larsa [2] is looked upon as one of the early inscriptions of the reign of Nebuchadnezzar. Langdon places it second among the inscriptions written during the period 600–593 B.C.[3] In this inscription the king tells us how Ebarra, the temple of Shamash at Larsa, had long lain in ruins; so buried in the sand that even the outline of its walls could not be traced. "In my reign," he adds, "the great lord Merodach took pity on that temple. He caused the four winds to come, and swept away the soil so that its walls became visible. Me, Nebuchadnezzar king of Babylon, his shepherd, his worshipper, he authoritatively commissioned to rebuild that temple." How easily might the strong impression made on the king's mind by this supposed act of Merodach, "the lord of the wind," have suggested that part of his dream in which he saw the fragments of the great colossus swept away by the wind, swept away, too, in order that something else might take its place! After listening to Daniel's interpretation of his dream, Nebuchadnezzar would see in this action of the wind, no less than in the marvel of the stone rising up into a great mountain, the work of the Enlil of the gods, *i.e.* of the Most High God Himself. The same effect would be produced on the less prejudiced members of the Chaldean priesthood. The fact that their god was styled "the Great Mountain" would help them to grasp at once the main outlines of the kingdom of the God of Heaven as revealed to them in their monarch's vision. The stone which smote the image was contemptible enough in itself in comparison with the gold, the silver, the brass, and the iron, but then it was cut out of the Mountain, *i.e.* out of the Deity, and it was cut out "without hands," [4] *i.e.* by divine instrumentality. Further, after smiting the image and shivering it to atoms, the

[1] *Altorientalische Forschungen,* 2nd series, vol. i. pt. i., p. 32, article "Shupria," by Winckler.

[2] *Building Inscriptions of the Neo-Babylonian Empire,* Nebuchadnezzar, No. 10: by Stephen Langdon. Paris, 1905.

[3] *Ibid.* pp. 21, 22.

[4] Cf. Dan. viii. 25, where it is said of the persecutor Antiochus Ephiphanes, "he shall be broken without hand."

stone itself became a great mountain and filled all the earth, became in fact "lord of the lands,"—another epithet and attribute of Enlil. The subject thus viewed, it seems impossible to conceive of any more telling figures by which the great truths concerning the Messianic Kingdom could be conveyed to a Chaldean audience.

But if the dream would thus prove most enlightening to those who first listened to its interpretation, it can be shown, also, as regards Nebuchadnezzar himself, that such a dream-vision was most natural, *i.e.* the king saw what he might almost be expected to see. "The night," says Bishop Hall, speaking of Solomon's dream-vision at Gibeon, "follows the temper of the day, and the heart so uses to sleep as it wakes." [1] We have seen an instance of this in that part of the vision in which the wind was seen to sweep away the shattered fragments of the image. Let us take another illustration, and begin by asking, What was the waking heart of this greatest of royal builders, when, like Solomon, he stood on the threshold of his long reign? [2] The India House Inscription gives us a sufficiently plain answer. It shows us that he must constantly have been planning the erection of temples and temple-towers, palaces and fortress-walls, mighty edifices to be piled up like mountains. Not only of the *zikkurats*, or temple-towers, does he use such expressions as "I raised its summit." [3] The ramparts of Babylon he has reared "mountain-high." [4] The temple of Shamash he has "constructed loftily." [5] The rebuilt and enlarged palace of Nabopolassar, as well as the new palace adjoining it on the north, he has reared "high as the wooded hills." [6] Whilst of the northern citadel he tells us, "On the flank of the wall of brick I made a great wall of huge stones the product of great mountains, and like the mountains I reared its summit." [7] Add to the above the famous Hanging Gardens—built for his favourite wife, a native of Media, to remind her of the mountains of her native land—and we shall come to the conclusion that there was no man more likely than Nebuchadnezzar to dream such a dream: to dream of a stone mysteriously cut out of a mountain—did not he himself cut stones out of the mountain?—which presently itself swelled up into a mighty mountain, and filled all the earth. Size, strength, and height, no less than

[1] Compare the words of Artabanus to Xerxes respecting that monarch's dream: "Whatever a man has been thinking of during the day, is wont to hover round him in the visions of his dreams at night." Herod. vii. 16.

[2] It was only his second year when Nebuchadnezzar saw the vision.

[3] Col. iii. 17, 69. [4] Col. iv. 13. [5] Col. iv. 34.

[6] Col. viii. 2, 63. [7] Col. ix. 22-28.

grandeur and magnificence, were in all this monarch's thoughts, and all find a place in his dream.

In the Book of Enoch,[1] in the portion called the Similitudes, chaps. xxxvii.–lxxi., which is assigned by Dr. Charles to some date between 94 and 64 B.C., there is a curious reference to the vision of Dan. ii. The passage is so interesting that I give it in full. The writer, after telling how he had been carried away by a whirlwind to the confines of heaven, where he had seen all the visions of that which is hidden, continues as follows:

"2 There mine eyes saw all the secret things of heaven that shall be, a mountain of iron, and a mountain of copper, and a mountain of silver, and a mountain of gold, and a mountain of soft metal, and a mountain of lead. 3 And I asked the angel who went with me, saying, 'What things are these which I have seen in secret?' 4 And he said unto me: 'All these things which thou hast seen shall serve the dominion of His Anointed that he may be potent and mighty on the earth.' 5 And that angel of peace answered, saying unto me: 'Wait a little and there shall be revealed unto thee all the secret things which surround the Lord of Spirits. 6 And these mountains which thine eyes have seen, the mountain of iron, and the mountain of copper, and the mountain of silver, and the mountain of gold, and the mountain of soft metal, and the mountain of lead, all these shall be in the presence of the Elect One, as wax before the fire, and like the water which streams down from above upon these mountains, and they shall become powerless before his feet. 7 And it shall come to pass in those days that none shall be saved, either by gold or by silver, and none shall be able to escape. 8 And there shall be no iron for war, nor shall one clothe oneself with a breastplate. Bronze shall be of no service, and tin shall be of no service and shall not be esteemed, and lead shall not be desired. 9 And all these things shall be denied and destroyed from the surface of the earth, when the Elect One shall appear before the face of the Lord of Spirits.'"[2]

In the above passage the author of the Similitudes, who is evidently a lover of the Book of Daniel and no mean interpreter of it, seeks, with the best intentions, to improve upon and supplement the vision of Dan. ii. Accordingly he takes the term "mountain," which in the Book of Daniel symbolises the developed Messianic kingdom, and transfers it to the world-kingdoms, since to him it bore quite a different meaning to that put upon it by a Chaldean audience. In making this change he was no doubt

[1] Cf. *The Book of Enoch*, pub. by S.P.C.K., 1917.
[2] *Book of Enoch*, chap. lii. 2–9.

PRINCIPAL CITADEL OF BABYLON BUILT BY NEBUCHADNEZZAR
(KOLDEWEY, FIG. 98)

influenced by such a passage as Jer. li. 25, where Babylon is addressed as a "destroying mountain." Compare also Ps. xlvi. 2. Further, he makes out the world-kingdoms to be six in number instead of four—possibly in order that the Messianic kingdom may be the seventh, though this is not stated—and intentionally reverses their order, that so, running up the stream of time instead of down, he may remind his readers that before the coming of Babylon, the Golden Kingdom, there were two other mighty world-powers, viz. Egypt and Assyria, that oppressed the people of God. Now, it is not his way to mention countries by name,[1] he loves rather to veil his allusions, at the same time giving quiet hints for the benefit of those who study the Scriptures and know their Bibles. It is from this source that he draws his name for Egypt, "a mountain of lead," in allusion to the well-known words in the Song of Moses, "They sank as lead in the mighty waters."[2] That passage is certainly in his mind, for only a little before in this same Similitude we find him saying of the kings and strong ones of the earth, "as lead in the water shall they sink before the face of the righteous."[3] That Assyria should be denoted by a mountain of soft metal is at first sight surprising, but this also receives explanation and confirmation from the page of Scripture. Micah, a prophet of the Assyrian period, tells how when the LORD cometh out of His place, "the mountains shall be molten under Him, and the valleys shall be cleft as wax before the fire, as waters that are poured down a steep place."[4] Now, these very words of Micah are distinctly referred to in the passage before us. And what was to happen indeed to all the "mountains," was to happen specially to the Assyrian mountain, the great world-power of Micah's day: it was to become "soft metal" at the coming of the LORD.[5] But *that* was by no means Assyria's former condition. So, then, when our author in the next two verses again refers to the metals of which the mountains were composed, he substitutes bronze for copper and tin for soft metal, *i.e.* he substitutes harder metals for the softer ones, since it is only in the presence of the Elect One that the strong mountains grow weak, that the brazen kingdom of Daniel—so called in allusion to the brazen arms of the Greeks—becomes a copper kingdom, and the military empire of Assyria is reduced to soft metal.[6] Finally, the utter destruction

[1] The mention of Media and Parthia in chap. lvi. 5, is considered an interpolation. See Charles' *Book of Enoch*, p. 109, footnote.

[2] Exod. xv. 10.

[3] Chap. xlviii. 9.

[4] Micah i. 4.

[5] Cf. Judg. v. 5.

[6] The mention again of both soft metal and tin in the list given in chap. lxvii. 4 has led Charles to suppose that the metal mountains are seven in number, and that "tin" has dropped out of the two lists in chap. lii. 2

of the world-kingdoms is traced to that momentous occasion "when the Elect One shall appear before the face of the Lord of Spirits": a striking reference to the sublime vision of Dan. vii. 13, 14.

To return to our main subject; when the dream-vision shown to Nebuchadnezzar was recalled and interpreted by Daniel, the impression made on that monarch was immense.[1] Forthwith he showed his reverence for the God of Daniel by ordering special, if not divine honours, to be paid to His prophet, as well as by prostrating himself at the feet of Daniel. Then, as his words show, he went on to ascribe to Daniel's God the attributes of his favourite divinities, Merodach and Nebo. "The king answered unto Daniel, and said, Of a truth your God is the God of gods, and the Lord of kings, and a revealer of secrets, seeing that thou hast been able to reveal this secret." We may justly compare with the above utterance, first, what the monarch says of Merodach in the India House Inscription. Thus, in col. ii. 44 he is styled "the Enlil of the gods," *i.e.* the supreme god. In col. iii. 35 he is "the king of the gods, the lord of lords." Again, in col. ii. 54–62 we are told how at the festival of the New Year—a very great occasion at Babylon—"the divine king of the gods of heaven and earth, the lord of the gods," takes up his abode in the shrine of the fates, and "the gods of heaven and earth with awe submit unto him." Daniel's God is admitted by the king to be supreme among the heavenly powers, like "the great lord Merodach." He is almighty; He is also all-wise, "a revealer of secrets," *i.e.* He is wise as Nebo, for Nebo, according to Babylonian ideas, "knows all that there is to know," and "to him belong wisdom and prophecy."[2] For the time being at any rate, "the God of Heaven" is admitted to the Enlilship, since He combines the attributes of both Merodach and Nebo.

and 6. This double omission of "tin" seems unlikely. Further, chap. lxvii. 4 does not belong to the Similitudes, but is an interpolation from the Apocalypse of Noah, and although the writer of that passage undoubtedly refers to chap. lii. of the Similitudes, yet the reference is a careless one, for instead of six, seven, or even eight metals, he only mentions *five*: gold, silver, iron, soft metal, and tin; leaving out copper, lead, and bronze.

That the "mountains," or world-kingdoms, in the Book of Enoch are really only six in number, may be deduced also from Rev. xvii. 10, where five, viz. Egypt, Assyria, Babylon, Persia, and Greece, are spoken of as already "fallen" in St. John's day, while the sixth "is," *i.e.* was then in existence.

[1] Witness the king's words in Dan. iv. 9, spoken many years after this.

[2] *Mudu mimma shumshu . . . sha shuddu u shushupu bashu*, as it is expressed on a statue, dedicated to the god Nebo by Bel-tartsi-iluna, governor of Calah, for the life of Rammanu-ninari III., king of Assyria, and his wife Semiramis, at present in the British Museum.

The astonishment displayed by Nebuchadnezzar at the revelation of the great secret must have been shared by many others who were present on that memorable occasion, so that the fame of the young Jewish prophet must have spread with lightning rapidity far and wide. The evidence of this is not far to seek. In the Book of Ezekiel there are two undoubted references to the events described in Dan. ii. The earlier, viz. that in Ezek. xiv. 14, 20, was written about fourteen years after the date of those events. The prophet there mentions Daniel as one of three holy men whose intercessions were known to have prevailed before God. Now, the story of Dan. ii. shows that on the occasion there described Daniel acted as intercessor, and by his all-powerful intercession saved, not only the lives of his friends, but also the lives of the wise men of Babylon. The second reference, found in Ezek. xxviii. 3, in a passage written some five years later, is still more telling. Daniel's holiness, and even his powerful intercession, would not alone account for his altogether remarkable fame at such an early age. There must have been something more. What that something was, appears very plainly in this later passage when taken in conjunction with the story of Dan. ii. Ezekiel is addressing the prince of Tyre, who so overestimated his wisdom and insight that he regarded himself almost as a god. Accordingly the prophet adopts a tone of keen irony: "Behold, thou art wiser than Daniel," he cries. *Wiser in what way?* The words that follow tell us: "*there is no secret they can hide from thee.*" Daniel, it is evident, fairly early in his career, must have established a world-wide reputation for wisdom by finding out some secret, something which only God could know. Also this discovery must have been published by him on some great occasion, and before a gathering of persons of position and eminence: for so only could the fame of this young Jewish captive have spread so rapidly and so extensively; not merely to the banks of Chebar and among his own compatriots, but even to the seagirt walls of Tyre and among heathen rulers. All these most legitimate inferences, so well pointed out by Hengstenberg, are seen to be so many actual facts in the light of the story contained in Dan. ii., so that Ezekiel's reference to the wonderful discovery described in that story is thus established beyond doubt. So, then, the first of the marvels contained in this Book of Daniel is proved to be true. Why should not this also be the case with the marvels that follow, for none of them surpasses this? What Daniel discovered was not merely the king's forgotten dream: but the history of the known world for long ages to come!

Those who refuse to receive Ezekiel's most conclusive testimony often urge as an objection against the early date of the Book of Daniel the fact that Jesus, the son of Sirach, writing about 190 B.C., in his list of Jewish worthies makes no mention of Daniel.[1] They point out that while Isaiah, Jeremiah, Ezekiel, and the twelve Minor Prophets collectively are all mentioned by him, not a word is said about Daniel. "If Daniel had been known to him," writes Dr. Charles, "with his roll of achievements unparalleled in the Old Testament, the writer could hardly have said, as in xlix. 15, that no one had ever been born like unto Joseph."[2] I answer that Daniel *was known* to him, seeing that he knew the Book of Ezekiel, as is shown by his reference to Ezekiel's vision of the cherubim,[3] and knowing that Book, he must at least have known of Daniel's fame for superhuman wisdom. The unique position in which he places Joseph finds a simple explanation in the fact that when we are looking fixedly in one direction we sometimes forget what can be seen in other directions. Now, the writer of Ecclesiasticus had his mind turned in the direction of the Book of Genesis when he said that there was none like Joseph.[4] This appears from both the preceding and succeeding context. In the verse that follows he mentions Shem, Seth, and Adam: in the verse that goes before he mentions Enoch, and tells us that there was none like Enoch for he was taken from the earth:[5] *i.e.* Enoch, like Joseph, is put in a place by himself in virtue of his translation from earth to heaven, the writer quite forgetting for the moment that the same thing had happened to Elijah and had been mentioned by him not so long before.[6] Further, his list of worthies leaves out Ezra as well as Daniel, and after stopping short with Nehemiah[7] darts back to the Book of Genesis, and finally, taking one tremendous bound, lights on Simon the son of Onias, the high-priest![8] To found an argument on the appreciations and omissions of a writer, at once so forgetful and so erratic, is useless. But even if the silence of this author were not capable of so simple an explanation, it would still count for nothing in view of Ezekiel's weighty testimony. It still remains, then, for those critics who look upon the Book of Daniel as the work of a later age, to explain to us the meaning of those telling words: "*Behold, thou art wiser than Daniel: there is no secret that they can hide from thee.*"

[1] Ecclesiasticus, chaps. xliv. to l.
[2] *Century Bible*, Daniel, p. xxxiv.
[3] Ecclesiasticus xlix. 8.
[4] *Ibid.* xlix. 15.
[5] *Ibid.* xlix. 14, 16.
[6] *Ibid.* xlviii. 9.
[7] *Ibid.* xlix. 13.
[8] *Ibid.* xlix. 14–l. 1.

6

The Messianic Kingdom (Daniel 7)

THE melting of the mountains in the passage from the Book of Enoch, quoted in the last chapter, answers to the breaking in pieces of the gold, the silver, the brass, and the iron before the impact of the stone cut out without hands. The writer of the Similitudes explains that all these metals will then be of no use at all and of no avail, and that they will be destroyed from the surface of the earth.[1] Compare Dan. ii. 35, " the wind carried them away, that no place was found for them." This, it is added, will happen at the time " when the Elect One shall appear before the face of the Lord of Spirits." In the Similitudes " the Lord of Spirits is the usual name for God, and " the Elect One " is the Messiah. Also, the appearance of the Elect One before the Lord of Spirits is a reference to the passage in Dan. vii. 13, 14. From this it appears that the author of the Similitudes looked upon Dan. ii. and vii. as parallel visions, since in dwelling on a theme suggested by chap. ii.—viz. the idea of the six mountains—he turns for a note of time to the vision of chap. vii. But far more important than this is the fact that he regards the vision of Dan. vii. 13, 14 as Messianic. His commentary on that passage runs thus : " And there I saw One, who had a head of days "—*i.e.* One who had the reverend and dignified appearance of an aged man—" and his head was white like wool, and with Him was another Being, whose countenance had the appearance of a man, and his face was full of graciousness, like one of the holy angels. And I asked the angel, who went with me and showed me all the hidden things, concerning that Son of Man, Who he was, and whence he was, and why he went with the Head of Days ? And he answered and said unto me, ' This is the Son of Man who hath righteousness, with whom dwelleth righteousness, and who revealeth all the treasures of that which is hidden, because the Lord of Spirits hath chosen him, and whose lot hath the pre-

[1] *Book of Enoch*, chap. lii. 7–9.

eminence before the Lord of Spirits in uprightness for ever.' "[1] To one who could write thus, the mysterious Being of whom he gives so wonderful a description evidently formed a subject of the deepest interest. He "was named," so he tells us, "in the presence of the Lord of Spirits . . . before the sun and the signs were created, before the stars of the heaven were made."[2] He is to share in the divine sovereignty,[3] and to sit on the throne of glory.[4] "His glory is for ever and ever, and his might unto all generations."[5] He is "the Righteous One,"[6] "the Elect One,"[7] and the Anointed One of the Lord of Spirits.[8] "His mouth shall pour forth all the secrets of wisdom and counsel."[9] He puts down the mighty from their thrones.[10] In him dwells the spirit of wisdom, and the spirit which gives insight, and the spirit of understanding and might.[11] He is to be the light of the Gentiles.[12] He is to sit on the throne of glory and judge the sinners according to their works.[13] He is to "judge the secret things and none shall be able to utter a lying word before him."[14] The mighty kings of the earth shall have to behold God's Elect One sitting on the throne of glory as judge.[15] At the general resurrection, when Sheol and Hell give back the dead, he shall separate the righteous from the wicked.[16] Finally, we are told that "all these things," viz. the six mountains of metal, the mountain of iron, the mountain of copper, the mountain of silver, the mountain of gold, the mountain of soft metal, and the mountain of lead, "shall serve the dominion of His Anointed that He may be potent and mighty on the earth."[17] The above extracts show unmistakeably a very wonderful growth and development of Messianic doctrine in the Jewish Church during the interval between the Old and New Testaments. The portion of the Book of Enoch known as the Similitudes is assigned by Charles and other eminent scholars to the period 94–64 B.C. Schürer places it as late as the time of Herod the Great. In any case there is a general, though not quite universal consensus of opinion, that the Similitudes are a product of the pre-Christian period.[18] It thus appears that before the coming into the world of our Lord and Saviour Jesus Christ, Jewish commentators had attained to marvellously clear

[1] *Book of Enoch*, chap. xlvi. 1–3. [2] *Ibid.* xlviii. 2, 3; cf. Prov. viii. 23, 27.
[3] *Ibid.* li. 3. [4] *Ibid.* xlv. 3. [5] *Ibid.* xlix. 2.
[6] *Ibid.* liii. 6. [7] *Ibid.* xlv. 3. [8] *Ibid.* xlviii. 10.
[9] *Ibid.* li. 3; cf. Prov. viii. 14. [10] *Ibid.* xlvi. 4, 5; cf. Luke i. 52.
[11] *Ibid.* xlix. 3; cf. Isa. xi. 2.
[12] *Ibid.* xlviii. 4; cf. Isa. xlii, 6, xlix. 6; cf. Luke ii. 32.
[13] *Ibid.* xlv. 3. [14] *Ibid.* xlix. 4. [15] *Ibid.* lv. 4.
[16] *Ibid.* li. 1, 2. [17] *Ibid.* lii. 4.
[18] See the Note at the end of this chapter.

views as to the divinity, character, and attributes of the Messiah, and more especially as to His office as the future Judge of mankind. What was not seen by them, though it had been revealed to Daniel, was His death as an atonement for the sins of men. In the words of Gabriel: "Seventy weeks are decreed upon thy people and upon thy holy city, to finish transgression, and to make an end of sins, and to make reconciliation for iniquity, and to bring in everlasting righteousness, and to seal up vision and prophecy, and to anoint the Most Holy." [1]

This single verse sets the Book of Daniel on a higher plane than the most wonderful of Jewish apocalypses, viz. the Similitudes of the Book of Enoch. But what concerns us most just now is the view taken by the author of those Similitudes of the vision of Dan. vii. 13, 14, seeing that one of an entirely different character is put forward by the critics with no small acumen and skill. The question as to the right interpretation of that passage is of the utmost importance, inasmuch as our Lord Jesus Christ on a most solemn occasion entirely endorsed the teaching of the Book of Enoch on this subject. "I adjure thee by the living God," says the Jewish High Priest, "that thou tell us whether thou be the Christ, the Son of God. Jesus saith unto him, Thou hast said":—*i.e.* thou hast said the truth—"nevertheless I say unto you, Henceforth ye shall see the Son of Man sitting at the right hand of power and coming on the clouds of heaven." [2] The reference here to Dan. vii. 13, 14, is unmistakeable. Our Lord claims to be the Person there described as "one like unto a son of man." He speaks of Himself as "coming on the clouds of heaven," just as that Person was seen by Daniel in the vision; and He asserts that He is on the point of receiving that delegation of divine power therein so strikingly described. The Jewish High Priest and Sanhedrim understood perfectly our Saviour's claim. In their eyes the mysterious Being seen in Daniel's vision was a Divine Being. Hence the High Priest declared that Jesus had spoken blasphemy, while the Sanhedrim with united voice exclaimed, "Art thou the Son of God?" [3]

Let us now turn to examine the view of this part of Daniel's vision, first put forward by Ephraem Syrus, *circa* A.D. 350, and of late revived by modern critics: a view so utterly at variance with that given in the Book of Enoch, as well as with that held by the Jewish teachers at the time of Christ and most solemnly endorsed by Christ Himself, that it becomes a duty for the Christian student to endeavour by a close study of the

[1] Dan. ix. 24. [2] Matt. xxvi. 63, 64. [3] Luke xxii. 70.

whole vision of chap. vii. to ascertain on independent grounds its actual meaning

The seer's most sublime description runs thus: "I saw in the night visions, and, behold, there came with the clouds of heaven one like unto a son of man, and he came even to the ancient of days, and they brought him near before him. And there was given him dominion, and glory, and a kingdom, that all the peoples, nations, and languages should serve him: his dominion is an everlasting dominion, which shall not pass away, and his kingdom that which shall not be destroyed." What first strikes us in this description is the incomparable grandeur and solemnity of it. So grand a setting calls, surely, for a worthy subject. Who is it, then, we ask, who comes thus with the clouds of heaven in a manner befitting only the Deity?[1] Who is it that is led by attendant ministers to be presented to the Ancient of Days and to receive from Him everlasting and world-wide dominion? No individual at all, answer the critics, but only the symbolic representative of a race of supernatural beings, viz. of the saintly Israel transformed.[2] Such an interpretation, when put before us, is distressingly disappointing, since the surroundings so evidently call for some great one. Further, we are conscious of a want of harmony in the interpretation of the next verse: "All the peoples, nations, and languages" are to "serve him." Now, to take the singular "him" in a figurative collective sense when put in such close contact with nouns of multitude, such as "peoples," "nations," and "languages," is, to say the least, bad taste and doubtful criticism. And no less strange is it to assign a figurative meaning to the "him," and a literal meaning to "the peoples, nations, and languages." We ask, then, on what grounds does this interpretation rest? And the answer is so clearly and fully given by the late Dr. Driver that I cannot do better than quote his words at some length.

"In the Book of Daniel itself," writes Dr. Driver, "there is nothing which lends support to the Messianic interpretation," viz. of this passage. "In the explanation of the vision which follows (vii. 15 ff.), the place occupied by 'one like unto a son of man' is taken, not by the Messiah, but by the ideal people of God: in *v.* 14 the 'one like unto a son of man' appears when the dominion of the four beasts, and the persecution of the 'little horn,' are both over, and receives a universal kingdom which shall never pass away; and in *vv.* 18, 22, 27, when the dominion of the four kingdoms corresponding to the four beasts is at an

[1] Ps. civ. 3; Isa. xix. 1.

[2] *Century Bible*, Dan. vii. 13.

end, and the persecution of the king corresponding to the 'little horn' has ceased, the 'saints of the Most High,' or (*v.* 27) the 'people of the saints of the Most High,' receive similarly a universal kingdom (*v.* 27), and possess it for ever and ever (*v.* 18). The parallelism between the vision and the interpretation is complete; the time is the same, the promise of perpetual and universal dominion is the same: and hence a strong presumption arises that the subject is also the same, and that the 'one like unto a son of man' in *v.* 13 corresponds to, and represents, 'the saints of the Most High' of *v.* 18, and the 'people of the saints of the Most High' of *v.* 27, *i.e.* the ideal Israel, for whom in the counsels of God the empire of the world is designed. If the writer by the 'one like unto a son of man' meant the Messiah, the head of the future ideal nation, his silence in the interpretation of the vision is inexplicable: how comes it that he there passes over the Messiah altogether, and applies the terms which (*ex hyp.*) are used of him in *vv.* 13, 14, to the people of Israel in *vv.* 18, 22, 27?"[1]

The argument, thus ably brought forward, is so specious that I have deemed it advisable to quote it *in extenso:* but it will be seen to lose much of its force when we recognise the fact that "the saints," who are looked upon by Dr. Driver as the true interpretation of "one like unto a son of man," *are already present in the vision before the appearance of that mysterious Being.* According to *v.* 21—which in point of time must be inserted between *vv.* 8 and 9, and is so inserted in the LXX.—Daniel saw the little horn making war with the saints and prevailing against them, before he saw the holding of the great assize (*vv.* 9, 10) and the execution of its sentence (*vv.* 11, 12), followed by the sublime vision of "one like unto a son of man": from which it follows that "the saints" *belong to the vision, and not merely to its interpretation.* They have already appeared in the vision as a persecuted people. It is, therefore, most unlikely that in its further development they should be represented in symbol by a single individual. But inasmuch as the kingdom given to "one like unto a son of man" is seen to be given also to "the saints," we are forced to conclude that the mysterious Person thus described is the God-appointed Head of "the saints."

But by far the most convincing proof of the fallacy of the view which Dr. Driver so ably maintains, will be found in a careful analysis of the whole chapter. The vision of Dan. vii. is divided into three sections thus: (i) *vv.* 2–6, (ii) *vv.* 7–12,

[1] *Cambridge Bible,* Daniel, p. 103.

(iii) *vv.* 13, 14. These three sections begin respectively with the words, " I saw in my vision by night," *v.* 2 ; " After this I saw in the night visions," *v.* 7 ; " I saw in the night visions," *v.* 13. The vision itself closes at the end of *v.* 14. The remainder of the chapter consists of questions and explanations. The whole passage may be briefly analysed thus :

Section (i), *vv.* 2–6. The four world-kingdoms, figured by four wild beasts, are seen rising out of the great sea, a particular description being given of each of the first three.

Section (ii), *vv.* 7–12. A particular description is given of the ferocious beast which represents the fourth kingdom, and of its ravages. Mention is made of its ten horns, and of the " little horn," which sprang up among them, and which is presently seen making war with " the saints "—see *v.* 21—until the coming of the "Ancient of Days." A great assize is then held, at which the " little horn " is condemned and judgment executed upon it. The other beasts are allowed to continue for a time, but are deprived of their power.

Section (iii), *vv.* 13, 14. " One like unto a son of man " is seen coming with the clouds of heaven, and is brought before the " Ancient of Days " to receive from Him universal and lasting dominion.

First explanation, *vv.* 15–18 ; given in answer to Daniel's question as to " the truth concerning all this " by " one of them that stood by," and exceedingly brief ; to the effect that the four beasts picture four kingdoms which will arise out of the earth, but that finally the kingdom will be given to " the saints of the Most High " who will possess it " for ever, even for ever and ever."

Further information desired by Daniel, *vv.* 19–22, as to the terrible fourth beast, its ten horns, and more especially as to the " little horn " which he had already seen making war with the saints and prevailing against them until the holding of the great assize.

Second and longer explanation, *vv.* 23–27, dealing with the points inquired about, and followed by a strengthened reiteration that the kingdom in all its greatness and universality will be given to " the people of the saints of the Most High " and that it will last for ever.

Abrupt end of the conversation, *v.* 28 a ; " Here is the end of the matter," *i.e.* " Do not ask any more." These are the words of the interpreting angel and not of Daniel. Compare the close of the vision in chap. viii., where, as here, as soon as the angel has done speaking, the seer goes on to tell us the effect of the vision upon himself.

It appears, then, from the above analysis that section (iii), the coming of "one like unto a son of man," *is left unexplained.* There is thus no solid ground whatever for the view that by "one like unto a son of man" we are to understand the "people of the saints of the Most High" transformed into a race of supernatural beings: not only is the context against such an interpretation, but the sublimity of the description, as stated above, suits only a Divine Being, although no hint is given as to who that Being is. That great question, like so many of our Lord's parables, was left unexplained, in order that His Church might find out the answer for herself, and this she was able to do. The writer of the Second Similitude, fully aware that the record of Daniel's vision contains no authoritative explanation of the mystery, pictures in his own person the earnest inquiries of the devout students of those early days to find out what had not been disclosed, "I asked the angel, who went with me and showed me all the hidden things, concerning that Son of Man, Who he was? and Whence he was? and Why he went with the Head of Days?"[1] and then proceeds to unfold in a wonderful way, as we have already seen, the person of the promised Messiah. The day vision of the Second Similitude, in which all is so sharp and clear and distinct, when placed side by side with the night vision of Daniel, resembles two pictures of the same landscape as seen in the broad sunlight and by the light of the moon. The seer's vision loses much of its entrancing grandeur and beauty, nevertheless we are grateful for the many striking details which the Apocalyptist has introduced on his canvas, forasmuch as they represent one of the earliest fulfilments of the promise with regard to this Book of Daniel referred to in our first chapter, "Many shall run to and fro, and knowledge shall be increased."[2]

If the question be asked, How comes it that our modern critics cannot see what was so clearly seen by the ancient Jewish expositors? the answer is that their inability to recognise the Messiah in the vision of Dan. vii. arises out of the estimate which they have already formed of Daniel's Book. To them it appears as a literary work of great power written more than 350 years after the times it describes.[3] They therefore argue that if by "one like unto a son of man" the writer had meant the Messiah, he would have been sure to make the angel say so when

[1] *Book of Enoch*, chap. xlvi. 2.

[2] Dan. xii. 4.

[3] Dr. Driver assigns the Book of Daniel to a date not earlier than c. 300 B.C., but more probably to the age of Antiochus Epiphanes. Daniel, *Cambridge Bible*, p. xlvii.

interpreting the vision to Daniel. To those of us, however, who see in the Book of Daniel, not a mere Jewish apocalypse, but genuine history, and who hold the belief that Daniel really saw the visions which he describes, this line of argument does not appeal. According to our view, Daniel only wrote down what he saw and heard. The interpretation of the vision is in no sense his, but only that of the interpreting angel. Had the angel given him an interpretation of that mysterious Personage, "one like unto a son of man," he would have been sure to have written it down. Likely enough, too—so one thinks—he would, had the opportunity been given him, have gone on to ask for such an explanation, just as he had already asked for an explanation of the fourth beast and of the "little horn"; but the angel, as we have seen, stopped him by saying abruptly, "Here is the end of the matter."

The Ruler of the fifth, or Messianic, kingdom is pictured in the vision by "one like unto a son of man" in contradistinction to the four previous kingdoms, which appear on the scene as wild beasts. Nevertheless it will be found that in two respects there exists a certain likeness between the Messianic kingdom and the first of those four kingdoms. In the Messianic kingdom the Ruler never changes: "His dominion is an everlasting dominion."[1] Also in the first of the four world-kingdoms, one ruler, viz. Nebuchadnezzar, is on the throne for forty-three out of the seventy years during which that kingdom lasts; and he reigns with such lustre that all his successors on the throne are put into the shade. Accordingly, Daniel, with prophetic eye foreseeing this, was able when interpreting the monarch's dream to say to him, "Thou art the head of gold." In the next place, it is said of the first kingdom in Daniel's vision in this seventh chapter that from being a beast of prey, viz. a lion with eagle's wings, its wings were plucked off, and it was "lifted up from the earth, and made to stand on two feet as a man, and a man's heart was given unto it"[2]: *i.e.* the kingdom, concentrated, so to say, in its great ruler, presently became humanised, and was so far a foreshadowing of the coming Messianic kingdom that it could no longer be depicted by a beast of prey. The historical fulfilment of this part of the vision of Dan. vii., which had already taken place at the time when the vision was shown unto Daniel,[3] may be summed up thus: Nebuchadnezzar began his long reign with a very rapid career of conquest in the West. *Then* he was a lion with eagle's

[1] Dan. vii. 14.
[2] *Ibid.* vii. 4.
[3] The vision belongs to the first year of Belshazzar. See Dan. vii. 1.

wings[1]: but *presently*, all his thoughts becoming centred on Babylon and on his home policy, he developed into a prince of peace. At intervals, indeed, expeditions to the West were still undertaken by him, as for instance in 588 B.C. when he besieged Jerusalem, and again in 568 B.C. when, according to the fragment of his Annals, he invaded Egypt.[2] But that war soon lost its charm for him is evident from inscriptions written comparatively early in his reign, as for instance that which describes the completion of the great temple-tower at Babylon.[3] The same feature appears with great clearness in a much later document, viz. the carefully drawn up India House Inscription,[4] the lofty poetic style of which entitles it to be looked upon as a literary work. In this inscription one brief passage, couched in quite general terms, is found sufficient to describe the monarch's warlike expeditions, while column after column is devoted to the various temples, fortifications, and palaces built by him at Babylon, the whole being prefaced and completed with the most earnest prayers and supplications to Merodach. Quite in agreement with the tone of that inscription is the historical record and the vision of Dan. iv., which will form the subject of our next chapter. In that vision the great king of Babylon is pictured as a giant tree, affording shade to the beasts, shelter to the birds, and sustenance for all. It was from this description that our Saviour drew His picture of the Messianic kingdom,[5] which, small as a grain of mustard seed at its first beginning, was presently to grow into a tree in which the birds of the heaven would come and lodge.

Note on the Date of the Similitudes

Dr. Charles is of opinion that the Book of Enoch in all its sections was written by the Chasids or their successors, the Pharisees. The portion called the Similitudes, or Parables, he assigns to the time of the later Asmonæan princes. These princes, who at first had been on the side of the Pharisees, went over to their opponents the Sadducees in 105 B.C., near the close of the reign of John Hyrcanus. Soon after this, the strife between the two parties, becoming more embittered, led to a terrible deed of bloodshed in 95 B.C., when six thousand Pharisees were put to the sword for insulting Alexander Jannæus at the feast of

[1] Cf. Dan. vii. 4, and Jer. xlix. 19, 22.

[2] *Keilinschriftliche Bibliothek*, vol. iii. pt. ii. pp. 140–1.

[3] *Building Inscriptions of the New Babylonian Empire*, No. xvii., by S. Langdon.

[4] *Records of the Past*, New Series, vol. iii. p. 104.

[5] Matt. xiii. 31, 32.

Tabernacles. These facts of history, as Charles points out, help to throw light on many expressions in the Similitudes, such as the following: "The kings and the mighty" (xlvi. 4), *i.e.* the unbelieving native rulers and their Sadducean supporters, who "denied the Lord of Spirits and his Anointed" (xlviii. 10) and the heavenly world (xlv. 1); who "persecute the houses of his congregations" (xlvi. 8); whose "power rests upon their riches" (xlvi. 7), and they place their hope in the sceptre of their kingdom and in their glory (lxiii. 7); who have oppressed God's children and his elect (lxii. 11), and shed their blood (xlvii. 1). For a short interval, indeed, during the reign of Alexandra, 79–70 B.C., the power was again in the hands of the Pharisees, but after her death her successors again went over to the side of the Sadducees. In 64 B.C. Rome appeared on the scene in the person of Pompey, and interposed in favour of Aristobulus II. As there are no references to Rome in the Similitudes, they can hardly have been written later than 64 B.C. Charles assigns them either to 94–79 B.C., or to 70–64 B.C.; more probably to the earlier interval. Schürer favours a later date, viz. the era of Herod the Great; but opposed to this is the fact that the Sadducees, who figure so largely in the Similitudes as the persecuting party then in power, did not take the side of Herod. That the Similitudes should be later than the time of Christ is ruled out by the fact that our Saviour quotes them in His teaching.

7

The Royal Builder

"Is not this great Babylon, which I have built for the royal dwelling-place?"
—Dan. iv. 30.

IT will be my endeavour in this and the following chapter to deduce from the inscriptions of the Neo-Babylonian Empire certain strong confirmations of the wonderful story told us in Dan. iv., and in attempting to do this I shall refer in the first instance, as is most natural, to the oft-quoted passage from the Assyrian history of Abydenus, preserved to us by Eusebius.[1] Abydenus, who lived about A.D. 200, gives as his informant Megasthenes, a writer of the age of Seleucus Nicator, 312–280 B.C. The passage runs thus:

"This also have I found concerning Nebuchadnezzar in the book of Abydenus. *On the Assyrians.* Megasthenes relates that Nebuchadnezzar became mightier than Hercules, and made war upon Libya and Iberia. These countries he conquered, and transported some of their inhabitants to the eastern shores of the sea. After this the Chaldeans say that on going up upon his palace he was possessed by some god or other, and cried aloud, 'O Babylonians, behold I, Nebuchadnezzar, announce to you beforehand the coming calamity, which my ancestor Bel and queen Beltis are alike powerless to persuade the Fates to avert. A Persian mule (Cyrus) will come, having your own gods as his allies. He will impose servitude upon you, and will have for his helper the son of a Median woman (Nabonidus),[2] the boast of the Assyrians (*i.e.* Babylonians). Would that before he betrayed my

[1] *Præp. Evang.* 41.

[2] The traditional text reads ἔσται Μήδης, "shall be Medes." But, as A. von Gutschmid points out, it is impossible to look on Μήδης here as a proper name. The presence of Πέρσης in the context compels us to take it in a gentilic sense. Since, however, the Greek for "Mede" is Μῆδος, not Μήδης, we are forced to regard the latter as the genitive feminine of the adjective and to suppose that υἱός has dropped out of the text. Further, to translate Μήδης "a Mede" would not be true to history, as the Medes could not be called "the boast of the Assyrians," neither are they distinguished from the Persians as a separate nation in the account left us of the capture of Babylon. To this it may be added that Nabonidus, the last king of Babylon, may very well have

citizens, some Charybdis or sea might engulf him and utterly destroy him! or that having betaken himself elsewhere, he might be driven through the desert, where there is neither city nor track of men, where wild beasts seek their food and birds fly free, a lonely wanderer among the rocks and ravines! and that I, before these things were put into my mind, had met with a happier end!' Having uttered this prophecy he forthwith disappeared, and Evilmaluruchus (Evil-Merodach) his son succeeded him on the throne."

It is admitted by the critics that the resemblances between the record of Daniel, chap. iv., and the above story cannot be accidental. "In both," writes Dr. Charles, "Nebuchadnezzar is on the roof of his palace: in both a divine voice makes itself heard (in the former work *to* the king, in the latter *through* him): and finally the doom pronounced in both is similar though its object differs. But neither form of the story is borrowed from the other, though that of Abydenus is more primitive, while that in Daniel has been transformed to serve a didactic aim." In this and the following chapter I propose to adduce from the contemporary inscriptions of Nebuchadnezzar and his father Nabopolassar certain facts, circumstances, and royal utterances, which have led me to an exactly opposite conclusion to the one just quoted; leaving it to a future chapter to show that the legend of Megasthenes is a gross distortion of the actual story, artfully concocted to serve a political purpose.

To lighten our subject, and at the same time to impart additional interest to it, let me begin at the point where the two stories come into closest contact. Both the Book of Daniel and the legend of Megasthenes represent the king as walking upon his palace at the time when the terrible calamity overtook him. "Upon" is the strict rendering of the Aramaic preposition in Dan. iv. 29, and it agrees with the ἐπὶ τὰ βασιλήϊα of Megasthenes. By this term the late Dr. Driver understood "on the roof of," referring to 2 Sam. xi. 2.[1] This, however, would give the idea of a flat roof, whereas the place where we may picture Nebuchadnezzar walking was anything but flat. If we except the top of the great temple-tower of Merodach, there was perhaps no point in the whole of Babylon from which a better view of the city could be obtained than from the Hanging Gardens. Of this ingenious structure,

been the son of a Median mother, seeing that his father was the high-priest of Haran, which, though included in the Babylonian Empire, must have been close to the Median frontier.

[1] *Cambridge Bible*, Daniel, p. 55.

which so awoke the admiration of antiquity, the great king, who so carefully describes all his other works, has, strange to say, left us no record. A possible explanation would be, that the Hanging Gardens were his latest work, or at any rate later than any of his extant inscriptions, that his madness followed soon after their completion, and his death, as there is some reason to suppose, soon after his recovery from his madness.[1] But this, again, seems unlikely, since they appear to have been constructed in a work which was executed fairly early in his reign, viz. the rebuilding of the old palace at Babylon, and were designed moreover according to Berosus to gratify the taste of a Median wife, presumably that Median princess, the daughter of Cyaxares, with whom for political purposes he was contracted in marriage even before his father's death.[2] But if over this building the inscriptions are silent, the ruins at any rate are eloquent. On the site of ancient Babylon and at the north-east corner of the rebuilt Old Palace, the explorer Koldewey found the remains of a remarkable structure, occupying an irregular oblong area and built on rows of vaults, the central row being the strongest, as though intended to bear the greatest weight.[3] All the other buildings at Babylon, with one exception, are found to be composed entirely of brick, but in this instance some stone has been used as well. Further, in one of the supporting cells the explorer believes that he has discovered the shafts of the hydraulic machine used to pump up water for the gardens, as described by Strabo.[4] The use of stone in the construction of the vaulted building tallies admirably with the following description of the Hanging Gardens given us by Josephus in an extract from Berosus: "Now in this palace, having built up lofty substructures of stone, and planted them with all kinds of trees, giving an appearance very closely resembling mountains, he wrought out and prepared the famous Hanging Gardens, to gratify his wife, who was fond of a mountainous country, having been brought up in Media."[5]

The Hanging Gardens, then, were lofty, resembling mountains. They therefore offered a good point of observation; and if we

[1] In *Josephus c. Apion*, i. 20, Berosus says that toward the close of his reign Nebuchadnezzar "fell into a feeble state of health and died." Hengstenberg argues very forcibly that the Greek expression here used—ἐμπεσὼν εἰς ἀῤῥωστίαν—signifies that his death was preceded by a lengthened state of debility, viz. by the madness recorded in Dan iv., and that the historian makes no mention of his recovery because it was followed shortly after by his death.

[2] Cory's *Ancient Fragments*, enlarged by E. R. Hodge, p. 88.

[3] See *The Excavations at Babylon*, by Robert Koldewey, pp. 91–100, also the plate given on p. 73.

[4] *Strabo*, xvi. 1, 5.

[5] *Josephus c. Apion*, i. 19.

identify them with the vaulted building described above, which stood close to the noble Ishtar Gate, it will be seen that they also stood on high ground, as the following extract from Koldewey bears witness: "The Kasr roadway lies high, 12·5 metres above zero, and slopes gently up from the north to the Ishtar Gateway. Before the time of Nebuchadnezzar it was considerably lower, but as he placed the entire palace on a level higher than that of its predecessor, he was forced also to raise the roadway. *In consequence of this we can to-day enjoy the glorious view over the whole city as far as the outer walls.*"[1] Besides being a lofty structure and standing on an elevated site, the position of the vaulted building was also a central one, from which the monarch could survey on all sides some of his principal works. To the north was the Northern citadel with its lofty rampart looking towards Sippar: to the east, the great outer wall of Babylon: to the south, the massive and lofty temple-tower of Merodach, E-temen-an-ki, "the temple of the foundation-stone of heaven and earth," begun by his father and completed by himself: to the west, the most daring of all his buildings, a fortress rising out of the bed of the Euphrates. It only remains to add that when walking upon this building the king was literally walking "upon the royal palace of Babylon," for, as Koldewey points out, the reason why the Hanging Gardens were looked upon as one of the seven wonders of the world lay in the fact that they were planted upon the roof of an occupied building, a building which on account of its coolness appears to have been in constant use.

It may well have been, then, that from the steep acclivities of these gardens the fatal words were spoken: "Is not this great Babylon, which I have built?" The ruins of Babylon, no less than the inscriptions, bear witness that this was no empty boast. Nebuchadnezzar was one of the greatest builders of antiquity, probably *the* greatest. He seems to have been possessed with a perfect rage for building: in his own expressive words, "My heart impelled me." Accordingly his inscriptions are most truly described as "Building Inscriptions"; and Langdon has found it possible from the nature of the various buildings, which form the principal subjects of the different inscriptions, as well as from the mention made in them of other buildings already completed, to arrange the inscriptions of Nebuchadnezzar in something of chronological order, at any rate for the earlier part of the reign,

[1] Koldewey, *Excavations*, p. 25. It is true that the lower parts of the vaulted building, being intended probably for cellars and storehouses, lie below the level of the palace in which it stands, but the superstructure, which the arches were intended to support, must have towered aloft.

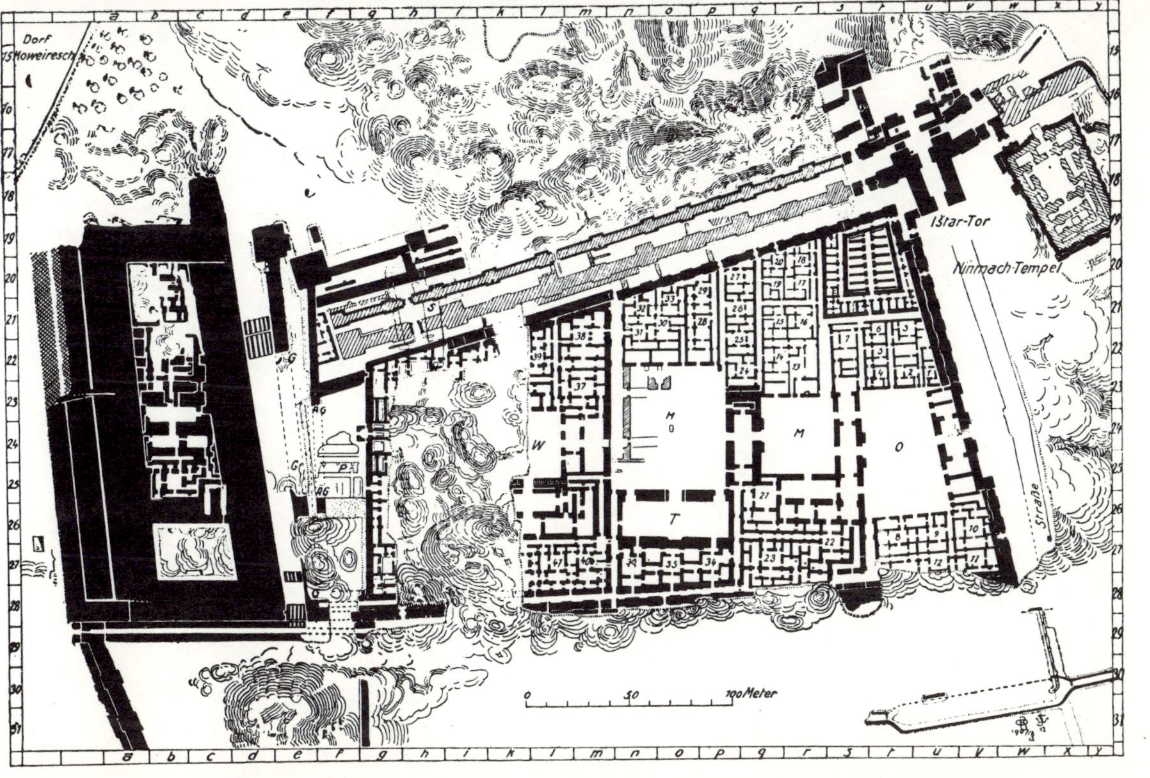

PLAN OF THE SOUTHERN CITADEL, SHOWING THE POSITION OF THE HANGING GARDENS BY THE ISHTAR GATE.

THE THRONE ROOM IS MARKED *T*, AND THE DARK BLOCK IS A FORTRESS BUILT IN THE BED OF THE EUPHRATES (KOLDEWEY, FIG. 44)

viz. 604 to 586 B.C.[1] For the later period, 586 to 561 B.C., we have only four inscriptions. One of these, the great Wady Brissa Inscription, must be placed *circa* 586 B.C. Another, a brief but important fragment from the Annals, refers to the king's 37th year, 567 B.C. But we are still at a loss as to the date of the two latest building inscriptions, and are unable to determine how long the royal builder continued his activities, what exactly were his latest works, and what their sequence.

The building inscriptions of Nebuchadnezzar which have so far been discovered are forty-nine in all. Many of them are six or eight-lined inscriptions, found chiefly on bricks, either stamped or written, and often found *in situ*, enabling the explorer to identify the different buildings. Indeed, so great is the help that the king gives us from these brick inscriptions, when taken in conjunction with the longer accounts found on tablets and cylinders, that it would be no very difficult thing to supply the modern tourist with "A Guide to Babylon, by Nebuchadnezzar." Of the longer inscriptions, some relate to special buildings, such as the great East Wall of Babylon, the Libil-khigalla canal, and various temples in Babylon and other cities. Others, about a dozen in number, take a wider range, and refer to various works besides the one which forms the special subject of each separate inscription. It is these longer and more comprehensive documents which, thanks to the literary method adopted, enable us to arrange the various buildings in something of a chronological order. They contain two very enlightening clauses: the first is introduced by the word *enuma*, "when," and describes more or less fully the various works already accomplished, often borrowing for this purpose from previous inscriptions. The second is introduced by *enumishu*, "then," and it is this clause which contains an account of the king's latest work, which led to the writing of the inscription. To put the matter in a nutshell, these documents run thus: "*When* I had done this and that, *then* I set to work to do what I am now about to relate."[2] Two other features enable us to arrange the inscriptions in something approaching to chronological order. In the first place, in the earlier inscriptions we seem to hear more or less distinctly the din of arms. Take, for instance, No. 4, which commemorates the building of the great East Wall and ends with the following prayer to Merodach, "Truly thou art my deliverer and my help, O Merodach. By thy faithful word that changes not, verily my

[1] *Building Inscriptions of the Neo-Babylonian Empire*, by Stephen Langdon. Paris, 1905.

[2] *Building Inscriptions*, pp. 2, 3.

weapons advance, verily they are dreadful: may they crush the arms of the foe."[1] Secondly, in the later inscriptions the literary style is changed, and we have what are called "historical redactions," so that henceforward the student "has to depend on lists of temples, new information, and the redactor's tendencies." Henceforward, according to Langdon, "the scribes seem possessed with the sole idea of telling what has been done, without reference to historical order."[2] This, however, only applies to the three or four great inscriptions which belong to the latter half of the reign; more especially to Nos. 14 and 15; the latter better known as the India House Inscription. This remarkable document, already repeatedly referred to, is described by Langdon as a "veritable marvel of the redactor's skill."[3] To the Bible lover it must ever be dear as a telling comment on the words of Nebuchadnezzar in Dan. iv. 30, which stand as a heading to this chapter.

The chief inscriptions of Nebuchadnezzar begin with an introductory hymn, in which the king describes the relation in which he stands to the great gods, more especially to the patron gods of Babylon and Borsippa. He is "favoured of Merodach, the beloved of Nebo," "the righteous king, the faithful shepherd, the contented one," "who loves the fear of their divinities, whose ears are attentive to their divine will, cultured and industrious, wise and prayerful, caretaker of Esagila and Ezida."[4] The longer inscriptions invariably close with a prayer, generally addressed to Merodach, or in the case of inscriptions from Sippar or Larsa to Shamash. In one of the Sippar inscriptions Merodach is joined with Shamash, while in a slab inscription from the Procession Street the prayer is made to Nebo and Merodach. Occasionally other divinities, such as Nebo and Ninkarrak,[5] are asked to intercede with Merodach or with Shamash and Merodach. In Inscription No. 12, describing the restoration of the temple of Shamash at Sippar, the prayer is addressed to that divinity. Not unfrequently the closing prayer is made to suit the subject-matter of the inscription. Thus, in the inscription describing the completion of E-temen-an-ki, the tower of Babylon, the prayer, which is addressed to Merodach, ends thus: "As E-temen-an-ki is established for ever, establish thou my royal throne unto the days of eternity! O E-temen-an-ki, unto me, Nebuchadnezzar, the king who restored thee, grant blessings. When with sound of many voices Merodach enters to abide in thee, recall to the mind of Merodach, my lord, my pious deeds!"[6]

[1] *Building Inscriptions*, p. 75.
[2] *Ibid.* p. 16.
[3] *Ibid.* p. 20.
[4] *Ibid.* pp. 61, 83, 155.
[5] *Ibid.* pp. 67, 95, 111, 115.
[6] *Ibid.* p. 151.

Among the forty-nine inscriptions of Nebuchadnezzar there is one which possesses a unique interest. It is a fragment of his annals, much obliterated. Enough is left to tell us that in his 37th year, 567 B.C., he invaded Egypt and encountered the army of Amasis.[1] On this occasion we may well believe that the prophecy of Jeremiah was fulfilled that Nebuchadnezzar should spread his royal pavilion on the brickwork at the entry of Pharaoh's house in Tahpanhes.[2]

In that famous and fatal utterance, "Is not this great Babylon, which I have built for the royal dwelling-place, by the might of my power and for the glory of my majesty ?" the king has in view all his buildings in that great city which he had done so much to enlarge.[3] Nevertheless it is evident that his thoughts centre chiefly on his palace, "the royal dwelling-place," on which he was walking at the time, and in which at the beginning of the story he describes himself as "at rest" and "flourishing." The order of Nebuchadnezzar's buildings at Babylon, roughly speaking, runs thus : fortifications, temples, canals, palaces. But to this order there is one exception, viz. the rebuilding of the old palace of his father, of which he says in the Wady Brissa Inscription, "Together with the restoration of the cities of the gods and goddesses, I have constructed the palace, my royal habitation, in Babylon."[4] It is probable that this great work was undertaken not later than 593 B.C. Nebuchadnezzar was a great temple-builder : he built temples in Sippar, Larsa, Ur, Erech, and other cities, besides the numerous temples, some seventeen in number, built by him in Babylon and its suburb Borsippa : but in building palaces he confined himself to his beloved Babylon ; in this, as he himself tells us, differing from his royal predecessors, who placed their dwellings in the cities of their choice, and only came to Babylon to the New Year Festival.[5] In the eyes of this king Babylon was the only city fit to be a royal residence. He speaks of it as "the city of the lifting up of mine eyes" ; and of the palace built by his father as "the house for people to behold, binding bar of the land, bright dwelling-place, abode of my royal power." But that palace had certain defects of construction : it was made of unburnt brick ; its foundations had been weakened

[1] *Vorderasiatische Bibliothek* 4, *Die Neubabylonischen Konigsinschriften*, p. 207.

[2] Jer. xliii. 8–13. For an interesting account of Tahpanhes and the actual spot on which in all probability the king of Babylon pitched his pavilion, see Flinders Petrie's *Ten Years' Digging in Egypt*, p. 50.

[3] Especially by building on the N.E. the long line of the great outer wall.

[4] *Building Inscriptions*, p. 173.

[5] *Records of the Past*, New Series, vol. iii. p. 117.

by a flood, and the raising of the Procession Street had caused its gates to fall in. Accordingly Nebuchadnezzar determined to pull it down and build up a new palace on the old site. The boundaries of that site are clearly defined by him. It stretched from the old city wall Imgur-Bel on the north to the canal Libil-khigalla on the south, and from the bank of the Euphrates on the west to Ai-ibur-shabu, the Procession Street, on the east.[1] The greater part of this site has been excavated by Koldewey, and it appears that the new palace of Nebuchadnezzar consisted of four courts stretching from east to west, with numerous buildings on their northern and southern sides.[2] The main entrance, known as the gate of Beltis, was from the Procession Street on the eastern side. This led through a double gateway into a large court, from which you passed by two double gates into a smaller court: thence on through a very massive double gateway into the third and principal court. On the south side of this third court was found the largest hall in the palace, measuring 52 metres by 17. Its longer walls were 6 metres thick, considerably in excess of those at the ends, as if to support a barrel vaulting. Three doors, of equal width, opened on the court. Opposite the central door was a doubly recessed niche, in which the throne must have stood; for this spacious hall, as indicated by its size and arrangements, no less than by the brilliant ornamentation in coloured tiles of the façade of the court in which it stood, was undoubtedly the throne-room of the Neo-Babylonian kings; and within its walls, as Koldeway suggests, may very well have been held Belshazzar's eventful feast.[3] The three courts just described represent the official part of the palace. The fourth and western court, which has not been fully excavated, appears to have contained the private apartments. In this portion the foundations show traces of what was probably the ancient palace of Nabopolassar. At the north-west corner of what still remains, there was found an earthenware coffin of unusual size, placed deep down in the brick-work, and bricked up, as this part of the building showed, in the time of Nebuchadnezzar. "The dead man," we are told, "must have been the object of the deepest reverence," for though the tomb had been plundered, there were found under the sarcophagus gold beads and a number of small gold plates with holes, as if they had been sewn on to a garment, also rectangular gold plates some-what larger, ornamented with moulded designs, one representing a bearded man offering before the symbol of Merodach, another

[1] *Records of the Past*, New Series, vol. iii. p. 118.
[2] Koldewey's *Excavations*, p. 67.
[3] *Ibid.* p. 103.

the gateway of a fortress with towers and battlements. The person of the deceased had evidently been arrayed in garments richly spangled with gold, and decorated with gold ornaments, which, taken in conjunction with the place and manner of his burial, suggest to us that he occupied a very important place at the court of Babylon. There is thus nothing at all unlikely in the suggestion made by Koldewey that we have here the tomb of Nabopolassar, the father of Nebuchadnezzar and the founder of the dynasty, by whom the original palace was built.[1]

Of the restored palace Nebuchadnezzar writes, "At that time the palace, my royal abode, binding bar of mighty peoples, abode of joy and happiness, whither I compelled tribute to be brought, I rebuilt in Babylon. Upon the ancient abyss, upon the bosom of the wide world, with mortar and brick I laid its foundation. Great cedars I brought from Lebanon, the beautiful forest, to roof it. A great wall of mortar and burnt brick I threw around it. My royal decisions, my imperial commands, I caused to go forth from it." [2] This palace appears to have been erected before the year 595 B.C. At some time after its erection the royal builder, as though apprehensive of an attack from the river, set to work to build up from the bed of the Euphrates a western outwork. In the foundations of this remarkable building were found chambers with walls of immense thickness as though to keep out the water. These may possibly have been used as dungeons. It is of this building that the king gives the following description: "For the protection of Esagila and Babylon, that evil may not be done against her, in the river Euphrates a great fortress in the river of mortar and brick I caused to be made. Its foundation I laid upon the abyss, its top I raised mountain-high." [3]

When the Old Palace had been rebuilt some years, we know not how long, the king began to find it too small. Accordingly he set to work to collect material for its enlargement, and made use of his Palestinian campaign in 588–589 B.C. to bring from the Lebanon a fresh store of cedar beams for the roofing; and after his return from that campaign "took a good look round," [4] as he tells us, to see in which direction to enlarge it. This soon led him to the conclusion that there was no more ground to be obtained in the Old City, seeing that he was unwilling to disturb the sacred Procession Street on the east, or to cross the Libil-khigalla canal on the south and thus encroach on the domain of Merodach.

[1] Koldewey's *Excavations*, p. 118.

[2] *Building Inscriptions*, p. 89.

[3] *Ibid.* p. 105.

[4] *Rapshish ashte'ema.* India House Inscription, col. viii. 41.

On the west he was hemmed in by the river. Thus the north was the only side which offered any opportunity for expansion. But to do this he must go beyond the old city walls, Imgur-Bel and Nimitti -Bel,[1] which bounded his palace on that side. This led to a northern extension of the citadel of Babylon and to the erection of a new palace outside the old town-walls. Accordingly the king built two " mighty walls," [2] the inner towering above the outer, to form " a fortification like a mountain," extending to a distance of 360 ells beyond the old walls. Between this fortification and Nimitti-Bel he erected a lofty terrace of burnt brick, much of which is still standing,[3] and on this terrace, in the incredibly short space of fifteen days,[4] raised his second palace, rearing it " high as the mountains." In this new palace there are signs that the original design was considerably enlarged, also that during the progress of the building the details of the plan were frequently altered. This shows, as Koldewey observes, that the royal builder must have insisted very specially and with great energy on his own wishes being carried out, for no architect would of his own free will alter plans so frequently during the course of building.[5] As if still apprehensive of attack from the north, the king presently built at a distance of 490 ells from Nimitti-Bel a third wall, faced in its lower courses with immense blocks of limestone bound together with dove-tailed wooden clamps laid in asphalt, which he thus describes : " Beyond the fortification of burnt brick I built a great fortification of mighty stones, the product of the great mountains, and raised its summit mountain-high." [6] After which comes the following imposing description of the New Palace. " That house I made to be gazed at : I had it filled with sculptures for the masses of the people to behold. The awe of power, the dread of the splendour of sovereignty its sides begird : and the bad unrighteous man cometh not within it. That the wicked man might not show his face against the wall of Babylon, his attacking spear I kept at a distance. Babylon I made strong like a mountain." [7] The last words well explain the king's reason for building the stone wall. The palaces of

[1] Imgur-Bel was the wall and Nimitti-Bel the rampart.

[2] The two walls formed one duru or "fortification," and as it rose up "like a mountain," it seems probable that the inner wall towered above the outer. Cf. the illustration given at p. 404 of Pinches' *Old Test.*, 1st ed.

[3] Koldewey's *Excavations*, p. 157, fig. 98.

[4] The same statement is made in an extract from Berosus quoted in *Josephus c. Apion*, i. 19.

[5] *Excavations*, p. 158.

[6] *Ibid.* pp. 177, 178.

[7] India House Inscription, col. ix. 22-44.

STONE WALL OF NORTHERN CITADEL BUILT BY NEBUCHADNEZZAR
(KOLDEWEY, FIG. 110)

Nebuchadnezzar were veritable fortresses, and even the drains, so necessary on low-lying ground and amid such vast masses of brickwork, are found to be carefully guarded by gratings of stone or burnt brick.

When the king had thus completed his new palace north of the old town-wall, he proceeded to unite it with the old palace so as to form one vast acropolis. His words are, "I joined it to the palace of my father, and caused the dwelling-place of my lordship to be glorious." [1] This statement is of importance, inasmuch as it helps to remove one great difficulty in the way of identifying the vaulted building with the Hanging Gardens. The vaulted building stands, as we have seen, in the north-east corner of the ruins of the Old Palace and within the old town-walls. But Berosus, when speaking of the palace built within fifteen days, which we know from the inscriptions was the New Palace, goes on to tell us that in this palace Nebuchadnezzar built up the lofty Hanging Gardens.[2] The explanation is, that while the two palaces were distinct groups of buildings, they were formed by Nebuchadnezzar into one vast whole, which would naturally be called "the palace," and within which stands the building that has been identified with the Hanging Gardens.

The enlarged palace of Nebuchadnezzar lies buried in the mound rightly named the Kasr or "Castle," seeing that it formed the acropolis of Babylon, of which only the southern half has so far been excavated. In area this enlarged palace must have more than twice exceeded that occupied by Nabopolassar. But its royal builder, as he himself admits, was still urged on by the lust of building and still apprehensive of attack from the north. Accordingly, at the northern end of the great outer wall of Babylon, called in the inscriptions the "East Wall," but which really runs from S.E. to N.W., he built what he calls an *appa danna*, literally "a strong nose," *i.e.* a great projecting platform, 60 ells broad, standing out from the wall, facing Sippar. On this platform, possibly standing somewhat back, he built up another lofty palace, which bore the name, "May Nebuchadnezzar grow old as the maintainer of Esagila and Ezida." [3] A glance at Koldewey's map of the site of Babylon [4] explains at once the king's description of the position of this palace and what he means by the term *appa danna*. The long low ridge, which runs from S.E. to N.W.,

[1] *Building Inscriptions*, Nebuchadnezzar, xiv. col. ii. 39. Berosus makes the same statement. Cf. Joseph. *Ant.* x. 11, 1.

[2] *Josephus c. Apion*, i. 19.

[3] *Building Inscriptions*, No. xiv. Cf. also p. 38.

[4] See Frontispiece.

marks the site of the great outer wall, so often referred to in the inscriptions. At the point where it terminates, almost due north of the Kasr, rises the square mound called Babil, which stands out from the line of the wall and faces the four points of the compass. Babil, which is only half the size of the Kasr, is the most northerly of the three mounds which mark the site of ancient Babylon. It still awaits excavation. Koldewey assures us that it contains many courts and chambers, both large and small, and mentions a sandstone slab found *in situ*, which describes it as a " palace of Nebuchadnezzar king of Babylon son of Nabopolassar king of Babylon." [1]

I have now described the palaces of Nebuchadnezzar and must return once more to the point from which I started. Two of the mounds of Babylon, viz. Babil and the Kasr, contain, as we have seen, those palaces. The third is the mound of Amran to the south of the Kasr, buried in which at a depth of 21 metres lies the famous temple of Merodach, Esagila. The great temple-tower, E-temen-an-ki, also sacred to Merodach, stood in the plain between Amran and the Kasr, a little to the north of the former. Both of these have been partially excavated, as well as a temple to Ninib the war-god, but the greater part of the vast mound of Amran is as yet untouched. The three mounds of Babylon stand on a straight line which runs nearly due north and south. If we prolong that line to a point where it meets the line of the south-eastern wall of the city, and then bisect it, we shall find that the point of bisection coincides with the central point of the eastern wall of the acropolis, where stood the Hanging Gardens. Further, if we suppose about a third of the city to have stood on the western side of the present course of the Euphrates, we shall come to the conclusion that these gardens formed the very centre of the whole. Then, too, since the ground falls away from them in every direction, they must have commanded a wide prospect on every side ; whilst close by stood one of the king's most splendid works, the noble Ishtar Gate ; [2] a double gateway, its walls covered with bulls and *sirrushes* [3] in high relief. This gateway, which stood on the old city walls, still rises to a height of 39 feet. The approach to it from the north lay between strong fortress walls, on which were rows of lions in relief, made of coloured tiles, some of them white with yellow manes, others yellow with red manes, against a ground of grey-blue.[4] Sights such as these still awaken our wonder even

[1] *Excavations*, p. 11.
[2] *Ibid.* pp. 33, 39.
[3] The four-legged " dragon of Babylon," *ibid.* pp. 46, 47.
[4] *Excavations*, fig. 16.

THE ISHTAR GATE

(KOLDEWEY, FIG. 24)

in this later age. How easily might they cause the heart of him, at whose fiat they were called into existence, to swell with pride as he looked down upon them from the steep slopes of the Hanging Gardens![1] In his inscriptions, indeed, Nebuchadnezzar is careful to utter prayers; but here, in the midst of his great works, he forgets the warning dream of a year ago, and indulges in an independent, godless, self-centred spirit, unconsciously betraying the leading motive which animated him in his proud building career: "Is not this great Babylon, which I have built for the royal dwelling-place, by the might of my power and for the glory of my majesty?" No sooner were the words spoken than with lightning speed the sentence of judgment fell: "O king Nebuchadnezzar, to thee it is spoken: the kingdom is departed from thee!"

[1] *Excavations*, fig. 46.

8

The Royal Wood-cutter

"Hew down the tree, and cut off his branches."—Dan. iv. 14.

IF the inscriptions of Nebuchadnezzar form the best commentary on the words, "Is not this great Babylon which I have built?" they also help in great measure to account for some of the leading features of the king's dream, as related in Dan. iv., so that when we compare them with the record given us in that chapter, we seem to see yet another instance of how men's dreams are moulded by their waking thoughts. Thus we can now see how easily one who had a strong admiration for the monarchs of the forest might come to dream of a great tree. We can also understand how entirely suitable in his eyes such a figure would be to portray the character of the kingdom which he had sought to establish at Babylon. For his own inscriptions show us that he meant his kingdom, centred in that city, to be just such a sheltering tree. Then again with respect to the command of the heaven-sent watcher for the tree to be cut down, we can see how naturally such a vision might dawn on one, who had himself cut down trees in the service of Merodach, and what a terrible significance it would have for him when the angel's words with startling suddenness revealed its meaning.

The reign of Nebuchadnezzar, which began with a rapid career of conquest, speedily assumed a totally different aspect. In the symbolic language of Dan. vii. 4, the lion with eagle's wings had its wings plucked off, was lifted up from the earth, made to stand upon its feet as a man, and a man's heart was given it. Inscription No. 17—according to Langdon the earliest of the inscriptions which belong to the second period of the reign, 600–593 B.C.—brings this out very clearly. In this inscription the king's empire is seen to be already firmly established. Not a word is said about war, and all his subjects from far and near—"the peoples, nations, and languages," of Dan. iv. 1—are summoned to help him complete the lofty temple-tower of Babylon. Already the great tree begins to loom large in the monarch's mind: witness the following extract:

"To raise the top of E-temen-an-ki towards heaven, and to strengthen it, I set my hand. I called unto me the far-dwelling peoples, over whom Merodach my lord had appointed me, the shepherding of whom was given me by the hero Shamash: and from all lands, and from every inhabited place, from the Upper Sea to the Lower Sea,[1] from distant lands, the people of far-away habitations, kings of distant mountains and remote regions by the Upper and the Lower Seas,[2] with whose strength Merodach the lord had filled my hand that they should bear his yoke. I summoned also the subjects of Shamash and Merodach [3] to build E-temen-an-ki."

Here follows a partially obliterated list of the peoples summoned, after which the recital continues:

"The kings of the remote district by the Upper Sea, the kings of the remote district by the Lower Sea, the princes of the land of the Hittites [4] beyond the Euphrates westward, over whom I exercise lordship by the command of Merodach my lord, these brought great cedars from the mountain of Lebanon unto my city of Babylon."

Babylon, then, in the monarch's intention is to be the centre towards which all the forces of the empire must converge. It is there that the great tree is planted "in the midst of the earth." [5] In the words of inscription No. 9, "The far-scattered peoples, whom Merodach my lord had given into my hand, I subdued under the sway of Babylon. The produce of the lands, the product of the mountains, the bountiful wealth of the sea within her I received. *Under her everlasting shadow I gathered all men in peace. Vast heaps of grain beyond measure I stored up within her.*" [6] In the Wady Brissa inscription the parallel passage runs thus: "*Under her everlasting shadow I gathered all men in peace. A reign of*

[1] *I.e.* from the Mediterranean to the Persian Gulf.

[2] Cf. Ezek. xxvi. 7. "Nebuchadnezzar king of Babylon, king of kings."

[3] *I.e.* the inhabitants of Babylonia proper. In the estimation of Nebuchadnezzar Shamash the patron god of Sippar here ranks next to Merodach the patron god of Babylon. For a possible explanation of this see Chapter IX. below.

[4] *I.e.* Syria.

[5] Dan. iv. 10.

[6] *Ana tsillishu darie kullat nishim dhabis upakhkhir. Urrie sheim dannutim la nebi ashtapakshu.*

abundance, years of plenty I caused to be in my land." [1] Place side by side with these extracts the record of Dan. iv., and the correspondence is very striking. "I Nebuchadnezzar was at rest in mine house, and flourishing in my palace. I saw a dream which made me afraid: and the thoughts upon my bed and the visions of my head troubled me." "I saw, and *behold a tree in the midst of the earth, and the height thereof was great. The tree grew and was strong, and the height thereof reached unto heaven,*[2] *and the sight thereof to the end of all the earth. The leaves thereof were fair, and the fruit thereof much, and in it was meat for all: the beasts of the field had shadow under it, and the fowls of the heaven dwelt in the branches thereof, and all flesh was fed of it."* [3] Clearly the great tree seen in the king's vision coincided exactly with that idea of empire which Nebuchadnezzar had placed before himself, and had so successfully striven to realise. It signified lofty greatness and far-extended rule, peace and prosperity, shelter and security, for all who dwelt beneath his sway. It was a visible representation of the monarch's own words, "Underneath her everlasting shadow I gathered all men in peace." In this tree there was "much fruit" and "meat for all," so that "all flesh was fed of it," for the king tells us that his reign was "a reign of abundance, years of plenty," and that in Babylon he has stored up "vast heaps of grain beyond measure." [4]

But there was another reason why according to natural laws the vision took this form in the mind of the royal dreamer. Nebuchadnezzar had a great admiration for the giants of the forest, and was a lover of the woodman's art. If there was one spot in the whole of his vast empire, with the sole exception of Babylon, more dear to him than another, it was the cedar forest in the Lebanon. The longest, and quite one of the most important inscriptions of Nebuchadnezzar, has been met with in the Lebanon. It was written, indeed, to record the long list of his building achievements, but specially his conquest of that much-coveted district, and is found carved in duplicate on the rocks of Wady Brissa, a valley west of the Upper Orontes, and at a point not far from that river, where the ancient road from Babylon to the Mediterranean passes between two steep cliffs. The inscription on the north side of the defile is written in archaic characters.

[1] Wady Brissa, Inscription B, col. viii. 34.

[2] Nebuchadnezzar in his inscriptions appears always impressed with size and height, but particularly with the latter. It will be noticed that in Dan. iv. 10, 11, he twice alludes to the height of the tree.

[3] Dan. iv. 4, 5, 10–12.

[4] For the granaries in Babylon see Jer. l. 26, R.V.M.

The closing portion of it, written in the Neo-Babylonian script, has been found some distance farther along the road, a few miles north of Beyrout, on the rocky pass of the Nahr-el-Kelb or Dog River, at a spot where the great military monarchs of Egypt and Assyria had already carved their effigies and the records of their conquests. The duplicate inscription at Wady Brissa, on the south side of the defile, is also written in the Neo-Babylonian script.[1] It contains some additional matter, notably the campaign in the Lebanon, and it is this fact which has led Langdon to conjecture that the archaic inscription was written in 588 B.C., when the Chaldean army was entering Palestine on its way to besiege Jerusalem; the Neo-Babylonian duplicate, on their return in 586 B.C. after the capture of that city; the campaign in the Lebanon taking place either during that interval or on their homeward march. This long and famous inscription[2] is dedicated to Gula, the goddess of health, for whom Nebuchadnezzar had built temples at Babylon, Borsippa, and Sippar. It is written on the older literary plan. After a brief introductory hymn we come to the *enuma* clause, which begins in much the same strain as the hymn, sounding forth the praises of the monarch, his divine right to the throne, and his faithfulness to Merodach and Nebo. Under their guidance he has undertaken marches to distant lands, by difficult paths, and through waterless tracts. "Their gracious protection was stretched out over me," says the king. "When I lifted up my hands to them, my prayer came before them, they heard my supplication." No wonder, then, as the context tells us, that from the great store of silver, gold, cedar-wood, and other things collected in these campaigns, offerings were made to Merodach and Nebo from year to year. His campaigning over, the king next gives us an account of the sacred edifices raised or restored by him, and of the provision made for the maintenance of the priests, beginning with Babylon and Borsippa. Interesting and minute details are then given of the bark of Merodach, in which he sailed upon the waters of the Euphrates at the New Year festival, also of the bark of Nebo, in which on the same occasion that god was brought from Borsippa to Babylon. This naturally leads on to a description of work done on the sacred streets of Babylon, along which at the New Year festival the images of the gods were borne after their voyage by water. As one of those streets, viz. the Procession Street, passed through the old town walls at the Ishtar Gate, the scribe proceeds to give an account of

[1] The two inscriptions are distinguished as A and B, A being the archaic.

[2] See Langdon's *Building Inscriptions*, pp. 153–175.

the bulls and standing serpents with which that gate was adorned, and mentions the completion of the old walls. He then turns to work done in the canals and in the bed of the Euphrates. After this comes a long list of temples, either built or restored, in Babylon and Borsippa, including no fewer than three temples to Gula in the latter city. Our attention is next drawn to the defences of Babylon, the great outer wall and the broad moat by which it was engirdled, as well as to the dyke near Sippar from the Tigris to the Euphrates, mentioned by Xenophon.[1] Then, after a list of offerings to be made at the New Year festival, followed by a second long list of temples which have been constructed in other cities, comes a declaration from the king that he has completed his work of temple-building and also another work which he undertook at the same time, viz. the rebuilding of the Old Palace at Babylon. With some account of this the long *enuma* clause [2] at last reaches its close. Its contents, indeed, belong properly to the subject of my last chapter, but for the sake of the *enumishu* clause,[2] which always contains the principal matter of an inscription, *i.e.* the subject which led to its being written, I have reserved the Wady Brissa Inscription to be treated of in this present chapter.

It is an almost unique thing for Nebuchadnezzar, or indeed any of the Neo-Babylonian kings, to give us any account of their conquests, but for once in the Wady Brissa Inscription this rule is broken, and we find in the *enumishu* clause an account of the campaign in the Lebanon. The record, though sadly obliterated in places, is yet of such deep interest and throws so much light on certain passages of Scripture, as well as on the special subject of this chapter, that I shall give it verbatim.

"At that time," says the king, "Lebanon, the cedar mountain, the luxuriant forest of Merodach, whose scent is fragrant, whose cedars" . . . Here the record becomes only partially legible for the next seven lines, but we are able to make out the words "another god" . . . "another king" . . . "my god Merodach, the king, for the brilliant palace of the prince of the gods of heaven and earth as an adornment" . . . Then the recital continues, "which a foreign foe ruled over and robbed of its rich abundance—His people fled, took themselves right off:—In the strength of Nebo and Merodach, my lords, to Lebanon I marched, I ranged my troops for scouring the country. Its enemy on the heights and in the valleys I drove out, and I made the heart of the country to rejoice. Its scattered peoples I gathered together, and restored

[1] *Anabasis*, ii. 4, 12.

[2] See the last chapter.

to their place. That which no other king had done, I did. The steep mountains I cut through, the rocks of the mountain I shattered, I opened the passes, a road for the cedars I smoothed. Before the king Merodach, mighty cedars, tall and strong, of costly value, whose dark forms towered aloft, the massive growth of Lebanon, like a bundle of reeds . . . I transported in the shape of rafts . . . by the Arakhtu into Babylon. *Tsarbati* wood . . . The people in the Lebanon I caused to dwell in security, I suffered no foe to rise up against them." [1]

Nebuchadnezzar was in Palestine at least four times. His wood-cutting in the Lebanon belongs to his second and third visits. In his first campaign to the West, in 604 B.C., he was acting as his father's viceroy. That was a far too anxious and critical time to allow of any opportunity for wood-cutting. The all-important question at that crisis was whether Babylon or Egypt should have dominion in the West. No sooner was this question settled in favour of the former,[2] than the young viceroy was compelled by the news of his father's death to hurry home across the desert in order to secure his succession to the throne. The king's next visit was in 597 B.C., at the close of the brief reign of Jehoiachin.[3] It was on this occasion that the wood-cutting took place described in inscription No. 17 and also in column iv. of the Wady Brissa Inscription. The object, as we have seen, was to obtain timber for the completion of the tower of Babylon, one of the king's earlier works, bequeathed to him, so to say, by his father. What a lively scene must the Lebanon have presented in the year 597 B.C.! What a babel of tongues was heard on all sides! What a variety of physical types, what diversity of costume was presented by that ever-shifting throng! But amongst all that motley multitude there was one figure which more than any other would have attracted our attention—the great king of Babylon himself, taking his part in the work. "As for me," he writes in the Wady Brissa Inscription, "I set my heart to the building of it," viz. the temple-tower. "Mighty cedars, which grew in the forest on the Lebanon, with my clean hands I cut down and assigned for its adornment." [4] Does he mean that he cut them down *with his own hands?* Yes! certainly: for otherwise the words "with my clean hands" would bear no meaning. Only a little further on in the inscription the king makes the same assertion, when speaking of the decoration of the shrine

[1] Wady Brissa, Inscription B, col. ix.
[2] 2 Kings xxiv. 7.
[3] *Ibid.* 11.
[4] Wady Brissa, Inscription A, col. iv.

of Nebo in his temple at Borsippa. All such acts were done by him most religiously, just as when in his boyhood's days he and his younger brother Nabu-shum-lishir, led on by their royal father Nabopolassar, had laboured on the lower stages of E-temen-an-ki. So then when the king speaks of his "clean hands," the words must be understood in a ritual, ceremonial sense, and possibly also in a moral sense.[1] But whichever way we take them, they must needs mean that the king cut down trees with his own hands. And, indeed, such a view is amply borne out by a remarkable passage in the prayer with which inscription No. 17 concludes: "O Merodach, my lord, champion of the gods, possessor of power, at thy command the city of the gods has been builded, its bricks fashioned, its street renewed, its temples completed. At thy exalted word, which changes not, *may my wood-cutting prosper! may the work of my hands come to completion!*"[2]

But should it be said that in the above passage the words "my wood-cutting" mean only "the wood-cutting done at my command," then we can point to a yet more convincing proof, still to be seen on the rocks of Wady Brissa. Between the fifth and sixth columns of the Neo-Babylonian inscription a figure is depicted in low relief, looking to the left, and attired in a pointed head-dress, closely resembling the mitre of a mediæval bishop, to which is attached at the back a kind of puggaree. This remarkable head-dress is the only part of the bas-relief in anything like fair preservation. Still enough is left to show that the figure is standing before a tree, which occupies the centre of the fifth column, and grasping it with the left hand, prepared apparently to cut it down with the right. Remembering, then, that the fourth column of the inscription, which is just to the left of the tree, contains the passage in which the king speaks of cutting down trees with his clean hands, and further that at the close of the inscription in a much-obliterated passage, which follows the account of his campaign in the Lebanon, the words twice occur, "an image of my royal person," we shall not think Weissbach fanciful when he writes at the foot of his plate representing this

[1] Cf. Ps. xxiv. 4.

[2] In his *Building Inscriptions of the New Babylonian Empire*, p. 151, Langdon renders the word *is-tag-ga-a-a* by "that in which I am interested." In his later work, *Die Neubabylonischen Königsinschriften*, p. 149, this word is translated "mein Holzfallen." As explained by this distinguished Sumerian scholar, *istagga* is a loan-word from the Sumerian GIS-TAG=the Assyrian *makhatsu sha itsi*, "timber-felling." For TAG=*makhatsu* see Syllabary C, 294, in Delitzsch's *Assyrische Lesestucke*. See also Rawlinson's *Inscriptions of Western Asia*, vol. v. 32, 21f. GIS, Assyrian *itsu*, appears in Hebrew as עֵץ.

bas-relief, "King Nebuchadnezzar fells with his own hand a cedar of Lebanon."[1]

The wood-cutting in the Lebanon in 597 B.C. throws a very vivid light on certain passages in the Book of the prophet Habakkuk. Hab. i. gives us a most graphic picture of the rise of the Chaldean power, as it appeared above the horizon of the Jews after the great victory over the Egyptians gained by the young viceroy Nebuchadnezzar at Carchemish on the Euphrates in 604 B.C. Hab. ii. belongs to a somewhat later date. It presupposes a time when the Chaldeans had made more conquests, and when men had become familiarised with their tyrannical treatment of subject nations. In ii. 9 the person of the Royal Builder comes in sight. His early career of conquest has had this for its aim, "to set his nest on high" and to place himself above the power of evil. By building walls round Babylon and raising up fortress-palaces he has sought to secure himself from calamity; like those birds of prey that "build their nests amid inaccessible rocks, along the steep side of gorges and defiles."[2] Already he is laying down the warrior's sword for the woodman's axe. On his way home from Palestine after his second visit in 597 B.C. he stops to fell timber in the Lebanon. Those huge beams are for the rebuilding of his own palace[3] as well as for the completing of the temple-tower. So, then, in the words of the prophet, "the violence done to Lebanon shall cover thee," *i.e.* shall recoil upon thee. "For the stone," writes the prophet, "shall cry out of the wall, and the beam out of the timber shall answer it": *i.e.* the very wood and stones, which the tyrant employs in his great buildings, shall bear witness to the robbery and injustice by which they were procured. "Woe," therefore, "to him that buildeth a town with blood, and establisheth a city by iniquity. Behold, is it not of the Lord of hosts that the peoples labour for the fire, and the nations weary themselves for vanity."[4] Here is a reference to that motley gathering in the Lebanon of peoples from all parts of the empire to cut down timber, so graphically described in inscription No. 17: "All peoples of scattered habitations, whom Merodach bestowed upon me, I compelled to do service."[5]

[1] *Wissenschaftliche Veroffentlichungen der Deutschen Orient Gesellschaft*, Heft 5 (1906).

[2] Hab. ii. 9, *Cent. Bible,* footnote *in loco.*

[3] Inscription No. 9, col. iii. 36.

[4] Hab. ii. 11–13. Compare Jeremiah li. 58, in his prophecy of the fall of Babylon.

[5] Compare the levy raised by Solomon, which was also for work in the Lebanon. 1 Kings iv. 6; v. 14; and ix. 15.

But the king's visit to the Lebanon in 597 B.C. was not only spent in wood-cutting. Like his royal predecessors on the throne of Assyria he devoted himself to the pleasures of the chase.[1] Along with " the violence done to Lebanon " Habakkuk mentions " the destruction of the beasts." [2] This also is illustrated on the rocks of Wady Brissa. A second bas-relief is found, in the archaic inscription on the north side of the road, which occupies the entire height of the inscription—no less than ten feet—and is carved on its left side. It represents a man—undoubtedly the king—holding with his left hand at arm's length a lion in the act of springing, while his right hand grasps a club with which he is about to despatch the brute. Strange to say no explanation of this bas-relief is found in the inscription, nor any lacuna in which it would be likely to occur. Weissbach suggests that the picture is intended to commemorate some special adventure that the king has had with a lion in the Lebanon : but this seems to me unlikely. As in the case of the other royal effigy, the meaning of this bas-relief must be sought in its position in the inscription. Now we notice that the king's figure is placed close to the dedication to Gula, " who enlarges the renown of my reign." Gula is the consort of Ninib, the god of war. She is also specially the goddess of health, and along with the epithet just quoted is described in the course of the inscription as " Gula the protectress of my life—who enlivens my spirit." Field sports, such as lion-hunting, are a mimic warfare. They require both strength and courage, and are attended with more or less bodily danger. We may, then, take the two bas-reliefs together, and look upon them, not merely as designed to show how the king spent his time in the Lebanon, viz. in hunting and wood-cutting, but rather to exhibit him to the inhabitants of that district as lord of the forest and its denizens, able to hew down the unsubmissive [3] and by his irresistible prowess to overcome the might of his foes.

The inscriptions and bas-reliefs of Wady Brissa, though a reminiscence of the great wood-cutting in 597 B.C., were as a matter of fact carved some ten years later, viz. during the interval 588 to 586 B.C., on the occasion of the king's third visit to Palestine, at the time of the siege of Jerusalem and at the close of the reign of Zedekiah. The conquest of the Lebanon, followed by a second wood-cutting described towards the close of the inscription, must be assigned to this interval. When, then, we remember that in the

[1] Cf. Dan. ii. 38.

[2] Hab. ii. 17.

[3] This thought may be compared with the text at the head of this chapter. He who has hewn down others is to be hewn down himself.

next year after the fall of Jerusalem, viz. in 585 B.C., commenced the thirteen years' siege of Tyre,[1] it seems exceedingly likely that the words "another god" . . . "another king," which occur in the earlier and half-obliterated portion of the description of the conquest of the Lebanon, refer severally to Melkarth the Tyrian Hercules, and to Ethbaal king of Tyre. As Nebuchadnezzar had claimed the cedar forest for Merodach, so Ethbaal may have claimed it for Melkarth. Tyre for the sake of her commerce had been friendly with Egypt, and therefore antagonistic to Assyria. Her traditional hostility to the Assyrians was now transferred to the Chaldeans, their successors in power. The Wady Brissa Inscription shows that it was the policy of Nebuchadnezzar to attach the inhabitants of the Lebanon to himself, that so they might guard the cedar forest from interlopers, such as the Tyrian king, and at the same time assist him to transport its sylvan wealth to Babylon.

On the occasion of this later visit to the Lebanon the great king had his headquarters at Riblah in the land of Hamath, as stated in 2 Kings xxv. 6. Riblah, on the right bank of the Upper Orontes is only ten miles E.N.E. of Brissa, the village which gives its name to the Wady. It was no doubt selected as forming a good strategic position, a centre from which roads branched out, northward by Hamath and Aleppo to Haran, eastward across the desert to Babylon by way of Palmyra, westward through the Lebanon to Phœnicia and so on by the coast route to Egypt, southward to Judæa by Cœle-Syria and the Jordan valley. But in Nebuchadnezzar's eyes, Riblah had this additional advantage that it was near "the glorious forest of Merodach." For although the still remaining cedar grove on the heights above Besherrah is rather more than thirty miles from Riblah as the crow flies, doubtless there were forest tracts very much nearer in the days of Nebuchadnezzar.

The tree which Nebuchadnezzar saw in his vision was conspicuous alike for its great height and for the shelter it afforded. In these respects it must have strongly resembled the cedars which he had been accustomed to cut down. Dr. Tristram, describing the cedar grove above Besherrah, observes that "in the topmost boughs ravens, hooded crows, kestrels, hobbys, and wood owls, were secreted in abundance, yet so lofty were the trees that the birds were out of ordinary shot."[2] No tree would so well convey the idea of ample shade and shelter as the cedar. It

[1] *Josephus c. Apion*, i. 21. The siege lasted from 585 to 572 B.C. Cf. Ezek. xxix. 17–20.

[2] *The Land of Israel*, p. 630.

was thus the apt symbol of a strong government, able to afford shelter and security to its subjects; whilst the far-stretching horizontal branches were no less suggestive of widely extended sway. Ezekiel, in his solemn warning to the king of Egypt, written only two months before the fall of Jerusalem, and at the very time when the king of Babylon had his headquarters at Riblah, describes the Assyrian monarchy in its palmy days under the Sargonids by this very figure. "Behold the Assyrian was a cedar in Lebanon with fair branches, and with a shadowing shroud, and of an high stature; . . . All the fowls of heaven made their nests in his boughs, and under his branches did all the beasts of the field bring forth their young, and under his shadow dwelt all great nations."[1] It has been asserted that the imagery of the king's dream in Dan. iv. is "clearly borrowed to a considerable extent"[2] from this passage. But against this we must remember, first, that the comparison of men to trees is a very frequent one,[3] and secondly, that just what Ezekiel does not mention, viz. the great fruitfulness of the tree, so emphatically stated in Dan. iv., is in exact correspondence with Nebuchadnezzar's own description of his kingdom. Speaking of his beloved Babylon he says, "Underneath her everlasting shadow I gathered all men in peace," and then adds immediately after, "vast heaps of grain beyond measure I stored up within her." It is, therefore, more reasonable to look upon the description of the vision in Dan. iv. as coming from the lips of the actual Nebuchadnezzar than to regard it as the imaginative composition of a later writer who borrows his imagery from the Book of Ezekiel. This view, it will be noticed, presupposes that Nebuchadnezzar was in some measure the author, or at any rate the inspirer, of his own inscriptions. In a later chapter further reasons will be adduced for believing that this was really the case. In Herodotus, book vii. 19, the historian tells us how Xerxes dreamed that he was crowned with a shoot of an olive tree, from which boughs spread out and covered the whole earth. If Xerxes could dream thus, influenced possibly by the recollection of some festal day, how much more easily might Nebuchadnezzar dream the vision of Dan. iv., his mind reverting to those happy busy days spent in wood-cutting on the heights of the Lebanon?

I have imagined the tree seen by Nebuchadnezzar in his vision to have been a cedar, but in the point referred to above it differed

[1] Ezek. xxxi. 3, 6.

[2] *Cent. Bible*, Dan. iv. 10–17, footnote.

[3] Cf. Judg. ix. 8; Ps. i. 3, xxxvii. 35, xcii. 12; Isa. x. 19, lxi. 3; Jer. xvii. 8; Matt. iii. 10, etc.

from the natural cedar, for "the leaves thereof were fair, and the fruit thereof much, and in it was meat for all."[1] But this need not surprise us, for we see stranger things in our dreams than cedars with leaves and fruit. These differences from the natural cedar would only serve to rivet the attention of the royal dreamer. That he had an admiration for the giants of the forest going beyond their utilitarian value may be gathered from the enthusiasm with which he speaks of "mighty cedars, tall and strong, of costly value, whose dark forms towered aloft."[2] Doubtless, then, he viewed with pleasure the great tree which so naturally rose up before him in his vision. Just such trees as this had he himself been accustomed to cut down in the Lebanon in the service of Merodach.[3] So, then, it would not surprise one who had a firm belief in spiritual beings, when "a watcher and an holy one"[4] was seen to descend from heaven and order the tree to be cut down; while the command to the beasts and the birds to get out of the way of the falling giant was all natural enough to one accustomed to work in the forest. True, the order given to leave the stump in the ground, encircled with a band of iron and brass, had something strange about it, for a cedar once cut down cannot spring up again. But the king's fears can hardly have been awakened until the angel began to disclose the inner meaning of the vision: "Let his portion be with the beasts in the grass of the earth: let his heart be changed from man's, and let a beast's heart be given unto him: and let seven times pass over him."[5] For now it was indicated, not uncertainly, that the great tree represented some person, and in Nebuchadnezzar's conception of the character of his kingdom whom could it so well represent as himself? That it did represent him, was proved unmistakably by the angel's closing words: "The sentence is by the decree of the watchers, and the demand by the word of the holy ones: to the intent that the living may know that the Most High ruleth in the kingdom of men, and giveth it to whomsoever he will, and *setteth up over it the lowest of men*."[6]

These last words must have fallen like a thunder-clap on the ears of the startled king, for they referred to a fact of which the monarch was perfectly cognisant, albeit in the course of his long

[1] Dan. iv. 12. [2] Wady Brissa, Inscription B, col. ix. 39–41.

[3] In that part of the Wady Brissa Inscription which refers to the king's doings in the Lebanon, the references to Merodach are remarkably frequent. Lebanon is "the forest of Merodach": the king goes thither "in the strength of Nebo and Merodach": the cedar beams are transported thence to Babylon "before Merodach the king": finally, Merodach is proclaimed "the lord" of his building operations.

[4] Dan. iv. 13. [5] *Ibid.* 15, 16. [6] *Ibid.* 17.

and successful career he must almost have lost sight of it, viz. the very humble origin of his family. Instead of "the lowest of men," the A.V. has "the basest of men." Dr. Driver is careful to point out that in Old English "base" means "low," "humble," not necessarily "wicked," and that the Aramaic word here used appears in its Hebrew form in Job v. 11, "He setteth up on high those that be low," and again in Ps. cxxxviii. 6, "Though the LORD be high, yet hath he respect to the lowly." [1]

The astonishing rise of the family of Nebuchadnezzar from the lowliest condition—hitherto known to us only from this Book of Daniel—is stated with the greatest plainness in an inscription of his father Nabopolassar, which for this reason as well as for its historical interest deserves to be reproduced as it stands.[2] The record runs thus:

"Nabopolassar, the just king, the shepherd called of Merodach, the offspring of Nin-menna,[3] great and illustrious queen of queens, holding the hand of Nebo and Tasmit,[4] the prince the beloved of Ea am I. When I *in my littleness, the son of a nobody,*[5] sought faithfully after the sacred places of Nebo and Merodach, my lords: when my mind pondered how to establish their decrees, and to complete their abodes, and my ears were opened to justice and righteousness: when Merodach who knows the hearts of the gods of heaven and earth, who sees the ways of men most clearly, had perceived the intention *of me, the insignificant, who among men was not visible,*[6] and in the land where I was born had designed me for the chieftainship and for the rulership of the land and people over whom I was nominated, and had sent a good genius to go at my side: when he had prospered all that I had done, and had sent Nergal, strongest of the gods, to go beside me—He subdued my foes, dashed in pieces my enemies:—the Assyrian, who from the days of old ruled over all men, *I, the weak, the feeble,*[7] in dependence on the lord of lords, in the strong might of Nebo and Merodach my lords, held back their feet from the land of Akkad and broke their yoke."

The emphasis with which Nabopolassar here speaks of his lowly origin is very marked. He is "the son of a nobody"; an expression, which, if it stood alone, might signify that he was

[1] *Cambridge Bible*, Daniel, pp. 51, 52.

[2] Langdon's *Building Inscriptions*, Nabopolassar, iv. p. 57.

[3] "The lady of the tiara," a name of Beltis, the wife of Bel-Merodach.

[4] The wife of Nebo.

[5] *Ina mitskhirutiya, apal la mammanim.*

[6] *Iashi, tsaḳhrim, sha ina nishim la uttu.*

[7] *Anaku, enshum, biznuqu.*

not of royal birth, and indeed is so used in the Assyrian inscriptions;[1] but as used by Nabopolassar it evidently signifies more. Not only is he not of royal birth, he is not even in society. In his own words he is "the weak," "the feeble," "the insignificant," "not visible among men."

It is thus that we realise the full significance of the angel's closing words, "setteth up over it *the lowest of men*"; words, which with true delicacy Daniel forbears to repeat. In this brief utterance, then, lies possibly the strongest evidence of the authenticity of this fourth chapter of Daniel, since the writer is thus seen to be well aware of a fact which must soon have faded from the knowledge of posterity, viz. the very obscure parentage of Babylon's greatest king. For the dazzling glory of that rapid career of conquest, followed by those long years of peace and prosperity, when temple arose after temple, palace after palace, to attest to future ages the might of their royal builder, must perforce have exercised such influence on the minds of men that future rulers would care more to show that they were sprung from Nebuchadnezzar than to inquire whom Nebuchadnezzar himself was sprung from. Such, at any rate, was the case before the sixth century B.C. had passed away.[2] Hence we may feel quite sure that by the time of Alexander the Great, or the still later period of the Maccabees, all recollection of the humble origin of the family of Nebuchadnezzar had entirely faded away. For it is ever the tendency of later ages to magnify great rulers as they recede into the past. Thus Megasthenes, in the extract quoted at the beginning of the last chapter, writing about 300 B.C., carries the arms of Nebuchadnezzar to Libya and even to Iberia. So, then, in this brief statement, "setteth up over it the lowest of men," we have a clear indication that the writer was a contemporary of Nebuchadnezzar, and might be supposed to be personally conversant with the events he records. This being granted, it is inconceivable how any contemporary writer, unless his narrative of the events leading up to the king's madness were a record of what actually took place, would ever have dared to make such a plain statement as to the very humble origin of the reigning dynasty and to put it into the lips of an angel as the telling close of a stern message of condemnation. Thus the words are a voucher, not only for the age of the Book of Daniel, but also for the truth of the story.

[1] Compare the Nimrûd Inscription of Tiglathpileser III., Rev. line 65, "Khulli, the son of a nobody, I set on the throne of his sovereignty."

[2] Compare the Behistun Inscription of Darius Hystaspes, col. i. 78, and iii. 80, where two impostors claim to be Nebuchadnezzar the son of Nabonidus.

9

The Personality of Nebuchadnezzar

"The Inscription paints for us in unfading colours a portrait of the man Nebuchadnezzar; it exhibits in the vivid light of actuality his pride of place and power and greatness, his strong conviction of his own divine call to universal empire, his passionate devotion to his gods, his untiring labours for their glory and the aggrandisement of that peerless capital which was their chosen dwelling-place."—Rev. C. J. Ball on the India House Inscription.

THE inscriptions of the Assyrian kings present us with more or less prosaic accounts of their warlike operations, embellished with ascriptions of praise to Ashur or to some war-god, and with a goodly amount of self-glorification, also not unfrequently with details of hideous cruelties, and ending with the account of the building or enlarging of some royal palace. But when we turn to the inscriptions of the Neo-Babylonian kings a great difference is observable. War is now made to take quite a second place, and is frequently not even visible, whilst the main body of the inscription is devoted to accounts of temple and palace building, introduced by a hymn in praise of some god, and ending in a prayer; a second hymn being sometimes inserted before the principal building operation described. The monarch, instead of boasting of his prowess in heaped-up epithets, now describes himself as the favourite of the gods, their dutiful worshipper, and the restorer of their shrines. That is, he puts his gods first and retires somewhat into the background himself; and yet, in spite of this, the royal personality becomes increasingly visible, and it is evident that the drawing up of the inscription is not left entirely to the court scribe, but that the king himself must sometimes have taken the pen in hand. This is especially the case with certain inscriptions of Nabopolassar, Nebuchadnezzar, and Nabonidus. No court scribe would have dared to speak of his royal master in the very humble terms employed by Nabopolassar, nor could any one but the monarch himself have expressed that intense delight with which Nabonidus records the recovery of the foundation cylinder of some ancient temple and reckons up the long centuries which must have elapsed since it was placed *in situ*. In the case of the great Nebuchadnezzar we have already been able to discover from his inscriptions certain traits in the character of that monarch as well as some personal tastes. We have found him a prince of peaceful pursuits, filled with a rage for building and a love of splendour and display. His activities are seen to spend themselves in raising bulwarks, in rearing temples and palaces, in clearing out canals, and in attending to the internal administration of the country. He appears before us as a monarch with strong imperialistic tendencies, bent on making Babylon the centre of a world-kingdom, and on displaying within her walls the splendour and magnificence of his rule. His lighter diversions are hunting and wood-cutting. In all these respects the portrait given of him in the Book of Daniel is found on examination to be strikingly accurate. What we have now to do is to inquire as to his religious knowledge and the degree of enlightenment possessed by him, also his disposition toward religion, in order that we may see how far in these respects the Nebuchadnezzar of the Book of Daniel corresponds with the Nebuchadnezzar of the monuments.

Both the Book of Daniel and the Neo-Babylonian inscriptions represent Nebuchadnezzar as a very religious man, and one whose religion possessed something of a monotheistic tendency. The sacred vessels of Jehovah's temple at Jerusalem are brought by him into the treasure-house of his god at Babylon, and we know from his inscriptions that the god meant is Merodach the patron-god of Babylon. This choice of Merodach was no doubt a deep conviction on the part of the Babylonians. They firmly believed that their god stood at the head of the pantheon. They also believed in "*great* gods," such as Sin, "king of the gods of heaven and earth," Shamash, "the judge supreme," Nebo, "the wise and knowing one," "who watches over the hosts of heaven and earth," and others besides. The expression "great gods" is one that occurs frequently in the inscriptions. Now we notice that Daniel, when recalling the king's forgotten dream, seeks to lead his royal master to a knowledge of the truth by telling him that a "great god"[1] has made known to him what shall be hereafter. But amongst these "great gods" it is perfectly clear that in the Neo-Babylonian inscriptions taken as a whole Merodach occupies the first place. Nebo and Shamash may seem at times to dispute his supremacy and to claim something of an equality, but these are only indications of certain fluctuations of religious feeling. Merodach is most certainly at the head of the Babylonian pantheon, and is so far exalted above the other gods as to give an almost monotheistic character to some passages in the inscriptions.

[1] This is the correct translation in Dan. ii. 45.

And here we may well pause to inquire how, in a religion characterised by "gods many and lords many," this monotheistic character is to be accounted for.

In ancient Babylonia Merodach was not always the chief of the gods. The country was anciently divided into several small city-states. Each city had a god of its own, whose rule extended just as far as the rule of that particular city, and no further. But as early as 3000 B.C. there was one of the gods, Enlil, the patron god of Nippur, a town some forty miles south-east of Babylon, who held the proud title "lord of the lands," *i.e* lord of the world. That this title meant something appears from the fact that Nippur, "the place of Enlil"[1]—for so it is expressed in the cuneiform writing—though never a city of any political importance, was yet in those early days the acknowledged religious centre of Babylonia. How the worship of Enlil became located at Nippur we cannot tell, but being thus located, it is quite possible for us to conceive how this god attained to the supremacy, with the result that his city was regarded as the Mecca of ancient Babylonia.

En-lil, "lord of the wind,"[2] was a Sumerian god. When the Sumerians left their mountain home in the north or north-west of Mesopotamia, it is probable that the Semitic Akkadians were already in possession of the plain of the Euphrates and the Tigris. Enlil, the storm-god, was their god of war. To him victories were ascribed and pæans sung in his temple at Nippur. Through the might of Enlil the invaders hoped, not merely to hold their own, but to sweep onwards and subjugate their foes. Hence they very naturally regarded him as their chief god and the principal object of their worship. In the course of time power passed from the Sumerians to the Semitic Akkadians with whom they were now intermingled. About 2225 B.C. a Semitic dynasty, believed to be of Amorite origin, established itself in Babylon, and Khammurabi,—the Amraphel of Gen. xiv.—the sixth monarch of this dynasty, was at last able, about 2123 B.C., to unite the various city-states under the sway of Babylon. It was now felt to be only right that Merodach, the patron-god of Babylon, should take the place of Enlil. This was accomplished in the following manner. Merodach was imagined as sent by the gods to conquer Tiamat, the dragon of Chaos. On his successfully achieving this difficult task, all the other gods were pictured as uniting to do him honour, and to bestow upon him fifty glorious names, representing so many attributes; until at the last Enlil, the head of the older pantheon, stepping forward, graciously bestowed upon

[1] In the ancient Sumerian EN-LIL′-KI.

[2] See above, Chap. V. p. 47.

him his own title, " lord of the lands," and resigned in his favour. From this time forward Merodach was looked upon as " the Enlil of the gods," and is so styled in the Neo-Babylonian inscriptions; whilst Babylon took the place of Nippur as the city of the gods. The gods who had gathered round the older shrine of Nippur were supposed now to assemble at E-sag-ila, the temple of Merodach at Babylon. Nippur itself, though a flourishing commercial city at the close of the Assyrian empire, is not so much as named in the inscriptions of the Neo-Babylonian kings. Indeed, according to Dr. Peters, the temple of the original Enlil in that city was destroyed by Nebuchadnezzar or one of his successors.[1] All this is most significant of the jealous care with which the religious supremacy of Babylon was guarded by the kings of the New Empire.

Previous to the rise of the New Babylonian empire, when Assyria held the reins of power, her warrior kings very naturally claimed the " Enlilship " for their national god Ashur. Hence Sennacherib, when dedicating an image to Ashur, extols his god as " king of the totality of the gods, lord of all gods, creator of the heaven of Anu, creator of mankind, dwelling in the resplendent heaven, the Enlil of the gods."[2] In fact, according to Jastrow, the supremacy of Ashur in Assyria was even more pronounced than that of Merodach at Babylon; but, as the same authority points out, there was this difference in the worship of these divinities: Ashur moved about from place to place as the centre of political power shifted from the old capital of Ashur to Calah and thence to Nineveh, while Merodach's home remained fixed at Babylon, " the town of the lord of the gods."

The Enlilship of Merodach, though subject to slight variations, is clearly visible all through the inscriptions of Nebuchadnezzar. It becomes most pronounced in No. 15, better known as the India House Inscription, to which frequent reference has already been made. It is of this inscription that Langdon writes, " It is a veritable marvel of the redactor's skill. Its sources are 14 and 19.[3] What is most striking about this composition is the Merodach tendency of the composer. As the cult of Nebo is glorified in 19, [so] Merodach is exalted by means of inserted prayers, changes of text, etc., in 15. I regard this composition," he adds, " as dating

[1] Peters' *Nippur*, vol. ii. p. 262.

[2] The same claim is made by Sargon, cf. line 121 of the remarkable tablet translated by F. Thureau-Dangin in his *Huitième Campagne de Sargon*.

[3] No. 14, at present in the British Museum, records the building of a fortress-palace at the northernmost point of the great outer wall of Babylon, the site of which is marked by the present mound of Babil. No. 19 is the Wady Brissa Inscription, carved in 586 B.C. as described in the last chapter.

at least after 570 B.C., at any rate it was composed after 14."[1] According, then, to this authority, No. 15 is the latest of the inscriptions of Nebuchadnezzar, and the Merodach tendency noticed by Langdon is of necessity a monotheistic tendency, for Merodach, who, as we have seen, is always foremost of the gods, appears in some passages of this inscription to stand alone. Now it is just in these monotheistic passages, these "*inserted prayers*" and "*changes of text*," that we seem to see the work of the real Nebuchadnezzar. Thus, immediately after the introductory passage, which describes the position occupied by the king with reference to Merodach and Nebo, there follows a hymn to those divinities, col. i. 23 to ii. 39, extracted from inscriptions 19 and 14. But in the middle of this hymn we meet with a prayer addressed to Merodach alone: col. i. 51 to ii. 11, and this prayer, be it noted, is *an entirely original addition, not found in any previous inscription.* Jastrow remarks with reference to it, "The conception of Merodach rises to a height of spiritual aspiration, which comes to us as a surprise in a religion that remained steeped in polytheism, and that was associated with practices and rites of a much lower order of thought."[2] This remarkable prayer runs thus–

"To Merodach my lord I prayed,
I addressed my supplication.
He had regard to the utterance of my heart,
I spake unto him:
'Everlasting prince,
Lord of all that is,
for the king whom thou lovest,
whose name thou proclaimest,
who is pleasing to thee:
direct him aright,
lead him in the right path!
I am a prince obedient unto thee,
the creature of thy hands,
thou hast created me,
and hast appointed me to the lordship of multitudes of people.
According to thy mercy, O Lord, which thou bestowest upon
all of them,
cause them to love thy exalted lordship:
cause the fear of thy godhead to abide in my heart!
Grant what to thee is pleasing,
for thou makest my life.'"[3]

[1] *Building Inscriptions*, p. 20.
[2] Jastrow.
[3] India House Inscription, col. i. 51 to ii. 1.

THE INDIA HOUSE INSCRIPTION

I would suggest that the above passage, coming so evidently from the heart, is the king's own composition, and the same may be said, perhaps, of a second prayer to Merodach, found at the close of the inscription, and also in No. 14.[1] This prayer reads thus–

"To Merodach my lord I prayed,
I lifted up my hands:
'O lord Merodach,
wisest of the gods,
mighty prince,
thou it was that createdst me,
with sovereignty over multitudes of people thou didst invest me.
Like dear life I love thy exalted lodging place:
in no place have I made a town more glorious than thy city of Babylon.
According as I love the fear of thy divinity,
and seek after thy lordship,
favourably regard the lifting up of my hands,
hear my supplication!
I verily am the maintaining king, that maketh glad thine heart,
the energetic servant, that maintaineth all thy town.'" [2]

The above prayer manifests the same intense love of Babylon, and pride in her adornment, which we meet with in Dan. iv. 30, and it is noticeable that the lines in italics in which this is expressed occur earlier in the inscription in the form of a statement, in a passage which reads thus–

"From the time that Merodach created me for sovereignty,
that Nebo his true son committed his subjects to me,
like dear life I love the building of their dwelling-place,
I have made no town more glorious than Babylon and Borsippa." [3]

Here they are repeated with some alteration, and inserted in the middle of a prayer, the reference to Nebo and Borsippa being struck out. Both the repetition and the alteration are indications that a second hand has been at work on this inscription, and there can

[1] No. 14 like No. 15 is considered by Langdon as one of the latest of Nebuchadnezzar's inscriptions.

[2] India House Inscription, col. ix. 45–65.

[3] Col. vii. 26–32.

be little doubt that it is the hand of the king himself,[1] whose heart is wrapped up in the glory and prosperity of his beloved Babylon, as witnessed by the whole tenor of this remarkable document no less than by his dream of sovereignty, as related in Dan. iv. Indeed the description in that chapter of the great tree with meat in it for all forms an apt parallel with the words, " I verily am the maintaining king—that maintaineth all thy town."

Our study, then, of Inscription 15 has led us to the conclusion that not only was there a tendency towards monotheism in the Babylonian religion, but that Nebuchadnezzar himself became increasingly monotheistic in his later years, a circumstance which might well be expected in view of the great miracles recorded in the Book of Daniel. Daniel, as we have seen, when interpreting the king's earlier dream, given in chap. ii., was able to reveal to him " the God of heaven " as the real Enlil, " the Great Mountain," and " Lord of the wind " ; and the monarch on that occasion was so far impressed by the discovery and interpretation of his forgotten dream that he freely acknowledged Daniel's God to be " the God of gods and the Lord of kings, and a revealer of secrets," thus putting Jehovah in the place of both Merodach and Nebo. Later on, in chaps. iii. and iv., he acknowledges the God of the Jews as " the Most High " and " the Most High God." I am now in a position to show that there were two ways in which he could do this without turning his back on, or abjuring, the Babylonian religion.

When Merodach became the Enlil, the other gods, as we have seen, bestowed on him their names and attributes. This fable of Babylonian mythology tended in the direction of monotheism, and paved the way for the identification of the other deities with Merodach, and for regarding them as so many manifestations of Merodach. This appears most clearly in a tablet known as the Monotheistic Tablet, from which the following is an extract :

> " Ninib is Merodach of the garden (?).
> Nergal is Merodach of war.
> Zagaga is Merodach of battle.
> Enlil is Merodach of lordship and dominion.
> Nebo is Merodach of trading.
> Sin is Merodach the illuminator of the night.
> Shamash is Merodach of righteousness.
> Rimmon is Merodach of rain." [2]

[1] The king who altered the plans of his architects—see above, Chapter VII. —would be the very person to alter the draft copies of his scribes.

[2] Pinches' *Old Testament*, p. 58, 1st edn., where for " Bel " read " Enlil."

How easy, then, would it be for the great king of Babylon, who was so devoted to his god, to add to this list and say-

"Jehovah is Merodach the revealer of secrets,"

thus acknowledging the God of Israel as one out of many manifestations of the Most High God!

Perhaps, however, there is more to be said for the supposition that for the time being Jehovah took the place of Merodach in the king's mind; and even this would not be altogether at variance with what we know of the history of religion at Babylon under the New Empire, as the following facts will show.

In the reign of Nabopolassar, the founder of the New Empire, for whom his son Nebuchadnezzar appears to have entertained a filial respect, Merodach found a formidable rival in the sun-god Shamash. Shamash was the patron-god of Sippar,[1] and Sippar lay some thirty miles to the north of Babylon, and therefore on the side of Assyria. In the closing days of the Assyrian monarchy northern Babylonia remained true to its Assyrian over-lord. But Sippar, it may be presumed, cast in its lot with Babylon and took the side of Nabopolassar when he broke loose from the Assyrian yoke. In any case that king appears to have entertained a great regard for Sippar, "the exalted city of Shamash and Malkat."[2] This regard showed itself in various ways: first, in a mundane way, by digging a canal to bring back the waters of the fugitive Euphrates to its old channel past the walls of Sippar;[3] secondly, in a religious way, by acknowledging the help given him by Shamash in overcoming the Assyrian. Thus, whilst in an inscription from the temple of Ninib at Babylon he declares that Merodach sent Nergal to go at his side and help him to defeat his foes,[4] in another inscription from Sippar he speaks thus: "When Shamash, the great lord, went at my side, I subdued the Subari," *i.e.* the Assyrians, "and reduced to heaps and ruins the land of my enemies."[5] And not only is the help of Shamash thus freely acknowledged, but Shamash himself is admitted to the Enlilship and his name placed before that of Merodach, even in an inscription which comes to us from Babylon, viz. that from the Ninib-temple just mentioned. Ninib was a war-god, and it is in describing the preparations made to rebuild his temple that the king uses the expression, "I mustered the workmen of the Enlil, Shamash and Merodach."[6] As this building of the temple

[1] The Biblical Sepharvaim.

[2] *Building Inscriptions*, Nabopolassar, No. 2, lines 12 and 13.

[3] *Ibid.* Nabopolassar, No. 2.

[4] *Ibid.* Nabopolassar, No. 4, line 15.

[5] *Ibid.* Nabopolassar, No. 3, col. i. 21.

[6] *Ibid.* Nabopolassar, No. 4, line 25, where for "Bel" read "Enlil."

of the war-god at Babylon took place apparently very soon after his victory over Assyria, it is clear that such language is suggestive of gratitude to Shamash, *i.e.* to the people of Sippar the town of Shamash, who appear to have helped him in the struggle. The above remarkable language is repeated by his son Nebuchadnezzar in the opening lines of Inscription No. 9, in which he speaks of himself as "the righteous king, the faithful shepherd, leader of the peoples, director of the subjects of the Enlil,[1] Shamash and Merodach." Again, in Inscription No. 17, describing the completing of the temple-tower of Babylon, Nebuchadnezzar tells us how he called together the far-dwelling peoples "over whom Merodach my lord has appointed me, whose shepherding Shamash the hero has bestowed . . . I also mustered," he adds, "the workmen of Shamash and Merodach," thus holding the balance very evenly between these two great gods, and anxious probably to attach Sippar closely to Babylon, seeing that the power most dreaded by him, viz. Media, lay to the north of Babylon and occupied the place of the old Assyria.

As Shamash was thus allowed to share the supreme power along with Merodach, in the early years of the New Babylonian empire,[2] so towards the close of that empire the same high honour was bestowed on the moon-god Sin. Nabonidus, the last of the Neo-Babylonian kings, was the son of the high priest of the temple of Sin in Haran. To Nabonidus, Sin and his son Shamash evidently meant more than Merodach and his son Nebo; and probably this is the explanation of this king's great unpopularity at Babylon, since such a preference on the part of their sovereign must have been most displeasing to the powerful priesthood of Merodach in that city. Nabonidus, in Inscription No. 3, speaks of the four winds as going forth at the command of Merodach,[3] whilst in Inscription No. 4 he speaks of them as going forth at the command of Sin and Shamash.[4] Again in Inscription No. 1, which commemorates the restoration of temples in Haran and Sippar in honour of Sin, Shamash, and his sister Anunit respectively, he first calls Merodach "the Enlil of the gods," and then

[1] By "the subjects of the Enlil, Shamash and Merodach," we may understand the people of Babylonia proper, of which Babylon and Sippar were the chief towns. Sippar, though doubtless much inferior to Babylon, must have been a place of considerable importance. It was considered an outpost of Babylon on the north, and, like that city, stood on either side of the Euphrates. The site was discovered by Rassam in 1881 in the mound of Abu Habba.

[2] Inscriptions 9 and 17 are believed by Langdon to have been written before 593 B.C.

[3] Langdon's *Neubabylonische Inschriften*, Nabonid. No. 3, col. ii. 10, 11.

[4] *Ibid.* Nabonid. No. 4, col. i. 51, 52.

later on bestows the title on the father of Anunit, *i.e.* on Sin, twice over describing her as fulfilling "the command of her father the Enlil."[1] If, then, Nabopolassar could include Shamash in the Enlilship along with Merodach, and if Nabonidus could bestow the title at one time on Merodach at another on Sin, it can be no matter of surprise to us to find Nebuchadnezzar, under the influence of the mighty miracles wrought before his eyes, bestowing on the God of the Jews the titles "the Most High" and the "Most High God."

It has been well remarked that the literary style of Nebuchadnezzar's latest document, viz. the India House Inscription, rises almost to the level of poetry.[2] The same feature strikes us in the Book of Daniel. This king inclines to a poetic style and readily falls into parallelisms, *not only in hymns of prayer and praise but in narrative as well.* Let us take some instances of this, first from the inscriptions and then from the Scripture narrative.

In col. i. 23–39 of the India House Inscription, occurs the following passage:

> "After that the lord my god had created me,
> that Merodach had framed the creature in the mother,
> when I was born,
> when I was created, even I,
> the sanctuaries of the god I regarded,
> the way of the god I walked in.
> Of Merodach, the great lord, the god my creator,
> his cunning works highly do I extol.
> Of Nebo, his true son, the beloved of my majesty,
> the way of his exalted godhead highly do I praise;
> with all my true heart
> I love the fear of their godhead,
> I worship their lordship."

Again, note the poetic rhythmical description of the king's early days, when in the might of Merodach he went forth conquering and to conquer, a passage which forms a beautiful contrast to the bald prosy circumstantial narratives of the exploits of Assyrian kings:

> "In his high trust,
> to far-off lands,
> to distant hills,

[1] Langdon's *Neubabylonische Inschriften*, Nabonid. No. 1, cf. col. i. 23 with col. iii. 23, 34.

[2] See the remarks of the Rev. C. J. Ball in *Records of the Past*, New Series, vol. iii. p. 103.

from the Upper Sea
to the Lower Sea,
steep roads,
blocked ways,
places where the path is broken,
where there was no track,
difficult marches,
roads through the desert,
I pursued :
and the unyielding I reduced,
I fettered the rebels.
The land I ordered aright,
the people I made to thrive.
The evil and bad among the people I removed.
Silver, gold, glitter of precious stones,
copper, palm-wood, cedar,
what thing soever is precious,
a large abundance,
the produce of mountains,
the fulness of seas,
a rich present,
a splendid gift,
to my city of Babylon
into his presence I brought."

The two hymns to Merodach given in the earlier part of this chapter are also very strongly marked with parallelism ; but it is less surprising to find this feature in hymns of praise than in prose narrative. Let us now turn to the Book of Daniel, and we shall find the same characteristic in the utterances of the Biblical Nebuchadnezzar. Dan. iv. 4, 5 presents us with the following instances of parallelism in prose narrative :

" I Nebuchadnezzar was at rest in mine house,
and flourishing in my palace.
I saw a dream which made me afraid,
and the visions of my head troubled me."

Another instance is afforded by the opening stanzas in which the king describes his vision–

" I saw, and behold a tree in the midst of the earth,
and the height thereof was great."

*　　*　　*　　*　　*

"The tree grew and was strong,
and the height thereof reached unto heaven,
and the sight thereof to the end of all the earth."

* * * * *

"The leaves thereof were fair,
and the fruit thereof much,
and in it was meat for all."

* * * * *

"The beasts of the field had shadow under it,
and the fowls of the heaven dwelt in the branches thereof,
and all flesh was fed of it."

The same feature meets us in the sentence uttered by the angelic watcher–

"Hew down the tree,
and cut off his branches,
shake off his leaves,
and scatter his fruit,
let the beasts get away from under it,
and the fowls from his branches."

* * * * *

"Let his heart be changed from man's,
and let a beast's heart be given him.
This sentence is by the decree of the watchers,
and the demand by the word of the holy ones."

That in the king's vision the angel should speak to him in his own literary style is what we should expect.

For parallelism in a hymn of praise we take the following beautiful and touching passage, in which the king describes how he recovered his senses after a long period of madness.

"And at the end of the days
I Nebuchadnezzar lifted up mine eyes to heaven,
and mine understanding returned unto me,
and I blessed the Most High,
and I praised and honoured him that liveth for ever;
for his dominion is an everlasting dominion,
and his kingdom from generation to generation;
and all the inhabitants of the earth are reputed as nothing,
and he doeth according to his will in the army of heaven
and among the inhabitants of the earth,
and none can stay his hand,
or say unto him, What doest thou?"

It must be freely admitted that this tendency to employ parallelism in prose recital as well as in devotional utterances which we have marked in the inscriptions of Nebuchadnezzar, is not confined to that monarch, but is met with in the inscriptions of other kings of the New Babylonian empire. Perhaps it may be regarded as an indication that their inscriptions were mainly drawn up by the priesthood. Nevertheless, such resemblances of style between the utterances of the Nebuchadnezzar of the monuments and the Nebuchadnezzar of Holy Scripture form part of the cumulative evidence in favour of the authenticity of the Book of Daniel. For we may well question whether a Jewish writer of the age of the Maccabees would be acquainted with the literary style of the scribes of the New Babylonian empire, or with the strong poetic tendencies of the real Nebuchadnezzar. Is it likely, we may well ask, that such a writer would be aware of the humble origin of this great king, of his deep religiousness, his intense devotion to his beloved Babylon, his fondness for great occasions, his love of splendour and display, his partiality, not only for the pleasures of the chase but also for the woodman's art? Could we expect him to be so exactly informed as to the ideal of a prosperous world-wide empire centred at Babylon which formed the aim of this monarch? Would he be likely to picture as a prince of peace one who in the other Scriptures appears rather as a man of war? Yet as to all these particulars, which may be gleaned from the contemporary Babylonian records, the writer of this Book is seen to be perfectly informed. Are we not, then, justified in regarding the Book of Daniel as genuine history, rather than as a religious romance, the work of a later age?

10

The Legend of Megasthenes

"Megasthenes relates that Nebuchadnezzar became mightier than Hercules and made war upon Libya and Iberia. These countries he conquered, and transported some of their inhabitants to the eastern shores of the sea. After this, the Chaldeans say that on going up upon his palace he was possessed by some god or other, and cried aloud, 'O Babylonians, behold I, Nebuchadnezzar, announce to you beforehand the coming calamity, which my ancestor Bel and queen Beltis are alike powerless to persuade the Fates to avert. A Persian mule (Cyrus) will come, having your own gods as his allies. He will impose servitude upon you, and will have for his helper the son of a Median woman (Nabonidus), the boast of the Assyrians (*i.e.* Babylonians). Would that before he betrayed my citizens, some Charybdis or sea might engulf him, and utterly destroy him! or that having betaken himself elsewhere, he might be driven through the desert, where there is neither city nor track of men, where wild beasts seek their food and birds fly free, a lonely wanderer among the rocks and ravines, and that I, before these things were put into my mind, had met with a happier end!' Having uttered this prophecy he forthwith disappeared, and Evilmaluruchus (Evil-Merodach) his son succeeded him on the throne."—ABYDENUS AP. EUSEBIUS.

IN the last three chapters I have striven to show some reasons for the belief that the story told us in Dan. iv. is a true story. I now turn back to explain to the best of my power the legend of Megasthenes, with which I started, and which stands at the head of this chapter. This legend, it will be observed, exhibits five points of contact with the story told us in the Book of Daniel.

(i) The calamity which befell Nebuchadnezzar is described in the Book of Daniel as happening when he was "at rest" and "flourishing in his palace," and in the legend, as taking place "after this," viz. after an unbroken career of victories and successes.

(ii) In Daniel the calamity is described as a certain kind of madness, viz. lycanthropy: in the legend it is spoken of as possession by some god. As, however, inspiration and madness were looked upon by the ancients as closely connected, this seeming difference must be counted a resemblance.[1]

(iii) In both stories the disaster happens to the king when he is walking upon his palace.

(iv) In one case—as Dr. Charles points out—a divine voice speaks *to* him; in the other a divine voice speaks *through* him. Thus, in either case he is the recipient of a message from heaven.

(v) The doom pronounced on Nebuchadnezzar in the Bible story, viz. that he should be driven from men and dwell "with the beasts of the field,"[2] or, as it is expressed in Dan. v. 21, "with the wild asses," is seen to bear the closest resemblance to the lengthy imprecation, which in the legend Nebuchadnezzar himself utters against "the son of a Median woman."

To the above it must be added that alike in the Book of Daniel and in the legend Nebuchadnezzar is represented as knowing that his kingdom will pass to others. In the former the bare fact has been unfolded to him by Daniel's interpretation of his vision of the great image, which was suggestive of an early transference of power.[3] In the latter he himself unfolds it to his subjects; not as a bare fact, but with very circumstantial details: it is the Persians who will upset his empire; they will be led by "a Persian mule," and will have the gods of Babylon on their side; they will be further helped by the treachery of a popular Babylonian. But while the contact between the two stories is thus seen to be so close as to make us feel certain that both have their origin in the same historical facts, the differences are at the same time so remarkable as to call for some explanation. Turning, then, to the legend, we notice that it comes before us in a Greek dress, and is in this respect just what we might expect from a writer of the age of Megasthenes, 312–280 B.C. Thus, mention is made of "some Charybdis," of "the Fates," and of

[1] Eusebius in his *Chronicon* comments on it thus: "In Danielis sane historiis de Nabuchodonosoro narratur, quo modo et quo pacto mente captus fuerit: quod si Græcorum historici aut Chaldæi morbum tegunt et a deo acceptum comminiscuntur; deumque insaniam, quæ in illum intravit, vel demonem quendam, qui in eum venit, nominant; mirandum non est. Etenim hic quidem illorum mos est, similia deo adscribere, deosque nominare demones." The Greek μάντις comes from μαίνομαι; whilst according to Plato προφήτης denotes one who puts an intelligible meaning to the ravings of the μάντις.

[2] "Beasts of the field" very frequently denotes wild beasts. Cf. Exod. xxiii. 29.

[3] This lies in the words "thou art the head of gold": thus identifying the empire of Babylon with the rule of Nebuchadnezzar. Also in the king's words as given in Dan. iv. 3, "His kingdom is an everlasting kingdom," there appears to be a realisation of the passing nature of his own kingdom of Babylon.

the Persians bringing the Babylonians into slavery, whilst the terms "Babylonians" and "Assyrians" appear to be used interchangeably as in the pages of Xenophon. But whilst thus Greek in form, the legend itself is undoubtedly Babylonian in origin. It belongs to a time when the personality of Nebuchadnezzar still figured large in the minds of men: to a time, too, very shortly after the Persian conquest, when indignation still burned fiercely in the hearts of Babylonian patriots against one who was regarded as the betrayer of his country. Its authors, according to Megasthenes, are "the Chaldeans," the same class of men who come before us so repeatedly in the Book of Daniel, and whom Herodotus helps us to identify with the priesthood of the god Bel-Merodach.[1] These men both in their faith and in their nationality were one with Nebuchadnezzar. Hence their story glorifies that monarch by crediting him with the gift of prophecy. But with Nabonidus, the "son of a Median woman," they have nothing in common. He is a Babylonian as distinguished from a Chaldean,[2] and probably a native of Babylonia rather than of Babylon itself: indeed, there is good reason for thinking that he hails from Haran, and that he cares much more for the worship of Sin and his son Shamash than for that of the Babylonian Merodach. Ur, Sippar, and Haran are more to him than Babylon, but especially Haran. Lastly, by his course of action, or rather inaction, he has betrayed his country.

Nabonidus, the last king of Babylon, is a character of whom we would gladly know more; but piecing together the few scraps of information which we now possess, we are able to make out the main outlines of his story. He was the son of Nabu-balatsu-ikbi, high priest of the temple of the moon-god Sin in Haran, a functionary who has left us a curious and unique autobiography,[3] from which we learn that he reached the advanced age of 104, his life extending from 653 B.C. to 549 B.C. The parentage of Nabonidus lets in a flood of light on his remarkable story. The post occupied by his father helps to explain his being called in the legend the "son of a Median woman," for Haran was so near Media that his mother may well have belonged to that nationality. But, more than that, it explains to us the puzzle of his life-story. In his early years, whether spent in Haran or in some other centre of moon-worship, he must have imbibed that strong attachment to the cult of Sin and Shamash which he manifested in later life. Thus all his chief inscriptions, with the exception of his famous

[1] Herod. i. 181. See Chapter IV. above.
[2] *Josephus c. Apion*, i. 20.
[3] See the note at the end of this chapter.

historical review on the stele discovered by Scheil,[1] are occupied with accounts of works done, not for Merodach and Nebo in Babylon and Borsippa, but for Sin, Shamash, and his sister Anunit, in Haran, Ur, and Sippar. How little he cared for Babylon is witnessed by the paucity of his remains found on the site of that city.[2] The first great work undertaken by Nabonidus, viz. the rebuilding of the temple of Sin in Haran, appears to have been of as much consequence in his eyes as the completion of the temple-tower of Merodach at Babylon was in the eyes of Nebuchadnezzar. Accordingly we find it described in very similar language. All his widespread armies, from the frontier of Egypt and from the Upper Sea to the Lower Sea, are summoned to take part in the work, as well as the kings, princes, priests, and people, whom Sin, Shamash, and Ishtar have committed to his care.[3] Merodach, it is true, is not forgotten. It was a dream-vision, sent by "Merodach the great lord and Sin the light of heaven and earth," which first prompted him to undertake the work. But whilst Merodach is there named first, he is practically subordinated to Sin, in whose honour the work is done. Along with his love of rebuilding temples Nabonidus manifests strong antiquarian and historical tastes. He delights in finding out from the foundation cylinders the histories of the temples he is rebuilding. Such tastes he would naturally acquire from his early surroundings. His aged father, who could look back to the days of Ashurbanipal, would delight to recall the past, and from his lips Nabonidus would early learn that sequence of historical events which he gives us on his stele.

Chosen by his fellow-conspirators to succeed Labarosoarchod,[4] the young son of Neriglissar, Nabonidus appears at the beginning of his reign to have been an undoubted favourite. The legend calls him "the boast of the Assyrians," *i.e.* the Babylonians; and the king himself tells us how at his election to the sovereign power "they all conducted me to the midst of the palace, cast themselves *en masse* at my feet, and did homage to my majesty. At the command of Merodach my lord was I raised up to the sovereignty of the land, while they cried aloud, 'Father of the land who hast no equal.'"[5] With this good start Nabonidus

[1] See *The Babylonian and Oriental Record* for September, 1896.

[2] Koldewey mentions only the Euphrates wall and the temple of Ishtar of Agade, identified with Anunit the sister of Shamash, whose worship along with that of her brother Nabonidus favoured. *Excavations*, p. 313.

[3] *Records of the Past*, New Series, vol. v. 168–170.

[4] This is a corrupt Greek form of the Babylonian Labashi-Marduk.

[5] Stele of Nabonidus, col. v. 1–12, and cf. *Josephus c. Apion*, i. 20.

began his reign well. He was careful to pay due respect to Merodach and to have his claim legitimised by the god.[1] In a spirit, not unlike that shown by Solomon of Israel, he beseeches Merodach to help one so unversed in the duties of kingship.[2] At his first New Year, the popular New Year feast at Babylon in honour of Merodach and Nebo was kept with kingly liberality. Large gifts of silver and gold were made to those gods and to Nergal, and 2,850 captives were dedicated to the service of their temples. Then a visit was paid to Erech, Larsa, and Ur, to make offerings to Sin, Shamash, and Ishtar. Soon after this we find the king making a royal progress in the West to cut down timber on Amanus [3] and probably to install a new prince at Tyre. Then, a little later, he seizes the opportunity presented by Cyrus' campaign against Astyages king of the Medes to rebuild the great temple of Sin in Haran, which had been laid waste by that people fifty-four years previously.[4] This was the great occasion referred to above. So far we have only reached the third year of the reign, and the next four years are a blank; the last ten, little better. It appears from the Annalistic Tablet of Cyrus that from his seventh to his seventeenth year Nabonidus lived in retirement at Temâ. When each successive New Year came round he refused to go to Babylon to renew his royal authority by taking the hands of Bel, and in consequence of this "Nebo did not go to Babylon, Bel came not forth, the New Year's festival did not take place." [5] Meanwhile the defence of the country was left in the hands of his son Belshazzar, so that year by year we meet with the notice, "The king was in Temâ: the king's son, the nobles, and his soldiers were in the country of Akkad." [5] How are we to explain this course of conduct on the part of Nabonidus? It may be that it was due to some extent to his age. If we suppose him to have been born in 614 B.C. when his father was aged thirty-nine, he would be fifty-eight years old at his accession, sixty-five in the seventh year of his reign, and seventy-five at the time of the capture of Babylon. Thus his age, taken along with his antiquarian tastes, would account for his not taking any active part in public affairs, at least in military matters, during the last ten years of his reign. But it does not explain his keeping away from Babylon at the New Year, when every motive of sound policy would have led him to be present at the great feast. Is it possible, then, that in his devotion to Sin and

[1] See next chapter.

[2] Stele of Nabonidus, col. vii. 45–56.

[3] *Records of the Past*, New Series, vol. v. p. 158.

[4] *Ibid.* vol. v. 169.

[5] *Ibid.* vol. v. 159–161.

Shamash he was madly bent on upsetting the supremacy of Merodach and Nebo by stopping the customary procession? Whatever may be the explanation, it is certain that in Babylon itself no course of action could have rendered him more unpopular. In the last year of his reign he awoke to his mistake, came out of his retirement, and appeared at Babylon at the New Year.[1] In the following summer he was at Sippar, a few miles to the north of Babylon, ready at last to take his part in the defence of his country. But it was too late, his country was undone, and his army in revolt, so that he was powerless to stay the advance of the Persians. On the 14th of Tammuz, June–July, Sippar was taken without fighting, and Nabonidus had to fly to Babylon. Two days later, Gobryas and the Persian troops entered Babylon without encountering any resistance, and ere long the last king of Babylon was a prisoner in their hands.[2] One of the latest acts of this unfortunate prince, and perhaps his crowning blunder, was his attempt to ensure the security of Babylon by gathering into it the gods from other cities, much to the displeasure, doubtless, of the priests and people of those cities, who would rightly ask, why should their defence be taken from them; while the priests of Merodach would be no less incensed at the slight put upon their god, as if he were unable to defend his own city. In their intense hatred of Nabonidus, the Chaldean priesthood appear to have been united, but in the feelings which they entertained towards Cyrus we shall find a broad cleavage in their ranks; a cleavage which finds some explanation in the Book of Daniel and is so far a confirmation of the authenticity of the historical portion of that Book. To see this we must study the legend of Megasthenes side by side with the Cylinder of Cyrus.[3] The tone of the inscription on the cylinder and the way in which it repeatedly speaks of "Merodach the great lord," show beyond all doubt that it comes from the same source as the legend of Megasthenes, viz. from the Chaldean priesthood of Bel-Merodach. Like the legend, the cylinder represents the gods of Babylonia as on the side of Cyrus. So enraged are they at Nabonidus' action in bringing their images into Babylon[4] that they complain to Merodach, who thereupon looks all round for a fresh king and finds the right man in Cyrus. Merodach himself also is angered with Nabonidus, and shows it unmistakably;[5] for when that king has hidden himself in Babylon

[1] *Records of the Past*, New Series, vol. v. p. 161, foot of page, "The king entered E-TUR-KALAMA," the temple of Ishtar of Agade (=Anunit) at Babylon.

[2] *Ibid.* vol. v. 162, line 16.

[3] *Ibid.* vol. v. 164.

[4] *Ibid.* vol. v. 162, lines 9, 10.

[5] *Ibid.* vol. v. 166, line 17.

in a place difficult of access, he is soon discovered and seized. In the words of this inscription, "Nabonidus the king, who revered him not, did he give into his [Cyrus'] hands." So far, then, the writer of the cylinder and the party whom he represents are seen to be in perfect agreement with the authors of the legend. But when we come to examine their feelings towards Cyrus we meet with the most marked difference. Of Cyrus the cylinder speaks throughout in the very highest terms, and in language so astonishingly like some passages in the Book of the prophet Isaiah as to force us to the conclusion that the writer was as certainly acquainted with that Book as the authors of the legend were familiar with the events recorded in Dan. iv.[1] Thus, we are told that Merodach "has sought for a righteous prince,[2] the wish of his heart, whose hand he holds: [3] he has called him by name,[4] Cyrus king of Anshan: for the sovereignty of the world he has proclaimed his name." [5] In strongest contrast to this the legend describes Cyrus as a "Persian mule," and evidently regards him with the same contempt as Nabonidus "the son of a Median woman," through whose treachery, joined with the help of the gods, he has been able to make himself master of Babylon. It is clear, then, that after the taking of Babylon the Chaldean priesthood were divided into two parties. Some, influenced it may be presumed by the Jews dwelling in their midst, and not unmindful how on one occasion in the past four young Jews by their prayers to the God of Israel had saved their order from destruction,[6] would be willing to view the course of events in something of the same light as the Jews, and to speak of Cyrus in much the same terms as the Hebrew prophet, only attributing to Merodach what the prophet attributed to Jehovah. Others, however, whose prototypes we seem to recognise in the Book of Daniel, had been brought into antagonistic relations with the Jewish captives,[7] and were also influenced by their dislike of foreigners, and more especially of the Persian rule, which had reduced Babylon, hitherto the seat of empire, to quite a secondary place, making her only one among other royal cities. These men, who had cut rather a sorry figure in the story of the events leading up to the king's madness, would seek to twist that story so as to hide

[1] The Book of Isaiah was evidently a favourite with Daniel and is thrice quoted by him. Cf. Dan. ix. 27 with Isa. xxviii. 22, and Dan. xi. 10, 40 with Isa. viii. 8. It is, therefore, quite conceivable that as "the chief governor over all the wise men of Babylon" he may have introduced it to the notice of the priesthood.

[2] Cf. Isa. xli. 2 and xlv. 13.

[3] *Ibid.* xlv. 1.

[4] *Ibid.* xlv. 3–4.

[5] *Ibid.* xli. 2, 25.

[6] Dan. ii. 12–24.

[7] *Ibid.* iii. 8–12.

their own discomfiture and Daniel's success, and at the same time to make use of it thus twisted to further their own seditious aims. So then, as Nebuchadnezzar was a name to conjure by in the early period of the Persian rule no less than in the closing years of the Babylonian empire,[1] they would not hesitate to take away the glory from Daniel and from Daniel's God and to give it to Nebuchadnezzar. Thus, in Megasthenes' legend, it is Nebuchadnezzar, and not Jehovah or Jehovah's prophet, who sees what is coming, and sees it with all clearness of detail. Further, in the popularity of Nebuchadnezzar and the unpopularity of Nabonidus they would find a double lever with which to stir up sedition. Nebuchadnezzar appears to have died soon after his recovery from his madness. "What was it," they might ask, "that hastened his end? Well, all men know that he was devoted to Babylon, and that his heart was wrapped up in the prosperity and greatness of his royal city. Imagine, then, how poignant was his anguish, when, with prophetic eye, he beheld so clearly what was coming, and foresaw the accursed treachery of the son of a Median woman, but for which the Persian mule could never have made us his slaves. Oh! what a sad end to the long and prosperous career of our greatest king was the sight of that coming inevitable catastrophe! Listen to his long-drawn utterance of woe on the traitor—the very last words that fell from his lips ere he was snatched from us!—'Would that, before he betrayed his fellow-countrymen, some Charybdis or sea might engulf him; or that having betaken himself elsewhere, he might be driven through the desert, where there is neither city nor track of man, where wild beasts roam, and birds fly around, a lonely wanderer among the rocks and ravines; and that I, before these things were put into my mind, had met with a happier end.'"

It is thus that I would seek to account both for the close contact and the wide divergence which strike us so forcibly when we place this fourth chapter of Daniel side by side with the legend of Megasthenes.

In conclusion, it is sometimes objected to the historical chapters in Daniel that they were so evidently written to serve a didactic purpose. My answer is: Be it so; for *that* was one object, and no unworthy object, of the Old Testament writers. But a story being written with a didactic purpose does not prove that story untrue. The legend of Megasthenes, according to the view given above, was also drawn up to serve a purpose. But that is not the reason why we refuse to give it credence. Our difficulty lies

[1] For evidence of this see the *Journal of Theological Studies* for October, 1915, pp. 46, 47.

in this: that we have no evidence to show that Nebuchadnezzar possessed such a marvellous gift of prophecy as is assigned to him in the legend.

Note

The inscription of the father of Nabonidus is given by Langdon in his *Neubabylonischen Inschriften*, pp. 288–295. See also pp. 57, 58. It was found by Pognon at Eski-Harran, a mile east of Haran, and possesses such unique interest that I venture to give an extract. The old priest has been telling with very natural pride and exultation how his son Nabonidus king of Babylon has rebuilt the temple of Sin in Haran and brought back the images of the gods. He then continues thus: "A thing which Sin the king of the gods had never done before, had never granted to any one, out of his love to me [he did for me,] because I reverenced his divinity and took hold of his robe. Sin the king of the gods lifted up my head and gave me a good name in the country. He gave me besides, a long life, years of joy of heart. From the time of Ashurbanipal king of Assyria to the sixth year of Nabonidus king of Babylon—the son the offspring of my heart —one hundred and four happy years before Sin the king of the gods he gave to my heart, and kept me alive. As for me, my eyesight is clear, my memory is excellent, my hands and feet are sound, my words are in high esteem, my eating and drinking are normal, and my teeth" . . . Here the record becomes illegible, but farther on the old man tells us how diligently he has performed his sacrificial duties; and then a note is added by some other hand to the effect that he himself was carried away by fate in the sixth year of Nabonidus king of Babylon, and received honourable burial at the hands of his royal son.

11

Belshazzar

THE fifth chapter of Daniel introduces us to Belshazzar, *i.e.* Bel-sharra-utsur, "Bel protect the king," the eldest son of Nabonidus the last king of Babylon. Before the discovery and decipherment of the cuneiform inscriptions the Belshazzar of Dan. v. was almost as great a puzzle as the Sargon of Isa. xx. 1 Commentators were then as much in the dark over this king as they still are over the " queen " of Dan. v. 10. But though there are some points in the story on which we may well desire further light, yet Belshazzar himself now stands before us as a very real person, and in fact one of the leading spirits of his age.

We have supposed Nabonidus born about 614 B.C., when his father Nabubalatsu-ikbi was aged thirty-nine. If we make a similar supposition with regard to his son Belshazzar, then his birth-year would be 575 B.C. This would make him fourteen years old at the end of the reign of Nebuchadnezzar, and nearly twenty at the time of his father's accession. Such suppositions agree with facts gleaned from the contract tablets. For instance, in the first year of Nabonidus, Belshazzar has a house of his own in Babylon, in the fifth year of Nabonidus mention is made of his secretary, and in the seventh year of his steward and secretaries. Most significant of all is the fact that in this latter year, when according to the above scheme Belshazzar would be twenty-six years old, we find him acting in northern Babylonia as commander-in-chief of the army.[1] As regards his religious tendencies Belshazzar was no doubt brought up in the cult of Sin, Shamash, and Anunit, to which his father was so strongly attached, and in which his grandfather, as high priest of the temple in Haran, held such a distinguished position. Thus, in a tablet dated the 9th of Nisan, the tenth year of Nabonidus, we find him sending by water sheep and oxen for sacrifice to the temple of Shamash at Sippar. On another occasion he sends a

[1] *Records of the Past*, New Series, vol. v. p. 159.

CYLINDER OF NABONIDUS, INSCRIBED WITH A PRAYER IN BEHALF OF HIS SON BELSHAZZAR

(BRITISH MUSEUM)

wedge of gold weighing one mana.[1] Yet again, he joins his father in sending animals for sacrifice. In the same way one of his sisters sends a silver cup weighing twenty-seven shekels as her tithe. Of another sister we are informed that she was dedicated by her father as a votaress of the moon-god Sin in the temple at Ur, and that he built a house for her close to the women's quarters, over which apparently she was called to preside.[2]

In the same year in which Belshazzar first appears as commander-in-chief of the army, 549 B.C., his grandfather Nabu-balatsu-ikbi died at the advanced age of 104 years. In 572 B.C., when Belshazzar, according to our scheme, was three years old, this venerable man received the office of *nash-padhruti* "sword-bearer," *i.e.* sacrificer, to Nebuchadnezzar in E-sha-turra,[3] the temple of Ishtar of Akkad—identified with Anunit the daughter of Sin—in Babylon. This appointment would tend to bring the boy Belshazzar into more or less close connection with the court of Nebuchadnezzar, and he was probably fully conversant with the circumstances of that king's madness, viz. the wonderful and tragic story told us in Dan. iv. Such a supposition lends additional weight to the stern reproof of Daniel, when before the conscience-stricken king he recalls that story to mind, and after relating it at some length, closes with the words, "And thou his son, O Belshazzar, hast not humbled thine heart, *though thou knewest all this.*"

But if Belshazzar in his early days had thus some acquaintance with court life, the question which most interests us is his exact relationship to Nebuchadnezzar. If we had only the Book of Daniel to go by, we should conclude him to be the undoubted son of that monarch, since the queen-mother, Belshazzar himself, and Daniel, all speak of Nebuchadnezzar as his father. In the light, however, of the inscriptions such a conclusion is seen to be a mistake. They reveal Belshazzar to us as the eldest son of Nabonidus, and therefore the heir apparent. They also make it clear that no tie of blood existed between Belshazzar and Nebuchadnezzar, at any rate on his father's side. Nabonidus, whatever his exact position in the state, was, according to his own statement, simply one of the conspirators who assassinated the boy-king, Labashi-Marduk, the grandson of Nebuchadnezzar and the last of his line.[4] But whilst the inscriptions thus show us

[1] Pinches' *Old Testament,* 1st ed. pp. 449–450.

[2] Yale Oriental Series, *Babylonian Texts,* vol. i. pp. 66–75.

[3] Probably the same as E-tur-kalama. Cf. Jastrow's *Religion of Babylonia and Assyria,* p. 311.

[4] Also stated by Berosus. Cf. *Josephus c. Apion,* i. 20.

our mistake, they also help us to understand why, in the narrative of Dan. v., Belshazzar is so frequently called the son of Nebuchadnezzar. Nabonidus, like many a usurper, was most anxious to legitimise his claim to the crown. Accordingly, on his celebrated stele, after telling us, as related in the last chapter, how his fellow-conspirators in the assassination of Labashi-Marduk unanimously elected him to be their king, he adds these words: "Of Nebuchadnezzar and Nergal-sharezer, the kings my predecessors, their delegate am I: their hosts to my hands they entrusted."[1] Then, a little farther on, he relates how in a dream he saw a meteor and the moon rising in conjunction, simultaneously with the rising of the star of Merodach (Jupiter), and was assured by Merodach that the omen was an auspicious one, and bidden to consult his predecessor Nebuchadnezzar—who also appeared on the scene—as to its significance.[2] In the same way we find dreams of a like character, seen by others, recorded as interpreted in favour of Nabonidus and his son Belshazzar.[3] All these are just so many indications of the extreme anxiety of the usurper to legitimise his claim. Such being the case, it is hardly conceivable that he would neglect the easiest and most effectual way of bringing about that end—so often practised in oriental monarchies—viz. the plan of marrying the wives of his predecessors, or their daughters. That he did so, can be shown as follows: On the celebrated inscription of Darius Hystaspes at Behistun mention is made of two impostors, who rose up in rebellion against that monarch, and attempted to seize the throne of Babylon by putting forward the claim, "I am Nebuchadrezzar the son of Nabonidus." The words are suggestive, and mean more than they say. To be descended from Nabonidus—who was not only a usurper but also a most unpopular king—would hardly be likely to ingratiate a man in the affections of the Babylonians. But if Nabonidus had allied himself by marriage with the family of Nebuchadnezzar, then to be sprung from Nabonidus might mean to be sprung from Nebuchadnezzar. Hence it seems highly probable that Nebuchadnezzar, the younger son of Nabonidus,[4] whom the impostors attempted to personate, was the son of a widow or daughter of the great Nebuchadnezzar. But with regard to Belshazzar the

[1] Stele of Nabonidus, col. v. lines 6, 7.

[2] *Ibid.* col. vi. The dream was probably understood to mean that Sin the moon-god and Merodach co-operated with and favoured the newly risen meteor, or "great star," which typified Nabonidus. Cf. Matt. ii. 2.

[3] Yale Oriental Series, *Babylonian Texts*, vol. i. p. 55.

[4] The usurper Nabonidus must have called his younger son Nebuchadnezzar in the same way that Hazael the supplanter of Benhadad named his son Benhadad. Cf. 2 Kings xiii. 3.

case is different. As we have seen, he was born many years before his father obtained the crown. Now, had his mother been a daughter of Nebuchadnezzar, there would have been no need for his father Nabonidus to be so very anxious to establish his claim : for he would have succeeded to the crown on the same grounds as his predecessor Neriglissar, who was a son-in-law of Nebuchadnezzar. Belshazzar, then, must be looked upon as the "son," *i.e.* grandson or descendant of Nebuchadnezzar, *only in the legal sense*. This explains the punctilious style in which the queen-mother addresses him in Dan. v. 11, "The king Nebuchadnezzar thy father, the king, I say, thy father." Evidently, as the whole narrative shows, it was a point of etiquette at the court of Babylon to speak of and treat Belshazzar as the legitimate son of the defunct Nebuchadnezzar.[1] And thus a term, which at first sight seems to imply imperfect knowledge on the part of the writer of the Book of Daniel, is found to be in perfect accord with what may be presumed to have been the actual state of things, and becomes a corroboration of the truth of the narrative.

We turn next to the "queen" of Dan. v. 10. So far she has not been identified. She was not the mother of Nabonidus. That lady, as we learn from the Annalistic Tablet, died in the camp at Sippara in the ninth year of Nabonidus.[2] But since she appears in Dan. v. in the character of queen-mother, and speaks with remarkable dignity and self-possession, it is reasonable to suppose that she was the widow of Nebuchadnezzar, whom Nabonidus had married, and who—now that her husband was a prisoner in the hands of the enemy—had assumed the post of queen-mother. Also, in the present imperfect state of our knowledge, we may perhaps look upon her as the Nitocris of Herodotus, to whom that historian ascribes the water-defences of Babylon, which were partly the work of Nebuchadnezzar and partly of Nabonidus. It would seem as though the informers of Herodotus, for some reason not clear to us, represented the water-defences of Babylon, erected by Nebuchadnezzar and Nabonidus, as the work of one who was queen to both.[3]

Our next question is as to the position held by Belshazzar. The Book of Daniel calls him "king." The critics point out

[1] Cf. 1 Chron. iii. 17, where Salathiel the son of Neri, who was descended from David through Nathan (Luke iii. 27, 31), is called the son of Jeconiah.

[2] *Records of the Past*, New Series, vol. v. p. 160.

[3] Herodotus, book i. 186, speaks of the water-defences of Babylon as the work of Nitocris. Nebuchadnezzar, in the India House Inscription, claims them as his work. Again, the historian attributes to that queen the quay-walls of Babylon and also the bridge over the Euphrates ; but it appears from Koldeway's *Excavations*, pp. 199–201, that these were the works of Nabonidus.

that in contemporary inscriptions he is always described as "the king's son," never as "king." How then, they ask, can we account for that title being given him in Dan. vi. 1? The answer is, first, that Belshazzar was a sub-king under his father Nabonidus. Nabonidus was king of the *empire* of Babylon; Belshazzar was merely king of Babylon. For the reigning monarch to appoint a sub-king over part of his dominions was a very common practice in ancient times. In 702 B.C. Sennacherib appointed Bel-ibni, a Babylonian of noble birth brought up at Nineveh, to be king of Babylon. Again in 699 B.C. he appointed his own son Ashur-nadin-shumu to the same post. In 668 B.C. Esarhaddon, dividing his empire, proclaimed his younger son Shamash-shum-ukin as king of Babylon, but yet in subordination to his elder son Ashurbanipal, whom he appointed king of Assyria. Neriglissar, the son-in-law of Nebuchadnezzar, styles his father, Bel-shum-ishkun, "king of Babylon"; but he could only have been a sub-king under Nebuchadnezzar. We may assume, then, that Belshazzar occupied a similar position to that held by Bel-shum-ishkun in the days of Nebuchadnezzar. But this is no mere assumption made in order to solve a difficulty. Evidence will be brought forward in a future chapter to show that Cyrus appointed his son Cambyses to succeed Belshazzar on the throne of Babylon, and that on the contract tablets of the first year of Cyrus Cambyses is styled "king of Babylon," while his father Cyrus takes the larger title, "King of the Countries." It is reasonable, therefore, to suppose that Belshazzar bore the same title that was afterwards given to Cambyses. At the same time it is more likely that in Dan. v. 1 the royal title is given to Belshazzar in the higher sense, either as sharing the supreme power along with his father, or as the *de facto* king. We must remember that for at least ten of the seventeen years of Nabonidus the defence of the country had rested on Belshazzar, while his father Nabonidus lived in retirement at Temâ. Also, that on the night of that fatal feast the person of Nabonidus had been in the hands of the enemy for well-nigh four months, so that during that interval in the eyes of the world at large Belshazzar would appear as the actual ruler. At any rate he would so appear in the eyes of the author of the Book of Daniel, writing after the event was over. For him, the reign of Nabonidus would end with his capture and he would view Belshazzar as the last of the Neo-Babylonian kings. But it is possible to adduce evidence to show that Belshazzar did actually share the supreme power along with his father and was associated with him on the throne. Thanks to a discovery made by Dr. Pinches, to whom Old Testament students owe so much, we are now in a position to show that for at least five years at the close of the reign of Nabonidus Belshazzar reigned along with his father. Among a collection of tablets from Erech, Pinches has deciphered one, dated the 22nd day of the additional month of Adar, the twelfth year of Nabonidus, which commences thus: "Ishi-Amurru, son of Nuranu, has sworn by Bel, Nebo, the lady of Erech, and Nana, the oath of Nabonidus king of Babylon and of Belshazzar the king's son, that on the 7th day of the month Adar of the twelfth year of Nabonidus king of Babylon I will go to Erech," etc., etc. On this tablet Pinches makes the following observations: "The importance of this inscription is that it places Belshazzar practically on the same plane as Nabonidus his father, five years before the latter's deposition, and the bearing of this will not be overlooked. Officially Belshazzar had not been recognised as king, as this would have necessitated his father's abdication, but it seems clear that he was in some way associated with his father on the throne, otherwise his name would hardly have been introduced into the oath with which the inscription begins. We now see that not only for the Hebrews, but also for the Babylonians, Belshazzar held a practically royal position."[1]

If Belshazzar was thus seated on the throne with his father, his offer of the *third* place[2] in the kingdom to any one who would interpret the mystic words is most intelligible. Clearly he regards his father, though now a prisoner in the hands of the Persians, as holding the first place, and himself the second place, so that the third place was the highest he had to offer. For though in the eyes of the world Belshazzar was now king, yet in the eyes of the Babylonians, as the contract tablets show, Nabonidus was looked upon as king down to that fatal night in which the palace was surprised and Belshazzar slain, that night of the final and complete, as distinguished from the partial, capture of Babylon.

But the critics point to a yet further difficulty, and ask how we can explain the first and third years of Belshazzar, mentioned in Dan. vii. 1 and viii. 1 respectively. They may be looked upon as the years of his reign as sub-king of Babylon; but it seems more natural to adopt Pinches' view, and to regard them as referring

[1] See the *Expository Times* for April, 1915.

[2] The form of the Aramaic word rendered "third" is unique. According to Baer, "Pro תְּלִיתָה reperitur Dan. v. 7 תַּלְתִּי (τρίτος), cum definito תַּלְתָּא (ὁ τρίτος) v. 16, quod tertium dignitate significat." In verse 16 the R.V. reads, "Thou shalt be the third ruler in the kingdom," thus agreeing with the Greek version of Theodotion, τρίτος ἐν τῇ βασιλείᾳ μου ἄρξεις. The R.V.M. reads, "Thou shalt rule as one of three," which approaches more nearly to the rendering of the LXX, ἕξεις ἐξουσίαν τοῦ τρίτου μέρους τῆς βασιλείας μου, with which compare verse 7.

to his joint reign with his father on the throne of empire. It will be said, however, that this system of dating is at variance with that adopted on the contract tablets by the Babylonians themselves, seeing that those tablets down to the very last are dated according to the years of the reign of Nabonidus, without any mention whatever of Belshazzar; and further, that the writer of the Book of Daniel betrays complete ignorance as to the existence of such a person as Nabonidus. My answer is, that the writer of this Book in mentioning the first and third years of Belshazzar most certainly adopts a different system of dating from that found on the tablets; but that he can hardly be charged with ignorance as to the existence of Nabonidus, since he represents Belshazzar as offering the *third* place in the kingdom to the successful interpreter of the mystic words. With regard to the system adopted on the tablets the explanation runs thus: When a father associates his son as co-regent, only one royal name, viz. that of the father, will continue to appear on the tablets, since the introduction of the son's name would involve the creation of a new era in the middle of a reign. The only exception to this would be when the two kings were able to date the commencement of both their reigns from the same New Year. Of this, as we shall see in a future chapter, the tablets furnish us with one notable instance.

At the close of Dan. v. Belshazzar is called "the Chaldean king"—*not* "the king of the Chaldæans." The term "Chaldean" is here used in an ethnic sense. Though Belshazzar himself was probably a Babylonian, at least on his father's side,[1] yet since Nabonidus had so completely identified himself with the family of "Nebuchadnezzar king of Babylon, the Chaldean,"[2] the writer very suitably calls him "the Chaldean king" in contra-distinction to "Darius the Mede" and to "Cyrus the Persian."

In the Annalistic Tablet, from the seventh year of Nabonidus onward, we are confronted year by year with the statement, "The king was in Temâ, the king's son," *i.e.* Belshazzar, "the *nobles* and the soldiers were in the country of Akkad." In very much the same light is Belshazzar brought before us in the opening verse of Dan. v.: "Belshazzar the king made a great feast to a thousand of his lords," where the Aramaic word translated "lords" comes from a kindred root to that translated "nobles" on the tablet.

[1] *Josephus c. Apion*, i. 20.
[2] See Ezra v. 12.

See Addendum on page 302

12

The Fall of Babylon

OUR studies in the Book of Daniel have now brought us to the story of the fall of Babylon given in Dan. v., and as the historical accuracy of that chapter has been much questioned since the discovery by Dr. Pinches of the contemporary native records, inscribed on the Annalistic Tablet and the Cylinder of Cyrus, it will be well for us to enter thoroughly into the subject by reviewing in succession, first the prophecy contained in Jer. l. and li., then the statements of the Book of Daniel and of the Greek historians, Herodotus and Xenophon, and lastly the contemporary cuneiform records, not forgetting the all-important contract tablets, which have the closest bearing of all on the subject now before us.

From the prophet's long prediction we select certain features which were to characterise the fall of the great imperial city, which the efforts of Nebuchadnezzar had rendered well-nigh impregnable. Jeremiah's prophecy was written in the days of the Median ascendancy and before the Persians under Cyrus had taken the lead. The prophet foretells that Babylon will be attacked by an invader from the north (l. 3, 9, 41), viz. "the kings of the Medes" (li. 11, 28), *i.e* the chiefs of the Median clans. The city is described as well provisioned (l. 26), with towering fortifications, broad walls, and high gates (li. 53, 58), agreeably with the statements of Nebuchadnezzar and the discoveries of Koldewey. Nevertheless she will be taken by stratagem, caught in a snare (l. 24). This stratagem is connected with her water-defences, of which Nebuchadnezzar gives such an eloquent description [1]: Jehovah "will dry up her sea and make her fountain dry" (li. 36). It is connected also with the course of the Euphrates through Babylon. The "passages," or ferries, which link the streets on the opposite sides of the river—as described by Herodotus [2]—will be taken by surprise, and the reeds burned with fire (li. 32). It will be successfully executed at the time

[1] India House Inscription, col. vi. 39–46.
[2] Book i. 186.

when a great feast is going on, at which all the principal men of the land are gathered together. "When they are heated, I will make their feast, and I will make them drunken, that they may rejoice, and sleep a perpetual sleep, and not wake, saith the LORD." "And I will make drunk her princes and her wise men, her governors and her deputies, and her mighty men: and they shall sleep a perpetual sleep and not wake, saith the king, whose name is the LORD of hosts" (li. 39, 57).

Such being the utterances of the prophet, we turn next to the historians, and first to the Book of Daniel, which, though not a history, claims to be a record of actual facts, and has historical notes scattered throughout it. The main point of agreement between the record of Dan. v. and the prophecy of Jeremiah lies in this, that the town is taken on the night of a great feast, and when a large gathering of the principal men were inflamed with wine (Dan. v. 1, 4). To this the critics will reply, that the author of the Book of Daniel is acquainted with the writings of Jeremiah, as he himself admits, and borrows his ideas as to the circumstances of the capture of Babylon from the predictions of that prophet. But this will not account for the very similar details furnished by heathen writers, who in all probability had never seen the prophecies of Jeremiah or even heard of his name. Let us take first the testimony of Herodotus. Babylon was captured by Cyrus in 539 B.C., and Herodotus, whose travels extended from 464 to 447 B.C., is believed to have visited Babylon in early manhood, only some eighty years after its capture. According to Herodotus, Cyrus approached Babylon in the spring of the year. The Babylonians met him without the walls, were defeated, and then retired within their defences. "Here," adds the historian, "they shut themselves up, and made light of his siege, having laid in a store of provisions for many years [1] in preparation against this attack; for when they saw Cyrus conquering nation after nation, they were convinced that he would never stop, and that their turn would come at last." [2] This led Cyrus to resort to stratagem. In the words of Herodotus, "He placed a portion of his army at the point where the river enters the city, and another body at the back of the place where it issues forth, with orders to march into the town by the bed of the stream as soon as the water became shallow enough." [3] After this he withdrew the less warlike portion of his troops to a place where Queen Nitocris had made a vast lake, into which the waters

[1] Cf. Jer. l. 26 and Dan. iv. 12.
[2] Herod. i. 190.
[3] *Ibid.* i. 191.

of the Euphrates were turned while she was lining with brick the quay-walls of the city. Repeating the plan of Nitocris, Cyrus, according to Herodotus—

"turned the Euphrates by a canal into the basin, which was then a marsh: on which the river sank to such an extent that the natural bed of the stream became fordable. Hereupon the Persians, who had been left for the purpose at Babylon by the river-side, entered the stream, which had now shrunk so as to reach about midway up a man's thigh, and thus got into the town. Had the Babylonians been apprised of what Cyrus was about, or had they noticed their danger, they would never have allowed the Persians to enter the city, but would have destroyed them utterly; for they would have made fast all the street-gates which gave upon the river,[1] and mounting upon the walls along both sides of the stream, would so have caught the enemy as it were in a trap. But, as it was, the Persians came upon them by surprise and so took the city. Owing to the vast size of the place, the inhabitants of the central parts—as the residents at Babylon declare—long after the outer portions of the town were taken, knew nothing of what had happened,[2] but as they were engaged in a festival, continued dancing and revelling until they learnt the capture but too certainly."[3]

Such, then, is the testimony of a very famous historian, who had been at Babylon, as he tells us, and conversed with the inhabitants as to the circumstances of the capture of their city at no very long interval after that tragic event took place.

We pass on next to the *Cyropædia* of Xenophon, one of the latest works of that historian, written about 360 B.C., a hundred years or so after Herodotus' visit to Babylon. The *Cyropædia* has been described as a "political and historical romance, containing the author's own ideas as to training and education." Such no doubt it is; but we must remember at the same time that it is the work of a minute and painstaking historian—the author of the *Anabasis*—and of one who had been in Babylonia and in the neighbourhood of Babylon.[4] The locality, therefore, no less than the subject-matter of his book, would lead him to take a deep interest in Babylon's fate and in the circumstances of

[1] Viz. at the "passages," or ferries, where boats plied to and fro; mentioned above in Jer. li. 32.

[2] Cf. Jer. li. 31.

[3] Herod. i. 191.

[4] Viz. at the battle of Cunaxa, fought some sixty miles to the north of Babylon.

her capture by the Persians. According, then, to Xenophon, Cyrus, impressed by the strength and height of the fortifications, thought first of starving out the city; but when the river was mentioned to him, and some comment made on its depth, he conceived the idea of draining off its waters by digging a trench round the town and at the same time leading the Babylonians to believe that he was preparing to blockade their city by forming a rampart with the earth thrown up out of the trench. This indeed they believed, and in the words of the historian, "laughed at his blockade, as being furnished with provisions for more than twenty years." After the trench was dug, Cyrus, according to Xenophon, "on hearing that there was a festival in Babylon, in which all the Babylonians drank and revelled the whole night, took, during the time of it, a number of men with him, and as soon as it was dark, opened the trenches on the side toward the river. When this was done, the water ran off in the night into the trenches, and the bed of the river through the city became traversable." After sending a force of men to test the depth of the river, on their reporting favourably, Cyrus addressed his officers and assured them that they would find little difficulty in overcoming a foe whom they had already defeated when sober, and who were many of them asleep and intoxicated. He concluded his address with the words, "Hasten, therefore, to arms, and I will lead you with the gods: and do ye, Gadatas and Gobryas, show us the way, for ye know it; and when we are within the city, guide us the quickest way to the palace." "Yes!" replied Gobryas, "we will: and I should not be surprised if the doors of the palace are now open, for the whole city seems to-night to be given up to revelry. We shall find, however, a guard before the gates, for it is always set." "It would not do to wait," said Cyrus; "we must advance, in order that we may take the men as much off their guard as possible." As soon as these words were spoken, they started on the march; and of those who met them, some were struck down and killed, some fled, and some raised a shout. Those with Gobryas joined in the shout with them, as though they too were revellers themselves, and, marching by the quickest way they could, arrived at the palace. The party with Gobryas and Gadatas found the doors of the palace shut, and those who were told off to attack the guards fell upon them as they were drinking by a large fire, and forthwith dealt with them as with enemies. As a great outcry and noise ensued, those who were within heard the uproar, and on the king ordering them to see what was the matter, some of them threw open the gates and rushed out. The men with Gadatas, as soon as they saw the gates unclosed, burst in, and pursuing those who fled back within, and dealing them blows, they reached the king, and found him in a standing posture with his sword drawn. Him the party with Gadatas and Gobryas overpowered, whilst those who were with him were killed, one holding up something before him, another fleeing, another defending himself in whatever way he could. Cyrus sent troops of horse through the streets, bidding them kill those whom they found abroad, and those who understood Syrian (*i.e.* the Babylonian language) he ordered to tell those who were within their houses to remain there, and to say that if any were found abroad they would be killed. These commands they carried out. Gadatas and Gobryas now came up, and, after first paying their adoration to the gods because they had avenged them on the impious king, they then kissed the hands and feet of Cyrus, shedding many tears in the midst of their joy and satisfaction. When day came, and those who held the towers perceived that the town was taken and the king dead, they surrendered them. Cyrus immediately took possession of the fortresses, and sent commanders with garrisons into them. He allowed the dead to be buried by their relatives, and ordered the heralds to make proclamation that all the Babylonians were to bring out their arms, giving notice at the same time that in whatever house any arms were found all the inmates would be put to death. Accordingly they brought their arms, and Cyrus deposited them in the towers that they might be ready if ever he should want to use them.[1] The historian then goes on to say that he ordered the Babylonians to go on cultivating the land, to pay their tribute, and to serve those under whom they were placed: also, that very soon after he held a public reception two days running, when the people crowded to meet him: after which he consulted his friends, and by their advice entered into possession of the palace.

I have given the narrative of Xenophon at some length because of its important bearing on the contemporary Babylonian records. Before I go on to those records, I ask my readers to glance back at the above extracts and notice how prophecy and history support one another. Thus: Jeremiah predicts that Babylon will be taken by some stratagem connected with her water-defences and her ferries across the Euphrates, and also that it will be taken when a great feast is going on and the Babylonians are off their guard. The two Greek historians tell us that it was so taken. What is the inference? It is twofold: first,

[1] *Cyropædia*, book vii. chap. v. 7–34.

that Jeremiah's utterances are true prophecy; and secondly, that the record of their fulfilment is genuine history: so that we are bound to believe these two main facts with regard to the capture of Babylon, since we cannot suppose either Herodotus or Xenophon to have known anything of the writings of Jeremiah. This being the case, we must also credit the Book of Daniel with being historically correct in the two following particulars: first, in its mention of the feast held by the king and his nobles, which agrees, as we have just seen, with the prophecy of Jeremiah and the record of the two Greek historians; secondly, in connecting the death of the king with the final assault on the palace, for this fact is corroborated by the testimony of Xenophon, whom we have proved to be a faithful witness in this particular by his agreement with the predictions of Jeremiah of which he could have no cognisance.

We may now go forward to investigate the accounts of the capture of Babylon given us in the contemporary cuneiform records, amongst which the Annalistic Tablet claims our first attention. This tablet, found by Rassam, and now in the British Museum, was first deciphered by Pinches, who published a copy of it with transliteration and translation in the *Transactions of the Society of Biblical Archæology* for the year 1880. A subsequent translation was given by Sayce in *Records of the Past*, New Series, vol. v. The original is inscribed on a tablet measuring 4 inches by 3½, in four columns, two on the obverse and two on the reverse. The tablet is of sun-dried clay: hence it is no wonder that considerable portions of it are illegible. The record breaks off at a point of deep interest, viz. the burial of Belshazzar and the installation of Cambyses as his successor. The events on the tablet are chronicled according to the seventeen years of the reign of Nabonidus, 556–539 B.C. Thus, in his sixth year, we have the conquest of Astyages the Mede by Cyrus king of Anshan. Then, in his ninth year, Cyrus is styled king of Persia, and his crossing the Tigris is recorded. After the eleventh year occurs a long lacuna, and when the record again becomes legible we are already plunged in the account of the final conflict between Babylon and Persia, which reads thus-

"[year 17] . . . Nebo to go forth from Borsippa. . . . In the month . . . the king entered E-tur-kalama.[1] In the month

[1] "The House of the Court of the Universe," the name of the temple at Babylon dedicated to Ishtar of Agade, identified with Anunit the daughter of Sin. See Koldewey's *Excavations*, p. 296, and Jastrow's *Religion*, p. 311.

. . . and the Lower Sea[1] revolted . . . Bel went forth: the Akitu festival[2] they duly held. In the month . . . the gods of Marad,[3] the god Zamama,[4] and the gods of Kish,[3] Beltis and the gods of Kharsakkalama,[5] entered Babylon. Up to the end of the month Elul [August–September] the gods of the country of Akkad,[6] those above the sky and those below the sky, entered Babylon. The gods of Borsippa, Kutha, and Sippara[7] did not enter. In the month Tammuz [June–July] Cyrus delivered battle at Upe [Opis] on the river Zalzallat [the Tigris] against the troops of Akkad. The men of Akkad raised a revolt. Some men were slain. On the 14th day of the month Sippara was taken without fighting: Nabonidus fled. On the 16th day Ugbaru [Gobryas], the governor of the country of Gutium, and the soldiers of Cyrus entered Babylon without fighting. Thereupon Nabonidus was captured after he had been surrounded in Babylon. Till the end of the month Tammuz [June–July] the shield-bearers of the country of Gutium surrounded the gates of E-sag-ila. No one's weapon entered E-sag-ila and the shrines, nor did a flag come in. On the 3rd day of Marchesvan [October–November] Cyrus entered Babylon. The roads before him were full of people.[8] Peace was established for the city, peace to the whole of Babylon did Cyrus proclaim. Ugbaru [Gobryas], his governor, appointed governors in Babylon, and from the month Chisleu [November–December] to the month of Adar [February–March] the gods of the country of Akkad, whom Nabonidus had brought down to Babylon, returned to their own cities. In the month of Marchesvan on the night of the 11th day Ugbaru [Gobryas] went against . . . and the son [?] of the king died. From the 27th of the month Adar [February–March] to the 3rd day of the month Nisan [March–April] there was weeping in Akkad, all the people smote their heads. On the 4th day Cambyses the son of Cyrus went to E-khad-kalamma-shumma.[9] The official of the temple of the sceptre of Nebo who bestows the sceptre . . . brought a message in his hand. . . ."

[1] The Persian Gulf.

[2] The New Year festival.

[3] Names of Babylonian cities.

[4] A war-god.

[5] "The Mountain of the World," the name of a temple adjoining Kish.

[6] Northern Babylonia.

[7] Borsippa was close to Babylon on the S.W., Kutha lay to the N.E., and Sippara about thirty-five miles to the N.N.W.

[8] Lit. "were black with people."

[9] "The House where the sceptre of the World is given"; the name of Nebo's temple in Babylon.

Such is the record on the tablet. Before we go on to study it, let me place before my readers the very brief account of the capture of Babylon given on the Cylinder of Cyrus. This priceless relic, brought from Babylonia by Rassam, is now in the British Museum. It was first translated and commented on by Sir H. Rawlinson in the *Journal of the Royal Asiatic Society* for the year 1880.[1] To the Bible-lover the inscription on the cylinder must be ever of the deepest interest. It appears to be the composition of a priest of Merodach, who must have come into contact with some of the Hebrew captives at Babylon, since his style and tone of thought are Hebraistic and argue some acquaintance with the latter part of the Book of Isaiah. In the words of Prof. Sayce, "The construction of the sentences more than once reminds us of the later Hebrew prophets. . . . The inscription in fact is one of the most Hebraistic which have come to us from Babylonia or Assyria, and in one important particular twice adopts a usage which is Hebrew and not Assyrian." [2]

The great theme of the Cylinder Inscription is that Cyrus is the chosen of Merodach, and that Merodach has given him the empire of Babylon. The part which bears on our subject runs thus

"Merodach, the great lord, the restorer of his people, beheld with joy his [Cyrus'] pious deeds and righteous hand. To his town of Babylon he commanded him to march: he caused him to take the road to Babylon. Like a friend and a comrade he went at his side. His vast army, innumerable as the waters of a river, put on their weapons and marched at his side. Without fighting and battle he caused him to enter Babylon; his city of Babylon he kept safe. In a place difficult of access Nabonidus, who did not revere him, he delivered into his hand. The men of Babylon all of them, the whole of Shumer and Akkad [southern and northern Babylonia], the nobles and the high priest, bowed low before him, they kissed his feet: they rejoiced in his sovereignty, their faces shone." [3]

Such, then, are the contemporary records of the Babylonians. Let us notice, first, the points in which they agree with the state-

[1] See also *Records of the Past*, New Series, vol. v. p. 164, and B. M. *Guide to the Babylonian and Assyrian Antiquities*, plate xxxi. and p. 172.

[2] This refers to the employment of the terms *sharru* and *malku*. In Assyrian *sharru*="king," and *malku*="prince." In Hebrew the meanings are reversed. The writer of the Cylinder adopts the Hebrew usage.

[3] Cylinder of Cyrus, lines 14–18.

CYLINDER OF CYRUS, WITH AN INSCRIPTION DESCRIBING HIS CAPTURE OF BABYLON

(BRITISH MUSEUM)

ments of the Book of Daniel and the Greek historians; and secondly, those points in which there is a seeming variance or even an apparent contradiction. We begin with the preliminary battle fought according to the tablet at Opis. This is the battle described by Herodotus as fought at a short distance from the city.[1] Our next, and much more important point, is the statement as to the death of the king on the night of the capture of Babylon. In this the Annalistic Tablet most probably confirms the statement of the Book of Daniel and of the historian Xenophon: *most probably,* because the characters translated "*and the son* of the king died" are partially obliterated and have been read, "*the wife* of the king died." On this point some weight must be given to the opinion of the eminent Assyriologist who discovered the tablet, and who speaks thus: "Where the tablet is damaged there is not room enough for the character for 'wife,' and the verb to all appearance is not in the feminine. The Rev. C. J. Ball and Dr. Hagen, examining the text in my room in the British Museum, many years ago, agreed with me that the traces point to *u mar,* 'and the son of.' I do not think," he adds, "that there is any doubt that the Book of Daniel is as correct as it can be."[2] A further reason in favour of the reading "son" lies in the fact stated shortly afterwards that the funeral ceremonies of the dead person were conducted by Cambyses. Why Cambyses should conduct the funeral of the queen it is hard to see; but if the sceptre of the city of Babylon was to pass from the hands of Belshazzar into those of Cambyses, there would be a marked suitability in Cambyses conducting the funeral of Belshazzar. A third point of agreement between the writer of the tablet and the historians lies in the statement that the attack on the palace was led by Ugbaru, in whom we have little difficulty in recognising Gobryas, who, according to Xenophon, was one of the two leaders of the attacking party. Xenophon speaks of him as the Babylonian governor of a wide district, who had been very badly treated by the Babylonian king and had gone over to the side of Cyrus;[3] whilst the tablet informs us that Gutium was the district which he governed.[4] A fourth point of agreement is found in the great reception held by Cyrus after the

[1] Book i. 190.

[2] See *The Fall of Babylon,* p. 14: a paper by the Rev. Andrew Craig Robinson, read before the Victoria Institute.

[3] *Cyropædia,* book iv. chap. vi. 1–4.

[4] Gutium lay east of the Tigris and north of Elam. It extended as far east as the Zagros mountains, and formed a part of Assyria proper. It has been identified with the "Goiim" of Gen. xiv. 1.

capture of Babylon, as described on the Cylinder of Cyrus quoted above. This is in perfect accord with the statement of Xenophon that very soon after the taking of the city Cyrus admitted to his presence the Babylonians, who flocked around him in overwhelming numbers.[1]

Having now reviewed the points in which the contemporary native records agree with the statements made in the Book of Daniel and in the pages of the Greek historians, let me pass on next to notice other points in which at first sight they appear to tell a different story. These may be stated thus: Neither the Annalistic Tablet nor the Cylinder of Cyrus makes any mention of the siege of Babylon or of the stratagem by which the town was taken, whilst both alike dwell with marked emphasis on the peaceful nature of Cyrus' entrance into the city. Here, then, are differences that demand an explanation, and difficulties that call for a solution; and it will be found that the true solution lies in our ascertaining the date of that eventful night on which Babylon fell and "the son of the king died."[2] This, fortunately, we are able to do; for the tablet and the cylinder are not our only contemporary sources of information. There is one more infallible still, viz. the contract tablets. At first sight nothing would seem more certain than the accuracy of the contemporary annals. But we have to take into account that these records are official. "In that fact," as Olmstead points out, "lies their strength and their weakness." "Like all official records, ancient or modern," says the same writer, "these documents have been edited to a degree of which it is difficult to conceive."[3] But when we turn to the business documents the case is different, and we meet with items of valuable information which cannot be called in question. Apply this to the date of the capture of Babylon. According to the Annalistic Tablet the soldiers of Cyrus, led by Gobryas, entered Babylon on the 16th of Tammuz (June–July). Between three and four months later, on the 3rd of Marchesvan (October–November), Cyrus came to Babylon in person, and on the 11th of the same month an assault was made, apparently on the palace or citadel, in which the king's son was slain. The impression given us is that the town of Babylon made a peaceable surrender on the 16th of Tammuz (June–July), but that the king's son was able to hold out in some fortress till nearly four months

[1] *Cyropædia*, book vii. chap. v. 38, 41.

[2] See Craig Robinson's masterly work, *What about the Old Testament?* p. 147; also his paper on *The Fall of Babylon and Dan. v. 30*, referred to above.

[3] *Western Asia in the Days of Sargon of Assyria*, pp. 8, 18, 19.

later. When, however, we turn to the business tablets, drawn up in the seventeenth, *i.e.* the last, year of Nabonidus, we find not a few which bear a later date, such as the 5th of Ab (July–August), the 11th, 18th, and 21st of Elul (August–September), the latest being the 10th of Marchesvan (October–November), the very day before the assault in which the king's son was slain. The conclusion to be drawn is, that the troops of Cyrus could only have entered into a part of the city on the 16th of Tammuz. Further, we are led to infer that when Cyrus entered Babylon in person on the 3rd of Marchesvan, he only entered the suburbs. The interval between the 16th of Tammuz (June–July) and the fatal night of the 11th of Marchesvan (October–November) would thus allow time for the execution of the stratagem by which the remainder of the city was taken. But why is no mention made in the native records of that stratagem? Because the pride of the Babylonian priesthood, who doubtless drew up the official records, required that it should not be mentioned, if only on the score that it would be derogatory to Merodach. The impression must therefore be given that the town was peacefully surrendered, and that Cyrus was the chosen of Merodach, the deliverer of Babylon, not its conqueror. To do this without at the same time outraging the truth, was no difficult matter; for, as far as we know from the Greek historians, the siege was not a bloody one. After the preliminary battle fought near Opis, the Babylonians retired within their walls, and went on with their busy commercial life, deriding the efforts of their besiegers, who, under colour of raising a rampart of circumvallation, were steadily preparing the stratagem, which enabled them to gain an entrance into the part of the town still untaken. There was thus no fighting till that last fatal night, when all was sudden, sharp, and soon over. For, as the sequel shows, whether told by Xenophon or recorded on the cylinder, Cyrus did his best to conciliate the inhabitants, and they for their part responded heartily to his efforts. Hence it was possible for the official documents to emphasise these facts and to represent the entry of Cyrus into Babylon as a peaceful one: which indeed it was, save for that single night of carnage, when the son of the impious king who had angered Merodach [1] was delivered up into the hands of his foes.

Note

The question as to how much of Babylon was occupied by the troops of Cyrus when they first entered the city on the 16th of

[1] Cf. the Cylinder of Cyrus, lines 9 and 33.

Tammuz (June–July) is one of great difficulty. The fact that for nearly four months longer, on business tablets drawn up there, the reckoning is still made according to the day, month, and year of the reign of Nabonidus, is conclusive evidence that during that period a great part of the city still held out against the besiegers. On the other hand, we have to place the fact, recorded on the tablet, that by the end of the month Tammuz the swordsmen of the country of Gutium, presumably the troops of Gobryas, were guarding the gates of Esagila, the great temple of Merodach, which lay only a little distance to the south of the acropolis.[1] If this were the case, then a considerable portion of the city must have been in the hands of Cyrus' army by the end of Tammuz.

With a view to solve this difficulty, and to show that only the suburbs were in the besiegers' hands, the Rev. Andrew Craig Robinson very cleverly argues that the swordsmen of the country of Gutium, who guarded the approaches to Merodach's temple, were troops *furnished to Nabonidus by Gobryas before he went over to the side of Cyrus.* This may have been the case, and yet it is not the impression given by the record on the tablet, since almost immediately after the notice of the peaceful entrance of Gobryas the governor of Gutium and the soldiers of Cyrus on the 16th of Tammuz comes the statement that by the end of that month the swordsmen of Gutium were stationed at the gates of Esagila, without any cessation having taken place in the sacred rites. The passage as it stands appears to describe the rapid but peaceful advance of the arms of Cyrus. As in the middle of Tammuz his troops entered Babylon without fighting, so by the end of the month they were quietly guarding the gates of the great temple, where all was going on as usual. Here, then, is an enigma which seems still to defy solution: if Merodach's temple were in the hands of the enemy, how could business in the city of Babylon be still transacted as under the rule of Nabonidus?

[1] See the plan of Babylon facing p. 1 of Koldewey's *Excavations*.

13

The Handwriting on the Wall

"The king was on his throne,
 The satraps filled the hall,
A thousand bright lamps shone
 At that high festival:
A thousand cups of gold,
 In Judah deemed divine,
Jehovah's vessels hold
 The godless heathen's wine."

BYRON.

THE closing scene on that eventful night of the fall of Babylon, the 11th of Marchesvan (October–November), 539 B.C., referred to at the end of the last chapter, and which is so vividly described in Dan. v., now comes before us in the bright light of reality. Thanks to the excavations of Koldewey, not only has the throne-room of the Neo-Babylonian kings been discovered, but the doubly-recessed niche opposite the central entrance, which marks the spot where the throne must have stood, and where doubtless the conscience-stricken monarch must have sat.[1] The Chaldeans are fond of wine: Habakkuk, describing their lust of dominion, compares them to a drunken man, who, in his insatiable thirst, must have more and ever more. But "wine," in the language of the prophet, "is a treacherous dealer, a haughty man": [2] it makes things appear otherwise than they really are, and fills the drunkard with a false sense of his own importance. So, then, "Belshazzar, whiles he tasted the wine, commanded to bring the golden and silver vessels, which Nebuchadnezzar his father had taken out of the temple which was in Jerusalem." [3] Those vessels had been placed by Nebuchadnezzar in Esagila, the temple of his beloved Merodach, and Esagila, according to the Annalistic Tablet, was

[1] See Koldewey's *Excavations*, p. 104.
[2] Hab. ii. 5.
[3] Dan. v. 2.

already in the hands of the enemy.[1] True; but Nabonidus had small reverence for Merodach, and doubtless had not scrupled to remove the treasure out of Esagila before it fell into the hands of the enemy. In his dealings with the gods this king had already acted in a hasty and presumptuous manner, when, much to the wrath of Merodach, he collected their images and brought them into Babylon.[2] Doubtless, then, he would not scruple to remove the vessels of Jehovah from Merodach's temple to his own palace. When these sacred vessels were brought before his son Belshazzar, "the king and his lords, his wives and his concubines, drank in them. They drank wine, and," inflamed therewith, "praised the gods of gold, and of silver, of brass, of iron, of wood, and of stone, which"—in the words of Daniel—"see not, nor hear, nor know."[3] So emphatic is the language that it makes us think that those very images of the gods, which, as just stated, Nabonidus had collected into Babylon, must have been in the room at that critical moment when "the King eternal, incorruptible, invisible, the only God,"[4] saw fit to assert His supremacy; that moment which the sacred record thus describes: "In the same hour came forth the fingers of a man's hand, and wrote over against the candlestick"—the chandelier or lampstand—where the light fell brightest, "upon the plaister of the wall of the king's palace"—the chalk or white gypsum, with which Koldewey found the walls washed over.[5] It was against this light background that "the king saw the part of the hand that wrote." But it was not at once seen by that festal assembly; for, as we are told at the outset, the king was drinking wine "*before*" his guests. Their faces were turned towards him; their backs were toward that part of the wall on which the hand was writing. Consequently they saw their monarch's face pale with fear and his whole frame unmanned; but they saw not the cause of it.

The heathen have a conscience, a code of right and wrong, as well as Christians. Belshazzar is by no means ignorant of Jehovah the God of the Jews. As I have already shown, he knew at first hand the facts concerning Nebuchadnezzar's madness, and must have been a witness in his boyhood's days to his wonderful recovery. He must have known how, on that occasion, his legal "father" acknowledged the God of the Jews as "the Most High God."

[1] Annalistic Tablet, Rev. lines 16, 17, "At the end of the month Tammuz the swordsmen of Gutium guarded the gates of Esagila."

[2] Cylinder of Cyrus, line 33. Cf. Annalistic Tablet, Rev., lines 9–12.

[3] Dan. v. 3, 4, 23.

[4] 1 Tim. i. 17.

[5] Koldewey's *Excavations*, p. 104.

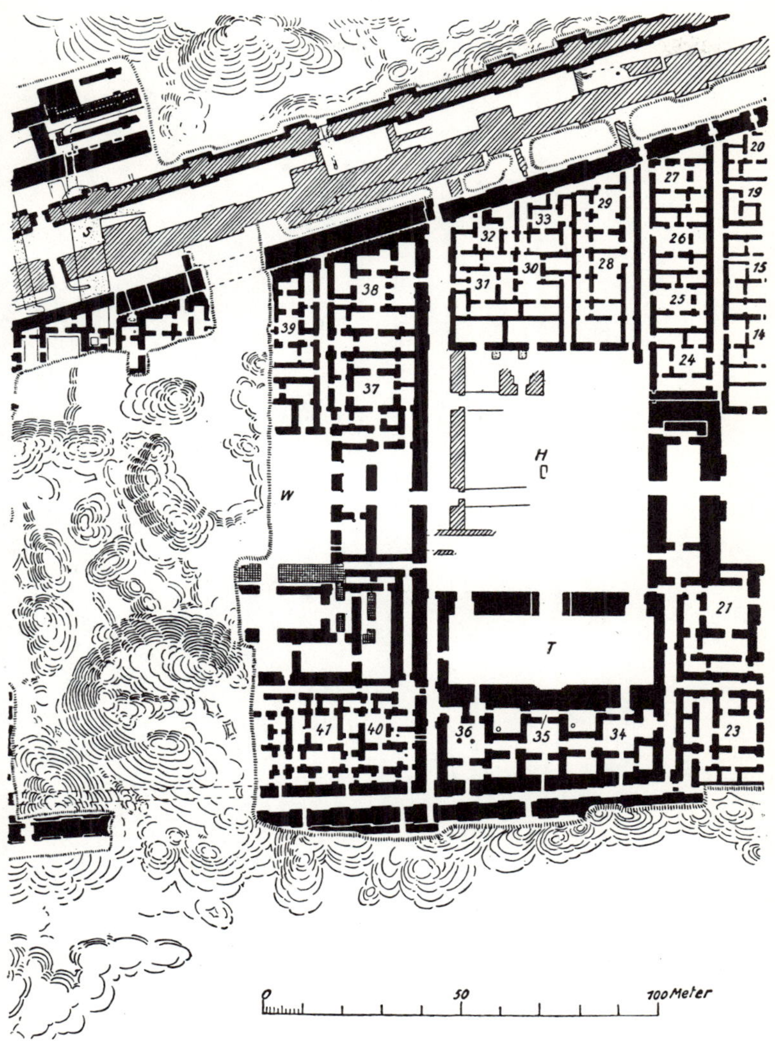

THE CENTRAL PART OF THE SOUTHERN CITADEL: THE THRONE ROOM OF THE NEO-BABYLONIAN KINGS IS MARKED *T*

(KOLDEWEY, FIG. 63)

All this he certainly knew, and Daniel taxes him with it. Besides, his very words to Daniel, if they betray a lack of personal acquaintance with the seer, show at the same time that he knew quite well who Daniel was: "Art thou[a] Daniel, which art of the children of the captivity of Judah, whom the king my father brought out of Judah?"[1] We cannot, therefore, shut our eyes to the sacrilegious conduct of Belshazzar, who, according to the chronological scheme suggested at the beginning of Chapter XI., would now be about thirty-six years old. It was one thing for a young king like Nebuchadnezzar, who at that time was ignorant of the might of Jehovah, to take in victorious war the vessels of His temple and place them in the temple of his own god at Babylon; it was another thing for a king, who had come to maturity, and who was cognisant of certain mighty acts wrought by the God of the Jews, to have those vessels fetched, and in a spirit of derision to praise the idol gods of Babylon while he drank wine out of them. Such an act, even for a polytheist, was one of daring sacrilege, and—as "conscience makes cowards of us all"—so the moment that mysterious hand was seen writing on the plaister of the wall, the king's conscience awoke, and he became a prey to the most abject terrors.

> "The monarch saw and shook,
> And bade no more rejoice:
> All bloodless waxed his look,
> And tremulous his voice:
> 'Let the men of lore appear,
> The wisest of the earth,
> And expound these words of fear,
> Which mar our royal mirth.'"

In his terror and alarm Belshazzar offers all that he has to offer to any of his wise men who shall interpret those mystic words. The third place in the kingdom shall be his, and along with it the insignia of royalty, the gold chain and the purple robe; those very insignia which Cambyses sent to the king of the Ethiopians, and concerning which Ashurbanipal says, when speaking of Necho I. of Egypt, "In clothing of *birmi* I clothed him, and a chain of gold as insignia of his royalty I made for him."[2]

At first the king's splendid offers are unavailing; but at the suggestion of the queen-mother, Daniel, the Jewish seer, who had shown such singular wisdom and insight in the days of Nebuchadnezzar, some thirty years ago and just a year before his madness,

[1] Dan. v. 13.

[a] should read, Art thou that David

[2] Cf. Herod. iii. 20, and the Rassam-cylinder of Ashurbanipal, col. ii. lines 10 and 11.

and who had been publicly honoured by that monarch in a most special manner in the early part of his reign, is brought into the banqueting-hall, and to him Belshazzar makes the same offer in words, which, as said above, show some knowledge of Daniel's origin and of his wonderful career, but no personal acquaintance. The aged statesman, now grown grey in the service of his adopted country, refuses to receive from Belshazzar those "rewards," which he was content to accept from Nebuchadnezzar. Sternly, and yet respectfully, he charges his royal master, in whose service he was still employed,[1] with sinning against light and knowledge, insisting on his perfect acquaintance with what had happened some thirty years before to Nebuchadnezzar his "father" at the hands of the Most High God: "Thou his son, O Belshazzar, hast not humbled thine heart, though thou knewest all this; but hast lifted up thyself against the Lord of heaven; and they have brought the vessels of his house before thee, and thou and thy lords, thy wives and thy concubines, have drunk wine in them: and thou hast praised the gods of silver, and gold, of brass, iron, wood, and stone, which see not, nor hear, nor know: and the God in whose hand thy breath is, and whose are all thy ways, hast thou not glorified."[2] No sooner has the prophet finished his stern accusation than the hand vanishes, and those four mystic words are seen inscribed on the palace wall, which in our Hebrew Bibles we find printed thus-

מְנֵא מְנֵא תְּקֵל וּפַרְסִין

They were written, as I hope to show, not in Babylonian, but in Aramaic—*i.e.* in the same language as this part of the Book of Daniel—and the characters employed were not the syllabic characters used in the Babylonian cuneiform, but those ancient alphabetic characters which we find in the oldest Hebrew and Aramaic inscriptions;[3] and from which are derived both the modern Hebrew characters and our own capital letters. The vowel points put to them in our Hebrew Bibles are very properly made to agree with Daniel's interpretation of the words. But we must remember that vowel points are a comparatively modern invention, and that as the characters stood on the palace wall they were without any such points, and were thus capable of being read in different ways. To show how they appeared on the wall, it will be best for me to write them in our own capitals, which, as

[1] Dan. viii. 1, 27.

[2] *Ibid.* v. 22, 23.

[3] Such as the Moabite Stone, the Siloam Inscription, and the Aramaic inscriptions from Zenjerli.

just stated, are the modern representatives of the ancient Aramaic characters. When so written they stand thus—the reading being from right to left-

NISRPU LQT ANM ANM

To suit our own mode of reading we must reverse them as follows :

MNA MNA TQL UPRSIN

Here the A, I, and U must not be looked upon as vowels, but as answering respectively to the letters Aleph, Yod, and Vau in the ancient Hebrew and Aramaic alphabet : the first, a soft breathing ; the second, possessing the consonantal value of the letter " y," but frequently used to represent the long " ē " ;[1] the third, with the consonantal value " v," but, like the Yod, sometimes used as a vowel, when it represents the long " ū." The Q represents the letter Koph, from which it is sprung, and like Koph must be credited with the consonantal value of the letter " k."

To the king and his lords these four words would appear as the Aramaic names of three weights, or, as we should say, three coins —weights taking the place of coins before the invention of coinage —the last of the three having appended to it the plural ending IN=*ēn*, and would therefore be read by them as follows :

Mĕnā mĕnā tĕqāl upharsēn [2]

i.e. " a mina, a mina, a shekel, and half-minas."

Inasmuch as Aramaic was the *lingua franҫa* of Western Asia and was much used in the world of commerce, Babylonian contracts were often stamped with Aramaic dockets, and weights, more especially, were inscribed with their value written in Aramaic characters, sometimes along with the cuneiform equivalents. On the lion-weights brought from Nimrud we often meet with the Aramaic MNA, " a mina." Also a lion-weight of the time of Sennacherib has been found marked in Aramaic PRS, *i.e. pĕrĕs,* of which *parsēn* would be the plural. This weight gives us the value of the *pĕrĕs,* for it bears the following Assyrian inscription written in cuneiform characters : *Mat Sin-akhi-irba shar (mat) Ashur* ½ *mana, i.e.* " the country of Sennacherib king of Assyria ½ mina." The *pĕrĕs* is also mentioned in an Aramaic inscription found at Zenjerli near the Syrian Antioch, written in the eighth century

[1] The values given to the vowels in *this* chapter are those found in *Mason and Bernard's Hebrew Grammar.*

[2] It should be stated for the benefit of the English reader that in Hebrew and Aramaic the " p " sometimes has the value of " ph," as in *upharsēn.*

B.C. by Panammu king of Samahla. In this inscription Panammu tells of a time of sore famine, when a *pĕrĕs* or half-mina, in value thirty shekels, "stood at a shekel," *i.e.* would only buy a shekel's worth of food. *Tĕqāl* is the Aramaic for the Hebrew *shĕqĕl*, "a shekel," the sixtieth part of a mina. See Ezek. xlv. 12.

A Babylonian, then, though he might not be so much at home in the Aramaic as in his native tongue, would yet certainly be as familiar with the appearance and meaning of the Aramaic words denoting weights, *i.e.* coins, written not in the Babylonian cuneiform but in alphabetic characters, as the Englishman who knows nothing of Latin is with the abbreviated Latin signs £ *s. d.* Further, we must not lose sight of the fact that the Neo-Babylonian kings—as we have seen in the case of Belshazzar himself—engaged as freely in commercial transactions as the humblest of their subjects.[1] At Babylon buying and selling and getting gain seem to have been in the very atmosphere of the place. This characteristic of the golden city appears to have continued long after her supremacy had passed away and to have furnished much of the imagery of St. John in Rev. xvii.[2] There can, therefore, be little doubt that Belshazzar read the four mystic words in the sense given above. But if he so read them, what cause was there for his extreme terror? Much, for various reasons. First, the sight of the supernatural is always alarming. Then, that human hand moving slowly along as it traced the words was suggestive of the presence in that hall of drunkenness and riot of an unseen Being silently registering some divine decree. For it was a belief among the Babylonians that the decrees of the gods were written on the tablets of fate up in heaven. Thus Nebuchadnezzar prays to Nebo, "O triumphant one . . . upon thine unerring tablet, which establishes the whole round of heaven and earth, decree me length of days." [3] The same idea in its lofty symbolic sense is embodied in the words spoken to Daniel by the Man clothed in linen: "I will tell thee that which is inscribed in the writing of truth." [4] This expression, "the writing of truth," is an exact parallel to the "unerring tablet," and denotes that which cannot fail of fulfilment but will most truly and certainly come to pass. In the Babylonian mythology the tablets of fate or destiny belonged to

[1] See the Appendix to this chapter.

[2] It is remarkable how little is said about this characteristic in the Old Testament. The Hebrew prophets seem to have been more impressed with the gross idolatries of Babylon than with her commercial proclivities.

[3] Langdon's *Inscriptions*, No. 11, col. ii. 17, 23–25.

[4] Dan. x. 21.

Merodach as the En-lil or supreme god, but they were in the keeping of Nebo, Merodach's vicegerent in these matters, who is styled, "the bearer of the fate-tablets of the gods, who regulates the totality of heaven and earth, holds the tablet, grasps the stylus, prolongs the days," [1] viz. of a man's life. Hence, Ashurbanipal says to Nebo, "My life is written before thee"; while, for the man who respects his inscription, Shamash-shum-ukin prays, "the days of his life may Nebo, the tablet-bearer of Esagila, inscribe for longer duration." On the other hand, a curse is often expressed in the prayer that Nebo may shorten the days of such and such a person.[2] Bearing, then, in mind Daniel's last words, "the God in whose hand thy breath is, and whose are all thy ways, hast thou not glorified," I am inclined to think that when the seer had ended his address, the king must have much more than half suspected the truth, and that he already regarded the mysterious writing as a transcript of what was actually recorded on the tablets of fate as to the duration of his life and kingdom; and all the more so, since, as Zimmern points out,[3] in the Babylonian way of looking at things, the idea plays a great part that the fate of men, and more especially that of kings, is fixed from of old. That the mysterious inscription meant, in any case, something different from what it appeared to mean, was indicated by the strange order in which the weights or coins were arranged; the shekel, which was only the sixtieth part of the mina, being dropped in between the mina and the *pĕrĕs* or half-mina, in much the same way as if the pence were seen placed between the pounds and shillings. Thus, in those mysterious words, arranged in so strange an order, and traced by the hand that "grasps the stylus," Belshazzar would not be slow to see some solemn message for himself. If he could only get at their meaning, he would know what that message was. It is in this sense that we may understand the words, "Whosoever shall read this writing and show me the interpretation thereof." [4] It is as if he said, "Whosoever can make any intelligible sense out of those words." This the wise men of Babylon were unable to do. But when Daniel was called in, he first delivered his solemn heart-searching address to the guilty king, and then taking the disappearing of the hand as a signal that the time was come to disclose the divine message, proceeded forthwith to unfold the

[1] Rawlinson's *Inscriptions of Western Asia*, vol. v. p. 52.

[2] Cf. *Die Keilinschriften und das Alte Testament*, edited by E. Schrader, p. 401.

[3] *Ibid.* p. 403.

[4] Dan. v. 7.

meaning of the four mystic words. He treated them, not as substantives, but as the past participles of three Aramaic verbs,[1] which have their very similar equivalents in Babylonian ;[2] and thus interpreted them as he went along : "MNA," pronounced *mĕnā*, "God hath numbered thy kingdom and brought it to an end" ; "TQL," pronounced *tĕqāl*, "thou art weighed in the balances, and art found wanting" ; till at last, coming to the final word, he gave it in its singular form, PRS, and treating it also as a past participle, accounted for its plural form, PRSIN, by declaring that it carried with it a further reference to the Persians, who, along with the Medes, were besieging the city at that time : "PRS," pronounced *pĕrās*, "thy kingdom is divided, and given to the Medes and Persians." The message, then, as read by Daniel, may be written thus-

NUMBERED NUMBERED WEIGHED AND DIVIDED

The repetition of the first word marks the certainty of the coming judgment, and is, as it were, the solemn death-knell of the Babylonian king ; the third word gives the reason of it ; and the last word, which because of its double meaning it is impossible to do justice to in an English translation, shows the course which that judgment will take.

What a tragic scene of alarm and confusion that banqueting-hall must have presented after Daniel had thus interpreted the writing, fancy can better paint than words describe. The king, indeed, so far recovers his presence of mind and self-respect as to order the promised rewards to be bestowed on Daniel, just as in Xenophon's description of the final scene he is pictured as meeting the foe in a standing posture with his sword drawn in his hand.[3] But all is now in vain ; nothing can avert the coming judgment. Unavailing is his bestowal of the rewards promised ; equally unavailing any resistance he may attempt to offer. Indeed, scarcely any opportunity is granted him for resistance. He is at once overpowered and done to death. So swiftly and irresistibly is the divine decree carried into effect, as signified by that one short sentence which concludes the tragic story : "In that night Belshazzar the Chaldean king was slain."

[1] The words are thus understood by the LXX. Cf. Dan. v. 7, 8, as given in that version.

[2] The equivalent Babylonian verbs are *manū*, *shaqālu*, and *parāsu* respectively. In the case of the second the Babylonian *sh* answers to the Aramaic *t*. The *u* before PRSIN—pronounced *parsēn*—is the conjunction "and."

[3] *Cyropædia*, book vii. chap. v. 29.

Appendix

On the commercial proclivities of the Neo-Babylonian kings

Dr. Pinches gives several examples of the commercial transactions indulged in by the kings and princes of the New Babylonian Empire.[1] Nergalsharezer, the son-in-law of Nebuchadnezzar, who presently succeeded his son Evil-Merodach on the throne, appears to have been a thorough man of business, freely engaging in trade thereby to increase his wealth. Labashi-Marduk, the young son and successor of Nergalsharezer, was not ashamed, as shown by the tablets, to engage in the business of a money-lender. Whilst with regard to Belshazzar himself the following extract from a tablet dated the eleventh year of Nabonidus exhibits him as a dealer in "clothes" or possibly "woollen stuffs":

"20 mana of silver, the price of the garments [which were] the property of Bel-sharra-utsur, the son of the king, which [are due] through Nabu-tsabit-qata, the chief of the house of Bel-sharra-utsur, the son of the king, and the secretaries of the son of the king, from Iddina-Marduk, son of Ikishâ, descendant of Nur-Sin. In the month Adar of the 1[1th] year, the silver, 20 mana, he shall pay. His house, which is beside the [plantation ?], his slave, and his property in town and country, all there is, is the security of Bel-sharra-utsur, the son of the king, until Bel-sharra-utsur receives his money. [For] the silver as much as [from the sum] is withheld, interest he shall pay.

"Witnesses: Bel-iddina, son of Remut," etc.

[1] See Pinches' *Old Testament*, 1st ed. pp. 430–451.

14

Darius the Mede, Independent or Not?

WE have now come to the great historical crux in the Book of Daniel. The great prophetical crux, as we have seen, occurs in chap. xi. of that Book, where an original prophecy of Daniel appears to have been overlaid and obscured by a Jewish targum of the age of Antiochus Epiphanes. The great historical crux meets us at the close of chap. v. in that brief statement, "*Darius the Mede received the kingdom, being about threescore and two years old.*" It admits, however, of a happier solution than the prophetical, thanks to the ever-increasing light which has come to us of late years from Babylonian sources. Indeed, our main difficulty now is, not so much to discover the Median Darius, as to decide which of two individuals has the stronger claim to represent that monarch.

Before we enter into this discussion, we must first endeavour to ascertain the position held by the Darius of the Book of Daniel. *Was he, or was he not, an independent sovereign?* The critics, in their anxiety to prove that the author of this Book interposes a Median empire between the Babylonian and the Persian—thus betraying his ignorance of the facts of history—look upon Darius the Mede as an independent monarch. They tell us that the words of Dan. v. 31, " Darius the Mede received the kingdom," mean that he received it from God, and in proof of their assertion point us back to verse 28, " Thy kingdom is divided, and given to the Medes and Persians." There is, however, a great difference between these two verses. Verse 28 is a prophetic statement as to the meaning of one of the four mystic words which make up a divine message. Verse 31 is an historical statement. In verse 28 it is understood without the shadow of a doubt that He who sends the message is Himself the Agent by whom it will be accomplished. But verse 31 is by no means so plain; and we might hang in doubt as to its meaning, were it not for a later passage which comes to our help. In Dan. ix. 1 we read, " In the first year of Darius the son of Ahasuerus, of the seed of the Medes, which *was made king* over the realm of the Chaldeans." Here is a chronological statement as to the date of one of Daniel's visions. It was seen, we are told, in the first year of the Median Darius, who " was *made king* over the realm of the Chaldeans." Made king by God ? What a needless statement ! All kings are made kings by God. But if we take the words to mean *made king by man,* then at once they become intelligible ; for they tell us that the date is reckoned, not according to the years of an independent sovereign, such, for instance, as the later Darius, but of a sub-king set over the realm of the Chaldeans, a Babylonian as distinguished from an imperial ruler. The Darius of Dan. v. is, then, a sub-king, and not an independent monarch as the critics would have us believe. But if this be so, the imaginary Median empire, which they think they see in this Book, and by which they interpret the vision of the four kingdoms in chap. ii., making Media out to be the second kingdom, is shown to be a mere fiction of their own creation.

The position held by the Median Darius being thus settled, our next object must be to identify this monarch. Where historical data are wanting, various identifications will naturally be put forward. Thus Darius the Mede has been identified with Nabonidus, with Astyages, with Cyaxares II., with Darius Hystaspes, with Gobryas, and finally with Cambyses the son of Cyrus. Before the decipherment by Pinches of the contemporary Babylonian records the first four may be said to have occupied the field. The claim of Nabonidus was advocated on the ground that he was the last king of Babylon before Cyrus, and must be looked upon as that Mede through whose treachery, or possibly incapacity, Cyrus, according to the supposed prophecy of Nebuchadnezzar quoted by Megasthenes,[1] was able to make himself master of Babylon. The claim of Astyages king of the Medes was made to rest, first on the conciliatory disposition manifested by Cyrus toward conquered kings, and then on the fact that Cyrus was related to the Median king either by descent or by marriage, and lastly on the argument that it would be sound policy on the part of Cyrus to gratify his Median subjects by making a descendant of Cyaxares viceroy of Babylon. The argument in favour of Cyaxares II., the son of Astyages, was based in part on the *Cyropædia* of Xenophon, who makes this monarch the king under whom Babylon was taken and goes on to relate that he gave his daughter in marriage to Cyrus with Media

[1] See Chapter X, above.

as her dowry.[1] It was also thought to be borne out by some lines in the *Persæ* of Æschylus,[2] and to be well-nigh established by the statement of Josephus in his *Antiquities*, x. 11, 4, " When Babylon was taken by Darius, and when he, with his kinsman Cyrus, had put an end to the dominion of the Babylonians, he was sixty-two years of age. He was the son of Astyages, and had another name among the Greeks." To the Higher Critics, Darius the Mede appears as a reflection into the past of Darius Hystaspes. They point out that Babylon was twice taken by Darius Hystaspes, also that it was under him that the Persian empire was first divided into satrapies, of which they see a backward reflection in the course of action pursued by Darius the Mede, as described in Dan. vi. 1.

However, for those who seek to interpret the historical portion of the Book of Daniel in the light of the contemporary inscriptions, the above identifications, though interesting to look back upon as the efforts of scholars, whether in a former and less privileged age, or in our own more enlightened times, may all very well be relegated to the limbo of the past. For if we follow the guidance of the Annalistic Tablet—so often referred to already—and the irrefutable evidence of the contract tablets, there are two persons, and only two, who can henceforth be looked upon as forming the original of the Darius of the Book of Daniel. According to the cuneiform records the choice must lie between Gobryas, Cyrus' governor in Babylon, and Cambyses the son of Cyrus. The claims of both these individuals to what we may call the vacant throne are very strong. According to the Annalistic Tablet, the general who led the troops of Cyrus into Babylon, and who—as borne out by the *Cyropædia* of Xenophon—conducted the attack on the palace, was Gobryas. It was the men with Gadatas and Gobryas who, according to that historian, overpowered the Babylonian king,[3] against whom both those generals had a special grudge.[4] Above all, according to the contemporary cuneiform record, Gobryas, in the early days after the capture of Babylon, was appointed Cyrus' governor in that city. In the words of the tablet, as translated by Pinches, " Cyrus promised peace to

[1] The identification of Darius the Mede with Cyaxares II. has been very ably worked out by Craig Robinson in *What about the Old Testament?* chap. xii., but it is not borne out by the cuneiform inscriptions.

[2] Cf. the *Persæ*, lines 771-774-

> *Μῆδος γὰρ ἦν ὁ πρῶτος ἡγεμὼν στρατοῦ·*
> *ἄλλος δ' ἐκείνου παῖς τοδ' ἔργον ἤνυσε,*
> *φρένες γὰρ αὐτοῦ θυμὸν οἰακοστρόφουν·*
> *τρίτος δ' ἀπ' αὐτοῦ Κῦρος, κ.τ.λ.*

[3] *Cyropædia*, book vii. chap. v. 30.

[4] *Ibid.* book iv. chap. vi. 4, and book v. chap. ii. 28.

Babylon, all of it. Gubaru [Gobryas] his governor appointed governors in Babylon." That the power of Gobryas was very considerable is further established by a contract tablet dated the fourth year of Cambyses, *i.e.* thirteen years after the capture of Babylon by Cyrus, on which a man undertakes to deliver a certain amount of early fruit at the king's palace: "If he does not bring it," adds the contract, "he will commit a sin against Gobryas the governor of Babylon." On these words Pinches well remarks that a failure to keep the contract will be a sin against Gobryas the governor, not against Cambyses.[1] This shows to what an extent Gobryas was entrusted with power, even though he may not have been governor of the city all through those thirteen intervening years. Another point in favour of Gobryas' claim to be the original of Darius the Mede, lies in the fact that Gutium, the country of which he was already the governor when he came over to the side of Cyrus,[2] formed a part of Media. Thus he may very well have been a Mede, or have been looked on as representing the Medes. That Cyrus should appoint a Mede as governor of Babylon is nothing remarkable; he was anxious to favour the Medes, who had revolted from Astyages and put themselves under his sway,[3] thus enabling him to go forward in his career of conquest. Indeed, the Medes were looked upon by the Persians as brothers, not as a conquered nation, so that under the Persian kings Medes were often advanced to high posts. As for the name "Darius," I shall hope to show that it was an appellative, a title of honour rather than a proper name. Gobryas may thus very well have been styled "Darius the Mede," while the age of threescore and two years, or thereabouts, agrees admirably with what we glean from the pages of Xenophon. That historian describes Gobryas as an old man when he came over to the side of Cyrus, and yet credits him with having sufficient energy to join Gadatas in leading the attack on the palace. Still, in spite of all these favourable points, I am inclined to give the precedence to Cambyses the son of Cyrus; and that, mainly on two grounds: first, Gobryas, unlike Darius the Mede, is never called a king, or described as having royal power, he is only a "governor";[4] secondly, Gobryas was not the successor of Belshazzar on the throne of Babylon. In both these respects Cambyses has incomparably the stronger claim, since it can be shown that for some nine months in the first year of Cyrus after the capture of

[1] *Expository Times*, April, 1915, p. 298.
[2] Annalistic Tablet, Rev. i. 15.
[3] *Ibid.* Obv. col. ii. 2, "The army of Istuvegu (Astyages) revolted against him, and laid hands on him: to Cyrus they delivered him."
[4] *Ibid.* Rev. col. i. 20.

Babylon, Cambyses occupied the same position in relation to his father Cyrus, both in the empire and on the throne of Babylon, which Belshazzar had held under his father Nabonidus; and also that Cambyses was appointed by his father Cyrus as the successor of Belshazzar. And this is what I understand the writer of the Book of Daniel to mean, when, after describing the circumstances of Belshazzar's death, he adds, "and Darius the Mede received the kingdom," *i.e. Darius received what had been Belshazzar's.*

The last tablet of the reign of Nabonidus, as we have seen, is dated the 10th of Marchesvan (October–November). For the remaining four or five months of that year, a period described in Babylonian fashion as "the accession year" of Cyrus, that monarch was king both of Babylon and of the empire. The earliest tablet of Cyrus is dated the 24th of Marchesvan (October–November) in his "accession year," and he is styled on it, "King of the Countries." In a tablet dated the 7th day of the following month, the month Chisleu (November–December), the style, though partly obliterated, reads thus-

"Cyrus king of . . .
. . . of Babylon." [1]

From which it seems probable that in the remaining months of his "accession year," after the capture of Babylon, Cyrus himself was styled "King of Babylon." This is rendered certain by tablet No. 1 in Strassmaier's *Cyrus*, in which though the day is wiped out and the month partly obliterated, yet the closing words stand out clear-

"accession year of
Cyrus king of Babylon and of the Countries."

Nevertheless, in spite of this, it can be shown that it was the intention of Cyrus that his son Cambyses should succeed Belshazzar on the throne of Babylon. The proof of this is as follows: The Annalistic Tablet, after describing the death of "the king's son" in the attack made on the palace by Gobryas on the night of the 11th of Marchesvan, goes on to describe the public mourning for him, which was held some three or four months later at the close of the year. The record reads thus: "From the 27th day of Adar [February–March] to the 3rd day of Nisan [March–April] a lamentation was made in the country of Akkad"—northern Babylonia, where Belshazzar had been in command of the army. "All the people smote their heads. On the 4th day Cambyses the son of Cyrus went into 'the Temple where the Sceptre of

[1] Cf. Strassmaier's *Inschriften von Cyrus König von Babylon*, No. 3.

the World is given.' The official of 'the Temple of the Sceptre of Nebo' *brought a message in his hand*" . . . Here the inscription becomes illegible, but enough has been told us to make it quite easy to guess what the purport of that message was. The public mourning for Belshazzar was doubtless a great occasion. It lasted just a week; the same period as the "grievous mourning" of the Egyptians over Jacob at the threshing-floor of Atad. It could only have been held with the consent and full approval of Cyrus. But we may go even further and say that it was probably initiated by Cyrus himself, either of his own accord or at the instigation of his advisers. The week of mourning began near the close of the Old Year, and ran on into the first three days of the New Year. At the New Year Babylon was probably full of people, who had come to keep the great New Year festival. This festival lasted certainly over the first eleven days of the month Nisan,[1] how much longer we cannot say. Cyrus, anxious doubtless to conciliate the Babylonians, and knowing that nothing was so likely to effect this as giving them a king of their own to succeed the dead Belshazzar, designed to place his young son Cambyses on the throne, and to give him the title, "King of Babylon," which had probably been given to Belshazzar. For this purpose he waited till near the close of the year to show all due respect to the dead monarch. Then, as soon as the week of public mourning was over, and when the vast throng of people were duly impressed with the kindness of the conqueror, on the very next day he sent his son Cambyses to the temple of Nebo, a temple which bears this significant name, "The Temple where the Sceptre of the World is given." Into this temple kings entered at the beginning of their reign. Thus Nabonidus says on his famous stele, "Into 'the Temple where the Sceptre of the World is given,' into the presence of Nebo, the prolonger of my reign, I entered. A righteous sceptre, a legitimate rod of authority enlarging the land, he entrusted to my hands."[2] Cambyses, by entering this temple immediately after the obsequies of Belshazzar were over, showed that he was about to succeed that monarch. And the message brought him by the temple official was no doubt looked upon as a message from the god confirming his claim. For in this predicament we may well believe that the Babylonian priesthood were as subservient to the monarch's will as the Parliament of Henry VIII. at the period of the Reformation. We must remember also that many of them were grievously incensed with Nabonidus for bringing the gods of the other cities into Babylon, and now that

[1] India House Inscription, col. ii. 57.

[2] Stele of Nabonidus, col. vii.

that king was a captive in the hands of his foes, and his son slain, were probably not unwilling to bar his possible return to the throne as a sub-king under Cyrus by welcoming the accession of the son of Cyrus. After the ceremony of Cambyses' visit to the temple of Nebo, it would appear to the people of Babylon that as Cyrus had taken the place of Nabonidus on the throne of empire, so his son Cambyses had taken the place of Belshazzar the son of Nabonidus on the throne of Babylon.

The above inference, so likely in itself, is abundantly confirmed by the evidence of the contract tablets. On the 4th of Nisan—the very day on which Cambyses went to the temple of Nebo—Cyrus is styled on the tablets "King of Babylon" for the last time for some nine months. Not till we come to the tablet dated 1.10.0, *i.e.* 1st year, 10th month, day uncertain, does he again bear that title. Further, the collections of Strassmaier and Peiser furnish us with no fewer than ten tablets during that interval on which Cambyses is styled "King of Babylon" and his father Cyrus "King of Countries." These tablets are dated as follows:

No.	Y. M. D.	Style
35	1 2 5	"Cambyses King of Babylon, Cyrus King of Countries."
36	1 2 9	"Cambyses King of Babylon, Cyrus King of Countries."
16	1 3 10	"Cyrus King of Countries, Cambyses King of Babylon."
42	1 4 7	"Cambyses King of Babylon, Cyrus King of Countries."
46	1 4 25	"Cambyses King of Babylon when Cyrus was King of Countries."
24	1 5 21	"Cambyses King of Babylon, Cyrus his father King of Countries."
72	1 8 9	"Cambyses King of Babylon, son of Cyrus King of Countries."
81	1 9 25	"Cambyses King of Babylon, when his father Cyrus was King of Countries."
426	0 9 25	"Cyrus King of Countries and Cambyses King of Babylon." [1]
98	1 0 8	"Cambyses King of Babylon, son of Cyrus King of Countries."

The mention of their two royal names on the above ten tablets of the first year of Cyrus, belonging to six different months, is a sure proof that he and his son Cambyses were reigning together

[1] The numbers in the first column refer to Strassmaier's *Cambyses* except in the case of the tablet dated 1.3.10, which is found in Strassmaier's *Cyrus*. The second column gives the year, month, and day. The tablet dated 1.5.21 is from Peiser's collection. Where a cipher stands the number is uncertain.

during the first nine months of that year, the former as " King of Countries," the latter as " King of Babylon." In three instances, viz. on the tablets dated 1.4.25, 1.9.25, and 0.9.25, this is expressly stated. The placing the name of Cambyses in eight cases before that of Cyrus is due to the fact that the contracts were drawn up at Babylon or at any rate in Babylonia. The only question that we have to determine is whether these tablets belong to the beginning or to the end of Cyrus' reign. The answer would seem to lie in the certainty that a paramount king like Cyrus would never allow a fresh era to commence during his reign. Thus, had Cambyses begun to reign as king of Babylon at the beginning, say, of Cyrus' seventh year, *that* year would never be allowed to be called the first year of their joint reign. It could only be called the seventh year of Cyrus king of the Countries, and the first year of Cambyses king of Babylon. However, by seating his son Cambyses on the throne of Babylon at the New Year, 538 B.C. —the year after the capture of Babylon—Cyrus brought it about that he and his son both had the same first year, as witnessed by the above tablets. The evidence of the contract tablets is thus seen to confirm in an admirable way the inference already almost forced upon us by the Annalistic Tablet, viz. that Cambyses went into the Temple of Nebo to have his title confirmed as " *King of Babylon*." Further, we learn from the same source that this reign of Cambyses as king of Babylon, which covered the first nine months of the year 538 B.C., terminated before the tenth month was over, for in a tablet dated 1.10.0 Cambyses is not mentioned, and the title " King of Babylon " is given to Cyrus. There are, however, in Strassmaier's *Cyrus* three tablets on which Cyrus is called " King of Babylon," which have been wrongly dated, so that they appear to fall into the nine months' interval, during which that title, as we have seen, was held by his son Cambyses. The first of the three tablets is No. 13, dated Cyrus (?) 1.1.10. This tablet is much obliterated. The name " Cyrus " is uncertain, as indicated by Strassmaier. Equally uncertain is the title " King of Babylon." Still more important is No. 18, the tablet alluded to above as 1.10.0, but which Strassmaier, by a slip, dates as 1.5.30. This tablet reads thus–

> " 576 sheep from the month Tebet,
> the 1st year of Cyrus king of Babylon,
> to the 30th day of the month Ab," etc.[1]

[1] The year begins with Nisan (March–April). Tebet answers to December–January. The 30th of Ab (July–August) would fall in the *second* year of Cyrus.

The inscription on this tablet shows that Cyrus was "King of Babylon" in Tebet, the tenth month of his first year. As no special day of the month is mentioned, the tablet should be dated 1.10.0, or possibly 1.10.1, if, as seems likely, the words "from the month Tebet" mean that the contract was entered into on the first day of that month. The learned editor, misled by the mention in the third line of the 30th day of Ab, the fifth month, has mis-dated the tablet 1.5.30. The third instance of misdating is No. 19, which Strassmaier registers as 1.7.16. On this tablet it will be found that the number of the year is uncertain. It is indicated by a single perpendicular wedge at the end of the fifth line, placed after the character for "year." This single wedge has led Strassmaier to register the tablet as belonging to the first year of Cyrus. But when we look closer, we notice that the character used as a determinative after numerals, and which ought, therefore, to follow this wedge, is wanting, *i.e.* the line is incomplete, and has been partially obliterated. Hence *the number of the year itself may be incomplete.* There may just as well have been two or three perpendicular wedges before the vanished determinative as one, *i.e. the tablet may quite as possibly belong to the second or third year of Cyrus as to the first.* It cannot, however, belong to a later year than the third, since this would require a different arrangement of the wedges. The year being thus uncertain, this tablet ought to be dated, not 1.7.16, but 0.7.16. The result, then, of our close investigation is that Cambyses was king of Babylon for the first nine months of the first year of Cyrus, or, to be more exact, from the 4th day of Nisan to at least the 25th day of the ninth month, Chisleu. In the next month, Tebet, Cyrus had taken back the title, and apparently removed Cambyses from his post. In perfect accordance with this result is the fact that in the Book of Daniel *we find only the first year of Darius the Mede mentioned.*

The tablets at which we have been looking are of interest as forming the only instances in which two royal names appear. This, as stated in a previous chapter, was rendered possible by both Cyrus and Cambyses beginning the first year of their reigns at the same New Year. Interesting, too, is the title which Cyrus chose for himself, as contrasted with that which he allowed his son to bear. The title "King of Babylon," which had contented the Neo-Babylonian kings, in whose eyes Babylon was the centre of the universe, would bear a very different meaning in the eyes of the newly-risen king of Persia, whose conquests stretched far and wide, and covered a far more extensive territory than the empire of Babylon. To him such a title would seem far too confined to describe his vast empire. Accordingly, even in his "accession year," we find Cyrus styling himself on the tablets, "King of Countries," occasionally along with the older title, "King of Babylon." The significance of this new title is well brought out in a tablet of the first year of Cyrus, which reads thus: "Cyrus king of the Countries, king of all their kingdoms."[1] Compare Ezra i. 2: "Thus saith Cyrus king of Persia, All the kingdoms of the earth hath the LORD, the God of heaven, given me."

The title "King of Babylon," which Cyrus bestowed on his son Cambyses, must not be looked upon as a mere title. A kingdom went with it, albeit a sub-kingdom. This we gather from Daniel's interpretation of the word PERES, "thy kingdom is divided and given to the Medes and Persians." If PERES had only meant "divided" in the sense of "broken to pieces," or "broken away from thee," then the prophet would not have mentioned the Medes, for the play being on the word "Persians" there was no need whatever to mention the Medes, but rather the reverse. But since the Medes are thus expressly mentioned as well as the Persians, we see that PERES has here its primary meaning, "divided into two parts," and that the sense is, "thy kingdom will be divided between the two brother-nations, the Medes and the Persians." Thus the prophet's word of interpretation and the two royal names and titles on the contract tablets reflect a mutual light on each other. The Babylonian empire must have been divided by Cyrus into two parts. One part would be added to the countries which already owned his sway, and the other given as a sub-kingdom to his son Cambyses, the "Darius the Mede" of the Book of Daniel. In acting thus the Persian monarch was attempting afresh what had been vainly attempted before by Assyrian kings. Thus Sennacherib had appointed his son Ashur-nadin-shumu king of Babylon in subordination to himself; an arrangement which only lasted six years, when his son was carried captive to Elam. Still more disastrous was the attempt of Esarhaddon, when he appointed his younger son, Shamash-shum-ukin, as king of Babylon under the suzerainty of his older brother Ashurbanipal, king of Assyria. Ashurbanipal, trying apparently to lord it over his brother, a most dangerous rebellion arose, which was put down with great difficulty and seriously weakened the strength of the Assyrian empire, leading the way to its ultimate downfall. The attempt of Cyrus, if not so disastrous in its issue, was equally doomed to

[1] See *Babylonian Expedition of the University of Pennsylvania*, vol. viii. part i. text 58.

failure. It only lasted, as we have seen, nine months. When it was terminated by the conqueror's strong hand, it must have left the unruly Babylonians in a state of great discontent. To this probably were due the two rebellions which broke out in the early years of Darius Hystaspes.

We are now approaching the most obscure part of our subject: the question as to why Cambyses is called "Darius," and also why he is described as a "Mede." As we have just been studying the significance of the prediction contained in the word PERES, it may be best to take the latter question first. According to the historical note in Dan. ix. 1, the new king of Babylon was "of the seed of the Medes," a Median by descent. In the case of Cambyses this could only have been on his mother's side. Now, Ctesias tells us in his *Persica*[1] that after the defeat of Astyages king of the Medes and the capture of Ecbatana, Cyrus married Amytis the daughter of Astyages, and that Cambyses was the fruit of that marriage. It was, then, as the child of a Median mother that Cambyses received the title "Darius the Mede." Such a title would be likely to gratify the Medes, who had voluntarily come over to the side of Cyrus when he went to attack Astyages;[2] for it not only honoured them, but assured them of some share in the government of the empire. It would also tend to conciliate the Babylonians, for their great Nebuchadnezzar, according to Abydenus, had married another Amytis of the same royal Median line. But it would be especially welcome to captive Judah. For Media, according to Isaiah's prophecy, chap. xxi. 2, had taken the chief part in putting down Assyria[3] some seventy years before, and just lately, in accordance with Jeremiah's prediction, chap. li. 11, 28, had helped to subjugate Babylon; so that the title of the young king of Babylon sounded in Jewish ears like a

[1] See the *Persica*, excerpts 2 and 10. It is only incidentally that Ctesias informs us that Cambyses was the son of Amytis. Of the different stories told us by Greek historians of the connection of Cyrus with the Median royal family that of Herodotus is the most legendary. If, as that historian states, Cyrus was Astyages' heir, his own daughter's son, it was a most unnatural thing for the old king to seek to make away with his grandson. Far more likely is the version of Ctesias. By marrying Amytis, as this writer shows, Cyrus came to be looked upon as the legitimate successor of Astyages, so that when the news of the marriage reached the Bactrians, with whom he was then at war, they at once gave in their allegiance to Amytis and Cyrus. It may be noted that the name Ἀστυΐγας, as written by Ctesias, corresponds more closely with the cuneiform Ishtumvigu than the Ἀστυάγης of Herodotus. Ctesias himself was a prisoner in Persia from 417 to 398 B.C., and was court physician to Artaxerxes II.

[2] Annalistic Tablet, Obv. col. ii. 2.

[3] See my paper in the *Journal of Theological Studies* for July, 1913.

fulfilment of prophecy, which indeed it was, for Persia was but a new friend, while Media had all along been the champion of freedom. Israel, when taken captive, had been distributed among the cities of the conquered Medes.[1] *Now*, the Medes were themselves the conquerors, and were able to avenge on Babylon, the successor of Assyria, the wrongs done of old to God's people. While these considerations, coupled with the fact that Babylon itself was to be put under the rule of a Median prince, fully explain the naming the Medes before the Persians in the interpretation of the word PERES ; it is at the same time impossible for the critics to charge the writer of this Book with any the least ignorance as to the pre-eminence already attained by the Persians at the time of the fall of Babylon. For not only does he inform us that the kingdom of Darius was a sub-kingdom, " received " from another, viz. from " Cyrus the Persian," but already in a vision of a slightly earlier date, viz. the third year of Belshazzar, he has seen the Medo-Persian kingdom exhibited as a ram with two horns. Both horns were high, but the one which came up last was the higher, *i.e.* Media was still a great power, but Persia was seen overtopping her.

It has been shown in what sense Cambyses could be called a Mede, but what are we to say of the name Darius ? Prof. Sayce insists that " the kings of Persia were contented with one name," and that " by that name they were known in all parts of their dominion." He also affirms that " the son and successor of Cyrus is Cambyses in Babylon as well as in Persia and Egypt." [2] It is quite true that in the few monuments of the Old Persian empire which still remain to us, as well as on the contract tablets, Cambyses is always Cambyses. But this is insufficient ground on which to base the statement that the Persian kings had only one name. The testimony of Herodotus and Josephus points the other way. Josephus, speaking of Darius the Mede, says that " *he was the son of Astyages and had another name among the Greeks*." [3] Both of these statements are deserving of notice. The first statement, viz. that Darius the Mede was the son of Astyages, approaches very nearly the statement of Ctesias that Cambyses was the son of the daughter of Astyages. But it is Josephus' second statement with which we are now most concerned, and I shall endeavour to show from the pages of this historian that the other name of Darius the Mede, by which he was known among the Greeks, and which appears for the moment to

[1] 2 Kings xvii. 6.
[2] *Higher Criticism*, p. 543.
[3] *Ant.* x. 11, 4.

have escaped the historian's memory, was the name Cambyses. The proof lies thus: When introducing Artaxerxes I., Josephus makes the following remark: "After the death of Xerxes the kingdom came to be transferred to his son Cyrus, whom the Greeks called Artaxerxes."[1] Here is an incidental proof that the Persian kings sometimes had two names, and it will be observed in this instance that the name Artaxerxes, by which this monarch was known to the Greeks, is the same name that we find alike on the monuments in Old Persian and on the Babylonian contract tablets. Hence it may be argued in the case of "Darius the Mede" that the other name by which he was known among the Greeks must have been the name Cambyses, since that is the name of the king, set up at Babylon by Cyrus after the capture of that city, which appears on the contract tablets; the name, too, of Cyrus' son and successor, as witnessed alike by the tablets and the Old Persian inscription at Behistûn. But Herodotus throws still further light on the matter. According to the father of history the names of some of the Persian kings, *e.g.* Darius, Xerxes, and Artaxerxes, were appellatives rather than proper names, and this is the view of modern authorities on the Old Persian language. According to Herodotus, Darius="Worker," Xerxes="Warrior," Artaxerxes="Great Warrior."[2] These meanings cannot be maintained, since in the Old Persian dress it is seen at once that the names Xerxes and Artaxerxes have no connection whatever.[3] Nevertheless modern scholars on philological grounds have so far endorsed the statement of the old historian as to attach the following meanings to the three names: Darius, "possessing wealth"; Xerxes, "a royal person"; Artaxerxes, "law of the kingdom," or "he whose kingdom is lifted up." If, then, in the case before us, the name Darius be an appellative, the bearer, as stated by Josephus, would have another name, which, as has just been shown, was probably the name Cambyses. Why the Persian kings were called in some instances by appellations of honour as in the case of Cyrus-Artaxerxes, who was known as Artaxerxes, in other instances by their own proper names, as in the case of Cambyses, who appears on the monuments as Cambyses, though styled in the Book of Daniel "Darius the Mede," is a question that cannot be determined.

In Dan. ix. 1 it is said of Darius the Mede that he was the "son," *i.e.* the descendant of Ahasuerus. The critics who take

[1] *Ant.* xi. 6, 1.

[2] Herod. vi. 98.

[3] In Old Persian, Xerxes is *Khshayârsha*; Artaxerxes, *Artakhshatra*; and Darius, *Darayavahush*.

Darius the Mede to be a reflection into the past of Darius Hystaspes see in this statement the confusion of a later age, since Darius Hystaspes was the father of Xerxes, and not his son. The answer is that Dan. ix. 1 speaks of a *Median*, not a Persian Ahasuerus, the tribal distinction between the Medes and Persians being very clearly recognised in this Book, no less than their close political relationship. In the Book of Tobit xiv. 15, the writer of that romance identifies "Assuerus" with the destroyer of Nineveh, *i.e.* with Cyaxares. It has been asserted that his object was to make his book harmonise with the Book of Daniel, in which case the closing verse would form an early comment on Dan. ix. 1.[1] But however that may be, the identification is a likely one for the two following reasons. In the first place, the writer of this Book of Daniel, looking on the Median Darius as a deliverer, would like to note his descent from an earlier deliverer of the Chosen People, viz. the king who had put down Assyria. Secondly, Cyaxares, as witnessed by the Behistûn Inscription, was the pride of the Median monarchy, just as Nebuchadnezzar was of the Babylonian;[2] so that it would be natural to describe a king of the royal Median line as sprung from Cyaxares. It is, however, a mistake to seek to identify the name Cyaxares with the name Ahasuerus. "Cyaxares" is in the Old Persian, *Uvakhshatara*"; whilst "Ahasuerus," Hebrew *Achash-verosh,* appears in Old Persian as *Khshayârsha,* in Greek as Xerxes.

[1] Oesterley in his *Books of the Apocrypha*, p. 365, regards the Book of Tobit as pre-Maccabean, and notes that there is no reference in it to the Maccabean struggle.

[2] In the early years of Darius Hystaspes, as we learn from the Behistûn Inscription, two impostors claimed to be sprung from Cyaxares, just as two had called themselves "Nebuchadnezzar the son of Nabonidus."

15

Darius the Mede, His Identity

IN continuance of our subject I propose in this chapter to consider some further details with respect to "Darius the Mede," which bear on his identification with Cambyses the son of Cyrus; and the first point that naturally presents itself is the age assigned to Darius, viz. "about threescore and two years." In the LXX version—so highly prized by the critics, but which seems, to say the least of it, a very free re-editing of the original, partaking in some passages of the nature of a commentary rather than of a translation—no exact age is assigned to Darius, although he is described as "full of days and honoured in his old age." But our concern must be not with this Greek version, but with the Aramaic original, and I shall endeavour, therefore, to throw some light on the number 62 which at present stands in the text.

According to the Sippara Inscription of Nabonidus, col. i. 26–28, Cyrus defeated Astyages king of the Medes and captured Ecbatana in the third year of the reign of Nabonidus.[1] It is also clear from the contract tablets that Babylon was taken by Cyrus in the seventeenth year of the reign of Nabonidus. If, then, Cyrus married Amytis the daughter of Astyages shortly after the capture of Ecbatana, Cambyses would be quite young when he was appointed by his father to succeed Belshazzar. He might very well be twelve years old. I shall now give some reasons for thinking that 12, and not 62, was the original reading in Dan. v. 31.

It is well known that inaccuracy in numbers is a common thing in the Old Testament, and the reason given is, that numbers were anciently indicated by letters of the alphabet, and that some of these letters being very much alike were often mistaken one for the other: *e.g.* in 2 Kings xxv. 8 we have "*seventh* day," where the parallel in Jer. lii. 12 reads "*tenth* day." In this case Z, the archaic form of the letter Zain which stands for the number 7, has been confounded with Ƶ, the archaic form of the letter Yod,

[1] *Records of the Past,* New Series, vol. v. p. 169.

which stands for 10. We shall find that a very similar mistake has been made with regard to the age of Darius the Mede. First, however, we must inquire whether the letters of the alphabet were used to denote numbers as early as the time of Daniel and the age immediately succeeding. The answer to this question does not admit of absolute certainty, but facts can be brought forward to show the very strong probability that they were so used.

In the first place, in Jer. xxv. 26, and again in li. 41, we find the cipher "Sheshach" used as a kryptogram for the name "Babel," *i.e.* Babylon. *Sh,* the last letter but one of the Hebrew alphabet, is here made to take the place of *b*, the second letter; and similarly *ch*, the twelfth letter counting from the end, is made to take the place of *l*, the twelfth letter counting from the beginning. Thus BaBeL becomes SHeSHaCH.[1] This is suggestive that counting by letters was in vogue in the age of Jeremiah and therefore of Daniel. But stronger is the evidence of the alphabetic psalms, which may almost be regarded as definite instances of such a use, the first letters of the first words of the different verses being made to follow the order of the letters of the alphabet. Thus verse 1 begins with Aleph, verse 2 with Beth, and so on; which is almost the same thing as giving to Aleph the value 1, to Beth the value 2, etc., etc. Another very strong indication that the letters were used as numerals before the age of Daniel lies in the fact that both in the Semitic and Greek alphabets the letters have the same numerical values down to the seventeenth letter, thus showing that the alphabetic system of numerals was in use before those alphabets parted company, *i.e.* before the ninth century B.C.[2] In the case of the Greek alphabet the earliest instance of alphabetic numeration which we possess dates only from the reign of Ptolemy II., 285–247 B.C. But when we turn to Semitic sources we find letters used as numerals as early as the eighth century B.C. Thus on the lion-weights from Nimrûd, Beth, the second letter of the Semitic alphabet, is used in the sense of "double." [3] Amongst the Jews the earliest example still extant occurs on the ancient silver shekels, which have been variously assigned to the age of Ezra, to that of the Maccabees, and to the time of the first revolt.[4] The value, however, of the evidence afforded by these shekels depends, not so much upon their age, as on their markedly conservative and religious character. The type of alphabet used on

[1] Cf. also Jer. li. 1, where "Leb-kamai" is a cipher for "Casdim," Chaldeans.

[2] See Isaac Taylor's *Alphabet*, vol. i. p. 197.

[3] *Corpus Inscriptionum Semiticarum*, vol. i. part 2, Nos. 2, 3, 4.

[4] See *The Money of the Bible*, pp. 27, 28, by G. C. Williamson.

them is archaic as compared with that found on the coins of the Asmonean princes, and on those of the second revolt. The coins, if not of the date of Ezra, are stamped with letters which copy the older forms: letters which differ little in shape from those employed in the Siloam Inscription, supposed to have been written in the latter half of the eighth century B.C. Further, the symbols stamped on the shekels, such as the seven-branched candlestick, along with such superscriptions as "Jerusalem the Holy," give them a distinctly religious character. When, therefore, we find on these coins the number of the year given alphabetically, so that 4W stands for *shĕnâh B, i.e.* "year 2," the strong presumption is that letters of the alphabet were used by the Jews as numerals in copying their sacred writings, certainly as early as the fifth century B.C., to which the type of alphabet used on the shekels points back; and further, that in this fact we have the key to some of the numerical discrepancies of Holy Scripture.

Now let us apply this use of the letters to the case at issue. The age of Darius the Mede, viz. 62, is expressed alphabetically by the letters Samekh Beth. We need not quarrel with the Beth, but Samekh, which stands for 60, must evidently be a corruption, if the Median Darius is the same person as Cambyses. We turn accordingly to the ancient Semitic alphabet, and study the various phases through which this letter passed in the sixth and fifth centuries B.C., to find what other letter could most easily be confused with Samekh. It then becomes evident that during the last quarter of the sixth century B.C. and the first half of the following century there was a remarkable resemblance between the letters Samekh and Yod, so that a carelessly written Yod might very easily be mistaken for a Samekh. This is best seen in the inscription on the Teima Stone.[1] In line 13 of this inscription Yod appears as the second letter, and in the following line Yod is the first letter and Samekh the third, so that we have the two characters in convenient juxta-position. Now, if for Samekh Beth we read Yod Beth, the age of Darius is reduced from 62 to 12; and, as we have seen, 12 would be a very likely age for Cambyses at the time of the taking of Babylon, supposing him to be the son of the daughter of Astyages and born about a year after the capture of Ecbatana. To show that this idea is not a fanciful one, we are able to point to a passage in the Book of Isaiah where this same mistake has been made; a passage where, through an error of the copyist, the letter Samekh has supplanted a Yod. The passage in question is Isa. vii. 8. It contains a prophecy which in its present form

[1] *The Biblical World*, June, 1909.

THE TEIMA STONE

has sorely perplexed the commentators. The words are: "Within threescore and five years shall Ephraim be broken in pieces that it be not a people." Duhm pronounces this "a very old gloss," on the ground that "a late annotator would almost certainly have dated the extermination of Ephraim from the destruction of Samaria in 731 B.C., about fifteen years after Isaiah spoke."[1] There is, however, no need to suppose a gloss; for if Yod be substituted for Samekh, "threescore and five" will resolve itself into "fifteen": and this is no doubt the true reading. Even so in Dan. v. 31, for "threescore and two" we should read "twelve."[2]

With regard to both the personality and the age of Darius the Mede, the Septuagint reading of the passage, already alluded to, if not to be trusted, is yet remarkable and deserving of attention. It runs thus: "The kingdom was taken away from the Chaldeans, and was given to the Medes and to the Persians. And Artaxerxes, who was of the Medes, received the kingdom. And Darius was full of days and honoured in his old age." The Septuagint is the earliest interpreter of the Book of Daniel; for, as is well known, there is a remarkable dearth of Jewish writings between the close of the Canon and the middle of the second century B.C., about which time the LXX version of the Book of Daniel was made. The Septuagint translator interprets, accommodates, and alters, according to his own ideas, so as to make the Book square with history as known to him. The abrupt way in which he introduces Darius is proof that the original text has here been doctored by him, and clumsily doctored. What was his motive? Was he aware that Cyrus appointed Cambyses to the throne of Babylon and that Cambyses could not have been sixty-two years old at the time of his appointment? Is it not possible that as Josephus identifies the Artaxerxes of Ezra iv. 8 with Cambyses, so in the present passage by Artaxerxes the translator means Cambyses? That some tradition of Belshazzar being succeeded on the throne of Babylon by Cambyses was still current so late as the third century of our era is evident from the *De Paschâ Computus* of St. Cyprian[3] (243 A.D.), usually printed in the appendix to his[4] works. A list is there given of the kings of Babylon, from Nebuchadnezzar to Cyrus inclusive, who are mentioned in the Old Testament. On this list, faulty and imperfect as it is, between the names Belshazzar and Cyrus occur the words, "Darius Cyri filius." The number 62 the LXX translator appears to have regarded with distrust, yet in view possibly of the power placed in the hands of Darius,

[1] See *The Cambridge Bible for Schools and Colleges* on Isa. vii. 8.

[2] It is a curious fact that in the Septuagint of Dan. ix. 27, this very number, sixty-two, is expressed by the letters ξβ.

[3] *read* by an unknown Christian writer [4] *for his read* St. Cyprian's

he deems it advisable to describe him as an ancient and honoured statesman. His use of the two names Darius and Artaxerxes is due possibly to the fact that he had before him two documents, one a copy of the Book of Daniel containing the name "Darius," and the other possibly some historical summary in which for the name "Darius" was substituted "Artaxerxes," and thus, feeling at a loss which to decide for, thought it better to include both.

But perhaps the best proof of the youthful age of Darius the Mede is to be found in that most touching story of the lions' den. For into whose presence did the presidents and satraps "come tumultuously"?[1] Into the presence of a man of sixty-two years, wielding the rod of empire? Hardly so; but they might break in thus on a boy of twelve. Again, with regard to the words, "Know, O King, that it is a law of the Medes and Persians, that no interdict nor statute which the king establisheth may be changed," which amounts almost to a threat. Can we credit the speakers with venturing thus to address a man of over sixty years? Once more we ask, who is it, whose whole heart goes out to the aged prophet in those fervid words, "Thy God, whom thou servest continually, he will deliver thee"? And yet again, who is it who passes the night fasting, cannot sleep for agitation of mind, rises early, goes in haste to the den, and calls out with a lamentable voice to know whether the God whom Daniel serves continually has been able to save him from the lions? Would an Oriental despot, hardened by sixty-two years' contact with the world and inured to bloody scenes, act thus? Hardly; but a young lad might. Thus the whole tone of the story is suggestive of the generous impulsive nature of a young heart as yet unspoilt. No elderly man would be likely to act in the way that Darius acted. In this matter of age the story speaks for itself.

Some, however, will be disposed to question whether the character just described can ever have belonged to a harsh cruel despot like Cambyses, who by his mad acts of impiety so outraged the religious feelings of his newly conquered subjects in Egypt. The best answer to this objection is that the Egyptian experiences of Cambyses were a test of his character. They brought out both what was good in him and still more what was bad. We must admit that he was "an impulsive, self-willed, reckless, ambitious despot, of the peculiarly Oriental type, possessed of considerable

[1] Dan. vi. 6. The Aramaic root *rĕgash*, translated in the R.V. "assembled together," but in the R.V.M. better, "came together tumultuously," is the word used in the Aramaic of the Targums in Ps. xlvi. 6, "the nations *raged*," and again in Isa. xvii. 12 of the "*rushing*" of the nations. In the Hebrew of Ps. ii. 1 it occurs in the opening words, "Why do the heathen *rage*?"

ability as a general, but with passions so strong and uncontrolled as to render the powers he possessed worthless for good." [1] Nevertheless, during the earlier part of his stay in Egypt it is admitted that "for a time at least he cultivated the good will of his new subjects, sought instruction in regard to the rites of their religion, and was initiated into certain of its mysteries; that he listened to complaints in regard to the profanation of temples by Persians and other foreign soldiers, and gave orders for their removal from the sacred precincts; that he secured the priests in the receipt of the temple revenues, and arranged for the due and continual celebration of the customary ceremonies and festivals." [2] Moreover it is from this very land of Egypt that we gain an insight into the good points of his character as well as corroboration of the truth of the story told us in Dan. vi., as I shall now show.

There are few archæological finds of late years which have excited more interest than the Aramaic papyri of the fifth century B.C. discovered in the island of Elephantiné, just below the First Cataract of the Nile. This interest culminated when it was made known that documents had been found disclosing the existence of a Jewish temple to Jahu (Jehovah) at that spot, built before the reign of Cambyses. In these records, dated the seventeenth year of Darius (Nothus), *i.e.* in 407 B.C., the Jews of Elephantiné, complaining to Bagoas the Persian governor of Judæa [3] of the destruction of their temple by the priests of the Egyptian god Khnub, speak thus: "When Cambyses came into Egypt he found this temple built. And though the temples of the gods of Egypt were all thrown down, no one injured anything in this temple." Now why did Cambyses in his destructive rage spare the temple of Jehovah? Because the Jews were not Egyptians? Because they were monotheists, much like the Persians in their religion? Yes! probably so. But that was not all. Cambyses had not forgotten his younger, happier days, only thirteen years before, when in a Jew he found the wisest and most trusty counsellor he had ever had. He had not forgotten his night of terrible anxiety, and that astounding miracle wrought by the God Jahu in behalf of His faithful servant. He had not forgotten the decree put forth by himself, in which he had called on all his subjects to tremble and fear before the God of Daniel. He had not forgotten—how could he forget?—these things. So whilst the temples of the false gods of Egypt were thrown down, the temple of the God Jahu was left untouched.

The number of satrapies created by Darius the Mede—viz,

[1] *Encyc. Brit.*, art. "Cambyses."
[2] *Ibid.*
[3] Cf. Josephus, *Ant.* xi. 7, 1.

one hundred and twenty—has been much commented upon. The critics look upon this statement as a confused tradition of what was done by Darius Hystaspes, and they point out that whilst Darius the Mede divided his sub-kingdom into one hundred and twenty satrapies, Darius Hystaspes divided the whole wide empire of Persia into a sixth part of that number. One answer to this objection is that Dan. vi. 1 speaks, *not* of satrapies, but only of satraps, and that it is still an open question whether the title always implied territorial jurisdiction. In the very limited number of Old Persian inscriptions "satraps" are only mentioned twice, viz. in the Behistûn Inscription of Darius Hystaspes. Darius speaks of "Dadarsis by name, a Persian, my subject, a satrap *in* Bactria," or "satrap *of* Bactria," for the words can be read either way. Then again, a little later, he speaks of "Vivana by name, a satrap *in* Harauvatis," or "satrap *of* Harauvatis."[1] The Babylonian version of the inscription, which is legible in this latter instance though not in the former, renders the word "satrap" by *pikhatu*, "governor." This word *pikhatu* had in Babylonian both a larger and a smaller meaning. It was applied to subordinates as well as to those who were set over them. Thus Gobryas the *pikhatu* of Gutium, when appointed by Cyrus *pikhatu* of Babylon, forthwith proceeded to appoint *pikhati* who were to act as his subordinates. The description given us in Dan. vi. 1, 2, is suggestive that in that passage we have to do, not with great territorial magnates holding the position of sub-kings in their respective provinces, like the satraps appointed by Darius Hystaspes, but with officials whose main duty was to collect the taxes. They were required "to give account" to the presidents, that so "the king should have no damage." This duty of collecting the revenue appears to have formed the original *raison d'être* of the office. The title of satrap, in Old Persian *khshatrapava*, is derived from *khshatra*, "kingdom," and *pa*—compare Latin *pascor, pavi*—"to maintain," and signifies "maintainer of the kingdom." The Babylonian kingdom, over which Belshazzar had been reigning as sole monarch for some three or four months before the capture of Babylon, was, according to the interpretation given by Daniel to the mystic word PERES, to be partitioned between the Medes and Persians. Let us suppose for the sake of argument that Darius the Mede received half of that kingdom, while Cyrus retained the other half and added it to the many countries already under his sway. Then, since the sub-kingdom

[1] See Prof. R. D. Wilson's *Studies in the Book of Daniel*, p. 213, where this question of the satraps is very fully and very ably discussed.

of the Median Darius contained certainly some of the richest land in the empire—the Babylonian satrapy according to Herodotus being the second richest, and only surpassed by the Indian—and was of considerable extent, though small compared to the vast realm immediately under Cyrus, it follows that the posts held by these one hundred and twenty satraps would be of considerable importance, even though they would not hold the rank of the satraps of Darius Hystaspes. In the Book of Daniel the word "satrap" is used by the writer of certain high officials under Nebuchadnezzar.[1] This has been called an anachronism. If it be such, then we see in it the anachronism of an old man writing in the early Persian period a story of the Babylonian past. But perhaps we may also take it as an index that the title "satrap" was used among the Persians themselves with some freedom, and not restricted to one special rank of grandees.

With regard to the description given us in the Book of Daniel of the style and title of the Median Darius as well as of his acts, the following passage from the pen of Dr. Charles well voices the objections put forward by the Higher Critics: "Darius is not conceived as a vassal king, but as an independent sovereign; for he enjoys the title of king (vi. 3, 7, 8, 9, 12, 13, etc.): as sole ruler divides the vast empire into 120 satrapies (vi. 1); and as absolute despot sentences all the rulers of these satrapies to death by a single decree (vi. 24). When he dies he is succeeded by Cyrus the Persian (vi. 28). That our text, therefore, regards Darius the Mede as the sole and absolute king of the Babylonian empire cannot be questioned."[2] In reply to this I would observe that there is nothing strange in the title of king being given to a vassal king. Shamash-shum-ukin, vassal king of Babylon under his brother Ashurbanipal, hesitates not to style himself "the mighty king, king of Amnanu, king of Babylon, powerful, discerning, the shepherd, the favourite of the Enlil, Shamash and Merodach, king of Shumer and Akkad." Indeed the wonder would have been if the title of king had been denied to such a ruler. Certainly no lesser title would have satisfied the pride of the Babylonians, whom Cyrus was so anxious to conciliate. What is still more to the point, Cambyses, whom we have identified with Darius the Mede, is, as we have seen, expressly styled "King of Babylon" on contract tablets of the first year of Cyrus. Then, that Darius should be allowed to divide, *not* "the vast empire," but that part of the late empire of Babylon which was assigned to the Medes, into one hundred and twenty satrapies for the purpose of collecting

[1] Chap. iii. 2.

[2] *Cent. Bible*, Daniel, p. 59.

the revenue and that " the king should have no damage," is just what a Persian monarch, and more especially a prudent monarch like Cyrus, would be sure to approve of. Probably he would feel, too, that he could safely leave such an act of internal administration to his young son, with prudent counsellors at his elbow, and under the guidance of a statesman so honoured and revered as Daniel. Further, as to the power of sentencing his subjects to death, this was no doubt possessed by the satraps of Darius Hystaspes; how much more in this present instance by the king's own son? The very circumstances of a vast Oriental empire, so lately subdued under the sway of a new master, made such a power a necessity; and we may feel quite sure that while Cyrus was pursuing his schemes of conquest, his son Darius-Cambyses was not the only subordinate ruler who possessed that power. " When he dies," continues Charles, " he is succeeded by Cyrus the Persian." But the Book of Daniel says nothing about the death of Darius, though it acknowledges, what we have seen to be the fact, viz. that Darius-Cambyses was succeeded on the throne of Babylon by Cyrus.[1] Lastly, this Book does *not* " regard Darius the Mede as the sole and absolute king of the Babylonian empire," but only as " made king " over that part of the late empire of Babylon which was assigned to the Medes, and which is called in chap. ix. " the realm of the Chaldeans." We may well suppose, though we cannot be sure of it, that Syria and Palestine and the western countries were not placed under the sway of Darius; while Shumer and Akkad and the country down to the Persian Gulf, with that part of ancient Elam—including Susa which was under Babylon—was looked upon as constituting " the realm of the Chaldeans." Darius publishes his decree " unto all the peoples, nations, and languages, that dwell in all the earth."[2] This is the very style adopted by Nebuchadnezzar. It is just the style we should expect a Babylonian king to adopt; how much more the youthful Cambyses? This consideration seems to make it unnecessary to substitute " in all the land " for " in all the earth," though the Aramaic word there used, like its Hebrew equivalent, undoubtedly bears the double sense.

But this is not all that can be said in defence of the style and authority assigned in the Book of Daniel to the Median Darius, *i.e.* to Cambyses as sub-king of Babylon. The tone and language of the Cylinder of Cyrus is sufficient to show that Cyrus had associated his son Cambyses with himself in the government of the empire: in fact, that Cambyses, despite his tender age, held

[1] Dan. vi. 28.

[2] *Ibid.* vi. 25.

exactly the same position in the Persian empire which Belshazzar had held under his father Nabonidus in the Babylonian. The following passage on the Cylinder of Cyrus will serve to illustrate my meaning: "Merodach, the great lord . . . established a decree. Unto me Cyrus the king his worshipper, and to Cambyses my son, the offspring of my heart, and to all my people he graciously drew nigh, and in peace before them *we* marched": *i.e. the king and his son as true shepherds*[1] *marched at the head of their people.* Compare also the following: "Let Cyrus the king thy worshipper and Cambyses his son accomplish the desire of *their* heart."[2] In view of such language I see nothing strange either in the administrative acts of Darius or in the terms of his decree as recorded in Dan. vi.

The sixth chapter of Daniel throws a remarkable light on a question about which we should otherwise be completely in the dark, viz. the cause of the removal of Darius-Cambyses from his post as king of Babylon. In endeavouring to provide for the systematic collection of the revenue Cambyses was certainly doing the very thing his father would most approve. But Dan. vi. shows us how the good intentions of the young king were entirely frustrated by the jealousy so frequently manifested by the Babylonians against foreigners placed in posts which they looked upon as their right. The story shows that his turbulent subjects were too much for Cambyses, and that he in turn was too much for them. They had sought, not in vain, to overawe him; and he, shocked at their duplicity, and mortified possibly by their conduct towards himself, as well as deeply impressed by the mighty miracle wrought, hesitated not to put those who had accused Daniel to death. Such an act must have aroused great indignation in Babylon, and would convince Cyrus that the wisest course was to withdraw his young son from a too prominent post, and take to himself the title, "King of Babylon," and probably to entrust a considerable amount of delegated power to his governor Gobryas, who was probably himself a Mede. Thus the Sacred Record is not only confirmed by contemporary Babylonian documents, but in its turn throws light on a remarkable act on the part of the conqueror, indicated in those documents, but never clearly stated, viz. the removal of his son from the throne of Babylon.

Note

The confusion of the letter Samekh with the letter Yod which appears to have taken place both in Isa. vii. 8 and in

[1] Cf. Isa. xliv. 28.

[2] Cylinder of Cyrus, Obv. lines 26–28 and 35.

Dan. v. 31 is a matter of such importance as to demand a note to itself.

From the time of the earliest Hebrew inscription extant, viz. the Calendar of Gezer, *circa* 1000 B.C., down to the end of the first half of the fifth century B.C., Yod maintained the same archaic form which we meet with on the ancient Hebrew shekels, *i.e.* exactly like our capital Z with the addition of a short central parallel bar on the left side of the transverse bar, thus Ƶ. After the first half of the fifth century B.C. this letter very quickly drew in its horns, so that by the end of the fourth century B.C. the "jot" (Matt. v. 18) was already the smallest letter in the alphabet. With Samekh the case was different.[1] This letter ran through a great variety of changes. In its most ancient form, as seen in the Gezer Calendar, it consists of three parallel horizontal bars, crossed by a perpendicular bar, which begins a little above the highest parallel, and is bisected by the lowest, thus ‡. A little later, during the ninth and the first half of the eighth century B.C., the perpendicular bar began at the highest of the parallels, thus ‡. This is the form of the letter on the Moabite Stone, the stele of Zakir king of Hamath, and the earliest of the Zenjerli inscriptions. After the middle of the eighth century B.C. the perpendicular bar, instead of crossing the horizontal bars, is merely drawn downward from the lowest, so that we have two horizontal parallels and beneath them a capital T, thus ⩧. This form of the letter is found on the Zenjerli inscription of Bar-rekub, 745–727 B.C. Presently, in order to write the character more easily, the three horizontal bars were exchanged for a zigzag, the perpendicular being added below, thus ≷. This is the form which the letter assumes on a contract tablet dated the first year of Nabonidus, 555 B.C. But a further change was soon to follow. During the closing decades of the sixth century B.C., and throughout the fifth century B.C., Samekh was drawn like a capital Z, tilted somewhat to the left side, and with two additional strokes added to it; first, as in the case of Yod, a short parallel bar on the left side of the transverse; secondly, a tail, drawn from the right-hand extremity of the lowest bar parallel to the transverse, thus ʒ. This form of the letter is found in use on a contract tablet from Babylon dated the fourth year of Cambyses, 526 B.C.; on an inscription from Memphis dated the fourth year of Xerxes,

[1] **The true forms of the Samekh are as follows:**

482 B.C.; on the lion-weight from Abydos; and on the bilingual inscription, Lydian and Aramaic, dated the tenth year of Artaxerxes, viz. 455 B.C., if, as seems likely, Artaxerxes I. be intended. In the above four instances this form of Samekh is found along with the archaic form of Yod described above, *from which it differs only by the addition of the aforementioned tail.*[1] The Teima Stone, already referred to, belongs to the same period, viz. the end of the sixth or the first half of the fifth century B.C. Finally, let it be noted that the possibility of a Yod being thus mistaken for a Samekh in Dan. v. 31 presupposes that the Book of Daniel was written not later than the middle of the fifth century B.C.

[1] *Corpus Inscriptionum Semiticarum*, vol. i. part 2. On Plate V., compare the Yod in 64a with the Samekh in 64b. Also on Plate VII., 108a, compare the three Samekhs and two Yods in a short inscription of five words. Again, on Plate XI., 122a, compare the Yods and Samekhs in אוסרי and אבסלי. A description by S. A. Cook of the bi-lingual Lydian and Aramaic inscription will be found in *The Journal of Hellenic Studies* for June, 1917.

16

The Evangelic Prophecy, The Interpretation

"Danielem prophetam juxta Septuaginta interpretes Domini Salvatoris ecclesiæ non legunt, utentes Theodotionis editione, et hoc cur acciderit nescio. . . . Hoc unum affirmare possum, quod multum a veritate discordet, et recto judicio repudiatus sit."—Preface to Jerome's translation of the Book of Daniel.

WITH regard to the interpretation of the astonishing vision at the close of the ninth chapter of Daniel, the difference between the orthodox view and that of the Higher Critics is immense, as great as the difference between light and darkness. Most truthfully may we say to our opponents respecting this prophecy, " between us and you there is a great gulf fixed," a gulf that cannot be bridged over, and yet, happily, not an impassable gulf. As many have undoubtedly gone from us to join you, so there is hope that with increasing light and a more careful study of this Book, not a few may see their way to return to the altogether nobler, grander, and more far-reaching view, held by the Church of Christ through the long course of centuries.

According to the traditional view the vision of Dan. ix. is pre-eminently a vision of the great Atonement for sin, as indicated not uncertainly by the note struck in its opening verse, viz. *v.* 24. Within seventy mystic weeks will take place the sacrifice of the death of the Messiah, whereby sin will be restrained, made an end of, atoned for; whereby also everlasting righteousness will be brought in, the visions of the prophets fulfilled, and the All-holy One manifested. The assurance given to the seer in the following verse that Jerusalem will be rebuilt is introduced almost parenthetically, though it carries with it the implication that the Jewish sacrifices will yet again be offered, until the time comes when Messiah shall make them to cease by the sacrifice of Himself. The time of Messiah's public appearance is definitely foretold. It will take place at the end of sixty-nine mystic weeks

—weeks of years—reckoned from the time of the going forth of the command for the restoration and rebuilding of Jerusalem. Shortly afterwards, viz. in the middle of the seventieth week, Messiah will be " cut off," *i.e.* He will meet with a violent death; and this death, being the true sacrifice, will put an end to the Jewish sacrifices. That closing week in which Messiah is to suffer will see a good feeling displayed by the masses of the people towards the Messiah and His adherents, despite His violent death at their hands in the middle of the week. The vision, thus placed in a definite historical setting and told with some detail, is painted against a dark background. The nation that finally rejected its lawful Prince, that put to death its own Messiah, shall see its city and sanctuary destroyed by the people of the coming Prince, that same Prince Messiah whom they have already put to death. They shall go under beneath the desolating deluge of war, when borne onward on the wing of abominations there comes the mysterious desolator; and the ruin will be complete. Yet though city and sanctuary have perished, an indication is given that the nation is not finally forsaken, in the closing assurance that wrath will be poured out on the desolator.

Such, then, is the traditional view; that of the critics is far different. To them Daniel's astonishing vision appears as an interesting period of past history picturesquely put into the form of an apocalyptic vision. They regard as the main subject of this apocalypse the surprising revival of the temple worship in the days of the Maccabees after its seemingly complete overthrow by a persecuting power. This glorious event is to take place at the end of seventy mystic weeks. The heathen worship of Zeus Olympius, set up in the temple courts by Antiochus Epiphanes, after a short time of triumph will in its turn be overthrown and brought to an end; the awful sacrilege which attended it will be purged away; the worship of Jehovah will be restored; the vision shown to the prophet will be realised, and the Holy of Holies reconsecrated. All this is looked upon as told in detail in *v.* 24. In the next verse it is disclosed that the seventy weeks are to commence from the going forth of a divine command for the restoration and rebuilding of Jerusalem. The end of the first seven weeks, *i.e.* the first forty-nine years, will see the appearance of an anointed prince, either Cyrus king of Persia or Jeshua the son of Jozadak the Jewish high priest, under whom that restoration will commence. For the next threescore and two weeks, or four hundred and thirty-four years, the restored city will stand as the centre of Jewish worship even though the times be troublous. At the close of the threescore and two weeks " an anointed one," viz. the then high priest

Onias III., will meet with a violent death, apparently a martyr's death, and "the people of the prince that shall come," viz. the heathen host of Antiochus, will destroy the city and sanctuary with a desolating flood of invasive war. The persecutor will then enter into covenant with many apostate Jews for a week—the last of the seventy—and during half of that week will succeed in putting down the pure worship of Jehovah. Borne along upon the wing of his heathen abominations, he will go proudly forward in his desolating career until his own time comes and heaven's vengeance is poured out on the desolator.

The Higher Critics are not the first commentators to refer this vision to the times of Antiochus Epiphanes and the heroic struggle of the Maccabees. The LXX took the same view of it, and showed their strong bias in a most remarkable way. The first twenty-three verses of this chapter will be found faithfully rendered in the Septuagint version, but when we come to the vision in *vv.* 24–27, at the close of the chapter, the original prophecy becomes scarcely recognisable: the translator has turned commentator, and as we study his commentary we marvel at the ruthless way in which he has dismembered, defaced, and then put together again, so as to suit his own preconceived ideas, what was once a glorious, far-reaching prophecy. It is as if some splendid painted window with all its glories of design and colour, which once adorned some noble monastic building, were ruthlessly broken to pieces, and then re-collected, and studiously though clumsily put together again, with the view to make it fit into the smaller east-end window of some ancient parish church. We look at the attempted restoration, and recognise the antiquity of its parts, but find great difficulty in making out the original design. Just so is it with the treatment which Daniel's vision has received at the hands of the Septuagint commentator; but happily in this case we have a copy of the original before us, and so can easily detect from what portion of it this and that fragment of the re-constructed prophecy has been taken, and also what patches, defacements, and alterations have been made by the ignorant though well-meaning restorer. To make this plain to the English reader, let me put side by side our own Revised Version and an English translation of the passage as it stands in the Greek Septuagint.

REVISED VERSION, DAN. IX. 24–27.

24 Seventy weeks are decreed upon thy people and upon thy holy city, to finish transgression, and to make an end of sins, and to make reconciliation for iniquity, and to bring in everlasting righteousness, and to seal up vision and prophecy, and to anoint the most holy.

25 Know therefore and discern, that from the going forth of the commandment to restore and to build Jerusalem unto the anointed one, the prince, shall be seven weeks: and threescore and two weeks,[1] it shall be built again, with street and moat, even in troublous times.

26 And after the threescore and two weeks shall the anointed one be cut off, and shall have nothing: and the people of the prince that shall come shall destroy the city and the sanctuary; and his end[2] shall be with a flood, and even unto the end shall be war; desolations are determined.

27 And he shall make a firm covenant with many for one week: and for the half of the

SEPTUAGINT VERSION, DAN. IX. 24–27 (CODEX CHISIANUS).

24 Seventy weeks were determined upon thy people and upon the city of Sion that the sin be accomplished, and to make the iniquities rare, and to wipe away the iniquities, and that the vision be understood, and everlasting righteousness be given, and the visions and prophet be accomplished, and to gladden a holy of holies.

25 And thou shalt know, and shalt understand, and shalt be gladdened, and thou shalt find commands to be responded to, and thou shalt build Jerusalem a city to the LORD.

26 And after seven and seventy and sixty-two[3] an anointing shall be removed, and shall not be, and a kingdom of Gentiles shall destroy the city and the sanctuary along with the anointed: and his end shall come with wrath and a time of consummation:[4] war shall follow war.

27 And the covenant shall have power with many: and it shall be built again[5] in

[1] The R.V.M. gives the traditional view by placing a comma after "seven weeks" and a colon after "threescore and two weeks."

[2] R.V.M. "the end thereof."

[3] Note the suppression here of the word "weeks," and the substitution of "years" for "weeks" in the parallel in *v.* 27.

[4] *I.e.* "conclusion," "end."

[5] Lit. "shall return and shall be built": a literal rendering of the Hebrew phrase.

week he shall cause the sacrifice and the oblation to cease: and upon the wing of abominations shall come one that maketh desolate; and even unto the consummation, and that determined, shall wrath be poured out upon the desolator.

breadth and in length even at a consummation [1] of times, and after seven and seventy times and LXII [2] years, till a time of consummation [1] of war: and the desolation shall be taken away through the prevailing of the covenant for many weeks: and at the end of the week the sacrifice and the drink offering shall be put an end to, and over the temple there shall be an abomination of desolations until a consummation: [1] and a consummation [1] will be granted to the desolation.

From the translation of the Septuagint version of Dan. ix. 24–27 just given, my readers will see that I have not spoken in too strong terms of the ruthless way in which the original has been dealt with. Let me now examine in detail some of the freaks of the translator.

To the rendering of the opening verse, *v.* 24, comparatively little exception can be taken, though the six clauses employed in the Hebrew to describe the bright future are seen to be amplified into seven by the insertion of the words–

"and that the vision be understood."

Towards the close of the verse, however, we meet with a more significant change. The translator by transposing letters has changed מָשַׁח, *mâshach,* "anoint," into שַׂמַּח, *simmach,* "gladden," This he does in order that he may make the great joy which the faithful are to feel at the rededication of the altar after the pollutions of Antiochus Epiphanes—as described in 1 Macc. iv. 56–59 —the climax of the coming brightness.

In *v.* 25 the changes are very great. Not a single clause of the original remains intact, and the date from which the prophecy was to commence disappears. The only idea which the verse retains in common with the Hebrew is the rebuilding of Jerusalem. The occurrence of the word מָשִׁיחַ, *mâshîach,* "anointed," in the original

[1] *I.e.* "conclusion," "end."

[2] Written ξβ in the Codex. Cf. Chapter XV. on the use of letters of the alphabet to express numerals.

of this verse, appears to have suggested to the translator the insertion of the clause, " thou shalt be gladdened " : thus showing unmistakably the direction in which his mind was looking, when at the close of the previous verse he made the same change.

The chief feature in *v.* 26 is the alteration of the period " threescore and two weeks " into " seven and seventy and sixty-two." This is another very clear indication of the view of the passage taken by the Septuagint translator, and which by his daring alterations he seeks to impress on his readers, as will become yet more evident when we come to examine the closing verse. Further, in order to make the subject of the prophecy more plain, the invading power is described by the Septuagint translator as " a kingdom of Gentiles " ; whilst, instead of the " cutting off " of " the anointed one," mentioned in the original, we have a double announcement : first, an anointing is to be removed ; and secondly, the anointed one is to be destroyed as well as the city and sanctuary through the wrath of an unnamed enemy. This is done to suit the facts of history. Onias III. was first removed from the high-priesthood in favour of his brother Jason. Then, a few years later, Menelaus contrived to supplant Jason by means of a heavy bribe, the money for which he procured by selling the sacred vessels of the temple. For this gross sacrilege he was reproved by Onias. The reproof was more than his proud spirit could bear, so in a fit of revenge he bribed Andronicus, the king's deputy at Antioch, to murder Onias.[1] Thus " the end " of the anointed came " with wrath."

In *v.* 27, the closing verse of the prophecy, the numbers which occur in the original in *v.* 25 are again introduced, and at the same time altered. Thus instead of

" seven weeks and threescore and two weeks,"

we now have

" seven and seventy times and LXII years."

This, if we understand " times " in the sense of " years," agrees so far as the number is concerned with that given by the translator in *v.* 26-

" seven and seventy and sixty-two,"

and it is in this repetition made by him, coupled with the fact that he has ventured to insert the word " years " where we should have expected " weeks," that we have the key to his strange performance. The matter may be explained thus : In unpointed

[1] 2 Macc. iv. 7, 23-26, 32-35.

Hebrew, *i.e.* when the vowel-points—a comparatively late invention—are omitted, the same characters שבעים stand for both "weeks" and "seventy." It was thus easy for the ingenious translator to read the words-

"seven weeks and threescore and two weeks,"

which occur in *v.* 25 of the original, as-

"seven and seventy and threescore and two."

All he had to do was to place an "and" after "seven," to read the first "weeks" as "seventy," and to leave out the second "weeks." This he accordingly did, and substituted it in *v.* 26 for the "threescore and two weeks" of the original. Then in *v.* 27, as we have seen, he introduced it again in the slightly altered form-

"seven and seventy times and LXII years,"

substituting "years" for "weeks." What was it that moved him to this repetition? The discovery that seven and seventy and threescore and two years make up one hundred and thirty-nine years, which brings us to the second year of the reign of Antiochus Epiphanes, reckoned according to the era of the Seleucidæ,[1] *i.e.* to about the time of the removal of Onias from the high-priesthood. Along with the numbers brought down from *v.* 25 and inserted in this last verse of the prophecy, the translator also brings down and inserts the promise of the restoration and rebuilding of Jerusalem. The object of this change is to make the rebuilding of the Holy City, after its destruction by Apollonius the general of Antiochus in 168 B.C.,[2] the chief feature of the vision. Had the promise of restoration been left in its proper place, viz. in *v.* 25, it would, as Wright points out, have been interpreted of the rebuilding and fortification of the city centuries before the Maccabean era. By placing it in this last verse the translator makes the promise point to the restoration of Jerusalem after the hard struggle of the Maccabees. With regard to the rest of the verse we note that the opening clause of the original—"He shall make a firm covenant with many for one week"—is strangely altered by LXX and developed into two clauses: (i) "the covenant shall have power with many," (ii) "the desolation shall be taken away through the prevailing of the covenant for many weeks": *i.e.* instead of "one week" we have "many weeks." It would almost seem as if the translator had begun to realise that the one hundred

[1] Cf. 1 Macc. i. 10. "He reigned in the hundred and thirty and seventh year of the kingdom of the Greeks."

[2] Cf. 1 Macc. i. 29–31.

and thirty-nine years, which he sets so much store by, would only bring him to the beginning of the troubles, viz. to 174 B.C., the year after the deposition of the high priest Onias, and therefore sought to make the prophecy indicate that "many *weeks*"—the word being here taken in its literal sense, as is indicated by the "LXII *years*" a little before—must elapse after that event before matters came to the worst through the forced cessation of the Jewish sacrifices and the setting up in the temple of "an abomination of desolations," to wit, a heathen altar built over the altar of Jehovah. This took place on the 15th of Chisleu, 168 B.C.,[1] just *one week* of years after the deposition of Onias. To indicate this our ingenious translator takes the words rendered in the R.V. "for the half of the week," and in the R.V.M. "in the midst of the week," and substitutes for them, "at the *end* of the week," *i.e.* at the end of the seven years which followed the removal from office of Onias, once more giving back to the word "week" its mystical meaning. Lastly, the taking away of the desolation is traced by him to the covenant having power with many during those "many weeks" which were to elapse between the deposition of Onias in 175 B.C. and the restoration of Jerusalem and re-dedication of the altar in 165 B.C.; thus directing his readers' thoughts to the heroic struggle of the brave Maccabees. For their sakes, so he suggests, "a consummation will be granted to the desolation."

The amount of ingenuity thus displayed by the Septuagint translator in his endeavour to adapt the prophecy to the era of the Maccabees is in itself one of the strongest proofs that it does not refer to that period. It is also a proof that the prophecy is no *vaticinium post eventum;* for, if it were, it would not require so much mangling to make if fit in with the facts of history. All the more striking then, is it, that the critics should have tried in their way to accomplish that in which the Greek translator has so egregiously failed. The modern critic is, indeed, too much of a scholar to mangle the text after the fashion of the translator.[2] He loves rather to indulge in emendations and slight alterations.

[1] 1 Macc. i. 54.

[2] The untrustworthy character of the Septuagint and the liberties taken by the translator are thus freely admitted by Driver, when comparing it with the received Hebrew text: "The Septuagint, though in isolated passages it may preserve a more original reading, as a whole has no claim whatever to consideration beside it: the liberties which the translator has manifestly taken with his text being quite such as to deprive the different readings, which, if it were a reasonably faithful translation, it might be regarded as presupposing, of all pretensions to originality—except, indeed, in a comparatively small number of instances in which they are supported on strong grounds of intrinsic probability."—*Cambridge Bible*, p. cii.

But when he has persuaded himself on any point, everything must give way to his fixed persuasion. What, then, is the interpretation of the prophecy in Dan. ix. offered by the critics? In the first place, they seek to identify the "seven weeks" of *v.* 25. Seven weeks of years, *i.e.* forty-nine years, is exactly the period between the taking of Jerusalem by Nebuchadnezzar in 587 B.C. and the decree issued by Cyrus for the return of the Jews in 538 B.C. Cyrus became king of Babylon in 539 B.C., and in 588 B.C., the year before the fall of Jerusalem, were most probably written those wonderful promises made to the prophet Jeremiah concerning the rebuilding of the Holy City and the return of her inhabitants, which are found in the thirty-first and thirty-second chapters of his Book. In those promises the critics see "the going forth of the commandment to restore and to build Jerusalem," and they point out that exactly seven prophetic weeks after they were given, Cyrus, "the anointed one the prince," appears on the scene and issues his edict for the return of the Jews. So far, so good: no exception can be taken to this first step. The next step is to determine the "threescore and two weeks." They are to close with the "cutting off" of "the anointed one," foretold in *v.* 26, *i.e.* according to the critics, with the foul murder of the high priest Onias III., which took place in 171 B.C., so that the last or seventieth week, for "half" of which, or "in the midst" of which, the temple sacrifices are to cease, may answer to the seven years 171 to 165 B.C. inclusive. Now, the interval between 539 B.C. and 171 B.C. is 368 years; but the sixty-two prophetic weeks equal 7×62, or 434 years. How is it possible, then, we ask, to identify a period of 368 years with a period of 434 years? The critic can do it. He attempts, and in his own fashion achieves, what would have daunted even the Septuagint translator. He explains that "the author of Daniel followed a wrong computation." He assures us that "the materials for an exact chronology, from the destruction of Jerusalem in 586 B.C. to the establishment of the Seleucid period in 312 B.C., were not at the disposal of a Jew living in Palestine, nor apparently of any Jew," and fortifies his hypothesis by referring to errors in excess believed to have been found in Josephus and in the Egyptian Jew Demetrius.[1] But this

[1] See *Century Bible*, Daniel, p. 107, footnote to *vv.* 26, 27. Ewald, who has his own far-fetched way to account for the discrepancy between 368 and 434 years, or as he gives it, 364 and 434 years—reckoning only to the accession of Antiochus Epiphanes—points out that a Jewish writer of the age of the Maccabees would be very unlikely to be so ignorant of the history from the time of Cyrus as to commit an error of this kind. For though the Jews "had no longer kings, there still remained a kind of kingdom in the institution of the High Priests and religious festivals; and the Sabbatical year itself, which

line of argument is not convincing. For, after all, why should a Jewish writer of 165 B.C. be deemed so ignorant of the chronology of the period 586–312 B.C., and more especially with regard to the two centuries of Persian rule, viz. 539–331 B.C.? Granted that the Jews had no reigns of native rulers by which to reckon, yet they had a succession of high priests, whose terms of office must surely have been recorded. Then again, on *a priori* grounds, this supposed ignorance seems most unlikely. *Our* ignorance of Jewish history during that period is easily accounted for, since we are dependent on the later Books of the Old Testament and the writings of Josephus, from either of which sources we can gather very little. But we cannot postulate that a gifted Jewish writer, whose Book is assigned by the critics to 165 B.C., would be equally ignorant. Certainly in the Persian period the Jews were not careless in recording exact dates, as we know from the Books of Haggai, Zechariah, Ezra, and Nehemiah, where mention is made of events which happened in the first and second years of Cyrus, in the second, fourth, and sixth years of Darius I., and in the seventh, twentieth, and thirty-second years of Artaxerxes I., in many cases with the addition of the month and the day. What is still more to the point, in the papyri found at Elephantiné we have private deeds drawn up in the fourteenth and twentieth years of Xerxes, in the sixth, nineteenth, and twenty-third years of Artaxerxes I., and in the third, seventh, and thirteenth years of Darius Nothus, along with a letter dated the 20th of Marchesvan, the seventeenth year of Darius. Thus from these two sources we possess quite a series of dated events extending from 539 to 409 B.C., the latest date being about the middle of that period, the materials for the exact chronology of which were, according to the critic, not at the disposal of any Jew in the days of Antiochus Epiphanes. Now, what is the impression left on the mind by a consideration of these facts? Is it not the exact opposite to the view of the critic? Do we not seem to realise that there were abundant materials from which any intelligent writer of the year 165 B.C., who chose to do so, could construct a correct chronological scheme of the last four hundred years? Surely, if the family documents from Elephantiné, all duly dated, have survived down to this twentieth century, there must have been abundance of dated documents of both a

was at that time kept up, required a continuous and careful calculation of the years." He adds that at that time the nation and kingdom had not so completely fallen into disruption as at the time subsequent to the second destruction of Jerusalem, when Josephus made in Rome his unsuccessful attempts at restoring a chronology.—Ewald's *Prophets of the Old Testament*, Eng. trans. vol. v. pp. 269, 270.

public and private nature still surviving at the time of the supposed apocryphal writer of the Book of Daniel, which would have enabled him to compute exactly the interval between the decree of Cyrus and the death year of the high priest Onias III. For the Jews of those days in their commercial transactions, as witnessed by the Elephantiné papyri, were quite as careful in recording the year, month, and day of the reigning monarch as the Babylonian merchants on their contract tablets,[1] and such data would afford very exact evidence as to the length of the reigns of successive Persian monarchs, as well as of Alexander and his immediate successors; whilst the chronology for the subsequent Seleucid period, as the critics themselves admit, was well known.

On the whole, then, the attempt made by the critics to assign this prophecy to the times of the Maccabees and to regard it as a Jewish apocalypse seems doomed to as complete failure as the extraordinary performance of the Septuagint translator.

[1] In Schrader's *Keilinschriftliche Bibliothek*, vol. iv. pp. 312–319, Babylonian contracts are given dated the fourth year of the infant son of Alexander the Great, and the seventy-eighth and ninety-fourth years of the Seleucid era.

17

The Evangelic Prophecy, Messianic View

"The several books that he [Daniel] wrote and left behind him, are still read by us till this time, and from them we believe that Daniel conversed with God, for he did not only prophesy of future events as did the other prophets, but *he also determined the time of their accomplishment.*"—Joseph. *Ant.* x. 11, 7.

LET me now turn to the Messianic view of the prophecy contained in Dan. ix. 24–27: the old traditional interpretation, of late so much out of fashion, which has, as it were, gone down for awhile, overwhelmed and submerged beneath the rising tide of modern criticism: the view that we have in this passage an exact prediction of the times of the public appearance of Messiah, and of His violent death by which the Levitical sacrifices would be abolished, as well as of the short interval during which His teaching would be popular with "*the many,*"[1] to wit, the prescribed term of Jerusalem's day of grace; other predicted events being the rebuilding of the Holy City "even in troublous times," and its destruction by the Roman armies under the leadership of Messiah,[2] a destruction helped on and accompanied by some hateful, desolating power, on which the vials of divine wrath would ultimately be outpoured. Before entering on this subject let me venture at the outset to express the hope that when my readers have studied the traditional interpretation as unfolded in this chapter, and compared it with that of the critics as given in the previous chapter, their unhesitating verdict will be, "The old is better": better in its congruity with the subject and substance of the prophet's prayer; better in that it requires no emendations of the original, no alteration or transposition of the clauses; better in its exact agreement respecting the times and seasons, as contrasted with that glaring chronological discrepancy of sixty-six years which renders the view of the critics on an exact prophecy like the present one untenable; better, too,

[1] In Dan. ix. 27, for "many" read "*the* many," *i.e.* the multitude.
[2] Cf. *v.* 26, "The people of the Prince that shall come."

and nobler far, in its stately august recital of the completeness of Messiah's great atoning work, no less than in its setting the violent death of Messiah over against the dark storm-cloud of retributive vengeance which was to overwhelm the nation that murdered Him.

The occasion of the vision is undoubtedly the prophet's prayer as given us in the earlier part of the chapter: a prayer indicating unmistakably the frame of mind that led to its utterance. It is the spirit of that prayer which must guide us to the right understanding of the vision by which it was answered.

It is, then, the first year of the Median Darius, *i.e.*, as we have seen, of Cambyses, who has been "made king" by his father Cyrus, not over the whole of the Persian empire, but only "over the realm of the Chaldeans," of which Babylon is the capital. The first year of Cambyses as king of Babylon synchronises with the first year of Cyrus, 538 B.C., viz. the year after his capture of Babylon, the same year which was to witness his decree for the return of the Jews to their own land. Daniel, who, as he tells us, has been studying the writings of Jeremiah—a statement well borne out by the language of his prayer—is impressed with the nearness of the hour for Israel's promised deliverance. But instead of hailing the approaching fulfilment of the promise, instead of hastening to meet the dawn of the coming day, we see him utterly overcome with a deep sense of the sin of the nation. Accordingly, like one who feels that there is a great obstacle in the way of the fulfilment of the divine promise, he goes straight to God, and gives himself to prayer, along with those outward signs of humiliation—fasting, sackcloth, and ashes—and in language, drawn chiefly from the Book of Jeremiah and also in part from the Book of Deuteronomy, makes a very full confession of the sins of his people with a frank admission of his own share in the national guilt. As we study that long and beautiful prayer, the matter which troubles the mind of this saint of God becomes more and more evident. It is the enormity of the nation's sin, and the fact that it has been so little repented of.[1] Can it possibly be atoned for? Can mercy in such a case as this rejoice against judgment? In this anxious, depressed state of mind the prophet feels that all he can do is to cast himself upon his God in prayer, to confess how well deserved the punishment has been, and at the same time to plead that Jerusalem is still God's holy mountain and the temple still His sanctuary.[2] So, then, after placing in strong contrast God's righteousness and the guilt and the shame

[1] *Vv.* 5–11 and 13.

[2] *Vv.* 16–18.

of the favoured nation,[1] he throws himself on the divine attributes of mercy and unchangeable love.[2] Israel stand in sore need of that mercy, for they have sinned greatly and have suffered the judgment threatened in the law of Moses.[3] God has been true to His threatenings. Never was nation so heavily punished; yet, sad to say, they have not repented, have not entreated His favour, as they ought to have done. God is righteous in *all* that He has done.[4] But *what has He done?* Punished them? *Is that all?* Let Israel's early history tell. Did He not bring forth His people out of Egypt, and win for Himself a glorious name in the sight of the heathen?[5] Since, then, they are still His people, Jerusalem still His city, and the mountain of the house still His holy mountain, the prophet feels that he can appeal even to the divine *righteousness*,[6] *i.e.* to God's just dealings. Surely it cannot be right, *i.e.* it cannot be for His glory, that Israel should continue to be a reproach among the neighbouring nations. For Jehovah's own sake,[7] then, he entreats God to look upon the desolations of His city and sanctuary, to cause His face to shine upon them; to bow down His ear, and hear; to open His eyes, and see.[8] As the prayer nears its close it becomes increasingly earnest and impassioned, till at last it ends in a veritable storming of heaven: "O Lord, hear; O Lord, forgive; O Lord, hearken and do; defer not; for thine own sake, O my God, because thy city and thy people are called by thy name."[9] Can it be believed that we are asked to look upon this striking utterance, poured forth from the heart of a saint and patriot in language taken from "the books" that he has been studying,[10] as an interpolation, in fact an addition to the text?[11] It is indeed an addition, but not in the sense that our opponents mean. It is an addition of the greatest value, first as showing the heart of a saint, and then because of the light which it sheds on the answer granted to his prayer.[12]

After summarising his prayer as a confession of his own sin and the sin of his people Israel, and a supplication before Jehovah his God in behalf of His holy mountain, the seer goes on to tell us that while he was speaking the answer was coming, and that the man Gabriel whom he had seen in an earlier vision,[13] being

[1] *Vv.* 7, 8. [2] *V.* 9. [3] *V.* 13.
[4] *V.* 14. [5] *V.* 15. [6] *V.* 16.
[7] *V.* 19. [8] *V.* 18. [9] *V.* 19.
[10] *V.* 2. [11] *Century Bible*, Daniel, p. 96, note to *v.* 3.

[12] The critic urges (*Century Bible*, p. 96) that the prayer of Dan. ix. cannot have been written away from Palestine. Has he omitted to notice the parenthesis of Dan. vi. 10? Has he forgotten the old song, "My heart's in the Highlands, my heart is not here"?

[13] Dan. viii. 16.

caused to fly swiftly, touched him, about the time of the evening oblation, and acting the part of a friend and teacher, intimated that he had something to reveal. The moment Daniel began to pray, so this messenger tells him, "a word went forth," [1] *i.e.* from God—a word of dismissal to Gabriel, as the succeeding context shows—for Daniel was greatly beloved, a special favourite of heaven. Being so signally favoured, let him now "consider the word [2] and understand the vision" which Gabriel has been commissioned to bring him. So we come down to the vision itself: and first, let it be noted that it is in strict correspondence with all that has gone before, and forms a real answer to the prophet's prayer. Daniel's thoughts had been occupied with the predicted seventy years which were to lead up to the deliverance from the Babylonian captivity. Those seventy years in this characteristically chronological vision are now suddenly expanded, as it were, into seventy weeks of years, that so by their very expansion and the use of the sacred number seven as a multiplier the saint's expectation may be awakened to gain a sight of something far more glorious, a deliverance infinitely greater than the deliverance from the yoke of Babylon. Since it was the greatness of Israel's sin that weighed on the prophet's spirit, and since in his own true summary of his prayer he places first the "confessing my sin and the sin of my people Israel"; so, in the answer to that prayer, first and foremost and as forming the main subject of Gabriel's communication, stands that glorious revelation of the Atonement, opened out in six consecutive clauses, of which the first three dwell on the doing away with sin, and the last three on the bringing in of the good things of the Gospel.[3] These good things are, of course, in the first instance for Israel, and it is implied that the Holy City—God's hearth and altar—will be the scene of the Atonement, which Gabriel thus describes-

"Seventy weeks are decreed upon thy people and upon thy holy city, to finish [or restrain] transgression, and to make an end of [or seal up] sins, and to make reconciliation [or atonement] for iniquity, and to bring in everlasting righteousness, and to seal up vision and prophecy [lit. prophet], and to anoint the most holy [or a holy of holies]."

Between the first three and the last three clauses there is probably a correspondence, thus: transgression is to be restrained, held back; everlasting righteousness is to be brought in. Sin is to

[1] In *v.* 23, for "commandment" read "word," and strike out the definite article.

[2] "Word" is here parallel to "vision."

[3] *V.* 24.

be made an end of, or—according to one reading—"sealed up" and as it were bound. Vision and prophecy are also to be sealed up, *i.e.* brought to an end by their fulfilment, or stamped as true and genuine by their accomplishment. Lastly, iniquity is to be atoned for, and this can only be done by the triumph of the Cross, ending in the anointing of the All-Holy One.

Once more: the first three clauses grow ever stronger till they reach a climax. Sin is first held back, then bound and confined, and lastly done away with, wiped out, by atonement being made. "To make reconciliation" is the same Hebrew verb which occurs so frequently in the Book of Leviticus, and is there rendered both in the A.V. and in the R.V. "to make atonement."[1] It should be so rendered here. Similarly in the last three clauses there is a progressive revelation of the good things of the Gospel. First, everlasting righteousness is brought in, brought forth on the scene, viz. "when he bringeth in the firstborn into the world" (Heb. i. 6). Compare Zech. iii. 8, "I will bring forth my servant the Shoot." "Everlasting righteousness" is a description of the coming salvation, which contains within it a promise of victory over death and the grave. See Isa. li. 6, 8. Secondly, "vision and prophecy" are to be "sealed up," or accredited, by their fulfilment: a fulfilment effected by Christ's holy incarnation, by His earthly life, and above all by His atoning death and His glorious resurrection and ascension. This fulfilment of the older Scriptures was a point on which our Saviour ever laid the greatest emphasis: "Behold, we go up to Jerusalem, and all the things that are written by the prophets shall be accomplished unto the Son of man" (Luke xviii. 31). "To anoint the most holy": lit. "*a holy of holies.*" This is an expression found in the Books of Exodus, Leviticus, Numbers, and Ezekiel. It occurs in all forty-two times. It is used to describe the innermost shrine of the temple and tabernacle eleven times, *i.e.* almost twice as often as its application to any other object. So, then, Gabriel's words here are best illustrated by his message to the Virgin Mother, "The Holy Ghost shall come upon thee, and the power of the Most High shall overshadow thee: wherefore also that which is to be born shall be called holy, the Son of God"; and further by our Lord's words to the Jews, "Destroy this temple"—this sanctuary or shrine, Gr. *ναός*—"and in three days I will raise it up" (John ii. 19). The predicted anointing of a holy of holies refers, not, I think, to the mystery of Christ's holy incarnation, nor even to His baptism when He was "anointed with the Holy Ghost and with power" (Acts x. 38);

[1] The Hebrew word, rendered "mercy-seat" in our English Bible, is from the same root, and denotes the place of atonement, "the propitiatory."

but rather to His royal anointing, when, after His atoning work was done, He was received up into heaven to sit at the right hand of the Father. It is our Saviour's coronation rather than His consecration which is here foretold. For after He had fulfilled "vision and prophecy," this was to be the reward of, as well as the testimony to, His most holy life, "Thou hast loved righteousness and hated wickedness: therefore God, thy God, hath anointed thee with the oil of gladness above thy fellows" (Ps. xlv. 7). It is in anticipation of this exaltation that He is called in this prophecy, "Messiah the Prince." Accordingly, shortly after His mediatorial kingdom had begun, we find St. Peter speaking of Him as exalted by God "to be a Prince and a Saviour for to give repentance to Israel and remission of sins."

We have now looked at the main subject of Gabriel's communication as given in *v.* 24. The next three verses, 25–27, give us the particular details. In defending the traditional view as against the theories of the critics, it is the chronological accuracy of these details which must chiefly engage our attention. The LXX, as we have seen, went to the daring length of doctoring and even altering the numbers; whilst the modern critics in pursuit of their theory are compelled to make excuses for an error of no less than sixty-six years. The traditional view has no need to resort to any such devices. One thing, however, it does require, viz. that in *v.* 25 a comma be placed after "seven weeks" and a colon after "threescore and two weeks." With this, and a few other slight alterations in the rendering, the passage will read thus—

"Know therefore and discern that from the going forth of a commandment [lit. 'a word'[1]] to restore and to build Jerusalem to Prince Messiah shall be seven weeks, and threescore and two weeks: it shall be built again with street and moat, even in troublous times. And after the threescore and two weeks shall Messiah be cut off, and shall have nothing [?]: and the city and the sanctuary the people of the coming Prince shall destroy; and the end of it shall be in the flood, and there shall be war unto an end—desolations are determined. And he shall make firm a covenant with the many for one week, and for half of the week he shall cause sacrifice and oblation to cease: and upon a wing of abominations shall come one that maketh desolate; even unto a consummation, and that determined, shall wrath be poured upon a desolator."

According to the traditional view the chronological interpretation of this remarkable vision runs thus–

[1] Not "*the* word."

457 B.C.[1]–33 A.D.=490 years=70×7 years=the "seventy weeks."

457 B.C. is the date of "the going forth of the commandment to restore and to build Jerusalem," viz. the decree of Artaxerxes I. for the restoration of the Jewish state and polity. Ezra vii. 1, 7, 11–26.

457–408 B.C.=49 years=7×7 years=the first "seven weeks" =the "troublous times" of restoration.

408 B.C.–26 A.D.=434 years=62×7 years=the "threescore and two weeks."

26 A.D. is the date of the manifestation of the Messiah at the beginning of His public ministry.

26–33 A.D. is the last or seventieth "week," ending with the death of Stephen, during which Messiah will "make firm a covenant with the many," *i.e.* with the masses of the people.

30 A.D. is the middle of this last "week," when Messiah by offering Himself on the Cross will "cause sacrifice and oblation to cease."

In order to maintain the traditional interpretation, it is essential, as stated above, that we should follow the punctuation of the A.V. in *v.* 25 by placing a comma after "seven weeks" and a colon after "threescore and two weeks." My readers will ask, why is this punctuation altered in the R.V.? Why did the Revisers place a colon after "seven weeks," and only a comma after "threescore and two weeks"? It was done in accordance with the Hebrew accents of the Massoretic or received text. In the case of the "seven weeks," or, as it stands in the original, "weeks seven," the Massoretes placed the accent Ethnach under the word "seven." In the case of the "threescore and two weeks," in the original "weeks sixty and two," they placed the accent Zakeph Qaton over the "two." Of these two accents Ethnach is the stronger disjunctive. Our Revisers, therefore, represented it by a colon placed after "seven weeks." The weaker accent placed over the "two" they represented by placing a comma after the "threescore and two weeks." But in thus letting ourselves be led by the accents we have to remember that though they are of the greatest value in indicating the connection or otherwise of any word with the words before and after it, and thus discovering to us the arrangement of the clauses, yet at the same time they are something more than mere marks of punctuation. They are accents in the true sense, and as such they lend

[1] To speak more strictly the period begins at some point in the year 458 B.C., and ends at some point in the year A.D. 33, but for the sake of making the calculations I have set down the figures as above.

themselves *to mark emphasis as well as pause.* Dan. ix. 25 thus affords us an instance of what is called emphatic accentuation.[1] The Massoretic punctuators desired to call attention to the fact that the sixty-nine weeks, which were to elapse before the appearance of the Messiah, are for a good reason divided into two periods of seven weeks and sixty-two weeks; a fact which explains why the smaller number stands first. Accordingly they put the stronger accent on the word "seven." Their action may be represented thus: "Know therefore and discern, that from the going forth of a commandment to restore and to build Jerusalem to Prince Messiah shall be weeks *seven* | and weeks threescore and two: it shall be built again," etc. For other examples of emphatic accentuation in the Book of Daniel take the following:

"Then these men assembled together, and found Daniel | making petition and supplication before his God" (vi. 11).

"In the first year of his reign, I Daniel understood by the books | the number of the years," etc. (ix. 2).

"Then this Daniel was distinguished above the presidents and satraps | because an excellent spirit was in him: and the king thought," etc. (vi. 3).

In the above three cases the strong disjunctive Ethnach, of which with few exceptions only one appears in each verse, and in verses of a single clause none, and which usually answers to our colon or semicolon, is placed under the word which precedes the vertical line. The Massoretes wished, then, in the present instance to mark out pointedly the separation of the "seven weeks" from the "threescore and two weeks" which follow. To represent sixty-nine weeks by "seven weeks and threescore and two weeks" would indeed be strange, if there were no reason for it, *i.e.* no reason for the division and no reason for putting the smaller number first. But there was a reason. Those first seven weeks were to witness the restoration and rebuilding of Jerusalem "even in troublous times"; for this too was a matter of anxiety to the seer, though it stood second to his greater anxiety with regard to the enormity of the national sin. Let it be understood, then, that according to the traditional view the first seven weeks are described as a period of reconstruction, while the following sixty-two are left a blank, there being nothing particular to record with respect to them.

I propose now to go through the prophecy, if not exactly *seriatim,* yet examining each particular clause, that so difficulties may be cleared up, obscurities removed, and the fulness and exactness of this astonishing revelation be made plain.

[1] See Wickes' *Hebrew Prose Accents,* pp. 32–35.

The prophecy begins with "the going forth of a commandment [lit. 'a word'] to restore and to build Jerusalem" as its *terminus a quo*. The language here employed has given rise to various questions, such as, whose "word" is it that is meant? when and how did it go forth? and, in what sense would Daniel be likely to understand these words of Gabriel?

Undoubtedly the "word" spoken of is a *divine* word, just as in *v.* 23 the angel says to Daniel, "At the beginning of thy supplication a word went forth." The "word," *dabhar*, there spoken of, as the context shows, is the divine command to Gabriel to reveal the vision to Daniel. Here it is a mandate from the throne of the Divine Majesty for the restoring and rebuilding of Jerusalem. Its object and purpose are thus clearly defined. But since the *time of its utterance* is not defined, and since *dabhar* here, as in *v.* 23, is without the definite article in the original, we must therefore with Ewald, and Francis Brown's Hebrew Lexicon, render it "*a* word," not "*the* word." To render it "*the* word" would be to relegate its utterance to past time, thereby leading the reader to suppose that the "word" intended was the promise made to Jeremiah referred to in *v.* 2; whereas, as a matter of fact, the time of the divine utterance is left quite undefined. In the next place, we turn to the question, how, or in what way, did the divine word go forth? Was it a word of *promise* or of *execution?* The preceding context leads us to decide in favour of the latter. "At the beginning of thy supplications," says Gabriel, "a word went forth, and I am come to tell thee": *i.e.* Gabriel's coming was the immediate result of a divine "word" ordering him to come. Similarly the decree of an earthly ruler for the rebuilding and fortifying of Jerusalem was to be the immediate result of a divine "word" to that effect; thus illustrating the language of the Psalmist, "He sendeth out his commandment upon earth, his word runneth very swiftly."[1] So, then, the opening words of Gabriel, as well as the whole tone of his communication, would lead Daniel to expect a divine "word," that would be uttered *in the future,* rather than to look back to one that had been already uttered in the past. Further, he would expect that the divine "word," being uttered, would be put into immediate execution, presumably by some earthly ruler. This ruler could scarcely be Cyrus. The decree of Cyrus encouraged the Jews to return and to rebuild Jerusalem, but it did not permit them to fortify their city as foretold in Gabriel's message. The newly risen Persian power, however liberal and conciliatory its policy, could hardly

[1] Ps. cxlvii. 15.

be expected as yet to trust its Jewish subjects to *that* extent; not to mention the fact that in the third year of Cyrus Daniel was told of much opposition still to be expected from Persia.[1] According to the traditional view the divine "word" was uttered in the seventh year of Artaxerxes I., 457 B.C., and found its execution in the decree put forth by that monarch, which is recorded in Ezra vii. 12–26. To this the critics object that Artaxerxes' decree is silent as to any command for the rebuilding or fortification of the city of Jerusalem. This is quite true as regards the mere wording of the royal letter. The king's decree is mainly concerned with the official recognition of the God of Israel. He ordains that the Jewish religion is to become the established religion of that part of his dominions, and that Ezra is to teach it to the heathen around. To assist him to do this Ezra is invested with both civil and ecclesiastical authority. Further, his countrymen are invited and encouraged to return along with him; while costly gifts to "the God of Israel" are made by the king and his counsellors, and the most ample provision for carrying on the worship of "the God which is in Jerusalem." Thus in the larger and loftier sense it might truly be said, "The LORD doth build up Jerusalem, he gathereth together the outcasts of Israel,"[2] and this, indeed, is the sense which suits best with Daniel's prayer. For the prophet had spoken to God of Jerusalem as "*thy* city," "*thy* holy mountain," "the city which is called by *thy* name," "*thy* sanctuary." In his eyes Jerusalem was the place of worship, the city which Jehovah had chosen to place His name there; and to him, to restore and build Jerusalem meant above all to establish again the temple worship: the very thing which Artaxerxes did to the fullest extent. At the same time Gabriel's assurance that Jerusalem would be built again "with street and moat" requires us to assign a literal meaning to his declaration as to the restoration of the Holy City. Can, then, Artaxerxes' decree be looked upon as a mandate for the rebuilding and fortification of the town? Apparently this was the light in which the Jews regarded it. They no doubt reasoned that he who showed himself so favourable to the worship of the God of Israel as to make it the established religion of that part of his dominions could not possibly object to the rebuilding of His city; and further, that Jerusalem, being thus rebuilt, must needs be fortified, if only with a view to its security and to the safety of the treasures it contained. Encouraged, therefore, by the royal mandate, the Jews acted accordingly, and proceeded to rebuild the town and raise again its walls. This

[1] Dan. x. 1, 13, 20.

[2] Ps. cxlvii. 2.

is evident from the letter written by their enemies to Artaxerxes, as given in Ezra iv. 7–16, in which they say, "Be it known unto the king, that the Jews which came up from thee are come to us unto Jerusalem: they are building the rebellious and the bad city, and have finished the walls and repaired the foundations."[1] This letter insinuates that the Jews are plotting rebellion, and warns the king twice over that if the walls be rebuilt, they will cease to pay all taxes to the king, and will carry into revolt with them all the country beyond the river, *i.e.* the whole of that wide district to the west of the Euphrates over which Artaxerxes had given Ezra civil authority. The Persian king, who like James I. of England appears to have been well-intentioned but easily swayed by evil and interested counsellors, after looking back into the records of the past and finding that Jerusalem had formerly been the capital of a great kingdom, issued a second decree, ordering the writers of the letter to see that the work ceased, at any rate till further instructions were issued. This second decree appears to have been carried out with great severity by the enemies of the Jews. The work was not merely stopped, but what had been built up was pulled down, so that in the twentieth year of Artaxerxes, 444 B.C., Nehemiah received through his brother Hanani the sad news, "The remnant that are left of the captivity there in the province are in great affliction and reproach: the wall of Jerusalem also is broken down, and the gates thereof are burned with fire." Nehemiah knew, doubtless, of the royal decree stopping the rebuilding of the walls, but he did not know, till his brother told him, of the severity with which it had been carried out. It is thus that the Books of Ezra and Nehemiah lead us into those "troublous times," viz. the "seven weeks," 457–408 B.C., which Gabriel's message foretold. Nehemiah's first visit to Jerusalem lasted from 444–432 B.C. The date of his second visit is not given, but the expression "after certain days," Neh. xiii. 6, is suggestive that it followed soon after the first. During Nehemiah's first visit there were troubles both within and without, as his Book abundantly testifies; and doubtless very grave causes for anxiety still continued, otherwise he would not so soon have returned after that first lengthy visit. With respect to his second visit at some time subsequent to 432 B.C., related in the last chapter of his Book, it has been objected that no indication is given of any work of rebuilding still going on; but then the record is so scanty that this is nothing to be wondered at. It should

[1] The section Ezra iv. 7–23 has evidently strayed from its proper place. Chronologically it should stand between Ezra x. and Neh. i. See *Century Bible in loco.*

further be noted that Gabriel's words are capable of a double meaning. We may either understand him to say that the rebuilding and fortifying of the town would extend over a period of forty-nine years [1]—which may very well have been the case for anything we know to the contrary—or, again, that the "troublous times," which were to witness the rebuilding, would extend over that period. From the latter half of those forty-nine years a solitary ray of light reaches us from the Elephantiné papyri in the letter sent by the Jewish community at that place to Bagoas the Persian governor at Jerusalem in 408 B.C., just at the close of the "seven weeks." The letter shows that a state of peace existed between Jerusalem and Samaria at that time; inasmuch as the Jews of Elephantiné openly tell Bagoas that they have also written to Delaiah and Shelemiah, the sons of Sanballat the governor of Samaria. What this somewhat surprising state of things means it is difficult to say. It would seem that either Sanballat must have changed his tactics and adopted a more friendly policy, or that the laxer members of the Jewish community at Jerusalem must have succeeded in ousting the party faithful to the régime instituted by Nehemiah.[2] On the whole, then, we freely admit that owing to want of information respecting that portion of Jewish history, we are unable to say why the period of rebuilding or the "troublous times"—whichever way we understand the angel's words—are limited to seven weeks of years, *i.e.* to forty-nine years. But the exact fulfilment of other periods in the prophecy, occurring in times about which we are better informed, makes us feel sure that did we but know the story of those earlier days, we should as easily recognise the suitability of the separating those first seven weeks from the sixty-two that follow, as we recognise the propriety of the distinguishing the last week of the seventy from the sixty-nine that precede it.

A difficulty in the traditional view arises from the fact that it is not expressly stated in Gabriel's words that the first seven weeks correspond to the time of rebuilding, or at any rate to the "troublous times." Possibly the Massoretes wished to make the sense plainer when they placed an emphatic accent after "weeks seven" and a lesser accent after "weeks sixty and two." Those first seven weeks were to witness something for which Daniel had earnestly prayed, viz. the raising up of the holy city out of

[1] *Cambridge Bible*, Daniel, p. 145 (2).

[2] It is also noticeable that the sons of Sanballat bear the Jewish names Delaiah and Shelemiah, both common names at that period—see Neh. vi. 10 and xiii. 13—whence some suppose that their father was a Jew by birth despite his Babylonian name Sanballat.

its state of utter desolation; while the remaining threescore and two weeks, so far as the prophet's prayer was concerned, were a blank except as they led the way to the coming of the Messiah. To that great event our attention is next directed. "From the going forth of a commandment to restore and to build Jerusalem to Prince Messiah shall be seven weeks and threescore and two weeks," *i.e.* 483 years, viz. the interval from 457 B.C. to A.D. 26, at which latter date the Messiah was publicly manifested to Israel, first by the great forerunner, and then by the opening of His public ministry. "I knew him not;" says the Baptist, "but that he should be made manifest to Israel, for this cause came I baptising with water."[1] "We have found the Messiah,"[2] are Andrew's words to his brother Simon. Indeed, that first chapter of St. John's Gospel may be looked upon as an inspired record of the fulfilment of this part of the evangelic prophecy.

מָשִׁיחַ נָגִיד, *Mâshiach Nâgid*—rendered in the A.V. "Messiah the Prince," in the R.V. "the anointed one, the prince"—I have given as "Prince Messiah," just as "Nebuchadnezzar the king" ="king Nebuchadnezzar," and "Saul the king"="king Saul." As both *Mâshiach* and *Nâgid* are titles, they are treated as proper names and appear in Hebrew without the definite article. With the compound title, *Mâshiach Nâgid*, "Prince Messiah," compare פָּקִיד נָגִיד, *Pâqid Nâgid,* "Chief Officer," the title of a temple official which occurs in Jer. xx. 1. Compare also אֵל גִּבּוֹר, *'El Gibbor,* "Mighty God," Isa. ix. 5; יָהּ יְהוָֹה, "*Jah-Jehovah,*" Isa. xxvi. 4; and in this Book of Daniel, ii. 25, compare טוּר רב, *Tur Rabh,* "The Great Mountain," a title of the god Bel there transferred to Jehovah "the God of heaven." In all these cases we notice the absence of the definite article from either member of the compound.

This is the only place in the Old Testament where "Messiah" is used as a title or proper name of the Coming One. In other passages we have merely "my," "thy," "his anointed." The facts that the title is here associated with the restored Jerusalem —indirectly indicated as the place where "Messiah" would be "cut off"—and that in Daniel's prayer Jerusalem is described as "thy holy mountain," are alike suggestive that it is taken from Ps. ii. 2, "The kings of the earth set themselves and the rulers take counsel together against the Lord and against his anointed," seeing that further on in that Psalm, viz. in *v.* 6, Jehovah gives to Zion that same name, "my holy hill," or "mountain," which we find in Daniel's prayer. The second Psalm is a very striking one,

[1] John i. 31.

[2] *Ibid.* i. 41.

with a distinct character of its own. It was referred to the Messiah by the ancient Jewish commentators, and was looked upon by the Early Church as prophetic of the united action of both Jewish and Gentile rulers which led to Messiah's violent death and so to His resurrection.[1] Further, the view given in it of Messiah's kingdom is in striking harmony with such passages as Dan. ii. 35, 44, and vii. 13, 14; whilst certain verbal correspondences also strike us, such as the use of the uncommon word, rendered "rage" in Ps. ii. 1, and "assemble" in Dan. vi. 6, 11, 15, which is not found in any other passage; and the word used to describe the power of iron to break in pieces other things, used both in Ps. ii. 9 and Dan. ii. 40.

The use of "Messiah" as a proper name in the vision of Dan. ix. is a stumbling-block in the eyes of the critics. Prof. Driver observes that if the Book of Daniel were written by Daniel this use in it of "Messiah" would be "extremely unlikely."[2] But why so? Surely some considerable space of time must have elapsed between the date of the composition of Ps. ii. and the era of Daniel. The Psalm is attributed to the age of David, Solomon, or of Ahaz. Take the latest of these, and we have an interval of nearly two hundred years: quite enough to allow of a descriptive becoming a title. In the Book of Zechariah, iii. 8, we have another title of the expected King. "I will bring forth," saith Jehovah, "my servant the Branch." Prof. Driver readily acknowledges that the term *Tsemach*, "Branch," or rather "Shoot," is here used as a proper name, and is therefore without the definite article in the original;[3] and further, that it is used as a title of the Messiah, a title borrowed from the words of Jer. xxiii. 5, "Behold, the days come, saith the Lord, that I will raise unto David a righteous branch." If *tsemach* from being a descriptive could become a title within less than a century, why not *mâshiach* in nearly double that time?

"And after the threescore and two weeks shall the anointed one be cut off": so the R.V.; but better, "shall Messiah be cut off," or "shall the Anointed One be cut off." For since there is no definite article before *mâshiach* in the original, we must either look upon it as a title, or render it with the critics, "an anointed one." In the view of the passage taken by the critics the words, "to anoint the most holy," in *v.* 24, refer to the re-dedication of

[1] See *The Speaker's Commentary*, Psalms, p. 175; and for the N.T. references to this psalm see Acts iv. 25, 26, xiii. 33, and Heb. i. 5.

[2] *Cambridge Bible*, Daniel, p. 144 (1).

[3] *Century Bible*, Zechariah, p. 197, footnote.

the temple or altar in the days of the Maccabees; the "anointed one" of *v.* 25 is either Cyrus or Jeshua the son of Jozadak, and the "anointed one" of *v.* 26 the high priest Onias III. In the traditional view the reference in all three cases is to Christ.

Messiah is to be "cut off," *i.e.* He is to suffer a violent death as contrasted with a natural one. The Hebrew verb here employed is often used in the Books of Exodus, Leviticus, and Numbers of being sentenced to death. Compare also Isa. liii. 8—where a different verb of a similar import is used—"he was cut off out of the land of the living."

"And shall have nothing": lit. "and there is not to him." The meaning is obscure, and perhaps intentionally so. We may supply the word "guilt," and see in the testimony of Pilate, "I find no fault in him," or in the utterance of the dying robber, "This man hath done nothing amiss," the fulfilment of this part of Gabriel's message. Or, again, the words may mean that He has no one to stand by Him, none to take His part, and may be best illustrated by our Lord's words to His apostles on the night of His betrayal, "Ye shall be scattered every man to his own, and shall leave me alone."[1] Lastly, we may take the somewhat similar meaning given in the R.V.M., "There shall be none belonging to him," and contrast the few disciples found in Jerusalem after the Crucifixion[2] with the multitudes who used to follow Him in the early days of His Galilean ministry, or even with the crowds who had welcomed Him into Jerusalem only a few days before. The short, terse expression, "and there is not to him," takes in all these, and probably was intended to do so.

[1] John xvi. 32.

[2] Acts i. 15.

18

The Evangelic Prophecy, Judgment Upon the Nation

OUR last chapter carried us down to the death of the Messiah. We resume our analysis of the vision in the middle of *v.* 26, where the judgment on the nation that put Him to death comes into view with the words, " And the city and the sanctuary the people of the coming Prince shall destroy." As we have seen, Jerusalem is to be rebuilt despite the sins of her kings, her prophets, priests, and people. But presently the rebuilt city will be again destroyed, because of this her crowning sin, viz. the murder of the Messiah.

" The people of the coming Prince " : lit. according to the Hebrew usage, " the Prince, the coming one," *Nâgid habbâ*. As stated above, " the Prince that shall come " is to be identified with " Prince Messiah " in the previous verse. The picture there is of Christ coming to save ; here, of His coming to inflict judgment. This, then, is one of the passages from which the Messiah appears to have received the appellation " the Coming One." " When John heard in the prison the works of the Christ," *i.e.* when he heard that Jesus in His miracles of compassionate love was doing the works that the Christ was to do, " he sent by his disciples and said unto him, Art thou he that cometh ? "—better, " Art thou the Coming One ? "—Gr. ὁ ἐρχόμενος=Heb. *habbâ*—" or look we for another," a different person ? John seems to have doubted for the time being whether the Coming One and the Messiah were one and the same Person. Maybe, in his mind at the time when he asked the question, the thought of the Messiah was associated with works of mercy and love and with the vicarious atonement to be made by the sacrifice of the Lamb of God, to whom he had pointed his followers : the thought of the Coming One, with the sterner work of justice and judgment.[1] Could it be, then, that they were

[1] That the title, " the Coming One," may also be used of Christ as coming to save is clear, not only from Ps. xl. 6, 7, but also from the fact that the Prince, who in *v.* 26 comes " to destroy the city and the sanctuary," is the same Person who, as stated in *v.* 27, will " cause the sacrifice and the oblation to cease," viz. by the sacrifice of Himself.

two different persons? This passage in Daniel might seem at first sight to lend itself to such a supposition, seeing that *Mâshiach Nâgid* comes to suffer, whilst *Nâgid Habbâ* comes to inflict judgment. In this connection it is noticeable that in Heb. x. 37 the title ὁ ἐρχόμενος, "the Coming One," is actually used of Christ's coming to put an end to the Jewish state and polity. The passage is an adaptation of Hab. ii. 3 in the LXX version, and runs thus: "For yet a very little while, he that cometh"—or better, "the Coming One"—"shall come, and shall not tarry." To this part of Daniel's vision our Saviour refers in the parable of the Marriage of the King's Son, Matt. xxii. 7: "But the king was wroth; and he sent his armies, and destroyed those murderers, and burned their city." It will perhaps be objected that the king in the parable is Almighty God. Be it so; but the avenging army is under the command of His beloved Son. Compare Ps. cx. 1, 2, 5, 6. Stier, writing on our Lord's parable in Matt. xxii., says, "If thou wilt see a most special testimony to the true wrath of God which broke forth after the times of longsuffering, and in due time, then look at the destruction of Jerusalem, and see how the wrath of God is come upon the Jews εἰς τέλος (1 Thess. ii. 16), *i.e.* עַד כָּלָה, ἕως τέλους, Dan. ix. 26, 27. The Lord refers precisely to this passage of Daniel." . . . "As at chap. xxiv. 15 He mentions 'the abomination of desolation,' so now He says πέμψας τὰ στρατεύματα αὐτοῦ, 'he sent forth his armies,' which corresponds to 'the people of the prince that shall come' in Daniel." . . . "Just when *Messiah the Prince* appears as the Messiah cut off, He comes as *the Prince* to destroy the city and the sanctuary. The Romans, as hostile hosts, serve the judging Lord and God of Israel, as angels of judgment." [1]

It is objected that any reference in *v.* 26 to the destruction of Jerusalem would be out of place before the first half of *v.* 27; and also that that catastrophe, which happened forty years after the cutting off of the Messiah, does not fall within the seventy prophetic weeks, 457 B.C. to A.D. 33. I answer that the series of events, which led to the final overthrow in A.D. 70, began some years before that overthrow. Further, that in the true suitability of things it is most natural to look upon *v.* 26b as describing the judgment to be inflicted because of the great national crime foretold in *v.* 26a. Even before that crime was committed, its punishment was invoked by the multitude: "All the people answered and said, His blood be on us and on our children." [2] And the moment it was committed that punishment was due. We note,

[1] *The Words of the Lord Jesus*, vol. iii. p. 139.
[2] Matt. xxvii. 25.

too, that our Saviour Himself very shortly before His death, realising the great crime that was so soon to be committed, had that terrible retribution distinctly before His mind, and found in it one of the bitter drops in His cup of anguish. He foresaw "the end thereof," coming with "the flood"[1] of invasive war, "wars and rumours of wars," war following upon war even "unto an end," desolations "determined" on the guilty city and nation by the offended Majesty of high heaven.

Gabriel having thus revealed the judgment coming on the rebellious city that murdered its lawful Prince, goes on in *v.* 27 to describe the Prince's popularity with His subjects during that last seventieth week. His words may be rendered thus: "He shall make firm a covenant with the many for one week." "He shall make firm," or maintain, "*a* covenant," *not* "the covenant," as in ix. 4, where God's covenant with Israel is intended, nor "the covenant" in the sense of the Jewish religion and ritual, as in xi. 22, 28, 30, 32; but "a covenant" in the sense of a bond of friendship, amity, and good will. Compare Ps. lv. 20, "He hath put forth his hands against such as were at peace with him: he hath profaned his covenant." Also we must translate "*the* many," *not* "many," thus giving the article its proper force. By "the many" are meant the multitude, the masses of the people as contrasted with their rulers. So in xi. 33 we should read, "the teachers of the people shall instruct the many," where the masses are contrasted with their religious guides. Compare also xi. 39 and xii. 3. On the other hand, in xii. 2, where the word is used without the article, our Revisers have given us the right rendering: "Many of them that sleep in the dust of the earth shall awake"; "many," not as contrasted with others who do not awake—which would be a denial of the universality of the resurrection—but simply as drawing attention to their vast numbers. The prophecy that Messiah would establish and maintain good relations with the masses of the Jewish people during that last week, A.D. 26–33, and that He would yet nevertheless meet with a violent death in the midst of that week, was fulfilled to the letter. Christ's teaching was popular with the masses. "The common people[2] heard him gladly," is St. Mark's observation with regard to the temper shown by the multitude almost on the eve of the Crucifixion. Again, only a few weeks later, the adherents of the crucified and risen Jesus of Nazareth are described as "having favour with all the people."[3] In those early days the Church of

[1] Cf. Dan. xi. 22; Isa. viii. 7, 8, xxviii. 2, 17, 18; Nah. i. 8.
[2] ὁ πολὺς ὄχλος. Mark xii. 37.
[3] Acts ii. 47.

Christ went forward by leaps and bounds among Messiah's own people. "Believers were the more added to the Lord, multitudes both of men and women."[1] "The number of the disciples multiplied in Jerusalem exceedingly; and a great company of the priests were obedient to the faith"[2]; and so great was the popularity of the new doctrine that the rulers became apprehensive for their own safety, witness their words to the apostles, "Ye intend to bring this man's blood upon us."[3] One would suppose, indeed, after reading the first six chapters of the Acts, that Christianity was about to take the place of Judaism among the Jews of Jerusalem. But this was not to be. The popularity of the new faith among the masses lasted down to the death of Stephen in A.D. 33, but no longer. Then the tide turned. "There arose on that day"—the day of the death of the first martyr for Christ—"a great persecution against the church which was in Jerusalem; and they were all scattered abroad."[4] "It would appear," writes Alford, "that not only the authorities of the Jews, not only the Sanhedrim, who appear to have been the only ones concerned in the death of Stephen, but the people of the Jews also took part in the persecution of the church: because it hardly could have been general, it hardly could have been such as to scatter them away from Jerusalem, which it did, unless it had been throughout the people themselves."[5] The death of Stephen thus formed a crisis in Messiah's dealings with His own people. Down to the close of that seventieth week, in A.D. 33, the covenant held firm, friendly relations were maintained between Him and them, the Crucifixion was the only break in those relations. It was, so to say, a dark line drawn across the bright spectrum; but only a line. But after the death of Stephen all was dark for the Jewish people, the covenant ceased to hold. Stephen himself, that great master of the older Scriptures, seems to have realised that a change was near at hand. The character of his preaching as described by his enemies is suggestive that he not only understood the details of Daniel's vision, but that it gave the tone to his public addresses. "We have heard him say that this Jesus of Nazareth shall destroy this place"[6]—compare *v.* 26, "The people of the coming Prince shall destroy the city and the sanctuary";—"and shall change the customs which Moses delivered unto us"—compare *v.* 27, "In the midst of the week he shall cause the sacrifice and the oblation to cease." That the "cutting off" of the Messiah and His violent death was much on the mind of

[1] Acts v. 14. [2] *Ibid.* vi. 7. [3] *Ibid.* v. 28.
[4] *Ibid.* viii. 1. [5] *Homilies on the Acts,* chaps. i.–x., p. 233.
[6] Acts vi. 14.

the first martyr, we know, not only from his dying utterances, but also from his words to the Sanhedrim, when he told them to their faces that they had been the betrayers and murderers of the Righteous One.[1] It will thus be seen why the seventy weeks are made to close with the death of Stephen. Also this fact, too often overlooked, is brought prominently into view, viz. that while the fate of the Jewish state and polity was sealed by the great crime of the Crucifixion, nevertheless a day of grace, as indicated in the parable of the Barren Fig-tree,[2] was prolonged for the people of Jerusalem for about three and a half years after that event, by that early popularity of Christianity among the masses ; which period ended with the death of the first martyr. By this second crime, or at any rate by the adverse spirit which was stirred up at the time, the nation may be said to have closed the door upon themselves. So, then, as the angel tells Daniel, "*seventy* weeks are determined upon thy people" ; *not* sixty-nine weeks and a half ending with the Crucifixion, but seventy weeks ending with the death of Stephen. This was to be the limit of Jerusalem's day of grace. For just as in Ezekiel's vision the glory of the LORD first mounted up and stood over the threshold of the Holy House, then hovered for awhile over the east gate of the court, and then passing away eastward stood over the Mount of Olives, ere it quitted the neighbourhood of the doomed city : [3] so Messiah, the true Glory of His people, remained near them for three and a half years after they crucified Him. For by His Ascension from the Mount of Olives they were allowed, so to say, to see His glory over that eastern hill, while for a short space He was proclaimed among them as exalted by God "with his right hand to be a Prince and a Saviour, for to give repentance to Israel, and remission of sins." [4] It would indeed have been a sad thing, if, when the great sacrifice for sin had been offered up at Jerusalem, no opportunity had been offered to the Jewish people to confess their crowning sin, and their trust in the atonement made by Him whom they in their blind rage had crucified. But in point of fact such an opportunity was given, and many both among the priests and the people accepted it. The apostles were charged by Christ to begin their witness for Him from Jerusalem ; [5] and that they understood their orders well is clear from St. Peter's words to the people after the healing of the lame man at the Beautiful door of the temple, "Unto you first God, having raised up his Servant, sent him to bless you, in turning away every one of you from your

[1] Acts vii. 52. [2] Luke xiii. 6–9. [3] Ezek. x. 4, 19 and xi. 23.
[4] Acts v. 31. [5] Luke xxiv. 47. Cf. Acts i. 8.

iniquities."[1] In order, then, to give His apostles the opportunity to make Him known to the people who had crucified Him, Messiah Himself established a pact with the multitude, which, except for a brief interval at the time of the Crucifixion, lasted for just a week of years, viz. from the beginning of His public ministry down to the death of Stephen.

"And for half of the week he," viz. Messiah, "shall cause sacrifice and oblation to cease": *i.e.* for the last half of the seventieth week, A.D. 30–33, Messiah, by the sacrifice of Himself, will put an end to the Levitical sacrifices. *Zebach uminchâh*, "sacrifice and oblation," both the animal sacrifices and the bloodless offerings. Compare 1 Sam. ii. 29, Isa. xix. 21, Jer. xvii. 26, and especially Ps. xl. 6 (7). As was shown by the rending of the veil of the temple at the time of the Crucifixion, the death of Christ put an end to the worship carried on in the temple. The Levitical sacrifices, indeed, continued to be offered down to the destruction of Jerusalem, but in the sight of Heaven the Jewish sacrifices ceased with the sacrifice of the death of Christ: the type of necessity gave place to the antitype. Hence the best commentary on this part of the prophecy is found in Heb. x. 4–9, where the writer interprets in its loftiest sense the language of Ps. xl. 6–8, putting the words into the lips of the Messiah. The passage runs thus-

"For it is impossible that the blood of bulls and goats should take away sins. Wherefore when he cometh into the world, he saith, Sacrifice and offering thou wouldest not, but a body didst thou prepare for me: in whole burnt offerings and sacrifices for sin thou hadst no pleasure; then said I, Lo, I am come, (In the roll of the book it is written of me) to do thy will, O God. Saying above, Sacrifices and offerings and whole burnt offerings and sacrifices for sin thou wouldest not, neither hadst pleasure therein (the which are offered according to the law), then hath he said, Lo, I am come to do thy will. He taketh away the first, that he may establish the second."

It is, then, this taking away of the Levitical sacrifices by "the offering of the body of Jesus Christ once for all,"[2] which is signified by Gabriel's words, "For half of the week he shall cause sacrifice and oblation to cease."

"And upon a wing of abominations shall come one that maketh desolate; even unto a consummation, and that which is determined, shall wrath be poured upon a desolator." These last

[1] Acts iii. 26.

[2] Heb. x. 10.

clauses are not to be looked upon as a repetition or enlargement of the statement made in *v.* 26 that the city and the sanctuary would be destroyed by " the people of the coming Prince." The reference there is to the armies of Rome, marshalled under Messiah Himself, which are to capture and destroy both city and temple. Here the vision points to a yet more terrible foe, which was to arise within the doomed city and stir up civil war : a foe soon to become notorious for its abominable pollution of holy places.

The Zealots, whom Josephus so sternly denounces as the direct cause of the destruction of Jerusalem,[1] received their name from their affected patriotism and pretended zeal for the Law. In reality they were robber bands, cut-throats and murderers, the Bolshevists of those days ; and are more truthfully described by their other name, Sicarii or Assassins. Herod the Great in his early days did much to put down these robbers, who had made their strongholds in the precipitous hillsides of Galilee. But in the last years of the Jewish state this evil broke out afresh in the same quarter. A strong band of these men had held the town of Gischala against the Romans ; but when they saw its capture to be certain, they contrived by a stratagem to make their escape to Jerusalem under the leadership of John of Gischala. Having made their way into the capital, they set to work to corrupt the younger men, and stirred them up to rebel against the Romans. Meanwhile they were joined by many like characters from all parts of the country, and were able by making themselves masters of the temple to turn it into a fortress, from which they could sally out into Jerusalem and commit any acts of tyranny and savage barbarity which might serve their purpose. There could be no better description of the prosperous career for the time being of atrocious wickedness, violence, murder, rapine, and pollution, engaged in so lightly by the Zealot army, and of the terrible gloom which it cast over Jerusalem, than those brief words of Gabriel, " Upon a wing of abominations shall come one that maketh desolate." These bold, determined, desperate robber-ruffians, who jested over holy things, and yet when it suited their purpose professed a zeal for the Law and a belief in the prophets, sailed forth boldly on their career of crime like some powerful bird of prey the terror of the flocks.[2] Theirs was a wickedness which for a while prospered exceedingly. They seemed to be borne along on the wing of their own abominations, buoyed up by the very atrocities in which they indulged, by their acts of sacrilege and violence. Their crimes were " abominations " in the truest

[1] *Wars of the Jews*, book iv. 3, 3.
[2] Cf. Isa. viii. 8 ; Jer. xlviii. 40 ; Hos. viii. 1.

sense, objects of detestation and horror, "desolating," *i.e.* appalling those who witnessed them, for such is the force of the two Hebrew words here used. Thus they seized the appointment to the High Priesthood, and elected by lot to that sacred office a rustic clown, whom they decked with the priestly robes and brought him forth as if on the stage, indulging in uncontrolled merriment over his awkwardness, while the more earnest-minded of the priests shed hot tears of indignation at this horrid profanation.[1] Josephus, speaking of the Zealots, says that they ridiculed the oracles of the prophets which they themselves were instrumental in fulfilling, adding that "there was a certain ancient oracle of those men, that the city should then be taken and the sanctuary burnt, by right of war, when a sedition should invade the Jews, and their own hands should pollute the temple of God." [2] Again, addressing his rival, John of Gischala, one of the principal leaders of the Zealots, just three weeks before the capture of the city, he says, "Who is there that does not know what the writings of the ancient prophets contain in them—and particularly that oracle which is just now going to be fulfilled upon this miserable city—for they foretold that this city should be taken when somebody shall begin the slaughter of his own countrymen! and are not both the city and the entire temple now full of the dead bodies of your countrymen! It is God, therefore, it is God Himself, who is bringing on this fire, to purge that city and temple by means of the Romans, and is going to pluck up this city, which is full of your pollutions." [3] There is some reason for thinking that the special oracle referred to by the Jewish historian is this vision at which we are looking, for it will be noted that *pollution* is the keynote on which the Jewish priest and historian harps. The Zealots have *filled Jerusalem with their pollutions.* More particularly have they *polluted the temple of God.* John had told Josephus that he had no fear of the city being taken because it was God's city. In answer to which Josephus replied in a tone of bitterest satire: "To be sure thou hast kept this city wonderfully pure for God's sake. *The temple also continues entirely unpolluted.*" [3] Again and again we find references to the horrible pollution of the temple. Thus: "Those men made the temple of God a stronghold for themselves." [4] . . . "When they were satiated with the unjust actions they had done towards men, they transferred their contumelious behaviour to God Himself and came into the sanctuary with polluted feet." [5] Ananus, one of the high priests, is represented as saying to the

[1] *Wars of the Jews,* book iv. 3, 8.
[2] *Ibid.* book iv. 6, 3.
[3] *Ibid.* book vi. 2, 1.
[4] *Ibid.* book iv. 3, 7.
[5] *Ibid.* book iv. 3, 6.

multitude, "Certainly it had been good for me to die before I had seen *the house of God full of so many abominations*, or these sacred places that ought not to be trodden on at random, filled with the feet of these bloodshedding villains."[1] Jesus, the eldest high priest next to Ananus, addressing the Idumeans who had been invited to Jerusalem by the Zealots, speaks in the same strain. After denouncing the Zealots as the very rascality and offscouring of the whole country, he adds–

"They are robbers, who by their prodigious wickedness have profaned this most sacred floor, and who are now to be seen drinking themselves drunk in the sanctuary." . . . "These profane wretches have proceeded to that degree of madness, as not only to have transferred their impudent robberies out of the country and the remote cities into this city, the very face and head of the whole nation, but out of the city into the temple also: for that is now made their receptacle and refuge, and the fountain-head whence their preparations are made against us. And this place, which is adored by the habitable world, and honoured by such as only know it by report, as far as the ends of the earth, is trampled upon by these wild beasts born among ourselves."[2]

The strong emphasis with which Josephus thus again and again describes this awful pollution leads us to think that the certain ancient oracle concerning the capture and purification by fire of the city and sanctuary after the Jews with their own hands had polluted the temple of God, can be none other than this vision of Daniel, seeing that this very clause, "upon a wing of abominations shall come one that maketh desolate," was undoubtedly understood to refer to the temple in the days of Josephus, as may be gathered from the Septuagint rendering of the passage: *καὶ ἐπὶ τὸ ἱερὸν βδέλυγμα τῶν ἐρημώσεων ἔσται*, "and upon the temple there shall be an abomination of desolations."[3]

The origin of the above somewhat remarkable reading of the Septuagint in which the Hebrew עַל כְּנַף, *'al kĕnaph*, "upon the wing," is replaced by *ἐπὶ τὸ ἱερὸν*, "upon the temple," may be thus explained: The Hebrew word כָּנָף, *kânaph*, "wing," is also used of the extremity of anything, *e.g.* the "skirt" of a robe,[4] the "border" of a garment,[5] the "uttermost part" of the earth,[6] the four "corners" of the earth.[7] Hence taken architecturally

[1] *Wars of the Jews*, book iv. 3, 10. [2] *Ibid.* book iv. 4, 3.
[3] Theodotion's rendering is similar with the omission of ἔσται.
[4] 1 Sam. xv. 27. [5] Num. xv. 38. [6] Isa. xxiv. 16.
[7] *Ibid.* xi. 12.

it would signify a "gable," or "battlements," or, above all, a "pinnacle," just as the Greek πτερύγιον—lit. "a little wing,"—is used in precisely the same sense in Matt. iv. 5. The Hebrew word *kânaph* being thus understood, the clause could be read, "And upon a pinnacle there will be abominations making desolate." Now if Zion, in the words of Micah, was "the tower of the flock," [1] —"the very face and head of the whole nation," as Jesus the high priest phrases it in the passage quoted above—then undoubtedly the temple was the "pinnacle" of that tower, its culminating point. Thus, then, the Septuagint were led to give as a translation what is really an interpretation, "And upon the temple there shall be an abomination of desolations." In this light, then, the clause would probably be understood by Josephus, and our Saviour Himself has set His seal to the correctness of this interpretation. His words as given in Matt. xxiv. 15 run thus: Ὅταν οὖν ἴδητε τὸ βδέλυγμα τῆς ἐρημώσεως τὸ ῥηθὲν διὰ Δανὶηλ τοῦ προφήτου, ἑστὸς ἐν τόπῳ ἁγίῳ, ὁ ἀναγινώσκων νοείτω· τότε οἱ ἐν τῇ Ἰουδαίᾳ φευγέτωσαν ἐπὶ τὰ ὄρη. "When therefore ye see the abomination of desolation, which was spoken of by Daniel the prophet, standing in the holy place, (let him that readeth understand) then let them that are in Judea flee unto the mountains." By "the," or "a," "holy place" there is not the least doubt that our Saviour points to the temple; also, with the Septuagint version before us, there can be no doubt that the passage in the Book of Daniel to which He refers is the one at which we are looking, since in the parenthesis, "let him that readeth understand," we find an echo, as it were, of the words of Gabriel, "consider the matter and understand the vision," "know therefore and discern." The sign thus mercifully given by Christ was not only unmistakable in its fulfilment, but allowed ample time for all who gave heed to it to escape like Lot from the doomed city; for the temple was seized by the Zealots and made their stronghold some three years before the town was first invested by the Romans, and then enclosed within a wall of circumvallation.[2]

The desolations and abominations wrought by the Zealots were destined to end in their own utter destruction. "Even unto a consummation and that determined," *i.e.* "Even unto the consummation determined upon, shall wrath be poured upon a desolator." [3] Josephus' long tale of horrors shows us how exactly

[1] Micah iv. 8.

[2] Cf. Lewin's *Fasti Sacri*, p. 348.

[3] The word "wrath" is not in the original, and has to be supplied in order to make up the sense. Perhaps it would be better, therefore, to adopt Dr. Charles' rendering, "Until the consummation that is doomed is poured out upon the desolator." See *Century Bible* on Dan. ix. 27.

this part of the prophecy was fulfilled. His ever-famous work, *The Wars of the Jews*, closes just where our prophecy closes, viz. with the outpouring of the vials of wrath on the desolator. Of the Zealot leaders, he tells us how the crafty John of Gischala was condemned to perpetual imprisonment, and how the brave Simon the son of Gioras, after being drawn by a rope into the Roman Forum amid the torments of those that drew him, was there slain in the hour of the triumph of Vespasian and Titus. Then at the close of his seventh and last Book he tells us the fate of the remnant of the Sicarii. These men after the fall of Massada, the last Jewish stronghold to be taken, fled to Egypt, and even up the Nile as far as Thebes. They were caught and brought back, put to torture, and on their refusing to acknowledge Cæsar as their lord were burnt to death. The one bright spot in them was their amazing courage, for even their children were found ready to face this fiery doom.

"Consummation" is an awkward term. The Hebrew word thus rendered simply means complete utter destruction. The expression "a consummation and that determined" is a hendiadys, signifying the complete irrevocable destruction which the Almighty means to bring upon the desolator. The phrase is a quotation from Isa. x. 23, "A consummation, and that determined, shall the Lord, the Lord of hosts, make in the midst of all the earth." The same expression is repeated in Isa. xxviii. 22.

To the traditional interpretation just given it is objected that "if the Revised Version of verse 27 be correct—and it is certainly the natural meaning of the Hebrew—a reference to the death of Christ is excluded altogether, for the verse does not then describe the final *abolition* of material sacrifices, but their temporary *suspension* for 'half of the week.'"[1] While admitting the correctness of the Revisers' rendering, "for half of the week," I would point out to my readers that the above objection is based on a wrong view of the purport of the revelation made to Daniel. Daniel's prayer had been *for his own people*, not for the world at large, and for his people *nationally* rather than individually. So, then, the answer to that prayer, brought by Gabriel, in its primary import only concerns Israel and Israel's nationality. As the angel says at the outset, "Seventy weeks are determined"—cut off, portioned off[2]—"upon thy people and upon thy holy city." From the higher spiritual point of view, *i.e.* from the divine standpoint, Israel's existence as a nation ends with the close of the

[1] *Cambridge Bible*, Daniel, p. 146.

[2] The word used is significant as indicating the strictness of the arithmetical calculations which form the framework of the prophecy.

seventieth week, A.D. 33. Their fall, their lapse, their casting away [1] dates from then; and what Gabriel unfolds is the great fact that for the last half week of their existence, viz. from A.D. 30–33, the Levitical sacrifices and ritual will cease in the sight of God. Here, again, the meaning is spiritual. As a matter of fact the sacrifices did not cease to be offered till the destruction of Jerusalem; but in God's sight they ceased with the sacrifice of the death of His beloved Son. At the end, then, of the seventy weeks, the period "determined," *i.e.* portioned off in the divine foreknowledge, Israel drops out of sight, and is lost, as it were, in the darkness. We know, indeed, from Christ's own words, as well as from those of His apostle St. Paul,[2] that they will come into the light again; but nothing is here said of their restoration to the divine favour. In this vision only one faint ray of light is shed on Jerusalem's dark future in the closing statement that heaven's wrath will be poured upon the desolator, *i.e.* on the ruthless power that polluted Jehovah's sanctuary and desolated His city. This predicted outpouring of wrath might give some slight ground for the hope that even in that darkest hour Jehovah had not finally forsaken His city and His people.

[1] Rom. xi. 11, 15.
[2] Matt. xxiii. 39; Luke xxi. 24; Rom. xi. 12, 15, 25–32; 2 Cor. iii. 16.

19

Chronology of the Seventieth Week

THE chronology of the last of the Prophetic Weeks is a matter of such importance as to demand a short chapter to itself. The Weeks begin in the year 458 B.C., the seventh year of Artaxerxes I.,[1] and they end in the year A.D. 33. As they are not weeks of days, but weeks of years, the question as to literal days, or even weeks and months, does not enter into our calculations: we are only concerned with the *years*. Thus with regard to the " cutting off " of the Messiah, which according to the evangelic interpretation is to happen in the middle of the seventieth " week," it is sufficient to show that Christ died on the fourth " day," *i.e.* in the fourth *year* of that " week." In other words, we have to show that He died in A.D. 29–30, the middle year of the " week " A.D. 26–33. What time of the year He died is of no consequence so far as this prophecy is concerned: nor is it necessary that the half of the "week" should be exactly three and a half years, *i.e.* three and a half prophetic " days," but simply a period extending from some point in the fourth year, A.D. 29–30, to some point in the seventh year, A.D. 32–33.

In our study of the Seventieth Week the first thing is to determine the year of its commencement, *i.e.* we have to ascertain the year in which Messiah was proclaimed by His Forerunner, John the Baptist, as already present in the midst of His people Israel; and we shall find that no fewer than three independent calculations point us to the year A.D. 26.

Of the Four Evangelists St. Luke is the one who possesses most fully the historic sense. He is more concerned than his brother Evangelists with the chronological framework which lies at the back of the Gospel Story. One epoch which strikes him as of great importance, and to ascertain which is necessary for the right interpretation of the vision of Dan. ix., is the beginning of the ministry of John the Baptist: the time when the cry of that

[1] Ezra vii. 8, 9. See p. 185, footnote.

herald-messenger first rang out, bidding men prepare for the coming kingdom. Accordingly, in chap. iii. 1, 2, St. Luke is careful to mark the date with a striking series of synchronisms. The first note of time, which he there gives us, is the fifteenth year of Tiberius Cæsar. Tiberius was associated with Augustus in the sovereignty of the empire in A.D. 12. His fifteenth year, therefore, was A.D. 26. Prof. Ramsay suggests that the ministry of John began in the summer of that year, some six months before that of Christ, John being six months older than our Saviour. In the next place, St. Luke tells us in chap. iii. 23 that "Jesus himself, when he began to teach, was about thirty years of age." Now, according to St. Matthew's Gospel, chap. ii. 1, Jesus was born in the reign of Herod the Great, and evidently near the close of that reign: compare Matt. ii. 19, 20. Herod died in 4 B.C., very shortly before the Passover.[1] Whence it has been reckoned that our Saviour was born either at the end of 5 B.C., or early in 4 B.C. This would make Him "about thirty" at the end of A.D. 26. Thirdly, we learn from John ii. 20 that at the first Passover in our Saviour's ministry the temple had been in building forty-six years. Herod the Great, its builder, began to reign in 37 B.C., and it was in his eighteenth year,[2] *i.e.* in 20 B.C., that he commenced the building of the temple. Hence at some point in the year A.D. 26 the temple had been in building exactly forty-six years; also, leaving out months and taking account only of years, that number would still hold good for part of the year A.D. 27, and presumably at the time of the first Passover in Christ's ministry. Thus three different calculations unite in pointing us to the year A.D. 26 as that in which Messiah was made manifest to Israel, and near the close of which He entered upon His ministry.

We have next to ascertain the duration of that ministry, that so we may be able to determine the year in which Messiah was "cut off." St. John mentions three Passovers during the ministry: the Passover of John ii. 13, already referred to; that of John vi. 4, shortly after the Feeding of the Five Thousand; and the Passover of John xii. 1, at which Christ suffered. Hence our Saviour's ministry must have extended over at least two years. But it can be shown that it extended over three years, and that

[1] *Ant.* xvii. 8. 1. The date of this Passover and of the death of Herod is ascertained from the fact that just a month before there was an eclipse of the moon, which happened in the night of March 12–13, 4 B.C., *Ant.* xvii. 6. 4.

[2] *Ant.* xv. 11. 1. In the *Wars of the Jews*, i. 21, 1, the building of the temple is assigned to Herod's fifteenth year; but Wiesler has shown in his *Chronologica Synopsis*, p. 152, footnote, that the number 15 is an error of the transcriber. Cf. also *Herzog's Encyclopædia*, xxi. 546.

it included another Passover which is not mentioned by the Evangelist, viz. the next after the Passover of John ii. 13. The argument hinges on the right understanding of Christ's words in John iv. 35, "Say not *ye*, There are yet four months and then cometh the harvest? Behold, I say unto you, Lift up your eyes, and look on the fields, that they are white already unto the harvest." Many commentators have looked on this utterance as a proverb, and it is quite true that there is a proverbial ring about the words, "Say not *ye?*" "Is it not a common saying among you?" But since the interval between sowing and harvest—to which, if they were a proverb, they would naturally allude—is *six* months, and not four, we must understand them otherwise, viz. as a note of time: "Say not ye *at this time of the year*, Yet four months till harvest? Behold, I say unto you, Lift up your eyes, and look on the fields, that they are white already unto the harvest. Look yonder! See that eager throng pressing forward out of the city. The good seed has already been sown there, and has sprung up with lightning speed. There lies the true harvest field, ready even now for the reaping!" It is thus the sharp contrast presented by the then state of the spiritual field as compared with the natural, which drew from our Saviour's lips this enigmatic saying. Here, then, is an additional reason for looking at Christ's words as a reference to the time of year. A proverb they could hardly be; but taken as a note of time they help to furnish a striking enigma.

Our Lord, then, after the first Passover of His ministry, leaving Jerusalem goes into Judea, and "tarries"[1] there for some eight months, baptising contemporaneously with John. At the end of that time, about the close of November or early in December, four months before the harvest—which began at the next Passover—He passes through Samaria on His way to Galilee, where He receives a warm welcome from those who had witnessed the miracles done by Him at Jerusalem in the early part of the year; and it may be presumed that He avails Himself of the door thus opened to Him, and "tarries" awhile in Galilee as He had done in Judea. Then follows the unnamed feast of John v. 1, to be present at which our Lord goes up to Jerusalem. *What feast could this be?* Certainly not the Feast of the Dedication, for that was held in the winter, viz. in the very month in which Christ went into Galilee. The next feast is that of Purim, which falls just a month before the Passover. This would require our Lord to spend less than three months in Galilee, and to rush away, as it were, from those who had accorded Him so warm a welcome.

[1] John iii. 22.

Besides, Purim was a vindictive feast, and its teaching was utterly alien to the spirit of Christ.[1] Further, that Christ should go up to the feast of Purim in John v. 1, and then absent Himself from the Passover of John vi. 4, which followed only a month later, is unthinkable. But if the unnamed feast of John v. 1 is not Purim, *it can only be a Passover or some feast subsequent to the Passover, i.e.* there is a Passover in Christ's ministry not mentioned by St. John, which falls between the Passover of John ii. 13 and that of John vi. 4. The ministry, then, which began near the end of A.D. 26, extended over the Passovers of A.D. 27, 28, 29, and 30, at the last of which Messiah was "cut off." If, then, we take the year A.D. 26–27, in which Jesus was pointed out by the Forerunner as Israel's Messiah, and in which He entered on His public ministry, as the first "day" of the Seventieth Week, then the year A.D. 29–30, embracing the Passover of A.D. 30 at which He suffered, will be the fourth "day," *i.e.* the middle of the week.

We have now to look at the second half of the "week," during which Messiah by the sacrifice of Himself on the Cross caused the temple sacrifices to cease in the sight of God. This has been already interpreted of the interval between our Saviour's death and the martyrdom of St. Stephen, and in justification of such an interpretation I shall avail myself of the researches of Prof. Ramsay. With regard to the results already arrived at, Ramsay is in perfect agreement, viz. that the Forerunner appeared in A.D. 26, possibly in the summer of that year, and that "the Crucifixion took place in A.D. 30, the fourth Passover in the public career of Jesus."[2] Then, when investigating the chronology of Early Church History, he goes on to place the appointment of the Seven Deacons in A.D. 32 and the death of Stephen in A.D. 33. In the latter year he also places the conversion of St. Paul, and states that according to the view put forward by him, A.D. 33 is the latest date for that event. He admits that the interval between A.D. 30 and A.D. 32 seems to him a short time for the Jewish Christian Church to realise the necessity for appointing Hellenistic Jews to official rank.[3] But, on the other hand, he finds

[1] At this feast the Book of Esther is read through at the Synagogue service. When Haman's name is mentioned the congregation stamp on the floor and call aloud, "Let his name be blotted out!" "Let the name of the ungodly perish!" while the children knock on the wall with wooden hammers, threatening with destruction, not only Haman, but the whole race of Amalek. Also when the reader comes to the names of Haman's ten sons, who were slain by the Jews, he does his best to read them through in a breath, thus signifying the suddenness of the destruction which overtook them.

[2] *St. Paul the Traveller*, p. 386.

[3] *Ibid.* p. 376.

it difficult to believe that repressive measures against the followers of Christ could have been delayed more than two years or three at the utmost. His conclusion runs thus: "It is therefore quite fair to date Stephen's death about two and a half or three years after the great Pentecost." [1] The year of Stephen's death being thus ascertained, with strong probability, if not with absolute certainty, we have now obtained the beginning, the middle, and the ending of that last great Seventieth Week, and can express the result in strict chronological sequence as follows:

A.D. 26–27: The proclamation of the Messiah by the Baptist.

A.D. 29–30: Messiah's violent death.

A.D. 32–33: The death of Stephen, at the close of Israel's day of grace, and very shortly before the conversion of the Apostle of the Gentiles.

It was pointed out in the last chapter that the extension of Israel's day of grace supplies the reason why the vision of the Seventy Weeks extends to some three years and more after the Crucifixion. But there is another and deeper reason for the selection of that limit which must not be overlooked. Beginning with the mention of Israel's sin and Israel's need, the vision of Dan. ix. passes on to Israel's "Glory" as Messiah comes upon the scene. In His rejection the national guilt is consummated. Nevertheless, mounting to His Mediatorial throne by the ladder of the Cross, exalted "to be a Prince and a Saviour," He still waits to be gracious to His own people, still maintains the "week"-long pact, thus giving His rebellious subjects time to send in their allegiance. But a second murder, that of His first martyr St. Stephen, puts an end to Israel's day of grace, and at the same time opens the way to a further development of the Messianic Kingdom. The murder of Messiah Himself had led the way to His being installed in the seat of power at Jehovah's right hand. The seeming defeat of the Cross had been a real victory: for then, as foretold in the second Psalm, the Almighty Ruler, seated on His heavenly throne, laughing to scorn the rage and malice of His foes, proclaimed the accomplishment of His fixed purpose-

"As for me,[2] I have set my king
Upon my holy mountain of Zion." [3]

But now a further step in the direction of the extension of the Kingdom was about to be taken. This is unfolded by Messiah Himself in the next stanza of the Psalm, *vv.* 7–10. He declares

[1] *St. Paul the Traveller*, p. 377.
[2] The pronoun is emphatic.
[3] Dan. ix. 16, 20.

that Jehovah has not only acknowledged His prerogative—viz. by the miracle of the Resurrection—but has given to Him, "the Firstborn from the dead," no merely Jewish kingdom, but world-wide sovereignty–

"Ask of me, and I will give thee the nations for thine inheritance,
And the uttermost parts of the earth for thy possession."

This second outrage, then, the death of His first martyr, shall be used by Him for this promised extension of His Kingdom. By means of it He will put forth His royal power, and scattering His servants from Jerusalem, will despatch them into all lands, thus fulfilling the prediction of the 110th Psalm–

"The LORD shall send forth the rod of thy strength out of Zion,
Rule thou in the midst of thine enemies."

With might irresistible, exceeding that of the Iron Kingdom, the forces of heathenism are broken down, while Messiah's true people, in numbers countless as the drops of dew, "offer themselves willingly" to serve under Him "in the day of His power." [1]

For the sake, then, of "Prince Messiah," the real subject of the prophecy, the vision which tells of His sufferings is carried down to that point at which His armies go forth into all lands, to bring them into subjection to the Cross of Christ. In the words of the historian-evangelist, "They therefore that were scattered abroad upon the tribulation that arose about Stephen travelled as far as Phœnicia, and Cyprus, and Antioch, speaking the word to none save only to Jews. But some of them were men of Cyprus and Cyrene, who, when they were come to Antioch, spake unto the Greeks also, preaching the Lord Jesus. And the hand of the Lord was with them: and a great number that believed turned unto the Lord." [2] Thus, a true evangelic fulfilment was given to the prophecy of Dan. vii. 27, "The kingdom and the dominion and the greatness of the kingdoms under the whole heaven, shall be given to the people of the saints of the Most High: his kingdom is an everlasting kingdom, and all dominions shall serve and obey him."

[1] R.V.M. *army*.

[2] Acts xi. 19–21.

20

The Scenes of the Two Visions Concerning the Jewish Church

THE two visions of Daniel, chaps. viii. and x.–xii., are very closely related. Not only are there many verbal points of connection between them, but the subject-matter of both is the same, viz. the perils awaiting the ancient Church of God at the hands of oppressive and persecuting world-powers. And for this reason both were shown to Daniel by the side of rivers, symbolical of those world-powers: rivers, over whose waters hovered, in one instance a Divine Presence, made known by a voice, in the other a Divine Person both seen and heard; affording in either case an assurance to the seer that He, from whom the vision came, would Himself control those powers, and not suffer His Church to be overwhelmed by them.

The earlier vision opens thus: "In the third year of the reign of king Belshazzar a vision appeared unto me, even unto me Daniel, after that which appeared unto me at the first. And I saw in the vision; now it was so, that when I saw, I was in Shushan the palace, which is in the province of Elam: and I saw in the vision, and I was by the river Ulai."[1] Belshazzar, as we have seen, was associated with his father Nabonidus in the sovereignty, and the passage is suggestive of the fact that a definite portion of the kingdom was placed under his sway. In chap. vii. 1 Belshazzar is called "king of Babylon," and it is not at all unlikely that his father may also have entrusted to him that part of ancient Elam which lay adjacent to Babylonia and was under Babylonian rule.

In the "vision which appeared unto me at the first,"[2] *i.e.* the vision of the Four Kingdoms in chap. vii.—shown to him two years before—Daniel had seemed to himself to be standing on the

[1] Dan. viii. 1, 2.
[2] Chap. viii. 2.

shore of the "Great Sea," the Mediterranean, looking west. That sea, out of which the four wild beasts—picturing the great heathen world-powers—were seen to arise, was symbolical of the sea of nations, and its very position was significant, since two of those powers, Babylon and Persia, sprang up on one side of it, and two, Greece and Rome, on the other side. It was no less significant as indicating the wider outlook of that vision, both in time and space, which has for its theatre the World of the Ancients, and in its scope takes in the remote future, casting a lurid light on that terrible persecution which the saints were to suffer at the hands of Papal Rome long after the Son of Man had received His mediatorial kingdom. Similarly, in these more contracted visions the scenes are no less admirably chosen. The mention of those two eastern rivers, the Ulai and the Hiddekel, is particularly striking as denoting the quarters most closely connected with those two world-powers, Persia and the Greek-Syrian kingdom, at whose hands the Jewish Church was to suffer, first, much opposition, and presently, the bitterest persecution. It is possible, indeed, that the vision of chaps. xi. and xii. has a further typical meaning; but the passage is one of great difficulty, as I have already shown in my first chapter. All that I would insist on here is, that the visions seen on the banks of the two rivers must not be mixed up and confused with the vision seen on the shore of the "Great Sea." To confuse the persecuting power of Dan. vii. with that of viii. and xi. is fatal. The circumstances attending the rise of each, as we have already seen, are entirely different. One power, that of chap. vii., is an upstart and usurper; the other is born in the purple.

In the vision of the world-kingdoms Daniel was not actually on the shore of the "Great Sea," but only seemed to be there. So, in these more contracted visions, he is not actually on the banks of the rivers mentioned, but only there in spirit. Nevertheless in the vision of chap. viii. the particularity of description in the opening verses is such as to give the distinct impression that some time or other he had been at Shushan—probably on business for king Belshazzar—and was thus familiar with the spot where, according to tradition, his bones repose.

Eastward, beyond the Tigris, towers the highland zone of the Zagros, range upon range of lofty limestone mountains, till the passes to the plateau behind them rise to 5000 and 6000 feet, and the peaks to over 11,000 feet. The width of the mountain belt averages 300 miles.[1] To the Semites looking up from the

[1] Myres' *Dawn of History*, p. 89.

Babylonian plain the southern portion of this mountainous region was known as Elam, "the Upland." Accordingly, in Isa. xxi. 2, where Elam is summoned to join Media in putting down Assyria, we find a play on the name, which might well be shown by a marginal rendering thus: "Up! Upland." To the Aryan tribes pressing forward from the east Elam was known as Uvaja, *i.e.* either the country "with good roads"—for through its mountain passes ran the trade routes from the East—or, the land "abounding in goats." The Elamites themselves called their country Haltamti. The second column of the great inscription of Darius Hystaspes at Behistûn is written in the Elamite language, in that branch of it usually known as the Neo-Susian. Like the ancient Sumerian it was an agglutinative tongue. Darius in his inscription, when enumerating in something of geographical order the countries which Auramazda has put under his sway, places Elam between Persia and Babylonia.

During the Assyrian period, Elam was the inveterate foe of the Assyrians and the firm ally of the Chaldeans. Against Elam Sennacherib directed five out of the eight campaigns described on the Taylor Cylinder. Elam was twice very severely chastised by Ashurbanipal, viz. in 660 B.C., and again in 645 B.C.; and so terrible was the vengeance on this latter occasion that one might suppose the nation wiped out. But Elam possessed a wonderful power of recuperation, and as a matter of fact outlived Assyria. Thus Nineveh fell about 606 B.C., but Elam was still a nation in the first year of Zedekiah 597 B.C., when the prophet Jeremiah predicted her approaching downfall.[1] In 586 B.C., only eleven years later, we learn from a prophecy of Ezekiel, that Jeremiah's prediction had been accomplished, and that Elam along with other great nations had gone down to the underworld.[2] In endeavouring to form some conjecture as to the causes which led to her overthrow, we must place the prophecy of Jeremiah side by side with the political conditions that existed in Western Asia at the time, so far as they are known to us. In the closing days of the Assyrian empire, when Cyaxares of Media was besieging the famous Assyrian cities, we learn from a fragment of Abydenus that a locust-like host—undoubtedly the Elamites—swarmed up from the sea and joined hands with Nabopolassar, the father of Nebuchadnezzar, in his attack on the southern border of Assyria.[3] On this occasion the ancient friendship between the Elamites and the Chaldeans was still maintained, and both must have rejoiced

[1] Jer. xlix. 34.

[2] Ezek. xxxii. 24, 25. For the date of this prophecy compare *vv.* 1 and 17.

[3] Cory's *Fragments*, new edition, 1876, p. 90.

together over the tragic downfall of their common foe. But when after the fall of Nineveh Babylon stepped into Assyria's place and took to herself the southern half of the old Assyrian empire, while the "mighty Medes" laid a firm hold on the northern half, the state of the political world was completely changed. The common danger being now removed, Elam would naturally be jealous of Babylon's success, whilst the Babylonian king, unable to effect further conquests on his northern frontier because of the strength of the Median kingdom, and having for his southern border the deserts of Arabia, would feel that he could only extend the limits of his empire on the east and west. From other parts of Scripture we learn what he did in the west, and here in this Book of Daniel we get a hint as to what he was able to effect in the east. On this side, indeed, he could not advance very far, for the small kingdom of Anshan, in the east of ancient Elam, destined to be the germ of the future empire of Persia, was a fief of the powerful Median kingdom, and thus formed a most effective barrier. Nebuchadnezzar would not dare to interfere with any dependency of his powerful Median ally, of whom he stood in goodly fear. He could, however, join with the Medes to destroy what remained of the Elamite power, obtaining as a reward for his services that part of Elam which lay nearest to Babylon. Now, in the prophecy of Jeremiah, chap. xlix, 36, it is foretold that Elam will be attacked from all quarters, and this prediction would receive a literal fulfilment if, as seems likely, she was attacked by Media and Anshan on the north and east, and on the west and south by the Chaldeans, both by land and sea, for what the Assyrians, an inland nation, had done in the days of Sennacherib, when they sailed across the Gulf to attack Elam, the Chaldeans, a maritime people, could much more easily effect.[1]

The part of Elam which fell to the lot of Nebuchadnezzar appears from this passage in Daniel to have included the city of Shushan, which was only some 200 miles to the east of Babylon. That Shushan lay within the bounds of the Babylonian empire is proved from the fact that in the list of Babylonian cities to which Cyrus, after the capture of Babylon, returned their gods, Shushan is mentioned along with Ashur.[2] This shows that Babylonian rule extended as far north up the Tigris as Ashur, the oldest

[1] See the account of Sennacherib's sixth campaign on the *Taylor Cylinder*.

[2] See the *Cylinder Inscription of Cyrus*, line 30, as read by Pinches and Weissbach. This is also Winckler's view. It is interesting to note that according to Sayce the discoveries of M. de Morgan on the site of Susa disclose the fact that in the early days of Babylonian history Elam was a Babylonian province and Susa the seat of a Babylonian governor.

capital of Assyria, and as far east as Shushan, the former capital of Elam. That Shushan lay on the eastern frontier of the empire, and that Nebuchadnezzar's kingdom could not have extended much beyond it, appears to be indicated by the fact that this great king drew his supplies of timber, not from the mountains of Elam, though comparatively near to Babylon, but from the much more distant forests of the Lebanon.

In the Assyrian period Shushan was the chief royal city of Elam, and the dwelling-place of the Elamite gods, famous for its sacred groves, its royal mausoleum, and the statues of no less than thirty-two kings, as well as for the treasures laid up in its palaces.[1] Doubtless it was still a place of importance under the New Babylonian empire, more especially as a military outpost and frontier town. In Persian times, which had already commenced when Daniel wrote his Book, Shushan, or Susa, speedily became one of the capitals of the empire, along with Ecbatana, Persepolis, and Babylon. It was, in fact, the favourite winter resort of the Persian kings, and so delightful was its situation and climate that by the reign of Darius Hystaspes it appears as the chief city of the empire, the place where Darius kept his treasure, and the terminus of the "Royal Road" from Sardis, which, according to Herodotus, it took ninety days to traverse.[2]

In his vision Daniel seemed to be in "Shushan the palace." The Hebrew word *birah,* translated "palace," is connected with the Assyrian *birtu,* "a fortress," and signifies the citadel of Shushan. Hence the marginal rendering, "Shushan the castle," is to be preferred, both here and in the Books of Nehemiah and Esther. In the Koyunjik Gallery of the British Museum, on one of the bas-reliefs from the palace of Ashurbanipal, we find a curious and interesting plan of the town and citadel of Shushan, as they existed in the middle of the seventh century B.C. The plan is in exact agreement with the lines of the ancient city as laid bare by Loftus. Nevertheless, across the picture is written in cuneiform characters, "The city of Madaktu." Madaktu was the name of another Elamite royal city, probably represented by a place named Badaca, about twenty-five miles from the site of Shushan. Hence it has been supposed that the sculptor has made a mistake in writing "Madaktu" instead of "Shushan." This bas-relief shows the city built on a narrow strip of land between two rivers. Near the junction of the rivers, standing on a hill or mound, is the "castle" or citadel. In the Persian period the famous Persian archers of the royal bodyguard, known as the Immortals,

[1] Inscription of Ashurbanipal on the *Rassam Cylinder,* col. vi.

[2] Book v. 52, 53.

had their long robes covered with scutcheon badges, on which were embroidered a conventional representation of the citadel of Shushan.[1] In the Book of Esther the "city Shushan" is distinguished from "Shushan the castle": chap. viii. 14, 15. So in our bas-relief the citadel is seen standing outside the walls, near the confluence of the two rivers: the town with its fortifications and houses a little to the right. Scattered houses and palm trees are seen in the foreground outside the walls, between the town and the larger of the two rivers. Many of the houses have chambers on the flat roofs, like that which Daniel used for his prayer-chamber.[2] In his vision Daniel tells us that he was "by the river Ulai," probably the larger of the two rivers depicted in the bas-relief as running close by the castle mound and across the immediate foreground. The word *ubal*, here used for "river," is an unusual one. It comes from a root meaning "to conduct," and might better be translated "canal." Another word from the same root signifies a "conduit." The Ulai was a very wide canal, 900 feet broad, joining the Kerkha (the ancient Choaspes) and the Abdizful (the ancient Coprates), the traces of which, though it is now dry, can still be seen. This vast canal joining the two rivers would be much used for water traffic, and must have proved a source of wealth to Shushan, which, as we have seen, was destined shortly to become the first of Persia's royal cities and to be restored to the same proud position which it had held under the native Elamite monarchs. In the visions of the Book of Daniel the immense wealth of the Persian empire is foretold. It is to be the Silver, *i.e.* the Monied Kingdom, and its mighty kings are to be strong through their vast wealth.[3] The idea of wealth and abundance was in the minds of the Babylonians connected with their system of canals, both because they helped to irrigate the land and make it fruitful, and also because—as in the case of the broad Ulai—they served for purposes of water-traffic. Such was the importance of these canals in Babylonia that both Nabopolassar and Nebuchadnezzar have left canal-inscriptions. The inscription of Nebuchadnezzar has reference to a canal at Babylon, which bore the name Libil-khigalla, "May it bring abundance."[4] This canal ran eastwards from the Euphrates along the south side of the southern citadel. Libil-khigalla had been in a ruinous state for some time, and the monarch gives the following account of the repairs executed by him: "Libil-khigalla, the east canal of

[1] *Story of the Nations: Media*, p. 337.
[2] *Cambridge Bible*, Daniel, chap. vi. 10, footnote.
[3] Dan. ii. 32 and xi. 2.
[4] The word *libil*, "may it bring," is from the root mentioned above.

Babylon, which for a long time had lain in ruins, blocked up with masses of earth, and full of obstructions, I cleared it out; and from the bank of the Euphrates to Ai-ibur-shabu I built its course with mortar and burnt brick. In Ai-ibur-shabu,[1] the street of Babylon, for the great lord Merodach I built a bridge over the canal, and made the roadway broad." Jeremiah has these canals in his mind, when in his long prophecy against Babylon he thus addresses her: "O thou that dwellest upon many waters, abundant in treasures, thine end is come, the measure of thy dishonest gain."[2] The use of the Hebrew word translated "measure," lit. "ell," and the mention of "dishonest gain," shows that the prophet connected the wealth of Babylon and her commercial greatness with the facilities for water-traffic offered by her canal system. The mention, then, of the Ulai, the broad canal of Shushan, as the scene of Daniel's vision is suggestive of the vast wealth and the immense resources of the fast-approaching Persian kingdom. For in front of this canal, as if to defend his treasures, stood the Medo-Persian ram, when against him from the west with the speed of some bird of prey, not touching the ground, came the Grecian he-goat with that notable horn between his eyes. "And he came," writes Daniel, "to the ram that had the two horns, which I saw standing before the river, and ran upon him in the fury of his power. And I saw him come close unto the ram, and he was moved with choler against him, and smote the ram and brake his two horns, and there was no power in the ram to stand before him."[3] A grand description this, of the swift irresistible career of Alexander, signalised by those great victories over armies much larger than his own at the Granicus, at Issus, and at Arbela, the last opening the way for him to Babylon, and so on to Shushan; Shushan, the very heart of the empire in more senses than one, for what the blood is to the human body, that the treasure laid up at Shushan was to the body politic of the Persian kingdom. Hence that last victory at Arbela touched a vital part, since it made Alexander master of the immense wealth stored up at Shushan; wealth which, wisely expended in the hire of Greek mercenaries, might have saved, or at any rate prolonged, the kingdom of Persia. "Once masters of this city," says Aristagoras, speaking of Susa to Cleomenes king of Sparta: "Once masters of this city, you may be bold to vie with Jove himself for riches."[4] And so, indeed, it proved, for the silver captured by Alexander at Susa amounted to no less than 50,000 talents, or

[1] *I.e.* "The oppressor shall not pass over it." Compare the description of 'The way of Holiness" in Isa. xxxv. 8, "the unclean shall not pass over it."

[2] Jer. li. 13, R.V.M.

[3] Dan. viii. 6, 7.

[4] Herod. v. 49

more than twelve million sterling! It was not, then, without a reason that the vision, which in its opening scene describes in so striking a manner the coming of the Greek kingdom into Asia, and the speedy downfall of the vast, unwieldy empire of Persia, should be shown to the seer at Shushan, and on the banks of its great canal, the Ulai.

When the vision was past, and while Daniel was pondering its meaning, there came from between the banks of the Ulai—*i.e.* from above the waters of the canal—a voice, undoubtedly the voice of Jehovah Himself, bidding Gabriel explain the vision to the seer. The fact that God's voice came from above the waters indicated that the vast resources of the Persian empire, typified by the broad Ulai, were under His control, and was suggestive that the decree, uttered against Babylon, would presently go forth against Persia—

> "A sword is upon her treasures, and they shall be robbed:
> A drought is upon her waters, and they shall be dried up."
> (Jer. l. 37, 38.)

Turning next to the scene of Daniel's latest vision, chaps. x.–xii., we read in chap. x. 4, "I was by the side of the great river, which is Hiddekel." In Gen. xv. 18 the Euphrates is called "The Great River," just as in Sumerian it is called *Pura Nun,* "The Great Water," or simply *Pura.*[1] But the Hiddekel, or Tigris, may well lay claim to the same title; for though its course is shorter, being only 1146 miles as compared with the 1670 miles of the Euphrates, yet in depth, volume, and velocity, it much exceeds the Euphrates.[2] The Sumerian ideogram for the Tigris—two horizontal wedges—bespeaks it the "swift" river. The Hebrew name Hiddekel corresponds to the Assyrian *Idiklat,* and signifies the "River of the Date-palm," Heb. *dekel.* From the word *Idiklat* the Persians, according to Sayce,[3] formed their name Tigra, with a play upon a word in their own language signifying "an arrow"; thus again reverting to the idea of swiftness.

What is the thought which underlies this mention of the Tigris as the scene of the vision of chaps. x.–xii.? Something utterly different from that suggested by the mention of the Ulai in chap. viii. The Ulai was a broad canal of still water, suggestive of traffic, and busy commerce, and power dependent upon wealth; the Tigris, a deep river with a rapid current, suggestive, not of the

[1] The Greek name "Euphrates" represents the Old Persian *Ufratu,* which comes from *Purat,* the Semitic form of the Sumerian *Pura.*

[2] Goodspeed's *History of the Babylonians and Assyrians,* p. 7.

[3] *Higher Criticism,* p. 96.

peaceful flow of commerce, but of the rush of mighty irresistible armies, "the rushing of nations, that rush like the rushing of mighty waters."[1] Isaiah had already compared the Assyrian invasion of the land of Israel in the days of Tiglathpileser to the Euphrates in flood: Isa. viii. 6–8. And in the vision of Dan. xi. the same figure is twice borrowed from that very passage to describe the movements of those great armies of invasion raised by the Seleucid monarchs, "the kings of the north." Thus in chap. xi. 10 it is said of Seleucus Ceraunos and Antiochus the Great, the sons of Seleucus Callinicus, "And his sons shall war, and shall assemble a multitude of great forces, which shall come on, and *overflow and pass through.*" And again in verse 40 we are told that "at the time of the end . . . the king of the north shall come like a whirlwind, with chariots, and with horsemen, and with many ships: and shall *overflow and pass through.*" In accordance, then, with the tone of the prophecy we may surely look on this mention, at the beginning of the vision, of the Tigris with its deep swift current as a type of those vast armies with which the Seleucid kings swept through the land of Israel.

But why, it will be asked, was not the vision shown to Daniel by the river Euphrates, which, as we have seen, was regarded as "The Great River," not only by the Hebrews, but also by the Sumerians, the ancient inhabitants of Babylonia, as well as being the river referred to by Isaiah? Doubtless because the Tigris, and not the Euphrates, was destined to have a special connection with the Seleucid dynasty. It was on the banks of the Tigris that Seleucus Nicator, the founder of the dynasty, built his great city of Seleucia, to take the place of Babylon and to form the capital of the eastern half of his empire. "What Seleucus did," writes Bevan, "was less to destroy Babylon than to transfer it to another site. It was usual, as Strabo observes, to describe a man of Seleucia as a 'Babylonian.' Seleucia was a very great city. According to Pliny, its free population was 600,000."[2] Seleucia, then, on the bank of the Tigris, was destined in the eyes of the nations to stand for a second Babylon, just as Babylon had stood for a second Assyria. And as the Assyro-Babylonian Euphrates had in a figure swept across the land of Israel, so presently would the Seleucid Tigris with its deep-rushing stream, "overflow and pass through." Again, the Tigris is chosen rather than the Orontes, on which stood Antioch the other Seleucid capital—also built by Seleucus Nicator, and from which the great Seleucid armies set out—because Antioch, unlike Seleucia, had no connection

[1] Isa. xvii. 13.

[2] *House of Seleucus*, vol. i. p. 253.

with Babylon, whilst the Orontes was too small a stream to represent the might of the Seleucidæ.

As Daniel, in chap. x. 4, calls the Tigris "The Great River," a name usually bestowed on the Euphrates, so toward the close of his vision he bestows on it another name, almost invariably used in Scripture of the Nile. This is the Egyptian loan-word *ye'or*, rendered "river" in Dan. xii. 5, 6, 7, both in R.V. and A.V. *Ye'or* had found its way into Babylonian as well as into Hebrew, and, if we may judge from the use of this word made by Nebuchadnezzar, it signifies, when not specifically used of the Nile, a great body of water, and is best translated by the word "flood." Nebuchadnezzar, when describing the vast water-defences constructed by him at Babylon, writes thus-

"that foes might not present the face,
the bounds of Babylon might not approach,
great waters
like the volume of the sea,
I carried round the land :
and the crossing of them
was like the crossing of the surging sea [lit. 'sea of waves']
of the briny flood" (*ya-ar-ri*).[1]

If, then, we substitute "flood" for "river," the striking passage which comes at the close of Daniel's latest vision will read thus-

"Then I Daniel looked, and, behold, there stood other two, the one on the brink of the flood on this side, and the other on the brink of the flood on that side. And one said to the man clothed in linen, which was above the waters of the flood, How long shall it be to the end of these wonders? And I heard the man clothed in linen, which was above the waters of the flood, when he held up his right hand and his left hand unto heaven, and sware by him that liveth for ever, that it shall be for a time, times, and an half; and when they have made an end of breaking in pieces the power of the holy people, all these things shall be finished."

By applying to the deep rapid river, on which the capital of the Seleucidæ was afterwards to arise, two terms—one, "The Great River," suggestive of the Euphrates ; and the other, the Egyptian

[1] In Assyrian the Nile is called *Ya'uru* and *Yaru'u*, and it has been questioned whether the *ya-ar-ri* of Nebuchadnezzar is not a different word ; but note that in Zech. x. 11 that identical expression, "the sea of waves," which Nebuchadnezzar uses in connection with *ya-ar-ri*, is there used in connection with *ye'or*. Hence it seems probable that the Babylonian *ya-ar-ri* is only another form of the Egyptian *ye'or*.

ye'or, pointing to the Nile—Daniel implies that before the onrush of the mighty waters of the Seleucid armies Judah must inevitably go under, and suffer an oppression, which could only be adequately pictured by the use of terms suggestive of the tyranny of an Egypt and Babylon combined. Isaiah's powerful description was thus to be realised yet a second time: "He shall come up over all his channels, and go over all his banks; and he shall sweep onward into Judah; he shall overflow and pass through; he shall reach even to the neck; and the stretching out of his wings shall fill the breadth of thy land, O Immanuel." In the strains of the Psalmist-

"If it had not been Jehovah who was on our side,
Let Israel now say;
If it had not been Jehovah who was on our side,
When men rose up against us;
Then had they swallowed us up alive,
When their wrath was kindled against us:
Then the waters had overwhelmed us,
The stream had gone over our soul:
Then the proud waters had gone over our soul."

But Jehovah *was* on their side, and when in the days of Antiochus Epiphanes the great crisis came, He was their Immanuel, "God with us." This was now to be shown beforehand to Daniel in a remarkable manner. In the earlier vision, as we have seen, a voice came from between the banks of the Ulai, viz. the voice of God; and, as at Sinai, a voice but no similitude. Since the date of that earlier vision Gabriel had been sent to inform Daniel of the coming of "Prince Messiah." And now a greater than Gabriel, even Messiah Himself—whose glorious appearance as described in chap. x. 5, 6, was to be seen yet again by St. John in Patmos—appeared to the Old Testament seer standing over the waters of the river.[1] The same development of revelation is noticeable in the world-visions of chaps. ii. and vii., *both* of which were shown to Daniel, though the former had been shown in the first instance to Nebuchadnezzar. Thus in the vision of chap. ii. we hear only of the kingdom of the God of heaven. Nothing is said as to the heaven-sent King, though it is quite true that a mysterious hint as to the Incarnation is contained in the mention of the "stone cut out of the mountain without hands." But in the later vision of chap. vii. the destined Ruler of the Divine Kingdom appears on the scene. "One like unto a son of man" is beheld "coming with the clouds of heaven," and is brought near to the Ancient of Days to receive from Him lasting and world-wide dominion.

[1] Cf. Dan. x. 5, 6 with Rev. i. 13-16.

The divine character of the Man clothed in Linen, who stood above the waters of the river, may be deduced, not only from His glorious appearance which so affected the seer, but also from the fact that He stood where attendant angels could not stand, viz. over the waters, while they were merely on the banks. Further, He is appealed to by one of these angels as knowing the future, knowing more than they know.[1] This knowledge of the future, along with an unmistakable tone of authority, appears also very clearly in the last words of this Book addressed by Him to Daniel, "Go thou thy way till the end be: for thou shalt rest, and stand in thy lot, at the end of the days"; so that despite the statement of chap. x. 11, that He is "sent," or rather along with that statement, we are compelled to recognise in this veiled Personality the Christ of the New Testament, and are led to place this closing vision of the Book side by side with that scene witnessed on the Sea of Galilee, when through the darkness a Figure was seen walking on the angry waters, whilst through the roaring of the tempest was heard a well-known Voice, saying to His terrified followers, "Be of good cheer: it is I; be not afraid."

APPENDIX 1

On the site of ancient Shushan and the reputed tomb of Daniel

The mounds of Shush, which mark the site of the ancient Shushan, are situated at the point where the rivers Kerkha and Abdizful most nearly approximate. Shush is distant ¾ of a mile from the Kerkha and 1½ miles from the Abdizful. The area covered by the ruins is 3½ miles in circumference. Within this circuit are four mounds, of which the western is the smallest but considerably the loftiest, rising to a height of 119 feet above the dry bed of the Scháour, the ancient Ulai. This western mound represents the acropolis, "Shushan the palace." At its foot and between it and the Scháour, is the reputed tomb of Daniel by common consent of Jews, Sabeans, and Mohammedans. Daniel, so the tradition runs, by his prayers obtained rain from heaven in a time of drought. For this reason the people of Shush obtained from the ruler of Irak permission for him to come to them, giving fifty men as hostages. His intercession was so effectual that they kept him till his death. When Persia was invaded by Abu Musa Alasha'ri under the khalif Omar in A.D. 640, this general entered the castle, and found a chamber under lock and key, and on

[1] Dan. xii. 6.

entering it saw in a stone coffin, wrapped in a shroud of gold brocade, the body of a man of great stature. On asking whose body it was, he obtained the reply, "The people of Irak called him Danyel Hakim or 'Daniel the Sage.'" This story he sent to Omar, who sent word back that the body should be reverently buried where the people of Shush could no longer have the benefit of it. Accordingly the stream which supplied the city with water —apparently a channel cut from the Ulai—was diverted, and a grave made in the dry channel; after which the waters of Shush were allowed to flow over the body of Daniel.

Appendix 2

A comparative table showing the marked similarity of language and description which characterises the two visions concerning the Jewish Church as related in the Book of Daniel

(1) "I was by the river Ulai," viii. 2. Cf. x. 4, "I was by the side of the great river which is Hiddekel."

(2) "I lifted up mine eyes, and saw, and behold," viii. 3. Cf. x. 5, "I lifted up mine eyes, and looked, and behold."

(3) "he did according to his will," viii. 4. Cf. xi. 3, "a mighty king . . . shall do according to his will"; also xi. 16.

(4) "he magnified himself," viii. 4; "the he-goat magnified himself," viii. 7. Cf. xi. 36, 37, "he shall magnify himself above every god"; "magnify himself above all."

(5) "and when he was strong, the great horn was broken: and instead of it there came up four notable horns toward the four winds of heaven," viii. 8. Cf. xi. 4, "and when he shall stand up, his kingdom shall be broken and shall be divided toward the four winds of heaven."

(6) "a little horn [lit. 'a horn from being little'] which waxed exceeding great," viii. 9. Cf. xi. 23, "he shall come up, and shall become strong, with a small people."

(7) "the glorious *land*," viii. 9. Cf. xi. 16, 41, 45.

(8) "it took away from him the continual," viii. 11. Cf. xi. 31, "they shall take away the continual"; also xii. 11.

(9) "the place of his sanctuary was cast down," viii. 11; "to give the sanctuary to be trodden under foot," viii. 13. Cf. xi. 31, "they shall profane the sanctuary."

(10) "it did *its pleasure*," viii. 12; also viii. 24. Cf. xi. 17, "he shall do his pleasure"; also xi. 28, 30; and xi. 32, "do *exploits*."

(11) " How long shall be the vision ? " viii. 13. Cf. xii. 6, " How long shall it be to the end of these wonders ? "

(12) " the transgression that maketh desolate," viii. 13. Cf. xi. 31 and xii. 11, " the abomination that maketh desolate."

(13) " I heard a man's voice between *the banks of* Ulai," viz. giving an order to Gabriel, viii. 16. Cf. xii. 7, " I heard the man clothed in linen, which was above the waters of the river," viz. speaking with authority in answer to a question put by one of the angels on the bank.

(14) " the vision belongeth to the time of the end," viii. 17 ; " it belongeth to the appointed time of the end," viii. 19. Cf. xi. 35, " even to the time of the end ; because it is yet for the time appointed " ; also xi. 40 and xii. 4.

(15) " Now as he was speaking with me, I fell into a deep sleep with my face toward the ground : but he touched me and set me upright," viii. 18. Cf. x. 9, 10, " when I heard the voice of his words, then was I fallen into a deep sleep on my face, with my face toward the ground. And, behold, a hand touched me, which set me upon my knees and upon the palms of my hands."

(16) " the latter time of the indignation," viii. 19. Cf. xi. 36, " till the indignation be accomplished."

(17) " shall stand up," *i.e.* shall arise, viii. 22, 23. Cf. xi. 2, 3, 4, 14, 20, 21.

(18) " understanding dark sentences," rather " skilled in ambiguities," viii. 23. Cf. xi. 21, " he shall obtain the kingdom by flatteries."

(19) " but not," viii. 22, 24. Cf. xi. 4, 6, 17, 25, 27, 29.

(20) " the holy people," viii. 24. Cf. xii. 7.

(21) " the Prince of princes," viii. 25, *i.e.* the Prince of angelic powers. Cf. x. 20, " the prince of Persia " ; x. 21, " Michael your prince," spoken of angels.

(22) " the vision . . . is true," viii. 26. Cf. x. 1, " the thing [lit. ' word '] was true."

(23) " shut thou up the vision ; for it belongeth to many days *to come*," viii. 26. Cf. xii. 4, " shut up the words, and seal the book, even to the time of the end " ; also x. 14, " the vision is yet for *many* days."

21

The Language Evidence

> "The language is one mark of evidence set by God on the book."
> *Lectures on Daniel the Prophet,* E. B. Pusey.

IF this chapter had been written at the close of the last century it would probably have been entitled, "The Language Difficulty." But so wonderful and enlightening are the archæological discoveries made in recent years that I have no hesitation whatever in calling it "The Language Evidence"; seeing that much of a linguistic nature which was formerly regarded as perplexing in the Book of Daniel has now through the progress of discovery become good and reliable evidence as to the authenticity of that Book and the period within which it was written.

When the late Prof. Driver wrote his valuable Commentary on the Book of Daniel—valuable, not so much for the views advanced as for the great mass of learning contained in it—he issued this famous dictum as to the period to which that Book must be assigned when judged from the standpoint of the language-

> "The verdict of the language of Daniel is thus clear. The Persian words *presuppose* a period after the Persian empire had been well established; the Greek words *demand,* the Hebrew *supports,* and the Aramaic *permits* a date *after the conquest of Palestine by Alexander the Great.*" [1]

Before his lamented death this dictum, or at any rate the latter part of it respecting the Aramaic, was considerably modified by its author, owing to a remarkable discovery which will be related in the course of this chapter.[2]

About half of the Book of Daniel, viz. from chap. ii. 4, to the end of chap. vii., is written in Aramaic, and, as stated in a previous chapter, the majority of scholars are of opinion that the whole

[1] *Cambridge Bible,* Daniel, p. lxiii.

[2] In his letter to *The Guardian* of November 6, 1907, Prof. Driver admits that the Aramaic spoken in Egypt in 408 B.C. "bears many points of resemblance to that found in the Old Testament—in Ezra, Daniel, and Jer. x. 11."

Book was originally written in this language and that the Hebrew portion is only a translation.

The Arameans—better known to us from the English Bible as " the Syrians "—are believed, like the Chaldeans, to have come in the first instance from Arabia, that prolific hive of Semitic peoples. In the Old Testament they appear before us in the story of Laban the Syrian, and again in the wars of David, in whose days we find Aramean states to the north and north-east of the Land of Israel, viz. Damascus, Zobah, Beth-Rehob, and Maacah, as well as Aram-naharaim to the east of the Euphrates.[1] Agreeably to these Old Testament notices some of the early Assyrian kings, viz. Shalmaneser I., 1325 B.C., Ashur-rish-ishi, 1150 B.C., and Tiglathpileser I., 1120 B.C., mention a tribe called the Akhlami, whom the last of these monarchs defines as " the *Aramean* Akhlami," and tells us that they dwelt on the Euphrates from the frontier of the Sukhi [2] as far north as Carchemish of the Hittites. These notices in the Old Testament and the Assyrian inscriptions lead us to look for the Arameans in the north of the Syrian Desert from Northern Palestine eastward to Haran. But further investigation has shown that this was not their first settlement. In Amos ix. 7, Jehovah says, " Have not I brought up Israel out of Egypt, and the Philistines from Caphtor, and the Syrians [Arameans] from Kir ? " Kir has not yet been found on the inscriptions, but it must have lain, as Hommel points out,[3] to the east of Babylonia and on the frontier of Elam, since in Isa. xxii. 6 it is mentioned in conjunction with Elam in the parallel clause : " Elam bare the quiver . . . and Kir uncovered the shield." This early eastward settlement of the Arameans after quitting the wilds of Arabia is confirmed by the cuneiform inscriptions. Agum-kakrimi, a Babylonian king of the seventeenth century B.C., styles himself " king of Padan and of Alman." Alman, or Arman, signifies the Arameans. Further, a geographical list tells us that Padin, *i.e.* " the Plain," lies " in front of the mountains of Arman," *i.e.* the Arameans.[4] These " mountains of Arman " were the hills east of the Tigris, at the foot of, and on the lower slopes of which, the Arameans made their early home, and from which, as recorded in the Book of Amos, they spread westward into the plain between the Tigris and Euphrates—called after them Padan-Aram, *i.e.* " the Plain of the Arameans "—and so further west into Syria.

It was against these eastern Arameans, from whom the western

[1] See 2 Sam. viii. 3–13 and Ps. lx. title.

[2] Cf. Job ii. 11.

[3] Hommel's *Ancient Hebrew Tradition*, pp. 204–208.

[4] Sayce's *Higher Criticism*, p. 200.

or Syrian branch had drifted away, that Tiglathpileser III., 745–729 B.C., conducted his first campaign. In his account of it he mentions by name no fewer than thirty-five different tribes, and finally sums them all up under one common designation as "the whole of the Arameans, who dwell on the banks of the Tigris, Euphrates, and Surappi,[1] as far as where the Uknu [2] falls into the Lower Sea." [3] Somewhat earlier Shamshi-Ramanu king of Assyria speaks of the countries of "Chaldea, Elam, and Namri, and the land of the Arameans" as in alliance with Babylon; and it is clear from the conjunction of names that he is speaking of these eastern Arameans, who had thus wedged themselves in between Assyria and Media in the north, and between Babylon and Elam in the south. It thus becomes evident that for some considerable time Babylonia had been ringed round from N.W. to S.E. with Aramean tribes, partly settled, partly migratory; and in consequence of this, as Dr. Albert Sanda points out, "the Aramaic language came more and more into acceptation at Babylon, and made its way upwards from the villages into the towns, and from the lower classes to the magistracy and into the higher circles of society." [4] Along with this upward current there would also be a downward current, since Aramaic was already the language of diplomacy and of commerce. This was due to its being so widely extended, and spoken in districts bordering on Elam, Babylonia, Media, Assyria, Asia Minor, Phœnicia, and Palestine. Hence we find the lion-weights from Nimrûd of the eighth century B.C. inscribed in Aramaic as well as in Assyrian, and contract tablets both from Nineveh and Babylon with Aramaic dockets: whilst the parley between the Assyrian Rabshakeh and the ministers of king Hezekiah shows very plainly that Aramaic formed a convenient channel of intercourse between Oriental diplomats in the year 701 B.C. If, then, the Book which bears his name was written by Daniel, a Jewish courtier and diplomat under both Babylonian and Persian kings, it is not surprising to find it written in Aramaic, a language which must often have been upon his lips, a language, too, more suitable than Hebrew to the wider outlook of his prophetic visions, and one that would make his Book available to a larger circle of readers.

At the close of the nineteenth century there were no Aramaic documents available for comparison with the Aramaic of the Book of Daniel. The inscriptions which we then possessed were

[1] According to Delitzsch the Shatt Um-el-Jamal.

[2] The Choaspes, the modern Kerkha, which flowed near Shushan

[3] The Persian Gulf.

[4] *Die Aramäer*, p. 20.

divided into three sections:[1] (i) those from Syria, Assyria, and Babylonia; (ii) those from Asia Minor, Arabia, and Egypt; (iii) those from Nabatea, and Palmyra. Of these, class (i) contained three inscriptions of the kings of Samahla in North Syria, belonging to the eighth century B.C., found at Zenjerli, some distance north of the Syrian Antioch and on the eastern slope of Mount Amanus, during the years 1888–91. They are of considerable religious, historical, and linguistic interest, but are too early to throw much light on our subject.[2] The inscriptions of class (ii) come to us from Egypt, and range from the end of the fifth to the beginning of the third century B.C. In language they have a close affinity to the Aramaic of the Book of Daniel, but the writers are not Jews and the subject-matter is too remote. The inscriptions of class (iii) come from Nabatea and Palmyra, and are of late date. They range from 70 B.C. down to about the third century of our era. Such light as was thrown by them on the Book of Daniel was supposed to argue a late date for that Book; but this view, which I shall have occasion to refer to later, has met with a complete check owing to a remarkable discovery made in the island of Elephantiné just below the First Cataract of the Nile in the early years of the present century. The story runs thus–

In the fifth century B.C. the twin fortresses of Jeb and Syené–answering to the modern Elephantiné and Assouan—the former being an island stronghold, the latter situated on the eastern bank of the Nile, stood confronting one another to guard the portals of the southern entrance into the Egyptian satrapy of the Persian empire. To reach that entrance from within you had to traverse Egypt proper and also Upper Egypt—the Pa-tu-risi, or "South Land" of the Egyptians, and the Pathros of the Old Testament–whence the prophet Ezekiel speaks of Egypt as extending "from Migdol to Syené, even unto the border of Ethiopia."[3] At this remote outpost, on the verge of the mysterious *hinterland* of Ethiopia, there was settled in the fifth century B.C. a flourishing colony of Jews, the possessors of houses and lands, and of a temple in which sacrifices were offered. They had been there, so they tell us, before Cambyses conquered Egypt in 525 B.C., and the probability is that they were sprung from the large Jewish population which had found its way as far south as Pathros even in

[1] Cook's *Glossary of the Aramaic Inscriptions*, pp. 2–4.

[2] For an interesting account of these inscriptions see E. G. H. Kraeling's *Aram and Israel.* New York Columbia University Press. 1918.

[3] Ezek. xxix. 10, R.V.M. The site of Migdol is about two miles from Suez.

the days of the prophet Jeremiah.[1] Indeed, for purposes of trade and commerce with the interior of Africa, Elephantiné under the Persian rule must have offered peculiar advantages. It is, then, from this Jewish source and from the Aramaic used by these Jews in the fifth century B.C. that we get our strongest light on the Aramaic of the Book of Daniel.

The first find at Elephantiné consisted of eleven documents, the contents of the deed-box of a Jewish family, stretching over three generations. They belong to the reigns of Xerxes, Artaxerxes I., and Darius Nothus, and cover a period of exactly sixty years, viz. from 471 B.C. to 411 B.C. They were found in a wooden box at the southern end of the island, and in a practically perfect condition, the strings tied round them being still intact and the seals unbroken. This discovery was very heartily welcomed by scholars. "Now for the first time," writes Prof. Sayce, "the Aramaic scholar has before him a series of connected and fairly lengthy documents, clearly written and but little injured, and furnished with exact dates. A fresh light is thus thrown on the history of the Aramean language, as it was spoken and written in the fifth century B.C., new words and meanings are added to the Aramaic dictionary, and new forms or idioms to the Aramaic grammar."

But the second find at Elephantiné, made only a few years later, was altogether so surprising as to throw the first into the shade; chiefly, indeed, on account of the intensely interesting nature of the subject-matter which it contained, but also to some extent because of the freer form of the Aramaic which it exhibited; the documents being written, not in the stiff legal phraseology of the title deeds first found, but in the more colloquial diction of everyday correspondence. The two finds, though so different in their character, are yet very closely connected. They belong to the same age, the same place, and the same people; and are, as we shall see, actually linked together.

In one of the legal documents, defining the boundaries of a piece of house property, it was noticed that the words occurred, "east of it is the temple of the God Jahu." This brief statement was quite enough at the time to whet the curiosity of every student of Biblical Archæology. But few of us could have imagined how fully the craving for further light and knowledge would shortly be satisfied by the discovery of these fresh treasures, which are believed to have come from the same spot as the first. They were unearthed in the chamber of a house excavated under the mound which marks the site of Jeb, the ancient name of Elephantiné.

[1] Jer. xliv. 15.

They consist of three documents, viz. a letter written and then copied out with some alterations, and also a short memorandum of the answer received. The letter was written in 408 B.C.—just three years after the latest of the legal documents—in the name of the Jewish priests, who formed the ecclesiastical heads of the colony at Elephantiné. It is addressed to Bagohi, the Persian governor of Jerusalem, and being penned only twenty-four years after Nehemiah's second visit to that city may be said actually to fringe on Old Testament history. Mention is made in it of the high priest Jehohanan, or John, whose name occurs in Ezra x. 6, and also of Sanballat the enemy of Nehemiah, who now appears definitely as the governor of Samaria. It also touches on the history given us in Josephus, for Bagohi is the Bagoas, who is represented in the *Antiquities* as dealing so hardly with the Jews, after the high priest John, *i.e.* Jehohanan, under strong provocation, had slain his brother Jesus in the temple.[1] The letter of the Jewish priests at Elephantiné shows that they were well aware of the covetous disposition of this man, and knew perfectly how they could most easily gain his ear. The immediate cause of the letter stands out on the face of it. The writers tell Bagoas how, in the absence of Arsames the Persian governor of Egypt, the Jewish community at Jeb have been subjected to very high-handed treatment, by the commanders, father and son, of the Persian garrisons stationed respectively at Jeb and Syené, who have been stirred up against them by the idolatrous priests of the Nile-god Khnub. Their temple, in which they offered sacrifice to Jahu the God of heaven, has been plundered, overthrown, and burned with fire, and they are not allowed to rebuild it. Three years ago, at the time when this calamity befell them, they sent a letter to Bagoas and to Jehohanan the high priest, but received no answer back. Ever since that time they have been mourning, fasting, and praying to Jahu the Lord of heaven, and are encouraged by the terrible retribution which has overtaken one of their persecutors to make a second appeal in the continued absence of the governor Arsames. If Bagoas will listen to them and redress their grievance, they assure him that he will be handsomely remunerated. Such is the gist of the letter, to which, as the memorandum shows, a favourable answer was returned. My readers will wish, however, to have these two documents placed before them *in extenso;* and indeed it is necessary for me to do

[1] As a punishment for the crime committed by John, Bagoas imposed a seven years' tribute on the Jews. They were required to pay fifty shekels out of the public funds for every lamb offered in the daily sacrifices. *Ant.* xi. 7, 1.

this in order to show their bearing on the Aramaic of the Book of Daniel. The letter reads thus–

"To our lord [1] Bagohi, governor [2] of Judah, thy servants, Jedoniah and his companions,[3] the priests who are in the fortress [4] of Jeb [say] Peace! [5] May our Lord, the God of heaven,[6] grant to thee peace abundantly at all times, and may He destine thee for favour [7] before king Darius [8] and the sons of the [royal] house [9] a thousandfold more than now,[10] and may He give thee long life! Mayest thou be happy and in good health at all times!

"Now thy servants, Jedoniah and his companions speak thus: In the month of Tammuz in the 14th year of king Darius, when Arsham departed and went to the king, the priests [11] of the god Khnub,[12] which was in the fortress of Jeb, made a joint conspiracy [13] with Waidrang, who was *fratara-ka* [14] here, saying, 'Let the temple [15] which belongs to the God Jahu,[16] the God which is in the fortress of Jeb, be taken away from thence.' Then the destroyer [17] Waidrang sent a letter [18] to his son Nephayan, who was

[1] "Lord," in the original *mârē'*. Cf. Dan. iv. 19 (16) and 1 Cor. xvi. 22, R.V.M.

[2] "Governor," *pĕchâh:* Dan. iii. 2, vi. 7 (8); Ezra v. 3.

[3] The word thus rendered occurs in Ezra iv. 9 and v. 3.

[4] A loan word from the Assyrian *birtu*, rendered in Dan. viii. 2, "palace," margin "castle," when speaking of the citadel of Shushan.

[5] Cf. Dan. iv. 1 (iii. 31) and vi. 25 (26).

[6] Dan. ii. 18; Ezra v. 11, vi. 9, vii. 12: a title characteristic of the Persian period.

[7] Lit. "mercies before king Darius." Cf. Dan. ii. 18, where the literal rendering is, "mercies from before the God of heaven."

[8] Darius Nothus, 424–405 B.C.

[9] Ezra vi. 10, vii. 23.

[10] Lit. "more than what now one thousand." Cf. Dan. iii. 19, which may be rendered literally, "one seven above what was seemly for heating."

[11] *Kĕmarîn:* used of idolatrous priests, 2 Kings xxiii. 5; Hos. x. 5; Zeph. i. 4.

[12] Khnub, or Khnumu, was the Nile-god of the Cataract, and as such the patron god of Elephantiné.

[13] The word translated "joint conspiracy" is an Old Persian word with a Semitic ending, akin to the Greek ἅμα.

[14] An Old Persian word, "chief in command." Compare the Greek πρότερος.

[15] The word for temple is the Sumerian *e-kur*, "mountain-house,"—see Chapter V. above—which found its way into the Assyrian and so into the Aramaic.

[16] In the Old Testament this form of the name Jehovah is found only at the end of proper names under the form "iah" in our English Bibles. Cf. Isaiah, Jeremiah, etc. It answers to the more contracted Jah, chiefly found in the later Psalms.

[17] "Destroyer." The word occurs in an inscription from Nerab of the seventh century B.C. See G. A. Cooke's *N. Semitic Inscriptions*, No. 6, line 10, "with a destructive death," etc.

[18] "Letter," *iggĕrâh*. Cf. Ezra iv. 8, v. 6.

commander of the forces [1] in the fortress of Syené,[2] saying, 'Let the temple which is in the fortress of Jeb be destroyed.' Whereupon Nephayan led out the Egyptians with the other forces. They came to the fortress of Jeb with their mattocks [?],[3] they went into this temple, they destroyed it to the ground, and the pillars of stone which were there they shattered them. Also it happened that they destroyed five stone portals, built of hewn blocks of stone, which were in this temple, and they burned [4] their lintels [5] and their hinges, which were of brass set in marble. And the roof, which was all of cedar beams, along with the stucco of the wall [6] and whatever else [7] was there—they burned all with fire. And the bowls [8] of gold and silver, and whatever else [7] was in this temple, they took and served themselves [of them]. Moreover our fathers built this temple in the fortress of Jeb from the days of the kings [9] of Egypt, and when Cambyses came into Egypt [10] he found this temple built: and all the temples of the gods of Egypt were thrown down, but no one injured anything in this temple. And when they"—viz. Waidrang and his soldiers—"acted thus, we put on sackcloth and fasted and prayed to Jahu the Lord of heaven, who showed us concerning this Waidrang.[11] The dogs have torn the chain from his feet, and all the riches which he got have perished, and all the men who prayed for evil against this temple—all are slain, and we have seen our desire upon them.[12]

"Also, before this, at the time when this evil was done to us, we sent a letter to our lord, and to Jehohanan [13] the high priest

[1] *Rabh-chayil*, "commander of the forces," a Babylonian compound word. Cf. Dan. ii. 14, "captain of the guard," and iv. 9 (6), "master of the magicians."

[2] Syené was on the right bank of the Nile opposite Elephantiné.

[3] A word of doubtful meaning.

[4] *Qîmu*: a verb found in the Assyrian.

[5] Lit. "their heads." Cf. Ps. xxiv. 7, 9.

[6] *Ushsharnâ'*: a word hitherto only found in Ezra v. 3, 9.

[7] "Whatever else." The word thus rendered is found in Egyptian Aramaic inscriptions of the fifth to the fourth century B.C.

[8] *Mizreqayyâ*. Cf. Exod. xxvii. 3.

[9] "Kings." Although this word is written in the singular, yet the duplicate shows that it is to be taken in a plural sense. The kings meant are the native kings of Egypt before the Persian conquest.

[10] 525 B.C. For Cambyses' slaughter of the priests of Apis and mockery of the idols of the Egyptians, see Herod. iii. 29, 37.

[11] *I.e.* allowed us to see the retribution that overtook him. He appears to have been thrown into chains and exposed to the semi-wild dogs of the East. Cf. Jer. xv. 3.

[12] A pregnant use of the verb="we have seen what we wished to see," "we have feasted our eyes upon." Cf. Pss. liv. 7 (9), lix. 10 (11); also line 4 of the Moabite Stone: "He [Chemosh] let me see my desire upon all my enemies."

[13] The Johanan of Neh. xii. 23.

and his companions the priests who were in Jerusalem, and to Ostan his brother—who is 'Anani [1]—and to the nobles [2] of the Jews; [but] they sent no letter to us.

"Moreover, since Tammuz-day, the 14th year of king Darius, to this day we have put on sackcloth and fasted; our wives have become as widows, we have not anointed ourselves with oil, nor drunk wine,[3] from that day to this day of the 17th year of King Darius: [and] meal-offerings, frankincense, and burnt-offerings have not been offered in this temple.

"Now, therefore, thy servants, Jedoniah and his companions, and the Jews—all the citizens of Jeb—say thus: If it seem good to our lord, think upon this temple that it may be rebuilt; since we are not permitted to rebuild it. Look upon the recipients of thy goodness and of thy favour who are here in Egypt. May a letter be sent from thee to them concerning the rebuilding of the temple of the God Jahu in the fortress of Jeb, as it was built in former times. And they will offer upon the altar of the God Jahu in thy name meal-offerings, and frankincense, and burnt-offerings; and we will pray for thee at all times, we, and our wives, and our children, and the Jews, all [of us] who are here. If thus it be done until this temple is rebuilt, then thou shalt have a fixed portion [4] before Jahu the God of heaven from every one who offers to Him burnt-offering and sacrifice, in value equivalent to a thousand talents of silver.[5] And concerning the gold—concerning *that* we have sent and given information. We have also sent the matter in a letter in our name to Delaiah and Shelemiah, the sons of Sanballat the governor of Samaria.[6]

"The 20th of Marchesvan, the 17th year of king Darius."

The answer to this petition is contained in the following brief memorandum:

"Memorandum of what Bagohi and Delaiah have said to me. Memorandum to this effect [7]: Thou art to say in Egypt before

[1] Ostan was his Persian, 'Anani his Hebrew, name.

[2] *Chōrim*, "nobles." See Neh. ii. 16, iv. 14 (8), etc.

[3] Dan. x. 3.

[4] *Tsĕdâqâh*, which generally means "righteousness," is here used of a portion fixed by law or agreement. In Neh. ii. 20 it is well rendered "right."

[5] Cf. what has already been said about the character of Bagoas as gathered from the pages of Josephus.

[6] The prominent position held by Sanballat in Samaria is indicated, though not plainly stated, in Neh. iv. 1, 2. Here we learn that he was sub-satrap of the district.

[7] Cf. Ezra vi., where the last word of *v.* 2 and the opening words of *v.* 3 should be rendered thus: "Memorandum: In the first year of Cyrus," etc.

Arsham concerning the house of sacrifice of the God of heaven, which was built in the fortress of Jeb from former times before Cambyses, which that destroyer Waidrang razed in the 14th year of king Darius, that it is to be rebuilt in its place [1] as it was in former times, and meal-offerings and frankincense are to be offered on that altar as was done in former times."

In perusing the above documents the reader will feel that next to the interest and surprise aroused by the discovery of a Jewish temple for sacrifice away from Jerusalem, what most impresses us is the feeling that in these papyri from Elephantiné we are brought nearer to the Old Testament than in any inscriptions previously discovered. I shall now hope to show that these remarkable documents are no less full of interest from the linguistic standpoint, since they enable us with confidence to assign a much earlier date to the Book of Daniel than the age of Antiochus Epiphanes. The critics, as we have seen, fix the date of that Book at 165 B.C. Now, the documents at which we are looking belong to 408 B.C., nearly two and a half centuries earlier, and rather more than a century after the date of Daniel, who was living in 535 B.C., " the third year of Cyrus." During the interval 535 to 408 B.C. very little change can have taken place in the language. If, then, it can be shown that the Aramaic in which the letter is written is essentially the same as the Aramaic of the Book of Daniel, then there is nothing, so far as regards the language, to prevent our referring the date of that Book to a period as early as the closing years of the life of Daniel. Let me endeavour, then, to put the matter so that an English reader may be able to form some judgment on the question, while at the same time a student of the Old Testament in the original will be able to gain a yet clearer view of the state of the case.

In the above letter, written on two sheets of papyrus in 30 lines of about 12 inches in length, as well as in the brief memorandum found with it, there are, if we omit proper names, 81 Nouns, Substantive and Adjective. Of these no fewer than 57 are found in Biblical Aramaic, and no fewer than 49 in the six Aramaic chapters of the Book of Daniel. Of the remainder the student will find the roots or equivalents of 19 in the Hebrew Lexicon;

[1] Cf. Ezra v. 15 and vi. 7. From the inscriptions of Nabonidus we learn that there was a strong feeling that temples, when rebuilt, should follow the exact lines of the old foundations. See *Records of the Past*, New Series, vol. v. p. 174, col. ii. 65.

1, viz. the word for "temple," is a loan-word from the Assyrian; 1, viz. the word rendered "destroyer," is from a root found in the Syriac; 1 is a word of doubtful meaning; and the remaining 2 are from the Old Persian. Of the 38 Verbs used in the letter, 32 are found in Biblical Aramaic, and of these 29 are in the Book of Daniel. The Prepositions, Adverbs, and Conjunctions are all found in the Book of Daniel, and also most of the compound particles; *e.g.* the word translated "when" in Dan. iii. 7 and "even as" in ii. 43 [1]; the word "till" in ii. 9 [2]; and the word rendered "aforetime" in vi. 10, (11), lit. "from before this." [3] And not only are verbs, nouns, and particles the same; but we notice certain peculiarities of form, expression, order, and syntax, already familiar to the student of Biblical Aramaic, such as the following:

(i) The use of the so-called Emphatic State, which according to the consensus of evidence and opinion probably answered, at least originally, to the Noun defined by the Article.[4]

(ii) The occasional use of the unit for the Indefinite Article.[5]

(iii) The freer use of the particle of relation in its threefold capacity, viz. as a Relative Pronoun, as a mark of the Genitive, and lastly as a Conjunction, in which case it is not infrequently joined to other particles.[6]

(iv) The frequent placing of a Proper Name before the Descriptive, when two Nouns are in apposition.[7]

(v) The use of the Active Participle in place of the Finite Verb.[8]

(vi) The similar use of the same Participle in conjunction with the Verb "to be." [9]

(vii) The use of the Passive Participle with afformatives of the Perfect to form a Perfect Passive.[10]

E. 1=Letter from Elephantiné, line 1.

1 כְּזִי or כְּדִי, according to difference of dialect. Cf. E. 4, 13.

2 עַד זִי or עַד דִּי. Cf. E. 27.

3 מִן קֳדָמַת דְּנָה, answering to קדמת זנה. Cf. E. 17.

4 Cf. E. 1, כהניא, "the priests."

5 E. 3, "*a* [lit. 'one'] thousandfold." Similarly E. 19, "*a* letter." Cf. Dan. ii. 31, "*a* great image"; iv. 19 (16), "for *a* while"; vi. 17 (18) "*a* stone."

6 E. 1, "*which* [are] in Jeb"; E. 5, "priests *of* the god Khnub"; joined on to a particle, E. 13, "*when* Cambyses."

7 E. 2, "Darius the king"=king Darius. Cf. Dan. iii. 1, "Nebuchadnezzar the king"=king Nebuchadnezzar.

8 E. 4, "[are] saying thus"; E. 23, "we are not permitted," lit. "they [are] not permitting us." Cf. Dan. ii. 8, "I know," lit. "I [am] knowing."

9 E. 15, "we *were* putting on"; E. 25, "it *was* built." In Dan. v. 19 this construction occurs nine times.

10 E. 17, "are slain." Cf. Dan. vii. 4, "were plucked off"; also vii. 10, "books were opened."

(viii) The use of the Verbal Noun governed by the Preposition ל to express a purpose.[1]

(ix) The use of the Preposition *qavêl* followed by the particle of relation to form Conjunctions.[2]

If to the above similarities of syntax and construction we add the use of similar words and phrases, it will then be evident even to the English reader that the type of Aramaic employed in these papyri of the year 408 B.C. bears such a striking resemblance to the Aramaic of the Book of Daniel as to allow of that Book being written as early as the year 535 B.C., "the third year of Cyrus," [3] and to make that date far more likely than the year 165 B.C. to which the critics so confidently ascribe the date of its composition.

But whilst the uninitiated will probably assent to this conclusion, it is quite possible that the Oriental scholar may demur on the ground of one striking difference between the Aramaic of the Elephantiné papyri and that of the Book of Daniel. It is this: that certain words—chiefly Relative and Demonstrative Pronouns—which in the former begin with a "z," Zain, in Daniel begin with a "d," Daleth.[4] This feature is very marked, and it has been regarded by some as a sign that the Book of Daniel is the work of a later age, inasmuch as certain late inscriptions from Palmyra and Nabatea, which date from about 70 B.C. and onwards, exhibit the same feature. There are, however, two very rational explanations of this phenomenon, both of which serve to show that the *d* consistently used throughout the Aramaic part of the Book of Daniel is no sign of late authorship. First, then, it is held by some authorities that the *d* sound and the *z* sound both sprang originally out of the *dh* sound, which is still preserved in the Arabic and still sounded in remote Bedawin dialects; but that whilst the Aramaic steadily modified the aspirate dentals to explosive dentals, the Hebrew modified them to sibilants. Thus the Arabic *dh* became *z* in Hebrew and *d* in Aramaic. Further, "It is impossible," writes an advocate of this theory, "to suggest that in Aramaic the *dh* first became *z* and then changed to *d*." In this case, then, the divergence is seen to be merely dialectal,

[1] E. 23, "that it may be rebuilt," lit. "for rebuilding it." Cf. Dan. vi. 3 (4), lit. "thought with a view to setting him"; also vi. 4 (5), 7 (8), 23 (24).

[2] This Preposition, so frequently used in Daniel in combination with Relatives and Demonstratives, is similarly used in E. 25, "*as* it was built." Cf. Dan. vi. 10 (11).

[3] Dan. x. 1.

[4] Thus for the Biblical דִּי, דָּא, דֵּךְ, דְּנָה, etc., we find in the Elephantiné papyri זי, זא, זך, זנה, etc.

and the *d* found in the Aramaic of the Book of Daniel cannot be regarded as any criterion of the age of that Book. The other explanation is that advocated by Prof. R. D. Wilson in his able article on "The Aramaic of Daniel."[1] According to this writer the Semites, from whatever source they adopted their alphabet, seem to have had only two signs, Daleth and Zain, to express the three sounds *d, dh,* and *z.* Daleth was always used to denote *d* and Zain to denote *z.* For the *dh* sound three methods were employed: (i) the Arabs invented a third sign by putting a dot over the Daleth; (ii) Hebrew and Babylonian expressed *dh* prevailingly by the *z* sign, but sometimes (iii) by the *d* sign. With regard to the Aramaic, according to Wilson, "the old Aramean inscriptions of Northern Syria and Assyria from the ninth to the seventh century inclusive, always use *z.*[2] The Palmyrene, the Syriac, and the Targums of Onkelos and Jonathan always use *d.* The Aramaic papyri from Egypt"—dating from the end of the fifth to the beginning of the third century B.C.—"use either with almost equal frequency. The earliest Nabatean inscription, dating from 70 B.C., always uses *z*; all the other Nabatean inscriptions use *d.*" The central portion of the Book of Daniel is thus the earliest Aramaic document known to us in which *d* takes the place of *dh.* But this usage, regarded by some as a sign of late authorship, was really in vogue long before the era of Daniel. The evidence of this, as Wilson points out, is furnished by the cuneiform inscriptions of Shalmaneser II., 860–825 B.C. In these inscriptions, when transcribing the name of a contemporary king of Damascus, the Assyrian scribe writes Dadda-i*d*ri instead of the Hebrew form Hadad-e*z*er; Dadda, which has the determinative of divinity before it, standing for Hadad, the Hebrew form of the name of the national god of Syria, and *idri* answering in Aramaic to the Hebrew *ezer;* thus showing that in the age of Shalmaneser II., *i.e.* as early as the middle of the ninth century B.C.,

[1] See *Biblical and Theological Studies* by the Members of the Faculty of Princeton Theological Seminary. New York. Charles Scribner's Sons. 1912. Prof. Wilson's article came to hand after I had written this chapter. My first impulse after reading it was to suppress the results of my own very limited investigations. Struck, however, with the fact that conclusions, at which I had arrived independently, tallied with those of this learned and lucid writer, and considering that any proof of the authenticity of the Book of Daniel must ultimately rest on cumulative evidence, I decided to let the results of my own studies see the light for the sake of any additional evidence they might contain.

[2] Viz. the inscription of Zakir king of Hamath of the ninth century B.C.; the inscriptions of Panammu I. and Bar-rekub, kings of Samahla near the Syrian Antioch, of the eighth century B.C.; and the Aramaic dockets found in Assyria from the ninth century B.C. onwards.

d was sometimes used to express the *dh* sound.[1] Further, since the actual native forms of the Syrian royal names are given us in the Assyrian inscriptions—as, for instance, in the annals of Ashurbanipal, where the name Ben-Hadad appears as Bir-Dadda, *bir* or *bar* being the well-known Aramaic equivalent of the Hebrew *ben*, "son" [2]—we may conclude that *d*, written to express the *dh* sound, represents the usage in districts where the pure Aramaic was spoken, such as the Syrian kingdom of Damascus; whilst the *z* found in the early inscriptions from North Syria and on the business dockets from Nineveh, is due to contact with the Hebrew and Phœnician.

The Aramaic of the Books of Daniel and Ezra is sometimes spoken of as the Western Aramaic, in order to distinguish it from the Syriac or Eastern Aramaic—to wit, the literary language which flourished at Edessa and Nisibis in North Mesopotamia some six centuries later. But both these terms are misleading: first, because of the interval of time which separated these two types of the language; and secondly, because of the introduction of a complete geographical misnomer. The Biblical Aramaic appears to have been the purer form of the language, rather than that spoken in Palestine; whilst the classical Syriac, as W. Wright points out,[3] does not represent the old Eastern Aramaic, but only a sister tongue. The modern representative of the old Eastern Aramaic according to W. Wright is the Neo-Syriac, still spoken in the mountains from Mardin and Midyad on the west to Lake Urumiah on the east,[4] a dialect more closely connected with the Mandaitic and that of the Babylonian Talmud than with the classical Syriac. Thus, for instance, the Infinitive Paël, which in the Syriac has the prefix *m*, is usually without that prefix in the Talmud Babli, the Mandaitic, and the Eastern Neo-Syriac, just as in the Biblical Aramaic.[5] On the other hand, the modern representative of the Western Syriac is the dialect spoken at Ma'lula in the Anti-Libanus. Both of these modern dialects have greatly modified the ancient grammar. The most interesting difference between them lies in the vocalisation, where the Eastern Neo-Syriac agrees more closely with the Biblical Aramaic than the Western. Thus נְהוֹרָא, *nĕhôrâ*, "light," Dan. ii. 22, is still pronounced *nĕhôrâ* in Eastern Neo-Syriac, but in Western Neo-Syriac appears as *nĕhûrô*. Similarly

[1] A yet earlier instance of this is found in the name of Adriel the Meholathite, the son-in-law of king Saul. A*d*riel is the Aramaic form of the Hebrew Azriel, "God is my help," for which cf. Jer. xxxvi. 26.

[2] Cf. Dan. vii. 13, *bar ĕnâsh*, "a son of man."

[3] Cf. *Comparative Grammar of the Semitic Languages*, p. 20.

[4] *Ibid.* pp. 201–2.

[5] *Ibid.* p. 183.

כָּהֲנָא, *kŏhănâ*, "priest," Ezra vii. 12, is to-day pronounced *kâhnâ* in the Eastern dialect, but *kôhnô* in the Western. Again, it has been usual till of late to distinguish the so-called Western and Eastern Aramaic by the prefix of the third person singular of the Imperfect. Thus the Western prefixes a *y*, the Eastern an *n*. But, as Prof. Wilson has shown, the *y*, according to all documentary evidence, was used in the East and West alike down to A.D. 73.[1] In the Mandaitic and the Talmud Babli the prefix is either *l* or *n*.[2] In Biblical Aramaic the *y* is invariably used except in the case of the verb "to be," where we find an *l* in the third person singular masculine and in the third person plural both masculine and feminine. The Mandaitic is the language of the sacred books of the Mandeans, or Gnostics, a half Christian, half heathen sect, of whom a miserable remnant still survives near Basra on the Lower Euphrates. The oldest portion of these books is believed to date from A.D. 700–900. The Babylonian Talmud is assigned to the close of the sixth century A.D. The fact that the Book of Daniel agrees with the Mandaitic and the Babylonian Talmud in omitting the prefix *m* in the Infinitive of the Paël and in using the prefix *l* in the case of the verb "to be," is another indication of some connection with Babylonia and the East, rather than with Palestine, as regards the author of that Book.

In concluding this short and imperfect sketch of the Aramaic of the Book of Daniel, instead of Dr. Driver's verdict—"*the Aramaic permits a date after the conquest of Palestine by Alexander the Great*"—I would suggest the following: "That in view of the evidence furnished, more especially by the Elephantiné papyri, as well as by other documents, *the Aramaic permits a date as early as the closing years of the prophet Daniel*."

[1] *The Aramaic of the Book of Daniel*, p. 267.

[2] *Ibid.* p. 269, where Prof. Wilson shows that this use of *l* in the Imperfect is no late feature of the language, but occurs in an inscription of the eighth century B.C.

22

Evidence of Foreign Words

IN the last chapter, when dwelling on the language evidence, I entered somewhat at length into the type of Aramaic which confronts us in the Book of Daniel. In the present chapter I propose to consider what is really the second part of the same subject, viz. the evidence afforded by the foreign loan-words which we meet with in that Book. There are in the Book of Daniel at the most some twenty words belonging to the Old Persian and also three Greek words. I shall hope to show that these Persian and Greek words, so far from presenting any real difficulty, supply most valuable evidence, alike as to the authenticity of the Book and as to the position occupied by its writer. They must, indeed, no longer be regarded as stumbling-blocks in our path, but rather as strong confirmations of the orthodox view that the Book of Daniel was written within and towards the close of the times which it describes, and that Daniel himself was the writer.

Let us take the Old Persian words first. It is of these that Prof. Driver wrote, "The Persian words *presuppose* a period after the Persian empire had been well established."[1] In this decisive dictum the learned Professor appears to have lost sight entirely of three important factors: first, the genius of the language in which the Book of Daniel is believed to have been written; secondly, the length of time during which that language had been in contact with the Old Persian; and thirdly, the position occupied by Daniel himself, if we assume him to have been the writer.

The Book of Daniel, as already stated, is believed by most scholars to have been written in Aramaic; and Aramaic, being widely dispersed, and acting as a means of communication between men of different races and languages, very easily incorporated foreign loan-words. Now, as regards the introduction of Old Persian words into the Aramaic, *that* would depend, not so much on the length of time that the Persian empire had been established,

[1] *Cambridge Bible*, Daniel, p. lxiii.

but rather on the length of time that the two languages, the Old Persian and the Aramaic, had been in contact. In the case of the Book now before us it would depend in great measure also on the position occupied by the writer; *i.e.* his position, national, social, and geographical. What race was he of? Did he hold daily intercourse with men speaking an Aryan tongue? Was the Old Persian likely to be often upon his lips at the time when he wrote his Book? Then, what of his whereabouts? Was his Book written in Egypt, Palestine, Syria, Babylonia, or even further east? As to the first of these questions there is happily no doubt whatever. The writer is evidently a Jew. He belongs to a race even then cosmopolitan; to a race, too, which possesses a rare facility for acquiring foreign languages. His social position—if we identify him with Daniel, the trusted statesman of the Median Darius—is all in favour of the introduction of Persian words, especially of such as find a place in this Book. In all probability he was as much at home in the Persian as in the Aramaic, and in his old age, as well as in the diplomatic service of his previous life, must often have conversed with men who spoke that language. But what of his surroundings? Where did he write his Book? The number of Persian words which it contains is suggestive that he wrote it in the East rather than in the West. And this supposition agrees well with what little we know as to the home of Daniel. He appears to have spent the greater part of his long life at Babylon. Once we find him, in spirit at least, on the banks of the Tigris; and once, by the Ulai at Shushan: and the notices in his Book, especially in the latter instance, favour the idea that he had been in these localities.[1] Moreover tradition declares that he spent the closing years of his life at Shushan, and that he was buried there.[2] Now, it was at the river of Shushan and on the banks of the Uknu,[3] as shown in our last chapter, that the inroads of the Arameans found their furthest eastern extension. The "land" of the Arumu, as we there saw, lay to the east of the Tigris. They had wedged themselves in between Babylonia and Elam on the south, and between Assyria and Media on the north. They formed, in fact, a number of buffer-states between the great empires on the Tigris and Euphrates and the Aryan peoples of Media and Persia. Shamshi-Rammanu, king of Assyria, 825–812 B.C., mentions together the lands of the Kaldu (Chaldeans), Elam, Namri, and the Arumu (Arameans). His predecessor, Shalmaneser II., 860–825 B.C., speaking of Namri,

[1] Dan. viii. 2, x. 4.
[2] See Loftus' *Chaldea and Susiana*.
[3] The Choaspes of Herodotus (book i. 188), and the modern Kerkha.

which lay between Assyria and Media, mentions certain fortresses, Bit-Tamal, Bit-Sakki, Bit-Shidi, whose first syllable *Bit* or *Beth*, *i.e.* "house" or "place," suggests that they were the outposts of a Semitic-speaking people—to wit, the Arameans.[1] Thus some three hundred years before the era of Daniel there was contact in the north between the Arameans and the Aryan Medes, whose language was the same as that of the Persians. The inroad of the Arameans into the southern district round Shushan took place about a hundred years later, in the reign of Tiglathpileser III., 745–729 B.C. Further, that monarch in the Slab Inscription from Nimrûd, when recording his eastern conquests, writes thus: "The land of Bit-Khamban, the land of Sumurzu, the land of Bit-Zualzas, the land of Bit-Matti, the town of Niqu, the land of Umliash, the land of Bit-Taranzai, the land of Parsua, the land of Bit-kabsi, as far as the town Zakruti of the distant Medes, I brought into subjection."[2] Here are districts apparently inhabited by a Semitic population, as indicated by the characteristic *Bit*, stretching right up to the Median frontier some two hundred years before the conquest of Babylon by Cyrus. This long contact, both in the north and south, between the Semites and the Aryan Medes, could not fail to introduce some Medo-Persian words into the Aramaic and more especially into the Eastern Aramaic, the Aramaic spoken in Babylonia where Daniel spent the most of his life, and in the district round Shushan, the traditional home of his later years. To these considerations it must be added that as a Jew he would be sure to be brought into contact with some of the descendants of the Ten Tribes, who, as Prof. Wilson points out, had been settled in the cities of the Medes for about two hundred years before the establishment of the Persian empire, and had now for some seventy years been under Median rule.[3] These captives had been settled in cities taken from the Medes; and all around them, or at any rate in their near neighbourhood, was a Median population, towards whom it may be supposed they bare a certain good will, since both they themselves and their Median neighbours had felt the oppressive power of a common foe. Would it then be anything strange, if these captive Israelites had adopted some Medo-Persian words into the vocabulary of their everyday life?

What has been so far advanced seems amply sufficient to account for the presence of Persian words in a book written in Aramaic by a Jew living in Babylonia and Susiana soon after the

[1] *Keilinschriftliche Bibliothek*, vol. i. pp. 142–143.
[2] *Records of the Past*, New Series, vol. v, p. 124
[3] See *Biblical and Theological Studies*, p. 302, and cf. 2 Kings xvii. 6.

Persian conquest; but the case becomes very much stronger when we take into account the special character of the Book now before us, as well as the position occupied by him who may well be accounted its author. Here is a work written by an old man, a courtier and a diplomat, a man in every way of a wide outlook, a religious imperialist. Certain portions of it are descriptive of scenes at court, in most of which he himself took a very prominent part. At the time when he writes his Book, he holds a very important post at the court of Persia, and converses in the Old Persian every day, either with the king his master or with the Median and Persian officials around him. Now, it is observable, and exactly what we should expect, that the Persian words in this Book occur chiefly in the descriptions given us of scenes at court, and that at least fourteen out of the twenty are of a legal, official, and state character, no less than eight being titles of office like the *frateraka* of the Elephantiné letter. Among these titles of office is an anachronism, just such as an old man who had lived in the employment of the state through the Babylonian and on into the Persian period might very easily be guilty of. I refer to the use in chap. iii. 3, of the Persian title "satraps," to describe certain high officials at the court of Nebuchadnezzar. This is just such a use of words as an aged servant of the public, busied in the affairs of the Medo-Persian kingdom, might very easily be led to make.

The fourteen Old Persian words, alluded to above, which belong to court life, and come so naturally from the pen of one long occupied in the service of his royal masters, are thus rendered in the Revised Version: "nobles," i. 8; "meat," or rather "royal dainties," i. 5, xi. 26; "pieces," ii. 5, iii. 29, lit. "limbs," describing a condign punishment, "you shall be made limbs," *i.e.* you shall be dismembered; "rewards," ii. 6, v. 17; "law," ii. 9, vi. 5, vii. 25; "satraps," "judges," "treasurers," "counsellors," or rather "justices," and "sheriffs," all in iii. 2; "counsellors," iii. 27, a different word to that used in verse 2; "chain," *i.e.* of office, v. 7; "president," vi. 2; "palace," xi. 45. That these thirteen words should be expressed in the Old Persian by a writer in the position occupied by Daniel is really nothing to be wondered at, nay, is almost what we might expect. But what shall we say of the following: "is gone from me," rather, "is sure," ii. 5; "time," ii. 16, iii. 7, iv. 36, vi. 10, vii. 12; "a secret," ii. 18, iv. 9; "kind," iii. 5, 10, 15; "matter," iii. 16, rendered "sentence" in iv. 17; "hosen," iii. 21; "sheath," vii. 15, R.V.M.? We may say that the word rendered "kind" is of uncertain derivation; that the two last words, "hosen" and "sheath," might very well be expressed in Old Persian, seeing that they refer to dress and attire, even though the former, like "satraps" in the same chapter, is somewhat of an anachronism, since it occurs in the description of a scene which took place in Babylonian times; and that the remaining four words are sufficiently accounted for by the writer's surroundings coupled with the length of time during which the Eastern Aramaic had been in contact more or less close with the Old Persian.

From what has been just said it will be seen that the Persian words in the Book of Daniel constitute no real difficulty, and that so far from compelling us to regard that Book as the work of a late writer in the Greek period, they are strongly suggestive of its having been composed in the Persian period and by a writer in the position of Daniel. Further, the long contact between the Aramaic and the Old Persian completely does away with any hesitation we might feel in ascribing it to the early years of the Persian period and within the lifetime of the prophet; whilst the internal evidence points in the same direction. The words of chap. i. 21, "And Daniel continued even unto the first year of king Cyrus," seem to furnish us with a date for the composition of the beginning of the Book; then the date of the prophet's latest vision, given us in chap. x. 1, viz. "the third year of Cyrus," coupled with the gracious assurance at the close of that vision, "Go thou thy way till the end be, for thou shalt rest and stand in thy lot at the end of the days," are indications that the Book was finished shortly after that vision and a little before his death. Thus we have in the Book of Daniel a work composed at the beginning of the Persian period by a Jew who had been long familiar both with the Aramaic and with the Old Persian.

Before we leave these Persian words, of which a fuller account is given in the Appendix to this chapter, we may pause to notice another valuable service which they render. Occurring, as they do, in the Hebrew portions of the Book as well as in the Aramaic, they serve to stitch together the different parts, and are a voucher for the unity of authorship of the whole, despite the fact that the work appears before us in two languages, part being in Hebrew and part in Aramaic. No less worthy of notice is the fact that we find them in the prophetic as well as in the historical portion of the Book, though, as one might expect, they are far more frequent in the latter. Thus the Persian words for "nobles," i. 3, "meat," i. 5 and xi. 26, "palace" xi. 45, occur in the Hebrew part of the Book, whilst the last two references are also in the prophetic portion, in which will be found likewise the Old Persian words rendered thus: "body," vii. 15; "time," vii. 12, 22, 25; and "law," vii. 25.

Turning now to the second part of our subject, what shall we say to the presence of three Greek words in this Book, if we assign it to a date as early as the commencement of the Persian period? We may say, in the first place, that there are only three Greek words to match some twenty Persian, and that had the Book been written in the time of Antiochus Epiphanes, more than a century and a half after the conquests of Alexander, having regard to the wonderful Hellenising of Western Asia caused by those conquests, we should certainly have expected to find more Greek words than Persian. *It is the fewness of the Greek words, coupled with the fact that they are only the names of musical instruments, that must prove fatal to the critics' theory that the Book was written in* 165 *B.C.*; fatal, also, to Prof. Driver's dictum, "the Greek words *demand* a date *after the conquest of Palestine by Alexander the Great.*"[1] Such a demand I utterly fail to see. Could nothing Greek make its way to Babylon before the days of Alexander? And if Greek musical instruments could reach Babylon, why should they not carry their Greek names with them, in the same way that the exports of the further East brought to the court of king Solomon were known by their Indian names?[2]

The names of the three Greek musical instruments mentioned in Dan. iii. as forming part of Nebuchadnezzar's band are as follows[3]:

קִיתְרֹס, *kîthĕrōs*, Gr. *κίθαρις*, the lyre, R.V. "harp."

פְּסַנְתֵּרִין, *pĕsantērîn*, Gr. *ψαλτήριον*, Ital. *salerio*, the dulcimer, R.V. "psaltery."

סוּמְפֹּנְיָה, *sūmpōnyâh*, Gr. *συμφωνία*, Ital. *sampogna*, the bagpipe, R.V. "dulcimer."

The possibility of these musical instruments reaching Babylon and carrying their Greek names with them, may, as we have seen, be taken for granted on *a priori* grounds; but the question as to the precise channel by which they came is doubtful, and forms a very fascinating theme, which, without in any way weakening the argument, allows of our wandering out of the narrow confines of probability into the broad regions of possibility.

In entering on such an interesting inquiry, our first aim must

[1] *Century Bible*, Daniel, p. lxiii. It will be noted that Driver ascribes a Palestinian origin to the Book of Daniel. It was more probably written in Babylonia or Susiana.

[2] 1 Kings x. 22, where "apes," Heb. *qophîm*, has been referred to the Sanskrit *kapi*; and "peacocks," *tukkîyyim*, to the Malabar *toghai*.

[3] See Stainer's *Music of the Bible*, revised by Galpin, pp. 57, 73.

be to study the relations that existed between East and West in the latter half of the sixth century B.C. Now, it is with regard to these relations that Prof. Driver writes, "Any one who has studied Greek history knows what the civilisation of the Greek world was in the sixth century B.C., and is aware that the arts and inventions of civilised life streamed then into Greece from the East, not from Greece eastward." Such a statement is most fallacious and misleading. In the first place, to find out whether the arts and inventions of the West reached the East, we must direct our attention, not to Greece, but to the lands of the East, to Phœnicia, Assyria, Babylonia, and Egypt; above all, not forgetting that there was a Greece in Asia as well as in Europe, and that this Asiatic Greece considerably influenced the civilisation of the Near East.[1] Secondly, the idea that the tide of commerce between two countries, both of them highly civilised, should flow only in one direction is inconceivable. Vessels carrying to the West, say from the port of Tyre, Oriental wares, would be sure on the return voyage to bring with them the wares of Greece. Indeed, this is no mere conjecture, for the prophet Ezekiel, writing in the ninth year of Zedekiah, *i.e.* the fifteenth year of Nebuchadnezzar —just three years, according to the LXX and Theodotion, before the scene pictured in Dan. iii.—when describing the extensive commerce of Tyre, tells us that Javan, *i.e.* Ionia or Asiatic Greece, traded with Tyre in vessels of brass. As Ezekiel wrote in Babylonia, we are warranted in thinking that some of these brazen goods from Greece found their way from Tyre to the mart of Babylon. Again, turning back to Assyrian times, we find Asiatic Greece in contact with Assyria in the days of Sargon II., 722–705 B.C. The Assyrian king, telling of his successful warfare against the Greek pirates, says that he "drew the Ionians out of the sea like fish." In 698 B.C. his son Sennacherib sent an expedition to Cilicia to put down a revolt fomented by a treacherous Assyrian governor, who had allied himself with "the peoples who dwelt in Ingira and Tarsus." These peoples are evidently the Greeks, who, according to Polyhistor, had made a descent upon Cilicia. They may be identified with those Ionian pirates who had already received chastisement at the hands of Sargon. But this was not the first time that an Assyrian army had been seen in those regions. Shalmaneser II. penetrated as far as Tarsus as early as 834 B.C. Sennacherib's expedition was sent, not merely to punish a rebellious vassal, but, as he tells us, to keep open the *girri Kue* or "Cilician Road," the great trade route from the West, which passing through

[1] See Hogarth's *Ancient East*, pp. 139, 143.

the famous Cilician Gates descended on Tarsus, and then, after reaching the north-east angle of the Mediterranean, branched off in two directions, eastward to the kingdoms on the Tigris and Euphrates, and southward along the Syrian and Palestinian coast to Egypt. Sennacherib's determination to keep this route open is in itself a voucher for the brisk commercial intercourse which existed between East and West well-nigh a century before the era of Nebuchadnezzar. According to Abydenus the battle fought at Tarsus was a naval one, in which the Assyrian defeated a fleet of Greek ships. He also records that Sennacherib built an "Athenian temple" at Tarsus, and erected columns of bronze on which his mighty deeds were inscribed. This statement receives a striking confirmation from the vivid account given by Sennacherib of his new method of casting bronze pillars, narrated on the same cylinder which records his expedition to Tarsus.[1] Polyhistor adds that Sennacherib rebuilt Tarsus after the likeness of Babylon, which is explained by Abydenus, who relates that he made the Cydnus pass through the middle of the city in the same way that the Euphrates flowed through the midst of Babylon. All this care bestowed on Tarsus is a further witness of the strong desire of the Assyrian king to encourage the commerce between East and West, and to ensure that a goodly share of the trade from Asia Minor should flow into Assyria.

Another instance of the way in which the West influenced the East is visible in architecture: not indeed to any great extent, for both in Assyria and Babylonia palaces and temples continued to be built in much the same style as heretofore. Still the Greek style, with pillars, entablature, and pediment, creeps in here and there. Sennacherib must have made use of it in his "Athenian temple" at Tarsus, which, it has been suggested, was an Ionic temple;[2] whilst his father, Sargon, on one of his bas-reliefs pictures a summer-house or small temple on the top of a hill with Ionic columns, on another a fishing pavilion with similar supports;[3] and, what is yet more surprising, in his representation of the shrine of the god Haldia at Mutsatsir the sacred city of Ararat, depicts a temple with banded columns and an unmistakable classical pediment.[4] But the most striking instance of all, and the one which bears most closely on our subject, is found in the palace at

[1] See *Cuneiform Texts from Babylonian Tablets in the British Museum*, part xxvi., published by order of the trustees.

[2] Hogarth's *Ancient East*, p. 131.

[3] See Botta's *Monuments de Ninive*, vol. ii. pl. 114, and Layard's *Nineveh*, vol. ii. p. 273.

[4] Maspero, *Passing of the Empires*, p. 59.

DECORATION OF THE FAÇADE OF THE THRONE-ROOM AT BABYLON, IN THE SO-CALLED IONIC STYLE

(KOLDEWEY, FIG. 64)

Babylon erected by Nabopolassar and then rebuilt and enlarged by Nebuchadnezzar. There, in the very centre of an extensive group of buildings, in the court of the throne-room, and on the outer wall of that hall of state in which possibly Belshazzar's feast was held, was found an elaborate and brilliantly wrought pattern in coloured tiles, recalling the most distinctive feature of the Ionic Order.[1] It is thus described by the late L. W. King of the British Museum: "The brick-work of the outer façade which faced the court was decorated with bright coloured enamel. Only fragments of the enamelled surface were discovered, but these sufficed to restore the scheme of decoration. A series of yellow columns with bright blue capitals, both edged with white borders, stood out against a dark blue ground. The capitals are the most striking feature of the composition. Each consists of two sets of double volutes, one above the other, and a white rosette with yellow centre comes partly into sight above them. Between each set is a bud in sheath, forming a trefoil, and linking the volutes of the capitals by means of light blue bands, which fall in a shallow curve from either side of it. Still higher on the wall ran a fringe of double palmettos in similar colouring, between yellow line borders, the centre of the latter picked out with lozenges, coloured black and yellow, and black and white alternately."[2]

If the volutes in the above description recall unmistakably the capitals of the Ionic Order, it will be found also that the buds in sheath with the shallow curves falling away from them are the same artistic details which have been met with at the Greek settlement of Naukratis in Egypt on the Pelusiac branch of the Nile.[3] Grecian decorative architecture found its way to the East by two routes: first, direct over land, as in the case of the temple at Mutsatsir and the pillared buildings with Ionic capitals depicted on the bas-reliefs of Sargon; secondly, as in the case of Nebuchadnezzar's throne-room, the artists may very well have been Greek captives taken in Egypt, since the same details have been found at Naukratis. According to Flinders Petrie it was in 650 B.C., in the reign of Psammetichus I., or possibly as early as 670 B.C., during the Assyrian wars with Tirhakah, that the Greeks settled

[1] Cf. the beautiful coloured plate, opposite p. 130 in Koldewey's *Discoveries at Babylon*. The plate is put in the wrong place: it should have faced p. 104, under the tissue leaf inscribed, "DECORATION OF THE THRONE ROOM."

[2] The Ionic capital, so famous in classical architecture, has been traced by recent investigators to the Hittites of Boghaz Kyöi. If this be so, we have here an instance of an architectural feature spreading eastward to Assyria and Babylon and westward to Greece. See H. R. Hall's *Ancient History of the Near East*, p. 535.

[3] *Egyptian Exploration Fund*, part i. pls. 3 and 7.

at Naukratis. Psammetichus, as we have seen, employed "brazen men from the sea" to help him conquer the Dodekarchy; and then out of gratitude for their assistance allowed them to settle in two camps on either side of the Pelusiac branch of the Nile. From this time onwards Greek mercenaries were employed in Egypt down to the days when the Persian rule was established in that country by Cambyses. Now, according to the Chaldean historian Berosus as quoted by Josephus, in 604 B.C., when Nebuchadnezzar was acting as his father's viceroy, he advanced against the governors whom his father had set over Egypt and the parts of Cœle-Syria and Phœnicia, and brought back captives from "the Jews, Phœnicians, and Syrians, *and the nations belonging to Egypt*," whom he planted in colonies in Babylonia.[1] Among "the nations belonging to Egypt" we may reckon the Greek mercenaries stationed at Daphnæ on the Pelusiac branch of the Nile, for the historian informs us in his *Antiquities* that the Babylonian king advanced as far as Pelusium,[2] whilst in another passage, when telling the story of the king's forgotten dream, he begins his account with the words, "Now *two years after the destruction of Egypt* king Nebuchadnezzar saw a wonderful dream."[3]

Among the possible work of these Greek captives taken in Egypt is a very curious relic, at present in the Museum at Florence, which is generally described as a cameo. It is not a cameo in the strict sense of the term, but an onyx with two shades of colour, originally the eye of a statue of the god Merodach. On it is carved a Greek head, helmeted and plumed, with a neck-piece attached; the whole being encircled with a finely cut cuneiform inscription, which reads thus: "To Merodach his lord Nebuchadnezzar has given this for his life." J. Menant, in his able article on this gem,[4] observes that the relic is unique: it differs from a helmeted head in the Greek style, and also from the Chaldean types known to us. As regards the workmanship of the engraving, he bids us distinguish between the inscription and the subject. "The head," he writes, "is executed with a certain rudeness; the graving tool has bitten into the depressions in an uneven manner. The profile seems to bury itself in the stone, instead of standing out in relief. The impression given is good; the work, mediocre." On the other hand, "the inscription," he declares, "shows great skill and familiarity with the [cuneiform] writing, and is traced with great clearness and delicacy."

[1] *Josephus c. Apion*, i. 19.
[2] *Ant.* x. 6, 1.
[3] *Ibid.* x. 10. 3.
[4] *Revue Archeologique*, Paris, 1885, p. 79.

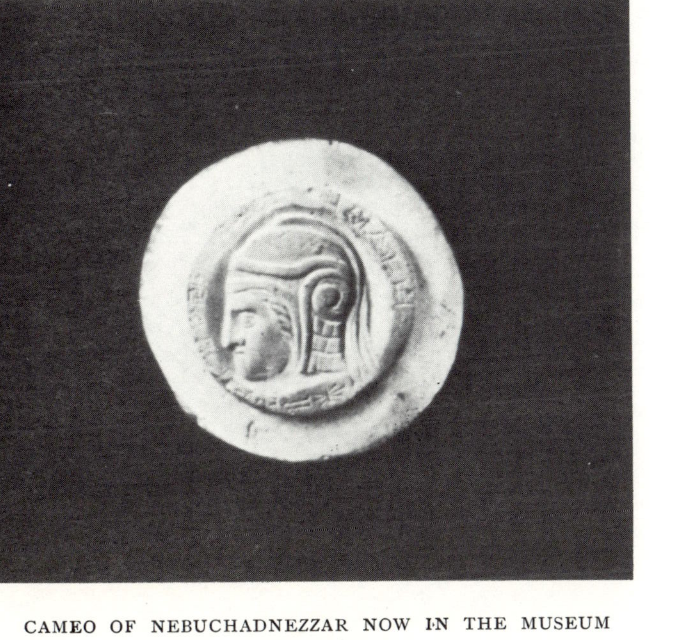

CAMEO OF NEBUCHADNEZZAR NOW IN THE MUSEUM AT FLORENCE

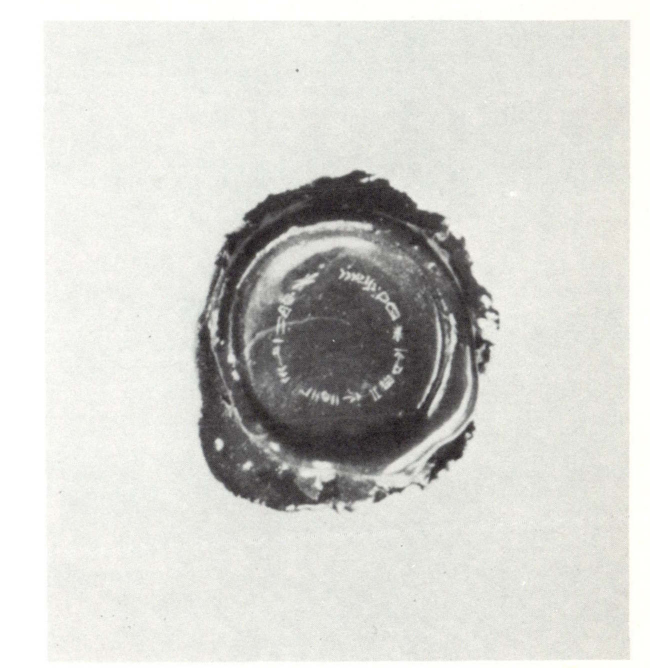

GEM IN THE MUSEUM AT THE HAGUE, WITH AN INSCRIPTION OF NEBUCHADNEZZAR

A close examination of a cast of this relic, kindly sent me by the Director of the Museum at Florence, quite confirms Menant's verdict that the head and the inscription are the work of two different artists, and that the latter belongs undoubtedly to the age of Nebuchadnezzar. With regard to the head I cannot see the "rudeness" of execution of which Menant speaks. The inscription called for fine work and is finely done; the head is bolder. There is a look of firmness and repose in the features, and a dignity of bearing in the carriage of the head. Also the curving lines of the helmet are smooth and flowing, and the drooping plume is very delicately cut. The unevenness of the depressions is due in part to the stone not having been cut true, for just at the tail of the helmet there is a decided bulge, which the artist has taken advantage of by allowing it to give a suggestion of the shoulder. The question then is, does this head belong to the time of Nebuchadnezzar, or is it the work of a later age? Menant thinks that it belongs to the age of Alexander the Great. Alexander, he observes, had a great liking for intaglios and a rich collection of them.[1] The eye may have belonged to some statue broken up by the Persians, and the head—intended for Alexander himself—may have been the work of some artist flatterer. At the same time, as he honestly admits, the lineaments are not exactly like those of Alexander as seen on any relics which have come down to us. With all due respect to the opinion of this scholar, I would venture to suggest that the head as well as the inscription is of the age of Nebuchadnezzar. The eyes of statues were sometimes simply polished stones. Sometimes an inscription was written across the stone in horizontal lines, as in the case of a statue dedicated by Nebuchadnezzar to the god Nebo, which bears an inscription very like that on our cameo.[2] Sometimes, as on a gem at the Hague Museum,[3] the inscription is traced in a circle on the slightly convex surface of the eye; the diameter of the circle measured to the outer edge of the characters being, in this instance, only $\frac{13}{20}$ of an inch. In the case of the cameo the diameter of the circle is $\frac{22}{20}$ of an inch, and the inscription is written, not on a nearly level surface, but *on the sloping rim of the eye, as if to leave more room for the head to be engraved in the centre.* The peculiar style of workmanship noticed by Menant—the head seeming to bury itself in the stone—is

[1] Pliny, *Nat. Hist.* book xxxvii. 4.

[2] See George Smith's *Assyrian Discoveries*, p. 385.

[3] For a sealing-wax impression of this gem I am indebted to the kindness of the Curator of the Museum at the Hague. The engraving is a microscopic marvel.

characteristic of Egyptian art of about that period, as may be seen in the head of Shabitoku, 703–693 B.C.[1] Further, the treatment of the plume, which is not erect but carried straight back over the head so as to droop down behind, is exactly what we see in the case of Shabitoku. The nearest approach to the helmet and neck-piece that I have been able to find, appears on the head of the Lycaonian soldier, whose funerary stele has been built into the south wall of Konieh, the ancient Iconium.[2] That monument is of an archaic character; also it is observable that the soldier carries a two-pronged spear, the double head of which resembles the spearheads found at Nebesheh in Egypt, an outpost of the Greek camp at Daphnæ.

In advocating the claim of the helmeted head to be regarded as a work of the age of Nebuchadnezzar, I do not mean to assert that we have here an actual portrait of that king, or that he ever appeared thus attired. It is sufficient if the work were executed under his patronage, or merely in accordance with his well-known cosmopolitan tastes. But it should be pointed out that the Græco-Egyptian artist in thus portraying the Babylonian king is giving us his idea of how a king should appear. For Herodotus, when speaking of Psammetichus I. of Egypt and the other members of the Dodekarchy, writes, "All the kings were accustomed to wear helmets."[3] Again, when relating how Apries sent Amasis to hold a peaceful parley with his rebellious army, he goes on to tell us how one of the malcontents "coming behind him put a helmet on his head, saying, as he put it on, that he thereby crowned him king."[4] With regard to the plume let it also be noted that according to Herodotus the Carians were the first to fasten crests on helmets.[5] These links with Egypt, coupled with the unmistakably Greek profile and the archaic style of treatment of some of the details, give ground for thinking that the head is the work of an Asiatic Greek brought by Nebuchadnezzar as a captive from Egypt at the time when he was sent by his father to put down the rebellion in that country.

That the king's head should be engraved on a stone intended to be placed as an eye in a statue dedicated to his god Merodach, and encircled with the words, "To Merodach his lord Nebuchadnezzar has given this for his life," *i.e.* either preserved, or to be preserved, is not such a strange thing as it might seem at first sight. Among the Hebrews the apple of the eye signified that

[1] See Maspero's *Passing of the Empires*, p. 360.
[2] Lewin's *Life and Epistles of St. Paul*, vol. i. p. 146.
[3] Herod. ii. 151.
[4] *Ibid.* ii. 161.
[5] *Ibid.* i. 171.

HEAD OF SHABITOKU
(FROM "PASSING OF THE EMPIRES," P. 360)

FUNERARY STELE OF A LYCAONIAN SOLDIER BUILT INTO THE S. WALL OF THE KONIEH, THE ANCIENT ICONIUM
(FROM LEWIN'S "LIFE AND EPISTLES OF ST. PAUL," VOL. I, P. 146)

which is most dear and most jealously guarded,[1] and a consideration of certain passages in the Book of Zechariah [2] suggests that as the picture of an eye portrays vigilance, so any figure drawn on the pupil of that eye would portray the object of that vigilance. Thus the king's image portrayed on the eye of his god would form a symbolical representation of the idea contained in Zech. i 8, "He that toucheth you toucheth the apple of his eye."

If there were Greek captives settled in colonies in Babylonia, there were also Greek soldiers of fortune in the army of the Babylonian king. The case of Antimenidas, the brother of the poet Alcæus, shows us the value set on these mercenaries and the doughty deeds they were sometimes able to perform in the service of their foreign employers. "Thou camest from the ends of the earth," sings the poet,[3] "wearing an ivory-hilted sword with gold settings, inasmuch as thou foughtest for the Babylonians and accomplishedst a great feat of arms, by slaying a warrior who fell short of five royal cubits by a mere handbreadth." [4]

But by whatever way the civilisation of Greece made itself felt in Babylon in the age of Nebuchadnezzar, whether by sea through the mart of Tyre, by land along the "Cilician Road" through the passes of the Taurus, or in a more roundabout way through wars carried on with Egypt, we seem to be led to Asiatic Greece as its source. Asiatic Greece was the probable home of the three Greek musical instruments mentioned in Dan. iii. In the words of James Kennedy, "The Asiatic Greeks of the sixth and seventh centuries B.C. surpassed the European Greeks, not only in commerce and philosophy, but in music. The story of Apollo and Marsyas, the adoption of the Lydian measure, the improvement of the lyre"—one of the three Greek instruments in Dan. iii.—"were all due to them.[5] They had founded a colony in Egypt, and supplied her army with mercenaries; they were to be found all along the Syrian coast, and in Syria and Cyprus they were subjects of Assyria and Babylon. They visited Babylon as prisoners of war, they must have visited it as traders also. That they should have introduced some rude but popular musical instruments into Babylon is not of itself improbable." [6]

[1] Deut. xxxii. 10; Ps. xvii. 8; Prov. vii. 2.

[2] Zech. ii. 8, iii. 9, iv. 10.

[3] Bergk's *Lyrici Græci*, iii. p. 160, Alcæus, 33.

[4] Not a span; but the breadth of the four fingers=nearly three inches.

[5] The writer might have added that Phrygia is credited with the invention of the reed-pipe.

[6] *The Book of Daniel from a Christian Standpoint*, p. 211.

Granted, then, that Greek instruments of music might have made their way to Babylon by three different routes, and either through the hands of traders, soldiers, or captives, there seems no reason whatever why they should not have carried with them their Greek names: for being strange and new to the Babylonians when first introduced, they would naturally continue to bear the names given them by those who introduced them.

But another objection of an entirely different kind to that which has so far engaged us has been made with respect to the occurrence of the names of two of these instruments in a work of the age of Daniel. It is objected that the words ψαλτήριον, *psalterion*, and συμφωνία, *sumphonia*, are not found in any Greek writer till a period much later than the time of Daniel. Thus ψαλτήριον is first met with in *The Problems*, usually attributed to Aristotle, 384–321 B.C., but possibly the work of a later writer, whilst συμφωνία occurs first in Plato, 427–347 B.C., in the sense of concerted music, but is not met with as the name of a musical instrument till the time of Polybius, 210–128 B.C. The best answer to this objection is supplied in the following words of James Kennedy: "The fact that a primitive kind of pipe is incidentally mentioned for the first time by a late author affords no proof that it was of late invention. Our knowledge of the everyday life of antiquity is extremely fragmentary and limited. Mommsen has pointed out that the stepping-stones, which are found in every street of every Italian town, are mentioned only once by any Latin author. The Ionians who wandered to Babylon were not great folk. . . . They were humble men, captives, mercenaries, artisans, merchants, at the best, doubtless much of the same class as the Europeans who traversed India in the days of the Great Moghul. But these vagabond Europeans, artillery-men, artificers, contributed more words for common objects to the native language than the English have done since Plassey. The 'symphonia' pipe is precisely one of the things that would pass—word and thing—from one to another in this stratum of society."[1] Further, in considering the appearance of Greek instruments in a Babylonian orchestra in the early part of the sixth century B.C., there is yet another factor in the case which must tell for much, viz. the character and tastes of the reigning monarch. Nebuchadnezzar, as we have seen, was devoted heart and soul to Babylon: no other place was so dear to him. But at the same time he was an imperialist. He meant his Babylon to be the centre of a world-empire, and he delights to impress

[1] *The Book of Daniel from a Christian Standpoint*, p. 210.

upon us how wide that empire was. In his account of the completion of the temple-tower of Babylon he tells us in a lofty poetic strain of the great distances from which his workpeople have been gathered. So, too, on the grand occasion described in Dan. iii., in the royal proclamation made by his herald he addresses "the peoples, nations, and languages," and gives a grandiloquent description of the state orchestra as composed of "cornet, flute, harp, sackbut, psaltery, dulcimer, and *all kinds of music*"; a description which, suitably to the pompous spirit of the age, is repeated no fewer than four times in the course of the chapter. The proclamation, if not drawn up by the king, is at any rate in accordance with his wishes, for it displays his power. He who can gather his subjects together to do his work from all quarters far and near, can also very easily collect into his orchestra *all kinds of music*, and if some of the instruments are Greek and bear Greek names, why, so much the better, and let the fact be duly published. The music of Greece must be laid under contribution to perfect the royal band, just as the art of Greece has been enlisted in the decoration of the royal palace.

If these Greek instruments in his band were thus welcome to Nebuchadnezzar as a sign of his boundless resources, it is quite possible that for an entirely different reason their names were not unwelcome to the prophet Daniel, when in his old age he wrote this Book. Nebuchadnezzar's kingdom had then passed away, and the second kingdom was already running its course. The third would most certainly follow in due time. Greek instruments of music had reached Babylon even in Nebuchadnezzar's days. Presently Greece would be there herself. The he-goat flying from the west would presently run upon the Persian ram in the fury of his power. With the coming of the brazen kingdom, "brazen men from the sea" would make their way to the furthest East. Where Grecian Art and Architecture were already present, Grecian Arms would follow. The wealth of the Silver Kingdom would be powerless to resist their advance. The fourth king might be far richer than all his predecessors, and by his riches he might stir up all against the realm of Greece; [1] but that tremendous effort would collapse: Greece would not go under, but would in her turn overwhelm Persia. Then Michael, Israel's all-powerful champion, who was now contending with the "Prince of Persia," would go forth to do battle with the "Prince of Greece." [2] But these later details had, perhaps, not yet been shown to the seer: they constitute a part of his latest vision. Still it was enough for him to

[1] Dan. xi. 2. [2] *Ibid.* x. 20, xii. 1.

know as he wrote down the Greek names of those three musical instruments that Persia, then supreme, was destined presently to give place to Greece.

Beside the Persian and Greek words at which we have been looking, it is deserving of notice that the Book of Daniel contains several Assyro-Babylonian words, such as might be expected in a book written at or near Babylon in the latter half of the sixth century B.C. Further, all the proper names in this Book are found in the Assyro-Babylonian or admit of a derivation from that source, the Hebrew names only excepted : a feature which hardly agrees with the hypothesis that it was written in the age of Antiochus Epiphanes. These Assyro-Babylonian words as well as the Persian and Greek words will be found discussed in the appendices to this chapter.

But the linguistic argument as to the date of the Book of Daniel and the region in which it was composed can be carried yet further by a close comparison of the foreign elements found in it with those found in other Aramaic documents whose age is approximately known. This has been very ably done by Prof. R. D. Wilson in his article on "The Aramaic of Daniel," in which he sums up thus-

"The Zakir inscription of 850 B.C.[1] has no foreign elements, except perhaps Hebrew. The Sendsherli inscriptions of the latter part of the eighth century B.C.[2] have Assyrian ingredients. The Egypto-Aramaic of the fifth century B.C. has Persian, Babylonian, Hebrew, and Egyptian terms, and perhaps one Latin and three Greek words. The Nabatean [3] has Arabic in large measure, one Babylonian, and a few Greek ones. The Palmyrene [4] has Greek predominantly, some Arabic, and two Sassanian or late Persian words. The Targum of Onkelos [5] has mainly Greek words, five Persian words, and some Hebrew and Babylonian elements. The Targum of Jonathan [5] has yet more Greek nouns and three verbs likewise, Aramaic in form, derived from Greek nouns, at least one Latin word, apparently no Persian words, and only one Babylonian word or form, except such as are found in the Scriptures,

[1] See the *Expositor* for June, 1908.

[2] Found near the Syrian Antioch. They are of the age of Tiglathpileser III., 745–729 B.C. See E. G. H. Kraeling's *Aram and Israel*.

[3] Of the Nabatean inscriptions the dated ones range from 70 B.C. to A.D. 95.

[4] The inscriptions of Palmyra belong to the first three centuries of the Christian era.

[5] The Targums of Onkelos and Jonathan in their present form are said to belong to the fourth century A.D.

and a considerable number of Hebrew words. The Syriac[1] (Edessene) has hundreds of Greek words, a considerable number of which are verbalised; a little Sanskrit, and in later works many Arabic nouns, especially names of persons and places. In New Syriac the foreign elements are predominantly Turkish, Arabic, and Kurdish loan-words.

"Therefore it being thus apparent that on the basis of foreign elements inbedded in Aramaic dialects, it is possible for the scholar to fix approximately the time and the locality in which the different dialects were spoken; all the more when, as has been shown in the case of Daniel, such a date and locality are required by the vocabulary of the pure Aramaic substratum and favoured, or at least permitted, by its grammatical forms and structure, we are abundantly justified in concluding that the dialect of Daniel, containing as it does so many Persian, Hebrew, and Babylonian elements, and so few Greek words, with not one Egyptian, Latin, or Arabic word, and being so nearly allied in grammatical form and structure to the older Aramaic dialects and in its conglomerate vocabulary to the dialects of Ezra and Egypto-Aramaic, must have been used at or near Babylon at a time not long after the founding of the Persian empire."[2]

To conclude, then, we may say that viewed from the linguistic standpoint there is no Book of the Old Testament which bears more clearly the stamp of its age than this Book of Daniel; no Book which indicates more clearly the region in which it was written as well as the personality of its writer. This is the Book of a pious Jew writing in a foreign land. The nationality of its author, his high social position, his daily surroundings and frequent intercourse with foreigners, his close contact first with the proud Babylonian monarch and later with the Medo-Persian ruler—all are in perfect harmony with the linguistic features of his work; are reflected, so to say, in his choice of the Aramaic, no less than in the Babylonian, Persian, and Greek words which appear on his pages. By force of circumstances and through the wider outlook of his heaven-sent visions he is cosmopolitan. But his heart is ever turning towards his native Zion, the home of his youth;

[1] Syriac literature, starting with the Peshitto version of the Scriptures, ranges from the second century onwards. It was at its best from the fourth to the eighth century, but kept up a flickering existence till the fourteenth century or even later. See *Encyc. Brit.* under "Syriac."

[2] See Wilson's article, "The Aramaic of Daniel," given in *Biblical and Theological Studies*, p. 304.

the windows of his prayer-chamber are ever open towards Jerusalem; and his petition is ever ascending in behalf of that sacred city and "the holy mountain" of his God.

Appendix on the Foreign Words in the Book of Daniel

1. *The Old Persian Words*

Old Persian, of which some twenty or more words are found in the Book of Daniel, belongs to the Aryan or Indo-European family of languages. The young student, who, unacquainted with the facts of philology, attacks it for the first time, is amused and lured on by finding words, as well as case and tense endings, which remind him of Greek and Latin, nay, even of his native English. He learns to his astonishment that *naman* is the Old Persian for "name," that *pathi* means a "road," *garb*, "to seize," "grip," *bar*, "to bear," *bu*, "to be," *sta*, "to stand"; that *antar* represents the Latin *inter*, and *apa* the Greek ἀπὸ; that "father" appears as *pitar*, "mother" as *matar*, and so forth; and resolves, maybe, to devote himself henceforth to the bewitching science of languages. Or, again, the effect on him may be somewhat different. It may seem to him that he is studying a mongrel language, and that Esperanto is no modern invention after all, but was discovered by the ancient Persians, long, long ago, as a channel by which they could make themselves intelligible to the nations of Europe. Then, indeed, he will be ready to say with Solomon, "The thing that hath been, it is that which shall be . . . and there is no new thing under the sun." [1]

The literature of the Old Persian is very limited. It consists of the inscriptions of the Akhemenian kings, Darius Hystaspes and some of his successors, which are found written in the Persian cuneiform at Behistûn, Hamadan, Persepolis, and Suez, along with an inscription of one line of Cyrus the Great on a monolith at Pasargadæ, and one or two brief inscriptions on vases and seals. These, with the exception of the inscription of Darius Hystaspes at Behistûn and that on the tomb of the same monarch at Naksh-i-Rustam, are short and offer but little scope, the same phrases occurring again and again.

It was not until many attempts had been made, extending over well-nigh half a century—the most successful being that of Grotefend—that the values of the forty characters employed in the Persian cuneiform were correctly ascertained, thanks, chiefly,

[1] Eccles. i. 9.

to the proper names which occurred in the inscriptions.[1] In 1844 the Norwegian scholar Lassen was able to read the short inscriptions found at Persepolis and the considerably longer one on the tomb of Darius. Only two years later the great inscription on the rock of Behistûn was successfully read by Rawlinson. Even though the values of the different characters had been correctly ascertained so as to secure an accurate transliteration of the Old Persian words, Rawlinson's great feat of translating the inscription would have been an impossibility but for the good work begun by Anquetil Duperron some seventy years previously but much improved by Burnouf only a short time before, whereby the language of the ancient sacred books of the Parsis—known as the Zend-Avesta—was made known to Europe. The Parsis of Bombay, as their name shows, came originally from Persia. Hence their ancient sacred language—called sometimes Zend, sometimes Avestan—is very closely related to the Old Persian. It was by means, then, of the Zend that Rawlinson was able to translate by far the longest of the Old Persian inscriptions, viz. that written by Darius on the rock of Behistûn about 500 B.C. Next to the Zend the Sanskrit, or ancient literary language of India, throws most light on the Old Persian. Accordingly, in seeking to ascertain the correct meanings of the Persian words contained in the Book of Daniel, scholars, after noting the traditional meanings affixed to these words by the Septuagint and other old versions, have recourse to these two ancient languages, the Zend and the Sanskrit, in order to test the accuracy of these meanings.

The following is a list of the Old Persian words in the Book of Daniel, together with some account of their composition and equivalents in the cognate languages and their derivatives[2]:

פַּרְתְּמִים, *partĕmîm ;* R.V. "nobles," Dan. i. 3, LXX οἱ ἐπίλεκτοι, Theod. φορθομμείν, Jerome *tyranni*, Est. i. 3, vi. 9, LXX ἔνδοξοι, Jerome in Est. i. 3, *inclyti*, in vi. 9, *tyranni*. Z *fratama*, Skt. *prathama ;* superlative of *pra*, "before." Cf. Gr. πρῶτος, Lat. *primus*, Eng. *first*. The comparative of this word occurs in the title *fratera-ka* found in the Elephantiné letter,

פַּתְ־בַּג, *path-bag ;* R.V. "meat," R.V.M. "dainties," Dan. i. 5, 8, 13, 15, 16, and xi. 26, LXX τράπεζα, δεῖπνον. From OP *pati-bajiy* ; cf. Skt. *prati-bhaga*, "an offering-to" a ruler, used of a share of small articles paid daily to the Rajah for household

[1] See *Booth's Discovery and Decipherment of the Trilingual Cuneiform Inscriptions*.

[2] OP=Old Persian, MP=Middle Persian, NP=New Persian, Z=Zend, Skt.=Sanskrit, AS=Anglo-Saxon.

expenditure. Composed of the OP patiy "to," Z *paiti*, Skt. *prati*, Gr. ποτί, and the OP *bajiy*, "tribute"; cf. Z *bagha*, "portion," Skt. *bhaj*, "to allot." In a fragment of Dinon's Persica, *circa* 340 B.C., this word is found transliterated into Greek as ποτίβαζις, and is defined as a meal of barley and wheaten cakes, which the Persian king partook of crowned with cypress and drinking wine out of an egg-shaped golden cup. See Athenæus, xi. 503.[1]

פִּתְגָם, *pithgâm*; R.V. "matter," Dan. iii. 16, LXX ἐπιταγή, Theod. ῥῆμα, R.V. "sentence," Dan. iv. 17 (14), Theod. ὁ λόγος, Est. i. 20, LXX νομός, Ezra iv. 17, LXX γραμματέα, v. 7 ῥήμασις, 11 ῥῆμα, Eccles. viii. 11 ἀντίῤῥησις. From OP *pati-gama*, "something going to," hence "sentence," "reply," and in a weakened sense, "matter"; cf. Z *paiti-jam*, Skt. *prati-gam*, "to go towards." Composed of OP *patiy*, "to," and *gam*, "to go"; cf. Z and Skt. *gam*, Lat. *venio* (for *guemio ?*), Goth. *quam*, Germ. *kommen*, Eng. *come*. Cf. MP *petgam*, NP *paigam*, *payam*, "message."

אַזְדָּא, *ozdâ*; R.V. "is gone," R.V.M. "is gone forth," Dan. ii. 5, 8; as if from a Semitic root *azad* taken as a form of Heb. *azal*, "to go forth." But according to Scheftelowitz an OP and Z word, *azaiti*, "to go." The LXX and Theod. render it ἀπέστη; Nöldeke regards the word as OP="certain," "sure." Cf. Skt. *addha*, "certainly," "truly." Also cf. Behistûn Inscription, § 10, *azda*, "knowledge." In Dan. ii. 5 the lit. rendering is "the word from me is sure," *i.e.* "what I say will certainly be carried out."

הַדָּמִין, *haddâmîn*, "pieces," lit. "limbs." R.V. "ye shall be cut in pieces"; lit. "ye shall be made limbs," Dan. ii. 5, iii. 29; LXX διαμελισθήσεται in iii. 29 (96). Cf. Z *handama*, NP *andam*, "limb." Possibly from a Semitic root; cf. Arabic *hadama*, "to cut."

נְבִזְבָּה, *nĕbhizbâh*; R.V. "rewards," Dan. ii. 6, v. 17, Theod. δωρεὰ. In ii. 6 for "gifts and rewards" the LXX has δόματα παντοῖα. From OP *ni-baz*, "to give," "allot." Composed of prefix *ni*, "down," "into," and *baz* connected with *baji*, "tribute"; see under *path-bag* above. The final syllable *bâh* has not yet been explained.

דָּת, *dâth*; R.V. "law," Dan. ii. 9, vi. 5 (6), etc., LXX and Theod. δόγμα, νόμος. Occurs also Deut. xxxiii. 2, Ezra viii. 36, and frequently in Esther. OP *dâta*, "law," Behist. § 8, Pass. ptcp. from *dâ*, "to place," "make." Cf. Skt. *dha*, *da-dhami*, Gr. τί-θημι, Goth. *domjan*, AS *deman*, Eng. *doom*.

דְּתָבַר, *dĕthâbhâr*; R.V. "counsellors," Dan. iii. 2, 3, or rather

[1] In Babylonian business documents of the reign of Artaxerxes I. mention is made of an official called (*amêlu*) *pitipabaga*.

"justices"; lit. "law-bearers," those who put the law into execution. The word has been found in Babylonian inscriptions from Nippur of the time of Artaxerxes I., 465–425 B.C. From *dâta*, "law," and OP *bar*, "to bear," Skt. *bhr*, Z *bar*, Gr. *φέρω*, Lat. *fero*, Goth. *bairan*, AS *beran*, Eng. *bear*.

זְמַן, *zĕman*; R.V. "time," Dan. ii. 16, iii. 7, vii. 12, etc., "season," ii. 21. Occurs also Neh. ii. 6, Est. ix. 27, 31, Eccles. iii. 1. From OP *zarvan*, "time," "age"; cf. Syr. *zebhan* found in Palmyrene, and Arabic *zamanoun*.

רָז, *râz*; R.V. "secret," Dan. ii. 18, etc., iv. 9 (6), LXX and Theod. *μυστήριον*, Skt. *rahas*, MP *raz*, NP *raz*, Syr. *araza*.

אֲחַשְׁדַּרְפְּנִין, *ăchashdarpĕnîn*, "satraps," Dan. iii. 2, vi. 1, etc., Ezra viii. 36, Est. iii. 12, etc., OP *khshătră-pâwan*, "protector of the kingdom." From *khshătră*, "kingdom," and *pâ*, "to protect." Cf. Z and Skt. *pa*, Lat. *pa*-vi, *pa*-scor, Gr. *σατράπης*, and on inscriptions from Asia Minor, *ἐξαιθράπης*, *ἐξατράπης*.

אֲדַרְגָּזְרִין, *ădargâzĕrîn*; R.V. "judges," Dan. iii. 2, 3. According to Marti, OP *handarza* or *handurzi-kara*, "making counsel," *i.e.* counsellors. Better perhaps with Scheftelowitz, "making firm regulations," *i.e.* rulers. Cf. Z *han-darez*, "to bind together" (where *ham*, before a dental *han*, answers to Gr. *ἅμα*, "together," and darez="to bind"), suggestive of the bond of law. With OP and Z *kar*, "to make," cf. Lat. *cre*-o.

גְּדָבְרִין, *gĕdâbherîn*; R.V. "treasurers," Dan. iii. 2, 3, LXX *διοικητάς*, supposed to be a parallel form of גִּזְבָּר, Ezra i. 8, vii. 21. From OP *ganja-bâra*, Babyl. *ganzabâru*, "treasure-bearer"; cf. Skt. *ganja*, "treasure," *ganjavâra*, "treasurer." From OP *ganja* comes Gr. *γάζα*.

תִּפְתָּיֵא, *tiphtayē*; R.V. "sheriffs," Dan. iii. 2, 3, LXX and Theod. *τοὺς ἐπ' ἐξουσιῶν*. A word of uncertain meaning; found also in Egyptian Aramaic. Behrmann compares the Skt. *adhi-pati*, "over-lord"; Scheftelowitz, the Z *vith-pati*, "head of clan." The rendering of the Greek versions agrees well with either of these.

כָּרוֹז, *kârōz*; R.V. "herald," Dan. iii. 4. Formerly referred to the Gr. *κῆρυξ*, by which it is rendered in the LXX and Theod.; but better from Skt. *krus*, "to call out." Cf. Z *khrus*, whence *khresio*, "herald." This root is widely spread in the Indo-Germanic languages; cf. Gr. *κράζω*, *κραυγή*, Lat. *garrio*, Eng. *shriek*. It appears to have early found its way into the Aramaic. On a seal in the shape of a scarabæus, given in *Corp. Inscript. Semit.*, part ii. vol. i. No. 86, is depicted a crier with the inscription *kârōz*.

זַן, *zan*; R.V. "kind," Dan. iii. 5, etc., 2 Chr. xvi. 14, Ps. cxliv. 13. Possibly a Semitic word, but according to some **authorities of**

Aryan origin. Scheftelowitz compares OP *zana*, "kind," Skt. *jana*, "race," "kind," Lat. *genus*, Gr. γένος, by which it is rendered both in the LXX and Theodotion in verse 5.

סַרְבָּלִין, *sarbâlîn* ; R.V. "hosen," Dan. iii. 21, 27. In dealing with this word it will be best for us to consider together the three words denoting articles of dress which occur in Dan. iii. 21, giving especial attention to the renderings of the ancient Greek versions, and no less to the equivalents in the cognate languages, that so we may seek to attach to each its proper meaning. The order, then, of the words in verse 21 runs thus—

Aramaic	*sarbâlîn*	*padhdhĕshîn*	*karbĕlâth*
LXX		ὑποδήματα	τιάραι
Theod.	σαράβαρα	τιάραι	περικνημῖδες
R.V.	hosen	tunics	mantles
A.V.	coats	hosen	hats

Whilst in verse 27 we have–

Aramaic *sarbâlin* LXX and Theod. σαράβαρα

A glance at the above shows us at once that in verse 21 σαράβαρα has fallen out of the LXX text.

To ascertain the meaning of these three words let us take the last first, as being that on which the least doubt rests. *Karbĕlâth* is undoubtedly the Assyrian *karballatu*, "helmet," "cap" ; a word found on Babylonian contract tablets of the reign of Nabonidus and also in the Babylonian version of the inscription on the tomb of Darius Hystaspes at Nakhsh-i-Rustem. Darius, enumerating thereon the different races subject to his sway, mentions three tribes of Scythians, one of which he describes as *Saka tigra-khauda*, *i.e.* "Scythians with peaked caps," like the comical figure described as "Skunka the Scythian," the last of the string of captives depicted on the bas-relief at Behistûn, who wears a cap like a fool's cap. *Tigra*, "sharp," [1] "pointed," is the same word which appears in the river-name Tigris, the "swift-darting" stream ; whilst *khauda* is rendered in the Babylonian version by *karballatu*, "cap." In its Greek form this word appears as κυρβάσία, "a Persian bonnet or cap"—so Liddell and Scott—which according to Herodotus was called the "tiara," [2] and is so rendered here by the LXX and Theodotion, the latter of whom changes the order of the words, putting the third word second.

The second word, *padhdhĕshîn*, is a word about which very

[1] According to Sayce *tigra* in Old Persian signifies an "arrow." *Higher Criticism*, p. 196.
[2] Book vii. 61.

little is known. It appears in the Syriac Peshitto in the sense of "tunic," "trousers," "gaiters." The LXX render it by ὑποδήματα, "sandals," "shoes"; Theodotion by περικνημῖδες, "trousers," "leggings." It therefore refers to the lower part of the body, and represents either the Persian trousers mentioned by Herodotus,[1] or, possibly, the long linen tunic worn next the body by the Babylonians, which Herodotus describes as "reaching to the feet."[2]

Karbĕlâth, then, refers to head-gear, and *padhdhĕshîn* to some covering for the legs or feet. Hence the probability is that the remaining word *sarbâlîn* signifies some clothing for the body. Also verse 27, coupled with the mention of their "garments," apparently *inner* garments, in verse 21, is suggestive of some loose *outer* clothing, such as would be especially liable to catch the flame. Now, the Aramaic *sarbâlîn* is evidently a Persian loan-word, as may be gathered from its Greek form, σαράβαρα, seeing that an Old Persian *r* sometimes takes the place of an Aramaic *l* and *vice versâ*.[3] Σαράβαρα would thus represent more closely the original word; and this, regarded as a compound made up of *sar*, "head," and *bar*, "to bear," would denote "head-gear," "head-covering," or still more literally, "what the head bears." In Persia the peasants, like the mill hands in the north of England, often place their shawls or mantles over their heads for protection from the weather: hence this word appears to denote a "mantle," a sense in which it is often used in the Talmud, and which also attaches to the Arabic *sirbal* derived from it. If it be objected that Daniel in chap. iii. is writing about Babylonian times, not about Persian, and that the heroes of the story are neither Babylonians nor Persians but Jews, the answer is twofold: first, he is writing his book in the early Persian period with a Persian atmosphere all around him; secondly, the Babylonian dress to some extent resembled that of the Persians, whilst the Jewish dress appears to have been the same as that of the Babylonians. The Babylonians according to Herodotus wore turbans on their heads: on their bodies tunics both upper and under, and also short cloaks. They did not, however, wear trousers, since the under tunic reached to the feet. Their shoes, according to the old historian, were of a peculiar fashion, not unlike those worn by the Bœotians. The Persians also wore shoes, as may be gathered from the bas-reliefs at Behistûn and Persepolis. The similarity of the Jewish dress to the Babylonian can be seen on the Black Obelisk, where

[1] Books i. 71, vii. 61. [2] Book i. 195.
[3] Cf. *Babirush*, the OP form of the Aramaic *Babhel*, "Babylon."

the soft caps, short cloaks thrown back over the shoulders, long tunics, and shoes of the Jewish tribute-bearers are all plainly discernible. It would thus seem that the rendering of the A.V. "coats," "hosen," "hats" is to be preferred to that of the R.V. "hosen," "tunics," "mantles," though perhaps it would be better still to render "cloaks," "sandals," "turbans," substituting in the margin "tunics" as an alternative for "cloaks," and "trousers" in the place of "sandals."

הַדָּבְרִין, *haddâbhĕrîn;* R.V. "counsellors," Dan. iii. 24, 27, iv. 36 (33), vi. 7 (8), LXX φίλοι, Theod. μεγιστᾶνες, δυνάσται. This is a Persian word as witnessed by the syllable *bar, bhar.* Compare *dăthâbhar, gizbar* above. Its meaning is uncertain. Scheftelowitz, on the ground that an Aramaic *d* represents a Persian *z,* derives this word from the Persian *h-n-z-b-r. H-n-z* in MP, NP *hanj,* "purpose," "plan." As the term "counsellors" is used in chap. iii. 2, 8, to translate the Persian word *dethâbhĕrîn,* Driver's rendering, "ministers," is to be preferred here.

נֶבְרַשְׁתָּא, *nebhrashtâ';* R.V. "candlestick," Dan. v. 5, LXX φῶς, Theod. λαμπάς. From the OP *bhraj,* "to shine," whence *bhrastra,* "light." Compare Z *baraz,* Skt. *bhraj.* The Gr. φλέγω and Lat. *fulgeo* come from this root. In the compound verb the prefix *ni*—MP *ne*—has in OP the force of "down" or "into." In some cases it is intensive; in others it leaves the meaning unaltered.

הַמְנִיךְ, *hamnîk;* R.V. "chain," Dan. v. 7, 16, 29. The more correct form of this word, המינכא, *h-m-y-n-k,* is given in the Massoretic text. Compare the MP *hamyânak,* "girdle," a diminutive from *hamyân,* which has the same meaning in NP. In the Targums it appears as *mĕnîk*—see Onkelos, Gen. xli. 42—in the Syriac as *hamnîk* and *hemnîk,* and in Greek as μανιάκης, by which it is here rendered in the LXX and Theodotion. According to Bevan it has the meaning "necklace" in the later Jewish Aramaic.

סָרְכִין, *sorekîn;* R.V. "presidents," Dan. vi. 2 (3), etc., LXX ἡγουμένοι, Theod. τακτικοὶ. From the OP *saraka,* apparently a diminutive from OP *sar,* "head." See above under *sarbâlîn.* In the Targums it has the meanings "officers," "overseers"; see Onkelos, Exod. v. 6, 10.

נִדְנֶה, *nidneh;* R.V. "body," Dan. vii. 15. Cf. 1 Chr. xxi. 27. Theod. ἕξις, lit. a "receptacle," "sheath," as in the margin. From *ni,* "down"—see above under *nebhrashtâ*—and *da,* "to place," referred to under *dâth* above. The Skt. *nidhana* has the same meaning. Cf. also Z *nidana,* MP *nidan,* "sheath."

אַפֶּדֶן, *appeden;* R.V. "palace," Dan. xi. 45; omitted by the LXX and transliterated by Theodotion Ἐφαδανῷ: and so the Vulgate *Apadno,* as though it were the name of a place. But the word is really Old Persian, and is met with in an inscription of Artaxerxes Mnemon (405–359 B.C.) found at Susa,[1] in which the king says, "This *âpadâna* Darius my ancestor made." As proved by the ruins at Susa *âpadâna* denotes, first, the pillared palace-hall of the Persian king; [2] then, in warfare, the royal headquarters, as in Dan. xi. 45, "the tents of his *palace*." In the Aramaic of the Targum on Jer. xliii. 10, it is used, as Driver points out, of the "royal pavilion" which Nebuchadnezzar was to "spread" at Tahpanhes in Egypt.

2. *The Assyro-Babylonian Words*

Besides the Old Persian words at which we have been looking it is worthy of notice that the Book of Daniel contains several Assyro-Babylonian words such as we should expect to find in a book written at or near Babylon in the latter half of the sixth century B.C. Such are the common nouns *âshaph*, "enchanter," chap. ii. 10, Assyrian *ashipu; attûn*, "furnace," iii. 6, Ass. *atunu; bîrah*, "castle," viii. 2, Ass. *birtu; zîv*, "brightness," ii. 31, Ass. *zîmu; karbĕlâ*, "mantle," or rather "hat," iii. 21, Ass. *karballatu*, Gr. κύρβᾰσις, "helmet," cf. Herod. vii. 64; *kĕthal*, "wall," v. 5, Ass. *kutallu; mĕlēk*, "counsel," iv. 27 (24), Ass. *milku; 'iddân*, "time," ii. 8, Ass. *adannu; pechâh*, "governor," iii. 2, Ass. *pikhatu; pechâr*, "potter," ii. 41, Ass. *pakhâru; shēgĕlâth*, "wives," v. 23, Ass. *shigrēti*. Note also the verbs *kĕphath*, "to bind," iii. 21, Ass. *kapâtu; kera'*, "to be distressed," Ass. *kurû*, "distress"; *nĕzaq*, "to suffer injury," vi. 3, Ass. *nazâqu*, "to injure"; *nĕthar*, "to strip off," iv. 11, Ass. *nashâru*, "to take away"; *pĕlach*, "to reverence," iii. 28, Ass. *palâkhu; tsĕlâ'*, "to pray," vi. 11, Ass. *tsullu; rĕchats*, "to trust," iii. 28, Ass. *rakhâtsu; sheyzîb*, "to deliver," iii. 28, Ass. *shûzubu*, a loan-word from the Shaphel conjugation of the Ass. *ezêbu*.

No less enlightening is the study of the proper names which occur in this Book. Elam, Shushan, Ulai, and Hiddekel have already been dealt with in Chapter XX. The others are as follows:

Nebuchadnezzar: a corrupt form of the more correct Nebuchadrezzar. It is found used throughout the Aramaic parts of the Old Testament. In the Hebrew both forms occur. As an instance of the interchange of the letters *n* and *r* some authorities point to Aram. *bar* and Heb. *ben*="son." C. H. H. Wright also

[1] Tolman's *Persian Inscriptions*, p. 90.

[2] For an attempted restoration of the *âpadâna* of Artaxerxes see Maspero's *Passing of the Empires*, p. 743.

instances Aram. *tĕreyn*, Heb. *shenyim*,[1] "two." In Babylonian the name appears as *Nabium-kudurri-utsur*, and admits of three explanations according to the meaning we affix to *kudurru*. Thus we have a choice of any one of the following: "Nebo protect (i) the crown, (ii) the boundary, (iii) the workman." In favour of (i), *kudurru*, Gr. κίδἄρις, is certainly used of the royal tiara;[2] whilst (ii) is a likely name for a usurper like Nabopolassar to bestow on his son. Nebuchadnezzar himself also recognises this duty of a king by adopting the descriptive epithet, "he who protects the boundaries."[3] In favour of (iii) it can be urged that his father Nabopolassar, when rebuilding the temple of Merodach, was proud to don the workman's cap—*kudurru*—and to work as a labourer; also, that he had an effigy of himself made wearing this attire, and caused his two sons to work along with him.[4]

Shinar, Dan. i. 2, Gen. xi. 1, or to transcribe the Hebrew characters more exactly, Shinear or Shingar, LXX Σεναὰρ. This is the Babylonian *Shunger*, answering to the Sumerian *Shumer*, the old name of South Babylonia.

Ashpenaz, Dan. i. 3. Friedrich Delitzsch regards Ashkenaz—see Gen. x. 3—as the primary form. In Babylonian Ashkenaz would be pronounced Ashgenaz; and since the letters *g* and *p* are very much alike in the ancient Semitic alphabet, and Josephus gives the name as 'Ασχανής, it is very probable that Ashkenaz is the true reading. Esarhaddon couples the country of Ashguza or Ashkenaz with the country of the Manna or Minni, as in Jer. li. 27. The name would thus mean a native of Ashkenaz.

Belteshazzar, Dan. i. 7. According to Friedrich Delitzsch this is an abbreviated name for *Bel-baladhsu-utsur*, "Bel protect his life." Prof. Wilson suggests *Bel-lidh-shar-utsur*, "Bel protect the hostage of the king." Both of these suggestions would agree with the statement of Nebuchadnezzar that the name given to Daniel contained the name of his god; whilst the abbreviation causes no difficulty, since Babylonian names, because of their length, were often thus abbreviated.

Shadrach, Dan. i. 7. According to Delitzsch=*Shudur-Aku*, "command of Aku," Aku being the old Sumerian name of the moon-god Sin, which is sometimes found in Babylonian names, *e.g.* *Kidin-Aku*, "servant of Aku."

Meshach, Dan. i. 7. Delitzsch regards this as a hybrid name, partly Hebrew, partly Babylonian=*Mi-sha-Aku*, "who is like

[1] A *t* in Aramaic answers to an *sh* in Hebrew.

[2] *Beiträge zur Assyriologie*, i. 636.

[3] *Inscriptions of Western Asia*, v. 55, 5.

[4] Schrader's *Keilinschriftliche Bibliothek*, iv. 5, col. ii. 59–iii. 18.

Aku ?" This was the name given to Mishael instead of his Hebrew name, *Mi-sha-El,* "who is like God ?" In pure Babylonian the name would be *Mannu-ki-Aku.* The change of *mannu-ki* into *mi-sha,* whether intentional or otherwise, is probably due to the correspondence between the two names.

Abed-nego, Dan. i. 7. A corrupt form of *Abdu-Nabû,* "servant of Nebo": a name found in a bilingual Assyrio-Aramaic inscription.

Hammeltsar: R.V. "the steward," A.V. Melzar; Theod. Ἀμελσάδ, as if the Babylonian *amel-Shadu,* "servant of the Mountain," *i.e.* the god Bel; but according to Delitzsch the Babylonian *matstsaru,* "keeper," with the definite article prefixed. The LXX identify this person with the Ashpenaz of verse 3, and render the name in both cases as Ἀβιεσδρὶ.

Arioch, Dan. ii. 14, Gen. xiv. 1. This is the Sumerian *eri-Aku,* "the servant of Aku." See Shadrach and Meshach above.

Dura, Dan. iii. 1. The Babylonian *duru,* "rampart." Hence the LXX reading, "He set it in the Plain of the Rampart." An inscription given in Delitzsch's *Paradies* mentions three places bearing this name. Further, a little below Babylon a small river called the Dura flows into the Euphrates, and near it are some mounds still called the Mounds of Dura. One of these, a huge rectangular brick structure, 45 feet square and 20 feet high, Oppert thinks may have formed the pedestal of Nebuchadnezzar's colossal image.

Belshazzar, Dan. v. 1=*Bel-shar-utsur,* "Bel protect the king." The LXX and Theod. confuse this name with Belteshazzar, the name given to Daniel, and write both names Βαλτασὰρ. Cf. Dan. i. 7, v. 1.

23

The Book of Daniel and Jewish Apocalypses

REFERENCE has been made in Chapters IV. and V. of this work to the Book of Enoch. This is one of those remarkable works written in the centuries just before and after Christ, and to which so much attention has been drawn of late—the Jewish Apocalypses. It is the most famous of such works, not only on account of its varied contents—for it is evidently a composite work, written by different authors and at different times—but more especially for the witness which it bears to the development of Messianic doctrine in the Jewish Church between the close of the Old Testament period and the coming of Christ, and also from the fact that it was evidently well known to our Lord and His apostles and finds an echo in many passages in the Gospels and Epistles and above all in the Book of the Revelation, not to mention the actual quotation made from it in the Epistle of St. Jude.[1]

The following description by Dr. Driver gives a very good idea of the nature of a Jewish apocalypse [2]:

"Its mode of representation was artificial. The disclosures which were the most characteristic element of apocalyptic prophecy were not made by the author in his own person. They were placed in the mouth of some pious and famous man of old—an Enoch, a Moses, a Baruch, an Ezra: from the standpoint of the assumed speaker the future was unrolled, usually under symbolic imagery, down to the time in which the actual author lived: the heavens were thrown open, glimpses were given of the offices and operation of the celestial hierarchy: God's final judgment both upon His own people and upon the powers opposed to it was described: the approaching deliverance of the afflicted Israelites was declared: the resurrection and future lot alike of the righteous and of the wicked were portrayed in vivid imagery. The seer who is repre-

[1] See *The Book of Enoch* by R. H. Charles, pp. xcv.–ciii.

[2] *Cambridge Bible*, Daniel, p. lxxviii.

sented as the author of the book, sometimes beholds these things himself in a vision or dream, but often he holds discourse with an angel, who either explains to him what he does not fully understand, or communicates to him the revelations in their entirety. Naturally there are variations in detail: the subjects enumerated do not appear uniformly with precisely the same prominence; hortatory or didactic matter is also often present as well; but speaking generally some at least of them are present in every 'apocalypse,' and constitute its most conspicuous and distinctive feature."

It will be noticed in the above description that attention is drawn to the artificial character of the Apocalypses. They are not actual prophecies in the sense of foretelling the future, but past history put into the form of prophecy; in order to do which the writer takes the name of some Biblical hero in the more or less remote past. They thus belong to the Pseudepigrapha–books with false titles—and are often referred to under that name. The pseudonymous character of these books and the assumption of the names of Biblical worthies, some of them inspired men, is opposed to our ideas of literary honesty, and appears the more strange to us when we discover that the writers were evidently earnest-minded religious men, although influenced in some cases by a strong spirit of religious and political partizanship. It is plain that we must not judge them by our standards. Nevertheless the matter calls for explanation, and explanations more or less satisfactory have been given by those who have studied the subject.

Dr. Charles, a great authority on the Pseudepigrapha of the Old Testament, speaking on the pseudonymity of the author of the Book of Enoch, says, "It was simply owing to the evil character of the period, in which their lot was cast, that these enthusiasts and mystics, exhibiting on occasions the inspiration of the Old Testament prophets, were obliged to issue their works under the ægis of some ancient name. The Law, which claimed to be the highest and final word from God, could tolerate no fresh message from God, and so, when men were moved by the Spirit of God to make known their visions relating to the past, the present, and the future, and to proclaim the higher ethical truths they had won, they could not do so openly, but were forced to resort to pseudonymous publication."

Dr. Oesterley, writing on the Apocalyptic literature, says, "All the known books belonging to it have false names in their titles, for which reason they are called the Pseudepigrapha. How are we to account for this apparent fraud on the part of writers who were clearly devout and earnest men? This strange procedure, as it appears to us nowadays, may to a large extent be explained if we remember that the apocalyptic writers almost certainly drew their material from popular tradition. Many of the ideas which receive various embodiment in this literature were derived doubtlessly from the common stock of the popular consciousness; their ascription to or association with the great heroic figures of antiquity, like Enoch, Abraham, Isaiah, or the twelve Patriarchs, may also be a feature from the popular consciousness. The men who reduced the various elements to writing, or utilised them for enforcing religious views or lessons, may, on this view, be acquitted from any charge of fraud or dishonesty: they implicitly trusted the popular tradition so far as to believe that the ideas to which they were giving expression really did go back to the heroic figures of old. Their estimate, moreover, of the function and importance of authorship probably differed fundamentally from that of the moderns; it was far less self-conscious, and was the natural outcome of a literary modesty which was *naïve*."

Dr. Samuel Davidson in his article on "Apocalyptic Literature" in the *Encyclopœdia Britannica* remarks, "Its object was to encourage and comfort the people by holding forth the speedy restoration of the Davidic kingdom of Messiah. Attaching itself to the national hope, it proclaimed the impending of a glorious future, in which Israel, freed from her enemies, should enjoy a peaceful and prosperous life under her long wished for Deliverer. The old prophets became the vehicle of these utterances. . . . Working upon the basis of well-known writings, imitating their style, and artificially reproducing their substance, the authors naturally adopted the anonymous (pseudonymous ?)."

Prof. Burkitt, writing about the false titles of the Pseudepigrapha, as Oesterley points out, makes a very significant remark. "There is," he says, "another aspect of pseudonymous authorship, to which I venture to think sufficient attention has not been given. It is this, that the names were not chosen out of mere caprice: they indicated to a certain extent what subjects would be treated and the point of view of the writer." Thus, for instance, Enoch, who "walked with God" and was eventually translated, is represented in the Similitudes as being carried off by a whirlwind during his life to the borders of heaven and seeing all the hidden and secret things; whilst Salathiel, who witnessed the destruction of Jerusalem by the arms of Babylon in the days of Nebuchadnezzar, is made to voice forth the perplexing questions which must have arisen in the minds of many earnest Jews when their Sacred City was a second time destroyed by the Roman Babylon. It is, indeed, a question whether the educated among the Jews were imposed upon at all; while for the masses the title might mean, what such and such a holy saint could or would have told us, had he been on the earth now.

The Book of Daniel is claimed by the critics as a Jewish apocalypse. "Daniel," writes the Rev. J. R. Cohu, is the typical Old Testament apocalypse." "The earliest of such apocalypses," writes Dr. Samuel Davidson, "is the canonical book of Daniel." Similarly Prof. H. T. Andrews, "Apocalyptic literature begins with the Book of Daniel." Dr. Charles speaks of "the pseudonymous character of this book." Prof. Driver in his moderate reverential strain, after describing the character of the Jewish Apocalypses, adds, "It is, of course, not for a moment denied that the Book of Daniel is greatly superior to the other apocalypses that have been referred to." Despite this consensus of opinion, for which doubtless many other authorities could be quoted, I venture to bring forward some reasons for thinking that the Book of Daniel is not an "apocalypse" in the sense in which the term is technically employed. To put the matter more plainly: the Book of Daniel, as I shall strive to show, is a *genuine* apocalypse as regards its visions, while the works at which we have been looking are admitted by all to be *artificial*.

To begin, then, I would observe that the Jewish Apocalypses are invariably plainly *linked on to the Old Testament.* Thus in the Book of Enoch we have that saint's descent from Adam; in the Book of the Secrets of Enoch a description is given of the translation of Enoch in his 365th year. The Book of Noah, fragments of which are found embedded in the Book of Enoch, has much to say of the fall of "the sons of God," makes mention of Noah's blameless life, his building the ark, and so forth. In the Testaments of the Twelve Patriarchs the connecting links with the Old Testament story are frequent. Thus Reuben refers to his act of incest; Simeon to his being bound as a spy; Judah to the reason why he was so called by his mother; and Naphtali to the blessing bestowed on that tribe by Jacob. The Assumption of Moses begins with Moses' charge to Joshua; the Ascension of Isaiah, with relating how Hezekiah called his son Manasseh into the presence of Isaiah, and how Isaiah made known to the king his son's future apostasy. The Syriac Apocalypse of Baruch professes to have been received by Baruch the son of Neriah in the twenty-fifth year of Jeconiah king of Judah, and tells how he was charged by God with a message to Jeremiah to leave the doomed city. In the Greek Apocalypse of Baruch that saint appears on the bank of a river, weeping over the captivity of Jerusalem and sorrowing that Nebuchadnezzar was permitted by God to destroy the Sacred City. In the Apocalypse of Salathiel, embedded in IV. Ezra, the link is supplied thus : " In the thirtieth year after the downfall of the City "—*i.e.* Jerusalem—" I Salathiel (who am also Ezra) [1] was in Babylon." Salathiel, *i.e.* " Shealtiel," according to legal descent was in the royal line of the kings of Judah,[2] and was accounted the son of Jehoiachin and legal father of his nephew Zerubbabel,[3] the " governor of Judah," who was presently to lead back the captives from Babylon to Jerusalem.[4] He would therefore be looked upon as the head of the Jewish community at Babylon, and all the more so seeing that his predecessor, " Jeconiah the Captive," [5] was not only in durance but was under the ban of heaven.[6] Accordingly the writer of the apocalypse, who adopts the rôle of Salathiel the " father " of Zerubbabel—a name which signifies " begotten at Babylon "—represents himself as living at Babylon in the thirtieth year after the fall of Jerusalem and as being the person to whom the supposed revelations were made.

In all the Jewish Apocalypses, then, we find plain unmistakable links with the Old Testament records of the worthies whose names appear in their titles, links of a simple, circumstantial character, by which these works appear as joined on to the Old Testament, albeit they are undoubtedly the product of a much later age. But when we come to the Book of Daniel, and regarding it for the time being as an apocalypse of the second century B.C., ask for the Old Testament worthy after whose name it is called and for the connecting link, we are pointed to two passages in the Book of Ezekiel concerning a certain saint and sage, apparently of the olden time, about whom no circumstantial, historical facts are known, mention being only made of his extraordinary power with God as an intercessor and of his well-nigh superhuman wisdom.[7] Now, it is quite true that the Book of Daniel admirably illustrates both the power with God and the wisdom of Ezekiel's Daniel, but it contains *no actual reference to those passages in Ezekiel.* For instance, in Dan. ii., where the writer tells how Daniel by his prayers found out the king's forgotten dream

[1] An interpolation.
[2] 1 Chr. iii. 17 ; Matt. i. 12.
[3] Ezra iii. 2, v. 2 ; Neh. xii. 1.
[4] Hag. i. 1 ; Ezra ii. 1, 2.
[5] 1 Chr. iii. 17, R.V.
[6] Jer. xxii. 28–30.
[7] " Our author got the name of his prophet from Ezekiel, who makes mention of a certain Daniel as having been especially pious and wise."—Cornill's *Introduction to the Canonical Books of the Old Testament*, p. 389.

and saved the lives of the wise men of Babylon, how easy it would have been for him to have introduced some mention of Noah and Job, and thus to have linked up the Daniel whose name he placed in the title of his book with the Daniel mentioned by Ezekiel! The fact that he has not done so, distinguishes his work from the other apocalypses. Perhaps, however, it will be said that the missing link connecting the Daniel of the Book of Daniel with the Daniel of Ezekiel is to be found in the fact that Ezekiel lived in Babylonia in the age of Nebuchadnezzar and that the saint and hero of the Book of Daniel belongs to the same country and the same age. This is true enough as regards Ezekiel; but if we look upon the Book of Daniel as an Old Testament apocalypse, it will no longer hold good of the Daniel mentioned by Ezekiel, who, by his being classed with Noah and Job, appears rather as a saint of the remote past than as a contemporary of Ezekiel.[1] Thus it still remains a fact that our Book, if treated as an apocalypse, is unlike the other apocalypses in that it *lacks any plain connecting link with the Scriptures of the Old Testament.*

But the above is by no means the only, or even the greatest, difference that exists between the Book of Daniel and the Jewish Apocalypses. To say nothing of the fact that this Book moves upon an essentially higher plane, this at least is evident, that while the Apocalypses contain scraps of Old Testament history, we find in the Book of Daniel *genuine historical facts derived from independent sources, as well as some linguistic features wholly lacking in the Apocalypses and altogether most surprising in a Jewish writer of the Maccabean age.* Placing these facts together, then, we are faced with the following remarkable literary phenomenon: A pseudonymous writer of the second century B.C. takes two notices found in the Book of Ezekiel of an ancient worthy who was famous alike for his wisdom and his piety, but of whom nothing else is known. Round this dim figure from the remote past he weaves a brilliant romance, illustrative both of the intercessory power of Ezekiel's Daniel, and also of his superhuman penetration in discovering secrets. Incorporated in his romance are found some surprising bits of genuine history, facts otherwise known only from contemporary cuneiform inscriptions or in one or two instances from the pages of profane historians, such as the lowly origin of the dynasty of the great Nebuchadnezzar, his personality and tastes, his idea of empire, and the generally peaceful character of his rule; the sovereignty of Belshazzar the son of the last king

[1] It is only the established authenticity of the Book of Daniel which allows us to identify its hero with the great, but otherwise dim, figure in Ezekiel, and to place that figure, not in the long ago past, but in the age of Nebuchadnezzar.

of Babylon, his death on the night of the capture of his palace, and the fact that he was succeeded, not by Cyrus, but by another ruler styled "Darius the Mede," who appears to have reigned for only part of a year. Stranger still, our author, who is supposed to have lived in Judea in the days of the Maccabees, has contrived to write his Book in what appears to be an Eastern type of Aramaic, and to scatter throughout it some twenty Old Persian words, which could hardly have been in use in the Aramaic of his day, though they may well be imagined as often on the lips of his hero who was prime minister at the court of Persia. These words are not confined to the historical part of his work, but one or two of them are introduced into his visions. For after crediting Nebuchadnezzar with two visions remarkably in keeping with that monarch's tone of thought as well as with his tastes and proclivities, he goes on in the latter part of his Book to give us his own visions, which are dated, not like the Syriac Apocalypse of Baruch or the Apocalypse of Salathiel by any reference to Jerusalem and her kings, but by references to the years of the kings who have been mentioned in the previous romance, Belshazzar, Darius the Mede, and Cyrus; he also makes mention of a Median Ahasuerus, otherwise unknown to history—for the Median kings have left no monumental records—and indicates quite incidentally that Shushan lay within the kingdom of Babylon, a fact hardly credited till confirmed by the Babylonian inscriptions. In all this he displays such a wonderful knowledge of ancient history, such an acquaintance with languages and dialects, and such literary craft and resourcefulness as we should hardly expect to find in a Palestinian Jew writing in the second century B.C. As we gaze at his masterpiece we are ready to echo the prophet's words, "Art thou wiser than Daniel?" wiser than the pseudonymous writer of this remarkable Book? What are we to say of such superhuman wisdom, of such a marvel of literature? Simply this: that the phenomena, which so utterly baffle us if we regard this Book as one of the Pseudepigrapha, are all clear enough if we look upon it as a contemporary record, a genuine work of the early Persian period. The fact is, that the critics, who cannot believe in miracles, have themselves constructed a theory which requires us to believe a miracle, inasmuch as their pseudonymous Daniel is seen to be as truly endowed with miraculous gifts as our historic Daniel.

Our comparison of the Book of Daniel with the Jewish Apocalypses suggests some causes of deep thankfulness to Him whose Providence has watched over this part of His Holy Word and furnished in these later days the means whereby His Church can withstand the attacks of hostile criticism. We thank Him—

(i) That the writer of this Book was led to incorporate history with prophecy in his great work, and to mention several facts in Babylonian history otherwise only known to us from the native cuneiform records;

(ii) That he was brought much into contact with a religiously minded albeit heathen king, of marked personality, who loved to record his doings and has left us many monuments of his great works at Babylon as well as an account of his exploits in the Lebanon;

(iii) That he wrote at a period when the Aryan-speaking peoples were being intermingled with the Semitic races, and that owing to this state of things, as well as to his position at the court of Persia, he was led to introduce several Old Persian words into the Aramaic in which his Book was written, and to represent the Babylonian monarch as uttering three Greek words when enumerating the "all kinds of music" of which his orchestra was composed;

(iv) That the two languages in which this Book has come down to us—part being in Aramaic, part in a Hebrew translation—form a voucher for the evil days through which it has passed, and help us in some measure to account for the signs of interpolation which appear in the long record of the eleventh chapter, which belongs to one of the Hebrew portions of the Book.

24

The Position of the Book of Daniel in the Canon of the Old Testament

"It is regarded as a palmary argument against the authenticity of the Book of Daniel that the Rabbis of the third and fourth centuries excluded it from the 'Prophets' and relegated it to the Kethubhim. Josephus includes 'Daniel' among the 'Prophets,' since the four books of the Kethubhim described by him cannot fit 'Daniel'; moreover he distinctly calls him a prophet."—*The Samaritans*, p. 360. By J. E. N. Thomson, D.D. Being the Alexander Robertson Lectures for 1916, delivered before the University of Glasgow.

THE fact referred to in the above brief extract is one that demands the attention of any writer who seeks to establish the authenticity of the Book of Daniel. I have therefore chosen as the subject of this chapter the position which that Book occupies in the Canon of the Old Testament Scriptures.

The formation of the Canon is a subject about which very little is known. As Dr. C. H. H. Wright observes, "There is nothing worthy to be regarded as real 'evidence' concerning the settlement of the so-called Canon of the Old Testament Scriptures. No one can prove when or by what authority the books of the Old Testament were arranged into three distinct divisions. It is vain to speak of three distinct canons, and to assign a date for the closing up of each division. These attempts rest on unhistorical conjectures."[1] These most true words were written with regard to the argument based by the critics on the position which the Book of Daniel occupies in our present Hebrew Bibles, where it stands last but two in the last of the three divisions of the Old Testament Scriptures, being followed only by Ezra-Nehemiah and the Chronicles. That position can be very well defended and satisfactory reasons can be given for the Book being thus placed. But, as the extract at the head of this chapter shows, *the present position of the Book in the Hebrew Canon is not its original position.* We have

[1] *Daniel and his Prophecies*, p. 50.

it on the authority of the Jewish priest-historian Josephus—one who in such a matter could make no mistake—that at the close of the first century A.D. the Canon of the Old Testament books was differently arranged from that at present accepted among the Jews; and it is also evident from the writings of the Early Fathers that a change must have been made in the arrangement of the Jewish Canon between the middle of the third and the end of the fourth century A.D.

The present Canon of the Old Testament as given in the Hebrew Bible is arranged thus–

I. The Law, comprising the five Books of Moses.

II. The Prophets, divided into two subdivisions: (i) the Former Prophets, viz. Joshua, Judges, Samuel, Kings;[1] (ii) the Latter Prophets, viz. Isaiah, Jeremiah, Ezekiel, and the Book of the twelve Minor Prophets: in all eight books.

III. The Kĕthubhim, or "writings," often called the Hagiographa or "Holy Writings," which are arranged thus: Psalms, Proverbs, Job, Canticles, Ruth, Lamentations, Ecclesiastes, Esther, Daniel, Ezra-Nehemiah, Chronicles: in all eleven books. The total number of books is thus 5+8+11=24. Hence they are sometimes called "The Twenty-four Writings." The first indication of this system of reckoning is found in the Ezra Legend, given in the fourteenth chapter of the Apocryphal book 2 Esdras, and in that part of the book which Oesterley—on the strength of the veiled note of time given in chap. iii. 1, "the thirtieth year after the ruin of the city," *i.e.* the Jerusalem of Salathiel—refers to A.D. 100. Ezra, we are told, being warned of God of his approaching end, becomes anxious for future generations. What can he do to help them? Shall he re-write the Law? God bids him make preparations, prepare many tablets, and secure the services of five men who can write quickly. Some of the things written he is to publish openly, and some are to be delivered in secret to the wise. Ezra, after drinking the cup of inspiration, undertakes the work with all diligence. At the end of forty days 94 books are written. Then he is commanded to publish openly the first books written, but to keep the last 70 for the wise. Whence it appears that the published books were 94 minus 70, *i.e.* 24. Josephus, writing at the same period as the author of 2 Esdras xiv., gives the number of books as 22, which later writers delight to point to as being the number of letters in the

[1] The prophets appear to have been the historians of Old Testament times like the monkish chroniclers of the Middle Ages. Cf. 1 Chr. xxix. 29, 2 Chr. ix. 29, xii. 15, xxvi. 22. Also some of their utterances are enshrined in the historical books.

Hebrew alphabet.[1] This fresh reckoning is explained from the list of Old Testament books given us by Origen, in which Ruth is joined on to Judges, and Lamentations to Jeremiah. Jerome was acquainted with both systems of reckoning. "Some," he tells us, "write down Ruth and Lamentations in the Hagiographa"–apart, that is, from Judges and Jeremiah respectively, which were included in the Prophets—"and think that they ought to be reckoned in its contents"—viz. in the Hagiographa—"and that thus the number of books of the ancient law is twenty-four." [2]

It is very interesting to notice that in the time of Christ the threefold division of the books of the Old Testament was already in existence, though, as we shall see, the distribution of the books between the Prophets and the Hagiographa was not the same then as now. Our Saviour after His Resurrection says to His Apostles, "These are my words which I spake unto you, while I was yet with you, how that all things must needs be fulfilled, which are written in the law of Moses, and the prophets, and the psalms, concerning me." [3] Our Lord here calls the third division "the psalms," probably because that Book formed the chief, and very likely the first, book in the Hagiographa of those days. But we can go back two centuries further and find good evidence that early in the second century B.C. a threefold division of the books of the Old Testament Scriptures was already in existence. In the Prologue to the Apocryphal Book of Ecclesiasticus, Jesus the son of Sirach, who translated that book from Hebrew into Greek, tells us how his grandfather, who bore the same name and was the actual author of the work, "when he had much given himself to the reading of the Law, and the Prophets, and other books of our fathers," was led on to write something himself. Then a little further on he speaks again of "the Law itself, and the Prophets, and the rest of the books." Now, the younger Jesus at the time when he wrote this Prologue was in Egypt, whither he had come, so he tells us, in the thirty-eighth year when Euergetes was king. The monarch meant is Euergetes II. The thirty-eighth year of his reign was 132 B.C. Hence his grandfather may be presumed to have flourished about 180 B.C. Thus we have reliable evidence that early in the second century B.C. the books of the Old Testament were classed in three divisions: the Law, the Prophets, and "the rest of the books."

The arrangement of the books of the Hagiographa in our

[1] Euseb. *Eccles. History*, vi. 25.
[2] Jerome, *Preface to the Books of Kings.*
[3] Luke xxiv. 44.

present Hebrew Bibles, according to Buhl,[1] is only found in German manuscripts. The ancient Palestinian Canon, given in a Hebrew Bible from Spanish sources dated A.D. 1009, runs thus: Chronicles, Psalms, Job, Proverbs, Ruth, Canticles, Ecclesiastes, Lamentations, Esther, *Daniel*, Ezra-Nehemiah. On the other hand, the Talmudic order, which seems to have been that of the Babylonian Jews, in the succession of the Prophets, places Isaiah after Jeremiah and Ezekiel, and arranges the Hagiographa thus: Ruth, Psalms, Job, Proverbs, Ecclesiastes, Canticles, Lamentations, *Daniel*, Esther, Ezra-Nehemiah, Chronicles. In both of the above lists it will be noticed that the Book of Daniel is excluded from the Prophets and placed near the end of the Hagiographa. This has often been urged as a proof of the late date of that Book as well as an indication that when the Canon was closed it was held in less estimation than the books of the Prophets. As regards those who drew up the Palestinian and Babylonian Canons such reasoning can easily be refuted, seeing that the Psalms, which undoubtedly formed the hymn-book of the second temple and as a collection was evidently drawn up for liturgical purposes, is placed in the same division. There is, however, no need for any such refutation, for it is possible to show from the pages of Josephus that the Book of Daniel must originally have been placed in the Prophets.

In book x. 2. 2, of his *Antiquities*, a work written in A.D. 93–94, Josephus tells his readers that Isaiah wrote his prophecies in books that posterity might judge of their accomplishment from the event. After which he adds, "Nor did this prophet do so alone; but *the others, which were twelve in number*, did the same." The books of the Prophets, instead of being only eight in number as in the Babylonian and Palestinian Canons, are here said to be twelve in number along with the Book of Isaiah, *i.e.* thirteen in all. How is this to be explained? The answer is supplied by a plain statement in the treatise of *Josephus against Apion*. In this work, which is an apology for Judaism, we meet with the following passage: "For we [Jews] have not an innumerable multitude of books [as the Greeks have], but only twenty-two books, which contain all the record of past times, which are justly believed to be divine; and of them, five belong to Moses, which contain his laws, and the tradition of the origin of mankind till his death. This interval of time was little short of three thousand years; but as to the time from the death of Moses till the reign of Artaxerxes king of Persia, who reigned after Xerxes, the prophets

[1] *Canon and Text of the Old Testament*, pp. 39, 40.

who wrote after Moses, wrote down what was done in their times *in thirteen books. The remaining four books contain hymns to God and precepts for the conduct of human life.*" [1] Here the second division, viz. that of the Prophets, is said to contain thirteen books —which agrees with what is stated in the *Antiquities*—while the remaining books, which form the Hagiographa, are stated to be only four in number and to contain "hymns to God and precepts for the conduct of human life." The description thus given points to Psalms, Proverbs, Ecclesiastes, and Canticles, as the four books meant, but in any case cannot fit the Book of Daniel. That book therefore, in the time of Josephus must have been placed in the Prophets, not in the Hagiographa. Agreeably to this conclusion we note that our Lord Jesus Christ, when referring to the *Book* of Daniel, speaks of "Daniel the prophet," while Josephus in no measured terms asserts Daniel's prophetic gifts, and declares that the revelations made to him mark him out as one of the greatest of the prophets.[2]

The earliest Canon of the Old Testament is found in an extract from the writings of Melito, bishop of Sardis, *circa* A.D. 180, preserved to us by Eusebius.[3] Writing to a Christian who wished to know *the number and order of the books of the Old Testament,* Melito tells how he had travelled in the country where those books were published in order to obtain accurate information, and then goes on to give the following list: "Five of Moses: Genesis, Exodus, Numbers, Leviticus, Deuteronomy. Joshua (son) of Nun, Judges, Ruth, four (books) of Kings, two of Chronicles,[4] Psalms of David, Proverbs of Solomon also called Wisdom, Ecclesiastes, Song of Songs, Job. (Books) *of prophets:* Isaiah, Jeremiah, the Twelve in one book,[5] *Daniel,* Ezekiel, Ezra." [6] In the above list the four books of Kings include the two books of Samuel, Lamentations is probably included with Jeremiah, and Ezra and Nehemiah form one book. It is further noticeable that the Hagiographa of Josephus, viz. Psalms, Proverbs, Ecclesiastes, and Canticles, along with the poetical book of Job, is here dropped in between the Former Prophets—*i.e.* the historical books, to which Chronicles is added—and the Latter Prophets, *i.e.* the prophets properly so-called, *among whom the Book of Daniel holds an honoured place.* Lastly, observe that Chronicles is the last of the historical books and Ezra the last of the prophetical.

Origen, A.D. 185–254, after stating as a well-known fact that

[1] *Josephus c. Apion,* book i. 8.

[2] *Ant.* x. 11. 7.

[3] *Eccles. History,* iv. 26.

[4] Its Greek name, Παραλείπομενα, means "The Things Omitted."

[5] *I.e.* the Minor Prophets.

[6] *I.e.* Ezra and Nehemiah.

the testamentary books of the Hebrews are twenty-two—as many as the letters of their alphabet—gives the following list: Genesis, Exodus, Leviticus, Numbers, Deuteronomy, Joshua, Judges and Ruth in one book, Samuel, Kings, Chronicles, Ezra first and second [1] in one book, Psalms, Proverbs, Ecclesiastes, Song of Songs, Isaiah, Jeremiah with Lamentations, *Daniel*, Ezekiel, Job, Esther.[2] Though the sum of the books is stated to be twenty-two, yet the above list contains only twenty-one, whence it is evident that the book of the Twelve Minor Prophets has been omitted through a scribal error. In the above list, though the threefold division is lost sight of, yet *the Book of Daniel still maintains its place among the prophets.* Also the four books which formed the Hagiographa of Josephus still cling together, and Esther, absent from Melito's list, is here specifically mentioned.

Jerome, A.D. 340–420, spent four years in the East, and in his later life retired to a monastery at Bethlehem. He obtained his information, so he tells us, from a Rabbi, who Nicodemus-like came to him by night. Special mention is made by him of the threefold division of the books of the Old Testament, which he enumerates thus: *The Law:* Genesis, Exodus, Leviticus, Numbers, Deuteronomy. *The Prophets:* Joshua, Judges with Ruth, Samuel, Kings, Isaiah, Jeremiah, the Twelve Prophets, Ezekiel. *The Hagiographa:* Job, (psalms) of David, Proverbs of Solomon, Ecclesiastes, Song of Songs, *Daniel*, Chronicles, Ezra, Esther.[3] Here the four books of the Former Prophets are followed by the four books of the Latter Prophets as in our present Hebrew Bibles. Also the four books of the original Hagiographa are still found together, Job being placed before them, probably on chronological grounds [4] and also as being a poetical book. But what chiefly strikes us is that *Daniel has been removed from the Prophets and placed in the Hagiographa.* The reason for this change appears also to be a chronological one, since this Book is now followed by Chronicles—a late book—Ezra and Esther. Further, the whole order of the Canon, if we except the moral and poetical books which formed the first Hagiographa, is now seen to be arranged so as to suit the three periods in the history of the Chosen People. The Law covers the period in which they were being formed into a nation and brought to the borders of their promised land; the Prophets, the period of their independence, when they dwelt in their own land under their own rulers; the Hagiographa—barring the Book of Job and the original four books, which were

[1] *I.e.* Ezra and Nehemiah.
[2] *Eccles. History*, vi. 25.
[3] Jerome's *Preface to the Books of Kings.*
[4] Buhl's *Canon*, p. 40.

still allowed to remain in the division in which they were first placed—the period of their depression, when they were first led captive by Babylon and then restored as vassals of the kings of Persia. This consideration quite sufficiently explains the changed position of the Book of Daniel, a Book so tellingly significant of the supremacy of Babylon and Persia over the Jewish people, while at the same time no less significant of the supremacy of the God of Israel over the rulers of those mighty empires.

With regard to the position in the Canon of the Book of Daniel, Jerome, passing from a subject on which he had been dwelling, makes the following remark : " Leaving the decision on this matter to the reader's judgment, I give this admonition, that Daniel is not reckoned by the Hebrews among the Prophets but among those who wrote the Hagiographa." [1] The tone of his words shows plainly that he looked on the arrangement of the Old Testament books then in use among the Jews as the original arrangement, and that with regard to the Book of Daniel he wished his readers to take note of what was evidently a surprise to himself, viz. that the Jews placed Daniel in the Hagiographa. His surprise would have been removed, had he been aware of the change made by the Jews in the order of the Canon.

It will be noticed in the reference made above to the prologue of Ecclesiasticus that Jesus the son of Sirach, the grandson of the author, appears to speak in a tone of disparagement of the books of the Hagiographa, calling them " other books of our fathers " and " the rest of the books," and telling us that his grandfather intended to contribute to them his quota. This renders it probable that at the time when he wrote, the books of the third division were not yet regarded as canonical, or at any rate as completed. But in any case, even when those books came to be regarded as an integral part of Holy Scripture, the placing of any book such as Daniel in the Hagiographa could hardly fail to depreciate that Book. The feeling of the Jews toward the Law has always been faithfully reflected in the sentiment expressed in the closing verses of the Book of Deuteronomy, " There hath not arisen a prophet since in Israel like unto Moses, whom the Lord knew face to face." The Prophets thus took quite a second place. And hence it would be natural to look upon the books of the Hagiographa as third in merit as well as in position. Accordingly the Jews of the Middle Ages compared the three divisions of the Canon to the three parts of the temple. The Law was the Holiest of All ; the Prophets, the Holy place ; the Hagiographa, the Outer Court. Somewhat

[1] Jerome's *Preface to the Book of Daniel.*

of this same feeling shows itself in our modern critics, when they point to the place which the Book of Daniel occupies in the present Hebrew Canon. Our reply to them must be twofold: first, that the present position of this Book is not the position which it originally occupied; and secondly, that we have no sufficient ground for thinking that those who placed the Book in its present position intended thereby to put any slight upon it, but only, as it seemed to them, to improve the order of the books, chiefly on chronological lines.

But it will be asked, how far does the order of the Old Testament books, first given to us by Melito, fall in with our Saviour's words in Matt. xxiii. 35, when, threatening the persecuting hypocrites of His day, He speaks thus: "That upon you may come all the righteous blood shed upon the earth, from the blood of Abel the righteous unto the blood of Zachariah the son of Barachiah, whom ye slew between the sanctuary and the altar"? The reference in the above passage is to the murder of Zechariah the son of Jehoiada, who was stoned in the court of the temple, as recorded in 2 Chr. xxiv. 20–22. The dying words of this Zechariah, "The Lord look upon it, and require it," compared with the above verse as well as with Gen. iv. 10, make it almost certain that he is the person here spoken of. Now, it is evident that our Lord is not speaking from the point of view of time, for the murder of Uriah, recorded in Jer. xxvi. 23, was chronologically later than that of Zechariah. Hence we must understand Him to be referring to the range of the Canon, and in effect to be saying, "From the first murder in Scripture down to the last." Was, then, the murder of Zechariah the last recorded in the then Canon? This is a question to which for lack of information we can give no decisive answer. In Melito's Canon Chronicles appears as the last of the historical books, and Ezra is placed at the close of all under the heading "Prophets." But Melito's Canon is not that of Josephus, for he places the Latter Prophets—Isaiah, Jeremiah, the Twelve, Daniel, Ezekiel, along with Ezra—at the close of his list; while the Canon of Josephus ends with the four books of hymns and moral precepts. If in the time of Josephus, or rather of Christ, Chronicles was the last book of the second division, then our Saviour's words would carry equal force. But on this point we are likely to remain uninformed.

Let me now clench the arguments advanced above. Christ's words in Matt. xxiv. 15, spoken about A.D. 30, and the statements of Josephus about the close of the first century, alike show that the Book of Daniel stood originally in the division called the Prophets. Melito, in the last quarter of the second century, places Daniel in the last part of his list, under the heading "Prophets" and just before Ezekiel. In Origen's Canon—a century and a half later—this Book occupies the same position with regard to Ezekiel. Thus for two centuries and more we have good evidence of the honourable position occupied by the Book of Daniel in the Old Testament Canon. Is it not, then, time that the critics should cease to point out to us that "Daniel" stands last but two in the Hebrew Bible? To quote the able writer whose words stand at the head of this chapter, "*The case against 'Daniel' is peculiarly weak!*"

Closely akin to the subject just dealt with is the question, what meaning should be attached to the expression "the books" in Dan. ix. 2? In the first year of Darius the Mede, who was made king over the realm of the Chaldeans, Daniel tells us that he "understood by," or "*in* the books, the number of the years, whereof the word of the LORD came to Jeremiah the prophet, for the accomplishing of the desolations of Jerusalem, even seventy years." Commenting on this passage Charles writes, "The books here are the sacred books, *i.e.* the Scriptures. The phrase implies the formation of a definite collection of Old Testament books."[1] In like manner Driver, laying due stress on the definite article, —overlooked in the Authorised Version—observes that "'*the* books' can only be naturally understood as implying that, at the time when the passage was written, some definite collection of sacred writings already existed."[2] My answer to these comments is, that in endeavouring to ascertain the reference which underlies this expression "the books," it is better to take an equally common meaning of the word and one in perfect harmony with the context, in preference to a meaning which, though it may suit the supposed late date of the Book of Daniel, occurs nowhere else in the Old Testament.

The Hebrew word *sēpher*, here met with in the plural and translated "books," undoubtedly often has that meaning, and is used in the singular, sometimes of inspired writings, such as "the book of the covenant," "the book of the law," or again of secular works, such as "the book of Jasher," but nowhere of *a collection of sacred books*. Further, "book" is not the primary meaning of the word. According to F. Brown's Hebrew Lexicon *sēpher* is a loan-word answering to the Assyrian *shipru,* which comes from the root *shapâru,* "to send." Hence its primary meaning is "a missive"; then, "a letter" from some king, prophet, or other influential person; finally "document," "deed," "writing,"

[1] *Century Bible,* Daniel, p. 95. [2] *Cambridge Bible,* Daniel, p. 127.

" book." In the Book of Jeremiah, with which the passage in Dan. ix. 2 is concerned, *sēpher* is used of law deeds, of a " book " or collection of written prophecies, and also of prophetic " missives " or " letters." Since there are two prophecies in the Book of Jeremiah concerning the seventy years' captivity, the word might be translated here " the writings," viz. of that prophet. Or, again, since the plural is sometimes used of a single letter—cf. Isa. xxxvii. 14, also 1 Kings xxi. 8 and 2 Chr. xxxii. 17 in R.V.M. —the reference may be to the particular " letter " given in Jer. xxix. 1–20, which contains one of those prophecies. In any case a reference to the weighty utterances of Jeremiah is what we should naturally expect here. The Jews at Babylon, as we learn from the Book of Jeremiah, formed the better part of the nation, and to them the promise of a return to Jerusalem was specially made. Cf. Jer. xxiv. with xxix. 1–20. They would, therefore, be sure to feel a great respect for the writings of this prophet or for any missive received from him. Again, we note that Daniel is speaking of the fulfilment of Jeremiah's prophecy as being close at hand, and the state of the political world evidently inspires him with confidence. The Lord has " stirred up the spirit of the kings of the Medes," [1] the long prophecy of Jer. l. and li. has been fulfilled, and it is the first year of a Median monarch on the throne of Babylon. Well, then, might the Jewish seer, himself a captive at Babylon, understand from the " writings," or " letter," of Jeremiah the great event so soon to take place. Thus the whole atmosphere of the passage, the writer, the context, the subject dealt with, all alike suggest, not any collection of sacred books such as might be found in a later age, but the writings of the prophet Jeremiah, and it would thus be better to render the word " the writings " with a marginal alternative " the letter."

[1] Jer. li. 11.

25

The Testimony of Jesus Christ

"Danielem, qui prophetis non esset adjectus, ne prophetam quidem fuisse aliqui putarunt: . . . prophetam vero eum fuisse confirmat Propheta maximus."[1]—Bengel on Matt. xxiv. 15.

AN orthodox critic, whose writings on the Old Testament are full of interest and expressed with great perspicuity, in a letter to a Church newspaper makes the following weighty remark:

"The way in which our Lord Jesus Christ's heart and teaching were interpenetrated by the Scriptures of the Old Testament is abundantly evident from the Gospels. But the sceptical critics of modern Germany, in their discussion of the Old Testament, completely ignore the opinions of Christ, as they do also the indubitable opinions of the Jews of New Testament times. These German critics deliberately leave out of view a whole mass of vital evidence bearing on the subject, which—sceptics or infidels though they may be—it is most unscientific for writers, professing to be serious historians, to rule out of court and treat as if it had no existence."[2]

The above remark is a most true one and very much to the point. Those who do not believe in the Divinity of Christ have yet no right to ignore His views respecting the Older Scriptures: views put forth by One who had made those Scriptures the subject of His constant study, and in His interpretation of them showed Himself free from all narrow Jewish prejudice; by One, too, allowedly the sublimest moral Teacher the world has ever seen, who in His lofty code of morality ever laid the greatest emphasis on the truth, and when put on trial for His life before a heathen judge uttered those weighty words, "To this end am I come into

[1] In allusion to the place which the Book of Daniel occupies in the present Hebrew Bible.

[2] See the letter of the Rev. Andrew Craig Robinson in the *Church Family Newspaper* for March 24, 1921.

the world, that I should bear witness unto the truth. Every one that is of the truth heareth my voice."[1] Jesus Christ has a right to be heard as a great critic of the Old Testament, a critic of lofty disinterested purpose, and One, who, in the matter now before us, was in one respect more advantageously situated than the critics of these later days, seeing that He lived within two centuries of the date when they suppose the Book of Daniel to have been written.

Now, what is the witness of Christ respecting this Book of Daniel, for it is evident from His position as a teacher, His tastes, and the time at which He lived, that He must know the truth of the matter; whilst from His lofty morality we are sure that He will tell us the truth, the whole truth, and nothing but the truth? How does Christ treat this Book, of which the critics form so low an estimate, regarding it as a religious romance with a pseudonymous title, and its prophetic portion as a Jewish apocalypse, a *vaticinium post eventum?* The answer is that this is the Book which Christ specially delights to honour. To Him its title is no pseudonym, but the name of a real person, "Daniel the prophet"—"the prophet" in the sense of one inspired of God to foretell the future, "what shall come to pass hereafter." Our Saviour in His own great Advent prophecy—Matt. xxiv.—uttered on the eve of His death, quotes this Book of Daniel no less than three times. First, in verse 15, after mentioning Daniel by name, he directs His followers to a special passage in his prophecies, bids them study it intelligently, and assures them that in its fulfilment they will find the signal for their departure from Jerusalem.[2] The passage in question is Dan. ix. 27, where the Septuagint paraphrase reads, "And upon the temple there shall be an abomination of desolations,"[3] while the original runs thus: "And upon the wing of abominations shall come one that maketh desolate." Further, in Dan. xi. 31 and xii. 11, the words occur in the original, "The abomination that maketh desolate," so that Christ, while pointing to the first of these three passages, viz. that in chap. ix. 27, appears at the same time to glance across the prophecies of Daniel as a whole, and, as it were, to put His seal to them as being genuine. Our Saviour's second reference to the Book of Daniel in the prophecy of Matt. xxiv. occurs in verse 21,

[1] John xviii. 37. Jesus declares His sovereignty to be specially exercised in bearing witness to the truth. See Westcott *in loco* in the *Speaker's Commentary*.

[2] Compare Matt. xxiv. 15 with Dan. ix. 23.

[3] The *Codex Syro-Hexaplaris Ambrosianus* has the singular, "abomination."

where He uses language very similar to that found in Dan. xii. 1, in order to describe the unparalleled woes that were to come at the close of the Jewish Age: " Then shall be great tribulation, such as hath not been from the beginning of the world until now." The third reference is in verse 30, where our Lord, describing His Second Coming, uses language borrowed from and pointing back to Dan. vii. 13, " They shall see the Son of Man coming on the clouds of heaven with power and great glory." Again, at a very solemn moment of His life, when put upon His oath by the High Priest as to whether He were the Christ or no, our Lord makes a second reference to this same passage in Daniel,[1] and declares before His judge that He is about to be invested with that divine glory and authority which Daniel saw bestowed on " one like unto a son of man." " I adjure thee," says the High Priest, " by the living God, that thou tell us whether thou be the Christ, the Son of God. Jesus saith unto him, Thou hast said," *i.e.* thou hast said the truth, I am the Son of God; " nevertheless I say unto you," viz. to the whole Sanhedrim, " Henceforth ye shall see the Son of Man;"—ye shall see Me in My human nature—" sitting at the right hand of power, and coming on the clouds of heaven." Our Lord thus plainly indicates Dan. vii. 13 as the passage from which He takes his favourite self-chosen name, " the Son of Man," the definite article prefixed to the title intimating that He is Himself the mysterious Being whom Daniel there describes as " one like unto a son of man." [2] And yet in spite of this solemn repeated assurance on the part of Christ, our modern critics hesitate not to tell us that Dan. vii. 13 refers, not to the incarnate Son of God, but to " a supernatural being," or " a body of such beings," in fact, " to the faithful remnant of Israel, transformed into heavenly or supernatural beings." [3] Further, let it be noted that the passage in Dan. vii. 13, 14, at which we have been looking, not only furnishes our Saviour with His favourite name, but also, as Hengstenberg points out, forms the groundwork of all His declarations concerning His Second Coming. See Matt. x. 23, xvi. 27, 28, xix. 28, xxiv. 30, xxv. 31.[4] In addition to the above it is worthy of notice that our Lord's description of the Resurrection in John v. 28, 29, runs on the lines of Dan. xii. 2; while the next verse, Dan. xii. 3, is paraphrased by Him in Matt. xiii. 43, when describing the future glory in store for the righteous: " Then

[1] Matt. xxvi. 64.

[2] " ὁ υἱὸς τοῦ ἀνθρώπου: videtur articulus respicere prophetiam **Dan. vii. 13**." Bengel on Matt. xvi. 13.

[3] *Century Bible*, Daniel, p. 78.

[4] Hengstenberg, *On the Genuineness of Daniel*, p. 224.

shall the righteous shine forth as the sun in the kingdom of their Father."

Such, then, is the singular honour bestowed by Christ on a Book which the critics reduce to the level of a Jewish apocalypse.

But our Lord's testimony to the Book of Daniel is not confined to the Gospel pages. Let us turn to the last and latest Book of Holy Scripture, entitled, "The Revelation of Jesus Christ, which God gave him to show unto his servants." Such is the lofty description of that wonderful Book from the *heavenly* standpoint. What is there told us is a revelation from the All-wise God, made to us through His Son, Jesus Christ. But when we look at this sacred Book from the *earthly* standpoint, it is plain that in the lower sense of the word it owes much of its inspiration to the Book of Daniel. And, indeed, there is nothing to be wondered at in this, seeing that our Saviour in His prophetic utterances had singled out that Book for such special honour, and that St. John was deeply imbued with the mind of Christ, and had no doubt learned from his Master to love and honour the Book of Daniel. Thus it is clear that this Book appealed, if we may venture so to say, alike to Christ the Revealer and to St. John the receiver of the Revelation.

In the Revelation, then, we catch frequent echoes of the Book of Daniel and note many quotations from it more or less exact. This is best seen by comparing the Greek of Theodotion's version with the Greek of the Revelation. But, indeed, it is so self-evident that the English reader can very well form his own judgment in this matter. The following are some passages of the Old Testament Book which are re-echoed in the Revelation:

(i) The ten days' trial: Dan. i. 12, 15, cf. Rev. ii. 10.

(ii) The things that shall come to pass hereafter: Dan. ii. 29, 45, cf. Rev. i. 19, and iv. 1.

(iii) The sweeping away of the fragments of the colossus of world-power so that "no place was found for them": Dan. ii. 35, cf. Rev. xx. 11.

(iv) The compelling all men to worship the image: Dan. iii. 6, cf. Rev. xiii. 15.

(v) Great Babylon: Dan. iv. 30, cf. Rev. xiv. 8, xvii. 5, xviii. 2, 10, 21.

(vi) "The gods of silver, and gold, of brass, iron, wood, and stone, which see not, nor hear, nor know": Dan. v. 23, cf. Rev. ix. 20.

All the above are taken from the historic portion of the Book of Daniel, and we notice that of the different stories told us in that Book the story of the lions' den is the only one without its echo. But, indeed, this story had already found an echo in the experience of St. Paul, cf. 2 Tim. iv. 17, and had also been directly referred to by the writer of the Epistle to the Hebrews. Cf. Heb. xi. 33, 34.

But it is when we turn from the historic to the prophetic portion of the Book of Daniel that the Revelation supplies us with something more than mere echoes. Two most important points in the visions shown to Daniel are made clear to us in the Revelation; and in either case the interpretation there given is found to be at deadly variance with that put forward by the Higher Critics. In the first place, the Revelation unfolds to us the appearances of Christ in the visions shown to Daniel. The sublime vision of Dan. vii. 13, 14, is interpreted to us in the Revelation in precisely the same way as in our Saviour's teaching on earth at which we have been looking. Thus, we have barely entered on the first chapter before the great subject is brought forward, and we are told with all definiteness Who it is that comes with the clouds of heaven, and is brought near to the Ancient of Days to receive universal and lasting dominion. "Behold," cries St. John, "he cometh with the clouds; and every eye shall see him, and they which pierced him."[1] It is the crucified Jesus who will thus come. His crucifixion, as He told the Jewish High Priest, was to lead the way to the glory with which He would appear invested at His Second Advent. Similarly, in a later vision, St. John sees "one like unto a son of man"—the very expression used in Dan. vii. 13—sitting on a white cloud, and coming to reap the harvest of the earth.[2] Having thus twice identified Him who comes with the clouds as the future Judge of mankind, St. John in the earlier passage goes on to describe His appearance. He was "clothed with a garment down to the foot, and girt about at the breasts with a golden girdle." Also "his head and his hair were white as white wool, white as snow": *i.e.* Christ appeared to His apostle just as the Ancient of Days, the eternal God, appeared to Daniel, that He might thereby signify His oneness and equality with the Father. Then the description is continued as follows: "His eyes were as a flame of fire; and his feet like unto burnished brass, as if it had been refined in a furnace; and his voice as the voice of many waters."[3] These marks enable us to identify the risen and living Redeemer who appeared to St. John with the Person seen by Daniel on the banks of the Hiddekel. "I lifted up mine eyes," writes the seer, "and looked, and behold a man clothed in linen, whose loins were girded with pure gold of Uphaz: his body also was like the beryl, and his face as the appearance of lightning, and his eyes as lamps of fire, and his arms and his feet

[1] Rev. i. 7. [2] *Ibid.* xiv. 14. [3] *Ibid.* i. 13-15.

like in colour to burnished brass, and the voice of his words like the voice of a multitude."[1] This awe-inspiring Being, seen by both prophet and evangelist, thus reveals His own identity in His message to the Church at Thyatira : "These things saith the Son of God, who hath his eyes like a flame of fire, and his feet are like unto burnished brass."[2] The effect of this vision both on seer and evangelist, as well as the conduct and action of Him who thus revealed Himself, was the same in either case. Daniel tells us that when he "saw this great vision, there remained no strength" in him. "My comeliness," he adds, "was turned in me into corruption, and I retained no strength." Thus he lay pale and motionless like a corpse, till Christ touched him, and first set him on his hands and knees, and then helped him to stand upright. All trembling he stood; so that loving words were still required before he was sufficiently recovered to receive the revelation about to be made to him.[3] St. John in like manner tells how he fell at Christ's feet as one dead, till the Saviour's loving, strengthening touch and the same "Fear not" which fell on the ears of Daniel greeted him likewise,[4] and enabled him to receive Christ's message to the Seven Churches. One difference, however, we notice: St. John came to himself sooner than Daniel; and this is just what we might have expected, for St. John had already that personal knowledge of Christ which had not been granted to Daniel. Further, the striking attitude and action of the Divine Being, who appeared to Daniel in his latest vision, was witnessed also by St. John in the Apocalypse. Thus in Dan. xii. 6, "the man clothed in linen," whom we have just identified as Christ, is described as standing "above the waters of the river," and holding up his right hand and his left hand to heaven in the act of swearing a solemn oath "by him that liveth for ever." The posture and action of the "strong angel" in Rev. x. 5, 6, are so similar that we are forced to identify Him with "the man clothed in linen," *i.e.* with Christ. With His right foot upon the sea and His left foot upon the earth, He lifts up his right hand unto heaven, and like Daniel's Visitant swears by Him that liveth for ever and ever. Thus the Old Testament vision and the New Testament apocalypse help to explain one another; and the Book of "the Revelation of Jesus Christ" supplies us with further confirmation, if any were needed, that the "one like unto a son of man" seen by Daniel is He who "came to visit us in great humility," and who will presently return "in His glorious Majesty to judge both the quick and the dead." In His own words, "The

[1] Dan. x. 5, 6.
[2] Rev. ii. 18.
[3] Dan. x. 8–11.
[4] Cf. Dan. x. 12 with Rev. i. 17.

Father gave him authority to execute judgment, because he is the Son of man" (margin, "a son of man"):[1] in which judgment, as the Revelation assures us, only those will escape whose names are found in the book of life; that same book of which it was said to Daniel, "at that time thy people shall be delivered, every one that shall be found written in the book."[2]

The second, and only less important point in the visions of the Book of Daniel, which is cleared up for us in the Revelation, is the identification of Daniel's Fourth Kingdom. The vision related in Rev. xiii., and which is continued down to a later stage in chap. xvii., should be read side by side with the vision of Dan. vii. Out of the sea there rises in St. John's vision, not, indeed, a succession of four wild beasts as seen by Daniel, but only one: thus indicating that three have already risen and passed away, so that this one must be the fourth and last. It is further identified with the fourth wild beast of Daniel by its having ten horns.[3] Daniel had described this fourth beast as "terrible and powerful, and strong exceedingly," but had not likened it to any particular animal. In the Revelation it is described as being an amalgamation of the three wild beasts which precede it in the Book of Daniel. It is like its immediate predecessor the leopard of the third kingdom. Its feet are like those of the bear of the second kingdom, and its mouth is like that of the lion of the first kingdom.[4] As being a heathen kingdom its power, which so impressed Daniel, is derived from Satan. "The dragon," we are told, "gave him his power, and his throne, and great authority." Presently this monster receives a death-stroke in one of its heads, from which to the surprise of all it recovers, and becomes an object of universal admiration and homage.[5] From this time forwards it enters on a second stage of its existence, in which it very closely resembles the "little horn," which sprang up on the head of Daniel's fourth beast;[6] for it has "a mouth speaking great things" and uttering "blasphemies against God"; also it is permitted "to make war with the saints and to overcome them."[7] In these two respects it exactly answers to the "little horn" of Dan. vii. But the second vision, viz. that in Rev. xvii., throws a yet stronger light on Daniel's vision; for the beast of Rev. xiii. 1 is now seen carrying a woman styled "the great harlot."[8] A "harlot" is the description of a Christian Church unfaithful to its Lord and

[1] John v. 27.
[2] Cf. Rev. xx. 15 with Dan. xii. 1.
[3] Cf. Rev. xiii. 1 with Dan. vii. 7.
[4] Rev. xiii. 2.
[5] Rev. xiii. 3, 4.
[6] Dan. vii. 8
[7] Cf. Rev. xiii. 5–7 with Dan. vii. 8, 11, 21, 25.
[8] Rev. xvii. 1.

Master, Christ; the adjunct "great" indicates that this Church is one of considerable importance. Whilst the fact of the woman being mounted on the ten-horned beast, *i.e.* the fourth kingdom of Daniel, shows that this Church has attained great temporal power—to wit, the power of the Fourth Kingdom. The seat of this power is thus described by the interpreting angel: "The seven heads are seven mountains on which the woman sitteth," [1] *i.e.* the seat of this strange power is the City of the Seven Hills. As Wordsworth points out in his Commentary on the passage, "In St. John's time Rome was usually called 'the Seven-hilled City.'" "There is scarcely a Roman poet of any note," he adds, "who has not spoken of Rome as a city seated on Seven Mountains —Virgil, Horace, Tibullus, Propertius, Ovid, Silius, Italicus, Statius, Martial, Claudian, Prudentius: in short, the unanimous voice of Roman poetry, during more than five hundred years, beginning with the age of St. John, proclaimed Rome as 'the Seven-hilled City.'" [2] Rome, then, is the seat of the faithless Church which was to wield the power of the Fourth Kingdom, as is further witnessed by the angel's closing words, "The woman whom thou sawest is the great city, which reigneth over the kings of the earth." [3] But if this be so, then the ten-horned beast, which carried the woman, and which we have seen to be identical with Daniel's fourth beast, must be the Roman power, which, wounded to death as a heathen empire, was destined to be resuscitated under the Papacy. Yet the critics will have it that the fourth beast in Dan. vii. is the Greek kingdom of Alexander and his successors!

On these two points, then, "the Revelation of Jesus Christ" —*i.e.* as explained in the opening verse, the revelation which God makes to His Church through Jesus Christ—is perfectly clear and distinct-

(i) Christ Himself is the mysterious Being seen by Daniel as coming "with the clouds of heaven."

(ii) Daniel's Fourth Kingdom is the Roman power: first in its earlier stage as a consular and imperial power, and then in its later stage, when as the "little horn" it depicts the Papacy. Yet in both these points the critics hold entirely different views: *i.e.* they are wiser than Christ: Christ the Teacher of the Gospel pages, Christ the Revealer of the Revelation! Now *that* Higher Criticism, which, consciously or unconsciously, claims to be higher than Christ, comes to us really from beneath. It is the dragon who gives it "his power and his throne and great authority."

[1] Rev. xvii. 9.

[2] *Wordsworth's Greek Testament*, on Rev. xvii. 1. The writer gives quotations from all the Roman poets enumerated.

[3] Rev. xvii. 18.

Additional Note

SINCE this work was sent to the press the recently discovered "Chronicle of Nabopolassar" has at last made us acquainted with the date of the fall of Nineveh as well as with the ebb and flow of war during those eventful years which witnessed the collapse of the Assyrian Empire and the rise of the New Empire of Babylon. It has also shed an entirely new light on the policy of Egypt during that period. Egypt, instead of pursuing the game of grab and endeavouring to secure for herself as large a portion as possible of the falling empire, is seen bolstering up Assyria as a bulwark against the irruptions of the Scythians. The record is so closely connected with the rise of the New Babylonian Empire that it is desirable to add a short resumé of its contents.

The "Chronicle" embraces the years 616 to 610 B.C. It was drawn up probably at Babylon, as witnessed by the scribal note at its close: "Whoso loveth Nebo and Merodach let him preserve this and not suffer it to leave his hands." The style of the cuneiform writing points to the Achæmenid period as the time of its composition. Throughout the record Nabopolassar is styled "the king of Akkad," but Babylon is seen to be his base of operations. The revolt of this monarch began probably with his seizure of Sippar—see p. 99 above—an event, which as shown by Mr. C. J. Gadd [1] the discoverer of the tablet, must have taken place during the interval 620 to 617 B.C. In the early part of 616 Nabopolassar is seen conducting a campaign against the Aramean tribes on the Middle Euphrates. He then returns to Babylon, followed by the united forces of Egypt and Assyria. In the autumn he defeats an Assyrian force on the east of the Tigris so that they have to fall back on the Lower Zab. In the following year he attacks Ashur the old capital of Assyria, situated on the Tigris some sixty miles below Nineveh, but is unable to take it, and is compelled to fall back on the stronghold of Takritain, the modern Tekrit, lower down that river. In the autumn the

[1] See *The Fall of Nineveh,* by C. J. Gadd, M.A., published by the British Museum, June, 1923.

Medes descend on the Assyrian province of Araphu east of the Tigris and south of the Lower Zab.

In 614 the Medes under Cyaxares attack Nineveh. They are unable to take it, but make themselves masters of Tabriz a few miles N.W. of the capital. They then march down the Tigris and capture Ashur. Here they are met by Nabopolassar, who concludes an alliance with Cyaxares; after which both parties return home.

In the following year the province of Sukhu on the Middle Euphrates revolts. Nabopolassar marches thither, and captures two towns built on islands in that river, but retires to his own land on the approach of the Assyrian king.

The record for 612 is much obliterated, but it is clear that Nabopolassar meets the king of the Scythians—who according to the accounts left us by the classical writers had hitherto acted on the side of the Assyrians—also that Cyaxares joins them, and that then all three armies, Babylonians, Scythians, and Medes, march up the Tigris and lay siege to Nineveh. The siege lasts from the month of Sivan (May–June) to the month of Ab (July–August), and three battles are fought during the course of it. Finally the city is taken by " a mighty assault " and with a great slaughter of the principal men [1]; after which we catch the name of Sin-shar-ishkun the Assyrian king, and are told of " the spoil of the city, a quantity beyond counting," [2] and also of how great Nineveh in her turn met with the fate she had so often meted out to others, and was turned from a fenced city into a ruinous heap. According to the " Chronicle " Nabopolassar was present at the siege of Nineveh, and when it was over marched westward to Nisibis, and then retracing his steps returned home by way of Nineveh. Whatever truth there may be in this statement we are sure from his own inscriptions that the Babylonian king can only have played a very subordinate part, for he speaks merely of his operations in Mesopotamia, and of how he thrust back the Assyrians from the land of Akkad.

Although Nineveh was taken, the Assyrians attempted to set up a New Assyria in the West by placing Assur-uballidh on the throne in Haran. Accordingly in the following year, 611, Nabopolassar marched up the Euphrates into the new Assyrian Kingdom, but did not venture to attack Haran.

In 610 we read of marches and counter marches of the Babylonian king in the New Assyria. Then in Marchesvan (Oct.–Nov.) the Scythians come to his help, and an attack is made on Haran.

[1] Nahum iii. 18

[2] *Ibid.* ii. 9.

Assur-uballidh is compelled to evacuate the city and to fly westward across the Euphrates; Haran is captured and with it an immense spoil. The curious extract from the Stele of Nabonidus, referred to on p. 19, footnote 2, is now found to refer, not to the Medes, but to the Scythians, and to describe the devastations committed by them, not at the time of the fall of Nineveh, but just after this capture of Haran.

In 609 Assur-uballidh the Assyrian king, along with a strong Egyptian force, recrosses the Euphrates, and attacks the Scythian and Babylonian garrison left in Haran. The siege lasts for two months, but is raised on the arrival of Nabopolassar, who appears to have defeated the Egyptians and Assyrians.

The catch-line at the close of the tablet tells us that operations were resumed by Nabopolassar in the following year, 608 B.C.; and if we could get hold of the next tablet of the series, the record for this year would no doubt tell us something about the expedition of Pharaoh-Necho against Carchemish, in endeavouring to oppose which the godly king Josiah met with his death. The title "King of Assyria" in 2 Kings xxiii. 29, is given not to Assur-uballidh, who had been driven out of Haran and was unable to retake it, but to the Babylonian monarch, Nabopolassar.[1] Now that Nineveh had fallen, Babylon was looked upon as having taken her place, seeing that the Babylonians were masters of the richest and most fertile part of the old Assyrian empire. Similarly in Ezra vi. 22, the Persian king Darius Hystaspes is styled "King of Assyria"; whilst in Herodotus, bk. i. 206, Tomyris queen of the Massagetæ addresses Cyrus as "King of the Medes."

[1] Cf. Josephus, *Antiquities*, x. 5. 1: "Now Necho king of Egypt raised an army, and marched to the river Euphrates in order to fight with the Medes and Babylonians who had overthrown the dominion of the Assyrians."

AUTHORITIES CITED

ABYDENUS. On the Assyrians. *See* Eusebius' Præparatio.
ALFORD, HENRY. Homilies on Acts I.–X. London, 1858.
ALTORIENTALISCHE FORSCHUNGEN. *See* Winckler.
ANDREWS, F. T. Apocalyptic Literature: in Peake's Commentary. London, 1919.
ANNALISTIC TABLET. *See* Records of the Past.
ARISTOTLE. The Problems.
Babylonian and Oriental Record. London. Sept., 1896.
Babylonian Expedition of the University of Pennsylvania. C. L. Fisher. Philadelphia. 1905, etc.
BAER and DELITZSCH's edition of Daniel.
BALL, C. J. *See* Records of the Past.
Behistûn Inscription of Darius the Great. Pub. by British Museum, 1907.
BEHRMANN, GEORGE. Das Buch Daniel. Göttingen, 1894.
Beitrage zur Assyriologie. 1889. Delitzsch and Haupt.
BENGEL. Gnomon Novi Testamenti. Now N.T. Word Studies Kregel 1971.
BERGK, THEODOR. Poetæ Lyrici Græci. Leipzig. 1866–7.
BEROSUS. *See* Josephus.
BEVAN, A. A. Short Commentary on the Book of Daniel. Cambridge, 1892.
BEVAN, E. R. House of Seleucus. London, 1902.
Biblical World. Chicago and New York. June, 1909.
BIRKS, T. R. The First Two Visions of Daniel. London, 1844.
BOOTH, A. J. Discovery and Decipherment of the Trilingual Cuneiform Inscriptions. London, 1902.
BOTTA, P. E. Monuments de Ninive. Paris, 1849.
BROWN, FRANCIS. Hebrew and English Lexicon. Oxford, 1906.
BUHL, FRANTS. Canon and Text of the Old Testament, trans. by Macpherson. Edinburgh, 1892.
BURKITT, F. C. Jewish and Christian Apocalypses, being the Schweich Lecture for 1913. Oxford, 1914.
CHARLES, R. H. Century Bible, Daniel.
—— Book of Enoch. Oxford, 1912.
—— The Apocrypha and Pseudepigrapha of the Old Testament. 1913.
CICERO. De Naturâ Deorum.
CLAY, ALBERT T. Babylonian Texts: Yale Oriental Series. New Haven, Connecticut, 1915.
Codex Alexandrinus.
Codex Syro-Hexaplaris Ambrosianus.
COHU, J. R. The Bible and Modern Thought. London, 1920.
COOK, STANLEY A. Glossary of the Aramaic Inscriptions. Cambridge, 1898.
COOKE, G. A. North Semitic Inscriptions. 1903.
CORNILL, C. Introduction to the Canonical Books of the Old Testament. London and New York, 1907.

Corpus Inscriptionum Semiticarum. Paris, 1881.
CORY, I. P. Ancient Fragments: enlarged by E. R. Hodges. London, 1876.
Ctesias, Persica of. *See* Gilmore.
Cuneiform Texts from Babylonian Tablets, etc. Pub. by the British Museum. London, 1896 f.
CYPRIAN. De Paschâ Computus: included in Sancti Cæcilii Cypriani Opera per Joannem Cestrensem (Fell). Oxford, 1682.
DAVIDSON, SAMUEL. Article on Apocalyptic Literature in Enc. Brit., 9th edn. Edinburgh, 1875.
DELATTRE, A. J. Revue des Questions Historiques. 1866 f.
DELITZSCH, FRIEDRICH. Assyrische Lesestücke. 1912.
Die Keilinschriften und das Alte Testament. *See* Schrader.
DINON. Persica.
DIODORUS SICULUS. Bibliotheca, edited by Dindorf. Paris, 1878.
DRIVER, S. R. Cambridge Bible, Daniel.
—— Century Bible, Habakkuk.
Egypt Exploration Fund. Naukratis, Part I., 1884–5. London, 1886.
Encyclopædia Britannica, 9th edn. Edinburgh, 1875–88.
Enoch, Book of. *See* Charles.
ETHERIDGE, J. W. The Targums of Onkelos and Jonathan Ben Uzziel on the Pentateuch. London, 1862.
EUSEBIUS. Chronicon.
—— Ecclesiastical History.
—— Præparatio Evangelica.
Expositor, The. June, 1908.
Expository Times, The. April, 1915.
GELLIUS, AULUS. Noctes Atticæ, edited by Gronovius. Leipzig, 1762.
GILMORE, JOHN. The Persica of Ctesias. London, 1888.
GOODSPEED, G. S. History of Babylonia and Assyria. London, 1903.
Guardian Newspaper. Nov. 6, 1907.
GUTSCHMID, A. VON.
HALL, H. R. Ancient History of the Near East. London, 1918.
HALL, JOSEPH. Contemplations of the Historical Passages of the Old and New Testaments, edited by Charles Wordsworth.
HENGSTENBERG, E. W. On the Genuineness of Daniel, trans. by Ryland. Edinburgh, 1848.
HERODOTUS. History.
HERZOG, J. J. Encyclopædia of Religious Knowledge. New York, 1891.
HOGARTH, D. G. Ancient East. London and New York, 1914.
HOMMEL, FRITZ. Ancient Hebrew Tradition, trans. by McClure and Crosslé. London, 1897.
HORTON, F. R. Century Bible, Amos.
JASTROW, A. Dictionary of the Targummin. London and New York, 1886–1903.
JASTROW, MORRIS. The Religion of Babylonia and Assyria. Boston, Massachusetts, 1898.
JENSEN, P. Die Kosmologie der Babylonier. Strassburg, 1890.
Jerome, The Works of, edited by Migne. Paris, 1877.
Josephus Flavius, Works of, trans. by Whiston. Kregel Publications 1960.
Journal of Hellenic Studies. London, June, 1917.
Journal of Theological Studies. London, July, 1913; October, 1915.
JUSTI, F. Handbuch der Zendsprachen. Leipzig, 1864.
JUVENAL. Satires.

Keilinschriftliche Bibliothek. *See* Schrader.

KENNEDY, JOHN. The Book of Daniel from a Christian Standpoint. London and New York, 1898.

KENNEDY, J. H. The Fourth Book of Hippolytus' Commentary on Daniel. Dublin, 1888.

KING, LEONARD W. A History of Babylon. London, 1919.

KOLDEWEY, ROBERT. Excavations at Babylon, trans. by Agnes Johns. London, 1914.

KRAELING, E. G. H. Aram and Israel. New York, 1918.

LANGDON, STEPHEN. Building Inscriptions of the New Babylonian Empire. Paris. 1905.

—— Neubabylonischen Königsinschriften. Leipzig, 1907.

—— Sumerian Grammar. Paris, 1911.

LAYARD, A. H. Nineveh and Babylon. London, 1853.

LEWIN, T. The Life and Epistles of St. Paul. London, 1875.

—— Fasti Sacri. London, 1865.

LIDDELL and SCOTT. Greek Lexicon, 8th edn. 1901.

LIVY. Annals.

LOFTUS, W. K. Chaldea and Susiana. London, 1857.

LUCRETIUS. On the Nature of Things.

MARTI, D. K. Daniel. Tubingen and Leipzig, 1901.

MASON and BERNARD. Hebrew Grammar. Cambridge, 1853.

MASPERO, G. The Passing of the Empires, trans. by McClure. London, 1900.

MEGASTHENES. *See* Abydenus.

MENANT, M. J. Un Cameo du Musée de Florence: in Revue Archéologique. Paris, 1885.

MYRES, J. L. Dawn of History. London and New York.

OESTERLEY, W. O. E. The Books of the Apocrypha, their Origin, Teaching, and Contents. London, 1915.

OLMSTEAD, A. T. Western Asia in the days of Sargon of Assyria. New York, 1908.

Onkelos, Targum of. *See* Etheridge.

Palestinian Targum. *See* Etheridge.

PEISER, F. E. Babylonische Verträge des Berliner Museums, 1890.

PETERS, J. P. Nippur. New York, 1897.

PETRIE, W. M. FLINDERS. Ten Years' Digging in Egypt. 2nd edn. London, 1893.

PINCHES, T. G. The Old Testament in the Light of the Historical Records of Assyria and Babylonia. London and New York, 1902.

PLINY. Natural History.

POGNON, H. L'inscription en caractéres cursifs de l'Ouady Brissa. Paris, 1891.

POLYBIUS. History.

POLYHISTOR, ALEXANDER. *See* Cory.

PUSEY, E. B. Lectures on Daniel the Prophet. Oxford and London, 1869.

RADAU, HUGO. Hymns and Prayers to the god Ninib, vol. 29, part 1, of Series A of The Babylonian Expedition of the University of Pennsylvania.

RAMSAY, W. H. St. Paul the Traveller. London, 1905.

RAWLINSON, H. The Cuneiform Inscriptions of Western Asia. London, 1861 f.

Records of the Past. New Series. London, 1888–92.

Revue Archéologique. Paris, 1885.

ROBINSON, A. CRAIG. The Fall of Babylon, a paper read before the Victoria Institute, Dec. 9, 1913.

—— What about the Old Testament, etc.? London, 1910.

—— Letter to the Church Family Newspaper, March 24, 1921.

SACHAU, E. Drei Aramaische Papyrus Urkunden aus Elephantiné. Berlin, 1908.

SANDA, ALBERT. Die Aramäer. Leipzig, 1902.

SAYCE, A. H. The Higher Criticism and the Monuments. London, 1894.

SCHEFTELOWITZ, ISIDOR. Arisches im Alten Testament. Berlin, 1903.

SCHRADER, EBERHARD. Die Keilinschriften und das Alte Testament. Berlin, 1902–3.

—— Keilinschriftliche Bibliothek. Berlin, 1889–1900.

SCHÜRER, E. A History of the Jewish People in the Time of Jesus Christ. Edinburgh, 1890–1.

Septuagint. *See* Swete.

Sibylline Books.

Similitudes, The. *See* Book of Enoch, under Charles.

SMITH, GEORGE. Assyrian Discoveries. London, 1875.

Speaker's Commentary. London: vol. iv. 1873; vol. viii. 1880.

STAINER, JOHN. The Music of the Bible. New edn. with supplementary notes by Galpin. London, 1914.

STIER, RUDOLF. The Words of the Lord Jesus, trans. by Pope. Edinburgh, 1870.

Story of the Nations: Media. *See* Ragozin.

STRABO. Geography.

STRASSMAIER, J. N. Die Inschriften von Nabuchodonosor, Nabonidus, Cyrus, Cambyses, und Darius. Leipzig, 1889–97.

SWETE, H. B. The Old Testament in Greek, vol. iii., containing both the Septuagint and Theodotion's version of Daniel. Cambridge, 1905.

TAYLOR, ISAAC. The Alphabet. London, 1893.

Theodotion. *See* Swete.

THOMSON, J. E. N. The Samaritans, being the Alexander Robertson Lectures for 1916, delivered before the University of Glasgow. Edinburgh and London, 1919.

THUREAU-DANGIN, FRANCOIS. Une Relation de la huitème Campagne de Sargon. Paris, 1912.

TOLMAN, H. C. Ancient Persian Lexicon. New York, 1908.

—— Guide to the Old Persian Inscriptions. New York, 1892.

Transactions of the Society of Biblical Archæology, vol. vii. part 1. London, 1882.

TRISTRAM, H. B. The Land of Israel. London, 1866.

Vorderasiatische Bibliothek, 4: Die Neubabylonischen Königsinschriften. 1907 f. *See* Langdon.

WEISSBACH, F. H. Die Inschriften des Nebukadnezzars im Wadi Brissa, in Wissenschaftliche Veroffentlichungen der Deutschen Orient Gesellschaft, Heft 5. Leipzig, 1906.

WESTCOTT, B. F. St. John's Gospel, in The Speaker's Commentary. London, 1880.

WICKES, W. A Treatise on the Accentuation of the Twenty-one so-called Prose Books of the Old Testament. Oxford, 1887.

WIESELER, KARL. Chronologica Synopsis, in Bohn's Theological Library, 2nd edn. London, 1877.

WILLIAMSON, G. C. The Money of the Bible. London, 1894.

Wilson, R. D., The Aramaic of Daniel, in Biblical and Theological Studies by the Members of the Faculty of Princeton Theological Seminary. New York, 1912.

—— Studies in the Book of Daniel. New York and London, 1917.

Winckler, Hugo. Geschichte und Geographie, in Schrader's Die Keilinschriften und das Alte Testament.

Wordsworth, Christopher. Greek Testament. London, 1870.

Wright, C. H. H. Daniel and his Prophecies. London, 1906.

Wright, William. Comparative Grammar of the Semitic Languages. 1890.

Xenophon. Anabasis.

—— Cyropædia.

Yale Oriental Series, Babylonian Texts. New Haven, 1915.

Zimmern, Heinrich. Religion und Sprache, in Schrader's Die Keilinschriften und das Alte Testament.

ADDENDUM

Note at the end of Chapter XI—"Belshazzar the king": Dan. v. 1. p. 120.

In a Babylonian poem of the age of Cyrus, written in the cuneiform script, which has been discovered and read by Mr. Sidney Smith of the British Museum, and published by him in his *Babylonian Historical Texts*, pp. 83–91 (Methuen & Co., 1924), will be found a very striking confirmation of the kingship of Belshazzar. The poem in question is a remarkable, and by no means friendly account of the doings of Nabonidus, the last king of Babylon and father of Belshazzar. Nabonidus in his 3rd year, 553 B.C., made an expedition against Tema in Arabia, the modern Teima, with the intention apparently of making it a second capital of the empire. Before his departure he associated his son with him on the throne. This act is thus described in the poem: [1]

"He entrusted a camp to his eldest, firstborn son,
The troops throughout the land he placed under his command
(lit. "he caused to go along with him").
He freed his hand: he entrusted the kingship to him.
Then he himself on a distant campaign set out.
The forces of Akkad [2] advanced along with him;
Towards the town of Tema in Amurru [3] he set his face.
He set out on a distant campaign, a road not within reach of old."

After the capture of Tema, Nabonidus remained there for at least eight, possibly for thirteen, years, as witnessed by the yearly entry in the legible part of the Nabonidus-Cyrus Chronicle: "the king was in Tema: the king's son, the nobles, and his troops were in Akkad." During these years Belshazzar was reigning as king in Babylon. Hence the references to the years of his reign in Dan. vii. 1 and viii. 1.

[1] I have somewhat altered Mr. Smith's translation, especially in the second line.

[2] Babylonia.

[3] The Amorite land, the West.

GENERAL INDEX

A

Abednego, 267
Abydenus, 65, 105
Agum-kakrimi, 227
Ahasuerus, the Median, 154–155, 274
Ahuramazda, 34
Ai-ibur-shabû, 72, 218
Akhlami, the, 227
Akitu festival, 127
Akkad, or Northern Babylonia, 90, 109, 115, 120, 127, 163, 164
Alcæus, 253
Alexander the Great, 29, 30, 31, 33, 91, 226, 246
Alford, 197
Alman or Arman, 227
alphabets, Semitic and Greek, 157
Amanus, 109, 229
Amasis, 71
Amran, mound of, 76
Amytis, 152, 156
Andrews, 271
Annalistic Tablet, 117, 120 ; account of capture of Babylon by Cyrus, 126–130, 133, 144, 152
Annals of Nebuchadnezzar, 69
Antioch, 220
Antiochus Epiphanes, 2, 3, 5, 6, 13, 14, 15, 48, 169, 170, 174, 176, 177, 222, 235
Anu, the god of silver, 34, 95
Anunit, 100, 101, 114, 115
appa danna, 75
Arakhtu, 83
Aramaic inscriptions, 228–229
Aramaic of Elephantiné, 235–237
Arameans, The, 227–228, 242–243
Ararat, Minni, and Ashkenaz, 18, 22–23
Arioch, 267
Aristobulus II., 64
Aristotle, 18, 254
Artaxerxes, meaning of name, 154
Artaxerxes I., 27, 166, 177, 188–189, 206, 230, 260, 261
Artaxerxes Mnemon, 265
Ashpenaz, 266
Ashur, the Enlil in Assyria, 95
Ashurbanipal, 113, 118, 135, 139, 151, 216
Ashur-nadin-shumu, 151
Ashur-rish-ishi, 227
Assyro-Babylonian words, 265–267
Astyages, 109, 143, 144, 145, 152, 153, 156
Atad, 147

B

Babil, mound of, 76
Babylon, the golden kingdom, 25–26 ; "the beauty of the Chaldeans' pride," 36–38 ; Merodach its patron god, 45 ; its great buildings, 66–77, 81–82 ; the centre of empire, 79–80 ; commercial centre, 138, 141 ; beloved of Nebuchadnezzar, 97 ; captured by Cyrus, 122-132 ; citadel taken on 11th of Marchesvan, 127, 131 ; Seleucia takes its place, 220
Baer, 119
Bagoas, 161, 231
Ball, 92, 101, 129
Barnabas, Epistle of, 22
Behistûn Inscription, 91, 116, 162, 258, 259, 260, 262, 263
Behrmann, 261
Bel and the Dragon, 26
Belesys, *see* Nabopolassar
Belshazzar, meaning of name, 114 ; eldest son of Nabonidus, 115 ; his age and upbringing, 114–115 ; early brought into contact with Nebuchad-

nezzar, 115; his "son" only in legal sense, 117; commander of the army for last ten years of his father's reign, 109; probably sub-king of Babylon, 118; business transactions, 141; slain in attack on palace, 125, 126, 127, 129
Belteshazzar, 266
Beltis, 72, 90, 127
Bengel, 286, 288
Bergk, 253
Berosus, 37, 38, 67, 74, 75, 115
Besherrah, 87
Bevan, A. A., 264
Bevan, E. R., 220
Birks, 33
Bishop Hall, 49
Bit, in names of places, 243
Black Obelisk, 263
Booth, 259
Borsippa, 26, 37, 70, 81, 82, 84, 97
Botta, 248
Brown, Francis, Heb. Lex., 30, 187, 284
Buhl, 279, 281
Burkitt, 270
Burnouf, 259

C

Calendar of Gezer, 166
Cambyses, according to Ctesias a Mede on his mother's side, 152; after the burial of "the son of the king" enters the temple of "Nebo who bestows the sceptre," 127, 147; "king of Babylon" on the contract tablets for first ten months in first year of Cyrus, 148; associated with Cyrus in the royal power, 164–165; conquers Egypt, 229; spares the temple at Elephantiné, 161, 233; his character, 160–161
Cameo of Nebuchadnezzar, 250–253
Carchemish, 85, 296
Carians, The, 29, 252
Chaldeans, The, 11, 35–44, 45; their mythology, 47–49; rise to power, 85; 107, 110, 120; fond of wine, 133, 140, 214, 215, 227
Charles, 3, 6, 50, 51, 54, 63, 64, 66, 164, 203, 269
Cicero, 34
"Cilician Road," The, 247
Codex Alexandrinus, 20
Codex Chisianus. *See* Swete's Old Testament in Greek, vol. iii. 171
Codex Syro-Hexaplaris Ambrosianus, 287
Cohu, 271
Contract tablets, 130-131, 141, 146 148-151
Cook, Stanley A., 167, 229
Cooke, G. A., 232
Cornill, 272
Cory, 37, 67, 214
Country of the Sea, 36, 41–42
Crœsus, 28
Ctesias, 152
Cyaxares I., 26, 37, 155
Cyaxares II., 143
Cylinder of Cyrus, its author acquainted with Book of Isaiah, 110-111, 121, 164–165; account of the capture of Babylon, 128–130, 215
Cyprian, 159
Cyrus, king of Anshan, 19, 111; of Persia, 126; approved of Merodach, 110–111, 128; takes Babylon by stratagem, 122–125; peaceful entry, 127–128; appoints Gobryas as governor, 127; makes his son Cambyses king of Babylon, 118, 146–149

D

d, *dh*, and *z* sounds, 237–239
Dadda-idri, 238
Damascus, 227
Daniel, a true patriot, 181; his early fame, 53; remarkable feature in his prophecies, 179; fond of Book of Isaiah, 111; his delicacy of feeling, 91; stern address to Belshazzar, 139; confession of sin, 180–181; his Aramaic resembles that of Elephantiné, 235–237; he was probably conversant with Old Persian, 242; his Book written near the close of his life, 245; and in the East, 240, 242; his tomb at Shushan, 223–224
Darius, meaning of name, 154
Darius Hystaspes, 28, 116, 152, 155, 154, 216, 262
Darius Nothus, 230, 232, 234, 235, 236
Darius the Mede, a dependent sovereign, 142–143; known by another name among the Greeks, 153;

possibly Gobryas, more probably Cambyses, 144–146; the story of Dan. vi. shows him a youth, 160; *threescore and two*, Dan. v. 31, a corrupt reading for *twelve*, 156–159; only his first year mentioned, 150
Date of Book of Daniel according to the critics, 2, 4, 226, 240, 241, 246
Davidson, 270, 271
Decree of Artaxerxes I., 188
Deioces, 26
Delattre, 43–44
Delitzsch, 266, 267
dhur rabh, 46
Dinon, 260
Diodorus Siculus, 39
Dodekarchy, the, 29, 252
Driver, 2, 3, 11, 19; Dan. vii. 13–14, his explanation of, 58–59, 61, 66, 90, 175; his dictum on the language of Daniel, 226, 240, 241, 246, 264, 268, 284
Duperron, 259
Dura, 267

E

Ea, the god of brass and also the sea-god, 34
E-barra, the Shamash-temple at Larsa, buried in the sand, 48
Ecbatana, 152
Egypt, invaded by Nebuchadnezzar, 71; conquered by Cambyses, 229; 227, 233, 242, 249, 250, 252, 253, 278
E-kharsag-gal-kurkurra, 45, 47
Elam, 22, 213–216, 227
Elephantiné, discoveries at, 161, 229–231, 177, 190
Elymais, 3
emphatic accentuation, 185–186
Encyclopædia Britannica, 33, 270
Enlil, the god of Nippur, 34, 45; his titles, 45, 47; as god of war attains the supremacy, 94; dwells in the Great Mountain, and becomes identified with it, 45; his supremacy and titles transferred to Merodach, 45, 94–95; in Assyria Ashur is the Enlil, 95; in Babylonia, Merodach generally, 45–47; sometimes Merodach and Shamash, 99–100; or even, under Nabonidus, Sin, 100–101
Enoch, Book of, 50–52, 55–57, 61, 63–64, 268, 269, 271
enuma and *enumishu*, 69, 81, 82
Ephraem Syrus, 22, 57
Epistle of Barnabas, 22
Erech, 42, 71, 119
E-sag-ila, the temple of Merodach at Babylon, 25, 39, 70, 73, 75, 76, 132, 133–134
Esarhaddon, 47, 151
Esperanto, 258
E-temen-an-ki, the temple-tower of Babylon, 43, 68, 70, 76, 79, 84
Ethbaal, 87
Etheridge, 7
Ethiopia, 229
Euergetes II., 278
Euphrates, 68, 76, 82, 219–221, 227, 228
Eusebius, 65, 105, 106, 278, 280
Evilmerodach, 66, 141
Ewald, 176–177
E-zida, the temple of Nebo at Borsippa, 70, 75
Ezra, 188–189
Ezra Legend, the, 277

F

Fate-tablets, the, 138–139
Florence Museum, 251
forced parallelism, a, 15
Four Kingdoms, the, 1, 4, 8, 13–22

G

Gabriel, 181, 183, 189, 190, 222, 225
Gellius, Aulus, 41
Gobryas, 11, 124, 125, 127, 129, 130, 132, 143, 144, 145
Goiim, 129
Goodspeed, 219
Gula, 81, 86
Gutium, 127, 129, 132, 134, 145
Gutschmid, 65

H

Hagiographa, 277, 278, 279, 280, 281, 282
Hague Museum, 251
Hall, Bishop, 49

Hall, H. R., 249
Hanging Gardens, 49, 66–68, 75–77
Haran, 87, 100, 107, 108, 109, 113, 114, 227
Hengstenberg, 53, 67, 288
Herodotus, 25, 26, 27, 28, 29, 30; visits Babylon, 38–39, 107, 117; account of capture of Babylon, 122–123, 154, 242, 252, 263
Herzog, 207
Hiddekel, 213, 219, 224, 290
Hippolytus, 22
Hogarth, 247, 248
Hommel, 227
Horton, 18
Hyrcanus, John, 63

I

Iconium, 252
Imgur-Bel, 72, 74
India House Inscription, 25–26, 49, 63, 70, 73, 74, 95–96, 97, 101, 121, 147
Inscriptions of Nebuchadnezzar, Extracts from, 69–70, 71, 73, 74, 75, 79, 81, 82–83, 84, 85, 86, 87, 96, 97, 100, 101, 102, 221
Inscriptions of Nabopolassar, Extracts from, 90, 99
Ionians, the, 29, 30, 247
Ishtar, 108, 109, 115
Ishtar Gate, 76, 81
Istuvegu (Astyages), 145, 152

J

Jason, 173
Jastrow, A., 20
Jastrow, M., 45, 46, 47, 95, 96
Jehoiachin, 83
Jensen, 34, 46
Jerome, 168, 259, 278; his canon of the O.T., 281–282
Jesus the son of Sirach, the younger, 278, 282
Josephus, 19; his view with respect to the Four Kingdoms, 21, 24; 37, 38, 67, 74, 75, 87, 107, 115, 120, 161; on the Zealots, 200–204; 207, 250; on the Canon of the O.T., 279-280
Juvenal, 35

K

Kaldu, the, 36
Kasdim (Chaldeans), 35
Kasr, the, 68, 75, 76
Kennedy, James, 253, 254
keseph, kaspu, 26
Kethubhim, 276, 277
Khammurabi, 45, 94
Khnub, the Nile-god, 161, 231, 232, 236
King, L. W., 249
Kir, 227
Koldewey, 19, 24, 43, 67, 68, 72, 73, 74, 76, 108
Kraeling, 229, 256

L

Labashi-Marduk, 108, 115, 141
Langdon, 47, 48, 63, 68, 70, 81, 84, 95, 97, 100, 101
Larsa (Ellasar), 48, 71, 109
Lassen, 259
Layard, 25, 28, 248
Lebanon, conquest of, 82–83; cedar grove, 87–88
Lewin, 203, 252
Libil-khigalla, 69, 73, 217
Liddell and Scott, 31, 262
Livy, 32
Loftus, 242
Lucretius, 31

M

Maccabees, the, 3, 5, 22, 91, 157, 178, 192, 274
Madaktu, 216
Mandaitic, 239–240
Marathon, 29
Marti, 261
Mason and Bernard, 137
Maspero, 248, 252, 265
Massoretes, the, 185, 186, 190
Medes, the, 152–153, 215, 243, 285
Media, one with Persia, 15; not "inferior to" Babylon, 18–19
Median Ahasuerus, the, 154–155
"Median Wall," the, 19
Megasthenes, 65, 66, 91, 105, 110, 112
Melito, his Canon of the O.T., 280; 283
Melkarth, 87

Melzar (R.V. "the steward"), 267
Menant, 250–252
Menelaus, 173
Merodach, head of the pantheon in the days of Nebuchadnezzar, 93, 96, 97; takes the place of Enlil, 45, 94–95; and thus becomes the god of gold, 34; "the king of the gods, the lord of lords," 52; bestower of sovereignty, 96, 97
Merodachbaladan, 36
Meshach, 266–267
Messiah, used as a proper name, 191–192
Migdol, 229
Minni, 23
Moabite Stone, 136, 166, 233
Monotheistic Tablet, 34, 98
Morgan, M. de, 215
Mushezib-Marduk, 38
Mutsatsir, temple at, 248, 249
Myres, 213

N

NABATÆAN Inscriptions, 237, 238
Nabonidus, son of the priest of Sin in Haran, 100, 107; autobiography of his father, 113; elected to the throne, 108; his archæological tastes, 108; rebuilds the temple in Haran, 108; lives in retirement for the last ten years of his reign, 109; angers the Babylonian priesthood, 110; taken prisoner in Babylon, 110, 127
Nabopolassar, a Chaldean, and founder of the New Empire, 37, 39, 49; of humble origin, 90–91; religiously disposed, 39, 84; drives out the Assyrians, 90; his supposed tomb, 72–73
Nabû-balatsu-ikbi, 107, 115
Nabû-shum-lishir, 40, 84
Nahr-el-Kelb Inscription, 81
Naksh-i-Rustam, 258, 262
Namri, 228, 242
Naukratis, 249, 250
Nebo, stands next to Merodach, 52; gives the sceptre, 127, 147; keeps the tablets of fate, 138–139
Nebuchadnezzar, meaning of name, 265–266; a Chaldean, 38; character of his inscriptions, 70; nature of his reign, 62–63, 78; loves display, 25–26; devoted to Babylon, 25, 97; his buildings, 71–77; offerings to Merodach and Nebo, 81; bas-relief at Wady Brissa, 84; admiration for forest trees, 89; cuts down cedars with his own hand, 83–84; invades Egypt, 63, 71; his idea of empire, 79–80; his personality, 92–104
Necho I., 135
Neo-Babylonian inscriptions, 92
Nergal, 98, 99, 109
Nergalsharezer, 141
Nergalushezib, 38
Neriglissar, 108
New Year festival, 71, 81, 109, 147
Nile, 221
Nimitti-Bel, 74
Nimrûd, 137, 228
Nimrûd Inscription, 91, 243
Ninib, god of iron, 34; 86, 98, 99
Nippur, 45, 94–95, 261
Nitocris, 28, 117, 122, 123
Nöldeke, 260

O

OESTERLEY, 155, 269, 270, 277
Old Persian, 244–246, 258–265
Olmstead, 130
Onias III., 170, 173, 174, 175, 176, 178
Onkelos, Targum of, 7, 256, 264
Opis, 127, 129, 131
Origen, Canon of O.T., 280–281, 284
Orontes, 80, 87

P

PADAN-ARAM, 227
Palestinian Targum, 7, 8
Panammu, 138
Pasargadæ, 258
Pathros, 229
Peiser, 148
Pelusium, 250
Persæ of Æschylus, 144
Persepolis, 258, 259
Persian royal names, 154
Persica of Ctesias, 152
Peshitto, 8, 257
Peters, 95
Petrie, 71

pikhatu, 162
pilum, the, 32
Pinches, 11, 119, 141, 143, 144, 145
Pliny, 220, 251
Pognon, 19, 113
Polybius, 31, 32, 254
Polyhistor, 37, 247
Porphyry, 22
Procession Street, 72, 73, 81
Psammetichus I., 29, 252
Pseudepigrapha, the, 1, 2, 8, 269–271, 274
Pura Nun, 219
Purim, 208–209
Pusey, 226

R

Radau, 47
Ramsay, 207, 209
Rassam, 100, 126, 128, 135, 216
Rawlinson, H., 84, 128, 139, 259
Riblah, 87, 88
Rimmon, 98
Robinson, A. C., 129, 130, 132, 144, 286
Roman Scheme, the, 14, 18, 22
"Royal Road," the, 216

S

Salamis, 29
Salathiel, Apocalypse of, 272, 274, 277
Samahla, 229
Samekh, the letter, 158–159, 165–167
Sanballat, 190, 231, 234
Sanda, A., 228
Sargon II., 24, 45
satraps, 161, 163
Sayce, 35, 126, 128, 153, 219, 227, 262
Scheftelowitz, 260, 261, 262, 264
Schrader, 11, 40, 45, 178
Schürer, 56, 64
Seleucia, 220
Sendsherli, *see* Zenjirli
Sennacherib, 5, 118, 151, 214, 215
Septuagint Version of Daniel, *see* Codex Chisianus
Septuagint, 22, 59, 156, 159, 170–178, 259, 260, 261, 262, 263, 264, 266, 267
Shadrach, 266
Shadû Rabû, 42, 45
Shalmaneser I., 227
Shalmaneser II., 242
Shamash, god of Sippar, 70, 79; 93, 98; sometimes joined with Merodach in the Enlil-ship, 99–101, 163; 107, 108, 109, 110, 114
Shamash-shum-ukin, 118, 139, 151, 163
Shamshi-Rammanu, 228, 242
Shinar, 266
Shumer, or Southern Babylonia, 128, 163, 164, 266
Shushan, or Susa, 215–219, 223–224
Sibylline Oracles, 22
Siloam Inscription, 158
Similitudes, the, 50, 52, 55, 56, 57, 61; date of, 63–64
Sin, 93; the moon-god of Haran, 98, 100–101, 107–109; 113, 114, 115
Sippar, or Sippara, 70, 71, 79, 81, 82, 99, 100, 110, 117, 127, 156
sirrush, the, 76
Smith, George, 251
Stainer, 246
Stele of Nabonidus, 108, 109, 116, 147
Stier, 195
Strabo, 38, 67, 220
Strassmaier, 46, 146, 148, 149, 150
Surappi, 228
Syene, 229, 233
Syriac, 239–240, 257

T

Tahpanhes, 71, 265
Targums, 7, 8, 160, 238, 256, 264, 265
Tarsus, 247, 248
Tasmit, 90
Taylor Cylinder, 214, 215
Taylor, Isaac, 157
Teima Stone, 158, 167
Temâ, 109, 118, 120
"Temple where the Sceptre of the World is given," 127, 147
Testaments of the Twelve Patriarchs, 2, 271
Theodotion, 119, 202, 247, 259, 260, 261, 262, 263, 264, 267, 289
Thermopylæ, 29
"The Twenty-four Writings," 277
Thureau-Dangin, 95
Tiglathpileser I., 227
Tiglathpileser III., 91
Tigris, 19, 82, 219, 220, 221, 262
Tolman, 265
Tristram, 87
Tyre, 87, 109

U

Ugbaru, *see* Gobryas
Uknu, 228, 242
Ulai, 212, 213, 217-219, 222, 223, 224, 225
Ur, 36, 42, 71, 108, 109
Urartu, 22, 23
Uruk, *see* Erech
Urumiah, Lake, 23
Uvaja, 214

V

Van, Lake, 23
Virgil, 31

W

Wady Brissa Inscription, 19, 69, 79; its contents, 80–83; 84, 86, 89, 95
Weissbach, 84, 215
Westcott, 287
Wickes, 186
Wieseler, 207
Williamson, G. C., 157
Wilson, R. D., 238, 240, 243
Winckler, 11, 22, 215
Wordsworth, Christopher, 293
Wright, C. H. H., 5, 7, 11, 17, 174, 276
Wright, W., 239

X

Xenophon, 19, 82, 107, 121; description of the capture of Babylon, 123–126; 129, 131, 140, 143, 144, 145
Xerxes, 28, 29, 30, 88; meaning of name, 154; 155, 166, 230

Y

ye'or, 221–222
Yod, the letter, 158–159, 165–167

Z

Zagros, 129, 213
Zain, the letter, 237
Zakir Inscription, 166, 238, 256
Zealots, the, 200–204
zebach uminchah, 199
Zend language, 259
Zenjirli Inscriptions, 136, 137, 166, 229, 256
zikkurat, 49
Zimmern, 139
Zobah, 227

SCRIPTURE INDEX

PRINCIPAL PASSAGES COMMENTED ON

PAGES
Dan. i. 7. *Belteshazzar—Shadrach—Meshach—Abed-nego* . . 266–267
21. *Daniel continued*, etc. 245
— ii. 2, 4, 5, etc. *The Chaldeans* 35–44
4. *in Aramaic*, R.V.M. 6
32–33. *gold—silver—brass—iron* 24–34
34. *a stone cut out without hands* 48
35. *a great mountain* (the Great Mountain) . . 42, 43, 45–49
38. *the beasts of the field* 86
39. *inferior to thee* (below thee) 18–20
45. *the* (a) *great God* 93
47. *of a truth your God*, etc. 52
— iii. 2, 3, etc. *See* Appendix on Foreign Words . . . 258–267
5, 7, 10, 15. Musical instruments with Greek names . . 246–255
26, etc. *Most High God* 17, 98–101
— iv. 10–16. The great tree 78–89
17. *the lowest of men* 89–91
29. *walking in* (upon) *the royal palace* 66
30. *Is not this great Babylon*, etc. ? 65–77, 97
32. *thy dwelling shall be with the beasts of the field* . . . 106
— v. 1. *Belshazzar the king* 117–119
1. *made a feast* 126
1. *to a thousand of his lords* 120
1. *and drank wine*, etc. 133
4. *they drank wine, and praised the gods of gold*, etc. . . . 134
7. The proffered rewards 135
7. *the third ruler in the kingdom* 119
10. *the queen* 117
11. *thy father :* repeated thrice 115–117
22. *though thou knewest all this* 114–115, 134–135
25–28. The four mystic words 136-140
28, etc. *Medes and Persians* 15
30. *Belshazzar the Chaldean king* 120
30. *was slain* 126, 128
31. *Darius the Mede* 142–167
31. *received the kingdom* 142–143
31. *being about threescore and two* (twelve ?) *years old* . . 156–160
— vi. 1. *an hundred and twenty satraps* 27, 161–165
6, 11, 15. *came tumultuously*, R.V.M. 160
10. *his windows were open in his chamber toward Jerusalem* . . 181
25. *Then king Darius wrote unto all the peoples*, etc. . . 164–165
— vii. Analysis of this chapter 59–60
1. *the first year of Belshazzar* 119–120
2, 3. *four great beasts came up from the sea* . . . 212–213

PAGES

Dan. vii. 4. The lion with eagle's wings 62, 78
5. The bear 18
5. The three ribs 18, 22–23
6. The leopard with four wings 30
7. The fourth beast, *terrible and powerful*, etc. 31–33
7. *diverse from all the beasts that were before it* 33, 292
7. *and it had ten horns* 16, 293
8. *there came up among them another horn, a little one* . 15, 16
9. *one that was ancient of days* 55
13. *one like unto a son of man* 57–62, 222, 288, 290
19. *whose teeth were of iron and his nails of brass* . . . 31
21, 22, 25, 27. *the saints* 58–61
— viii. 1–14. A vision concerning the Jewish Church 16–18
1. *the third year of king Belshazzar* 119-120
2. *I was in Shushan the palace*, etc. 215–217
2. *and I was by the river Ulai* 217–219
3. *a ram which had two horns* 15
5. *an he-goat came from the west* 30
6. *he came to the ram, which I saw standing before the river* . 218–219
9. *out of one of them came forth a little horn* 15–16
16. *I heard a man's voice between the banks of Ulai* . . . 222
20. The unity of the Medo-Persian kingdom 4, 15
25. *broken without hand* 48
27. *I was astonished at the vision*, etc. 13
— ix. 1. *the first year of Darius* 150
1. *the son of Ahasuerus* 154–155
1. *which was made king* 142–143
1. *over the realm of the Chaldeans* 36–164
2. *the books*, with emphatic accent 186, 284–285
3–19. Daniel's prayer 180–181
23. *the* (a) *commandment* (word) *went forth* 181–182
24–27. R.V. compared with the LXX 168–178
24–26a. The Evangelic Prophecy 182–193
26b–27. The Evangelic Prophecy 194–205
27. *a firm covenant with (the) many for one week* 206–211
— x. 1. *the third year of Cyrus* 245
1. *thing* (word) and *vision* 9
4. *the great river which is Hiddekel* 219–221
5, 6. *a man clothed in linen*, etc. 222–223, 290–291
8–11, 15–19. Effect of the vision on Daniel 291
21. *the writing of truth* 138
— xi. 1. *the first year of Darius the Mede* 150
2–xii. 4. A prophecy obscured by a targum 5–7
2. *the fourth shall be far richer than they all* 28
10, 40. *overflow and pass through* 12, 220
38. *the god of fortresses* 3
— xii. 2, 3. *many of them that sleep*, etc. 288–289
4. *shut up the words and seal the book* 9–10
4. *run to and fro* 10–12
5, 6, 7. *the river* (flood) 221–222
6. *the man clothed in linen—above the waters of the river* 12, 223, 290–291
8. *I heard but I understood not* 9
9. *Go thy way, Daniel* 10, 223

PAGES
Ex. xv. 10 51
Ezra i. 2 151
8 261
— iv. 7 6
8 159
17–24 189
— v. 15, vi. 7 235
— vii. 12–26. Decree of Artaxerxes 188
— viii. 36 261
Ps. ii. 1, 2, 6, 8, 9 . . . . . 191–192, 210–211
— cx. 2 211
Isa. vii. 8. *three score and five* (fifteen ?) *years* 158–159
— viii. 8. *overflow and pass through* 12, 111, 210, 222
— xiii. 17 28
— xiv. 25 5
— xix. 1 58
— xxi. 1 36
— xxxv. 8 218
— xxxix. 6, 7 36–37
— xli. 2, 25 111
— xliv. 28 165
— xlv. 1, 3–4, 13 111
Jer. xliii. 8–13 71
— l.–li. 121–123
— l. 26 80
Ezek. x. 4, 18–19 198
— xi. 22–23 198
— xiv. 14, 20. *Noah, Daniel, and Job* 53, 272–273
— xxiii. 14–15 41
— xxvii. 13 30
— xxviii. 3. *Behold, thou art wiser than Daniel* 53–54, 272–273
— xxxi. 3, 6 88
Hosea xiii. 7 30
Amos v. 19 18
— ix. 7 227
Micah i. 4 51
Hab. ii. 3, LXX 195
5 133
9, 11–13, 17 85–86
Zech. iv. 10 10
— x. 11 221
Matt. ii. 19–20 207
— xiii. 31–32 63
— xxii. 7 195
— xxiv. 15. *the abomination of desolation, which was spoken of by Daniel the prophet* 287
21. *great tribulation, such as hath not been*, etc. 288
30. *the Son of man coming on the clouds of heaven* 288
— xxvi. 64. *the Son of man coming . . . coming on the clouds of heaven* 57, 288
— xxvii. 25 195
Luke iii. 1, 2 207
— xiii. 6-9 198
— xxii. 70 57

PAGES
John ii. 13, 20 ; vi. 4 ; xii. 1 207
— iii. 22 ; iv. 35 208
— v. 1 . . . . 208, 209
27 292
— vi. 4 209
Acts ii. 47 196
— iii. 26 198–199
— v. 14 ; vi. 7 ; v. 28 ; viii. 1 ; vi. 14 197
— vii. 52 ; v. 31 198
— xi. 19–21 211
Heb. x. 37 195
Rev. i. 7, 13–15. *Behold, he cometh with clouds*, etc. 290
17 291
— ii. 18 291
— x. 5, 6 291
— xiii. 1, 2, 3, 4, 5–7 292
— xiv. 14. *on the cloud . . . one sitting like unto a son of man* . 290
— xvii. 1 . . . . 292, 293
9 293
— xx. 15 292

APOCRYPHA

2 Esdras 277
Tobit xiv. 15 155
Ecclesiasticus xliv.–l. 54
Bel and the Dragon i. 7 26
1 Maccabees i. 10 174
29–31 174
54 175
— viii. 13, 14 33
2 Maccabees iv. 7, 23–26, 32–35 173

THE END